Living with Grief:
Children and Adolescents

Edited by
Kenneth J. Doka & Amy S. Tucci
Foreword by U.S. Senator Tom Harkin

HFA
HOSPICE FOUNDATION
OF AMERICA

This book is part of Hospice Foundation of America's *Living With Grief* ® series

This book is part of HFA's *Living With Grief*® series.

Ordering information:

Call Hospice Foundation of America: 800-854-3402

Or write:
Hospice Foundation of America
1621 Connecticut Avenue, NW #300
Washington, DC 20009

Or visit HFA's Web site:
www.hospicefoundation.org

Assistant Editor: Keith Johnson
Cover Design: The YGS Group
Typesetting and Design: MillerCox Design, Inc.

Publisher's Cataloging-in-Publication Data
(Prepared by Quality Books Inc.)

Living with grief : children and adolescents / edited by
Kenneth J. Doka & Amy S. Tucci ; foreword by Thomas
Harkin.
p. cm.
Includes bibliographical references and index.
LCCN 2007935973
ISBN-13: 978-1-893349-09-4
ISBN-10: 1-893349-09-8

1. Grief in children. 2. Grief in adolescence.
3. Bereavement in children. 4. Bereavement in adolescence.
5. Loss (Psychology) in children. 6. Loss (Psychology)
in adolescence. 7. Children and death. 8. Teenagers
and death. 9. Children--Counseling of. 10. Teenagers--
Counseling of. I. Doka, Kenneth J. II. Tucci, Amy S.
III. Hospice Foundation of America. IV. Title: Children
and adolescents.

BF723.G75L585 2008   155.9'37'083
                QBI07-600334

Dedication

For Hospice Foundation of America President David Abrams,
whose leadership, vision, humor, and friendship we cherish.

Kenneth J. Doka
Amy S. Tucci

Contents

Foreword

U.S. Senator Tom Harkin

To paraphrase the late Senator Hubert H. Humphrey, the moral test of a society is how it treats those at the dawn of life, the children; those in the shadows of life, the sick and needy; and those in the twilight of life, the elderly and dying. The modern hospice movement plays an indispensable role in helping America pass this moral test.

My two brothers, dying of cancer, were cared for by hospice professionals in the final weeks of their lives. But I was introduced to the hospice movement many years earlier by a very special friend, Jack Gordon, a former Florida state senator and founder/CEO of the Hospice Foundation of America. I admired Jack as person of principle, passion, and progressive convictions. He sought political power not to "be somebody," but to get things done for others, including the most needy among us. And Jack brought that same sense of mission to advancing the hospice movement in the United States. Jack's life was tragically cut short two years ago, but his work is being ably continued by his wife and my dear friend, Myra MacPherson, an HFA director, and by the dedicated staff and volunteers of the Foundation.

One of Jack's inspired creations was HFA's annual live-via-satellite tele-conference, designed to reach a national and international audience with the most current research, theory, and practice in the field of bereavement. This year's 15th annual *Living With Grief*® Teleconference focuses on the experience of grieving children and adolescents, and the ways that hospice professionals, parents, teachers, and others can best support them as they cope with death and bereavement.

This book, "Living with Grief: Children and Adolescents," is a sourcebook for participants in the teleconference and for all of us who care about our youth. It includes chapters by academics and professionals. It also includes four remarkable first-person "voices" of children—those at the beginning of life struggling to understand the end of life and the grief that accompanies it.

In the United States, some 2.5 million children and young people under age 18 have experienced the death of a parent. An estimated 1.8 million young people in the U.S. currently are grieving the loss of a sibling. In Iraq, Afghanistan, Sudan, and other war zones, millions of children live in the constant presence of violence, destruction, death, and loss. Many thousands of children in the U.S., especially on military bases, are grieving and grappling with the death of their father or mother in combat. In many cases, these children are not adequately tended to because a parent or parents are also deep in grief.

We know that children who have lost a parent, sibling, or other close loved one are at significantly increased risk of depression, anxiety, post-traumatic stress symptoms, low self-esteem, and lower academic performance. It is an urgent challenge for us to understand how children and adolescents grieve, and how we as parents, professionals, and other adults can comfort and care for them in their grief.

Advancing this understanding is the worthy aim of this volume, and of the 2008 *Living With Grief*® Teleconference. As readers and/or participants, you are committed to the compassionate treatment of those at the beginning of life, in the shadows of life, and at the end of life. Senator Humphrey would be grateful to you, and so am I.

Tom Harkin is a U.S. Senator from Iowa and a longtime leader in the fight to improve health care. As co-chair of the Senate Rural Health Caucus, he has successfully pushed legislation to bring health professionals to small towns and rural areas. He authored the 1990 Americans with Disabilities Act, the landmark legislation that protects the civil rights of more than 54 million Americans with physical and mental disabilities. As the Chairman of the Senate education funding subcommittee, Senator Harkin has worked to expand school counseling and other school safety programs, and improve teacher training.

Acknowledgments

It is always a pleasure to acknowledge those who enrich our work and our lives. First and foremost is the staff of the Hospice Foundation of America. While small, it manages to accomplish so much each year. David Abrams, HFA's president, offers advice, counsel, and suggestions at each stage of the book. He keeps us grounded. Others at HFA provide both direct and indirect support, assisting the foundation's work so that the book can reach fruition. They include Sophie Viteri Berman, Keith Johnson, Kristen Baker, Susan Belsinger, Marcia Eaker, Lisa Veglahn and Krista Renenger. Of course, we both need to thank the contributing authors who met demanding deadlines with fine chapters that continue to push our field forward.

Although some acknowledgments are shared by both editors, each has an individual support system to acknowledge and thank.

Together, we would like to acknowledge the legacy of the late Jack Gordon, founder and former chair of The Hospice Foundation of America. The annual *Living With Grief*® teleconferences and the supporting books were part of his vision to provide education and support to those in hospice who deal daily with the dying and the bereaved.

In addition, we want to acknowledge the book's extraordinary Voices authors, who shared their grief experiences, and the organizations that helped connect us: The Compassionate Friends, The Hospice of the Florida Suncoast, and the Children's Grief Center of El Paso.

I would like to acknowledge and thank my co-editor, Amy Tucci. She is a joy to work with, and I hope this is the beginning of a series of professional collaborations.

I also wish to thank my administrators and colleagues at The College of New Rochelle for maintaining a stimulating environment that allows me to write and edit. I need to thank so many, including President Stephen Sweeny, Vice President Dorothy Escribano, Dean Guy Lometti and Assistant Dean

Marie Ribarich. Diane Lewis and Vera Mezzaucella provide critical assistance, as did Mary Whalen—now moved on to another division of the Graduate School. Colleagues at the College of New Rochelle as well as the Association of Death Education and Counseling (ADEC), and The International Work Group on Death, Dying and Bereavement, are always there to offer encouragement, inspiration, and friendship.

I, of course, need to acknowledge those in my personal life who are a source of joy. My son, Michael, and his wife, Angelina, my grandson Kenny, and granddaughter Lucy make it all seem so worthwhile. My godson, Keith Whitehead, continues in college, hopefully graduating before the next book is out. Other members of my intimate network of family, friends and neighbors—including Kathy Dillon; my sister and brother, Dorothy and Franky, and all of their families; as well as Eric Schwarz; Dylan Rieger; Larry Laterza; Ellie Andersen; Jim, Karen, and Greg Cassa; Paul Kimbal; Don and Carol Ford; Allen and Gail Greenstein; Jim and Mary Millar; Robert and Tracey Levy; Linda and Russell Tellier; Jill Boyer; Fred and Lisa Amore; Chris and Dirotta Fields; Lynn Miller; James Rainbolt; Scott and Lisa Carlson; Tom and Lorraine Carlson; Matt Atkins; Kurt Mulligan; and Don and Lucille Matthews—provide respite, friendship and most importantly, laughter.

—Kenneth J. Doka

Without Ken Doka, who brings so much expertise and dedication to HFA's *Living With Grief* ® series, this book would not be possible. We make a good team in a yin and yang way that I cherish, and I look forward to many more years of partnership directed at HFA's educational efforts.

I want to individually acknowledge Keith Johnson, assistant editor of this book, whose eye for detail and organization is invaluable during the editing process. He will ably assume the managing editor role for HFA's 2009 book; he has earned it after two years of hard work as assistant editor.

Neal Cox of MillerCox Design was creative, unflappable and even pleasant during the many revisions we insisted upon, and Greg Sindlinger and Brenda Trone of the YGS Group kept printing and distribution on schedule, an enormous task given the large girth of this book.

I thank HFA's Board of Directors for its faith in me, and I thank Jack Gordon for taking a chance on me four years ago.

My good friend, Jill Young Miller, has always been a source of professional inspiration and personal support. We have weathered the good and the bad together for more than two decades.

I want to thank my parents, Ann and Peter Stromberg, for their many gifts to me—a respect and appreciation for writing, an enduring work ethic, and a recognition that life is worth embracing at every turn, or at least whenever a good opportunity presents itself.

Finally, none of my work could be accomplished without the love and support of my husband, Michael, and my children, Nicholas and Rebecca. I thank them for putting up with me.

—Amy S. Tucci

Developmental Perspectives

Robert Kastenbaum (2000) described childhood as "the kingdom where nobody dies." These words, drawn from poet Edna St. Vincent Millay, represent our tendency to think of childhood as a time free from worrisome anxieties about death. Adults try to protect children from death—keeping secret the illnesses of family members, avoiding discussions of dying, and limiting exposure to death by preventing children from participating in funeral rituals. Yet, as Kastenbaum points out, such efforts are ineffectual. Children see death around them—in the deaths of pets and other animals, in their video games, in TV shows and movies, and in their music, books, and jokes.

Charles Corr's chapter reinforces this concept. From the earliest ages, he says, children try to understand death. Maurer (1966) noted that one of the first abstract concepts children grasp is "all gone," which he views as an early precursor to the concept of *nonbeing*. Corr reviews a number of approaches that attempt to assess and explain how children learn to recognize death. He recommends listening to the child and offers sage advice to adults as they help children who are grappling with death or loss. Julia Marquez's poem echoes Corr's points.

David Balk describes how the orientation toward death begins to shift as a child enters adolescence. Scholars used to assume that by late childhood the child had an "adult" understanding of death—recognizing the finality, irreversibility, universality, inevitability, and nonfunctionality of death. But Balk says that although adolescents have the ability to cognitively understand death, their preoccupation with self—their solipsism—makes it hard for them to identify death with themselves. Their "personal fables," as Balk calls them, do not allow for the possibility of personal death. When a peer dies (and in adolescence such deaths are often traumatic and sudden), this fable is deeply shaken.

Kenneth Doka's chapter completes this section. Doka agrees that orientation toward death continue to change through the lifecycle. He describes how certain events conspire to create an awareness of mortality in adults and how, in later life, adults recognize that life is drawing to a close. Thus, the human orientation moves from recognition of death to realization of mortality to a final resignation as death draws near.

The chapters in this section all emphasize that perspectives toward death continue to develop throughout the lifecycle and that this development is not only cognitive but affective as well. Young children have a "short feeling span"—meaning they can sustain strong emotions only for limited periods (Crenshaw, 1991). It is not unusual, for example, for a young child to cry bitterly over a loss, then cheerfully resume play, only to cry again later. As children get older, they are able to sustain strong emotions.

The ability to empathize with others generally develops with age. Very young children are egocentric, and loss is often viewed only from a personal perspective. As children age, they understand the many relationships that surround them and the differential impact of loss on those relationships. For example, a number of years ago, one of the editors of this book received a call from a friend who was troubled that his 6-year-old son, on hearing of his grandfather's death, cried and angrily shouted, "Who's going to take me fishing now?" The man thought he had sired a self-centered brat. The editor assured him that the reaction was normal for the boy's age. Five years later, the same boy responded to the death of his aunt by hugging his mother and saying, "I'll miss Aunt Sheila, but she was your sister." The older child, even in his own grief, could reach out to comfort his mother in her loss.

Children also develop spiritually. Robert Coles (1990) describes children as "spiritual pioneers." By that, Coles means that children are constantly trying to understand spiritual questions. For example, when a 3-year-old child holds up a dead bird and asks "Why?" the child is attempting to find some sense of existential meaning. Coles uses the metaphor of pioneers to explain that most children have not internalized spiritual schemas and are still exploring, attempting to develop or apply spiritual answers even without a fully developed cognitive map.

This spiritual questioning continues in adolescence. Adolescents are further refining their critical thinking skills and taking in new information from a variety of sources, and spiritual questioning is a natural aspect of their intellectual development. In addition, part of the struggle for identity is to affirm one's own beliefs. The adolescent says, "I know what my parents and religious teachers have taught me, but what do *I* believe?" Doka says this spiritual questing continues throughout adulthood, as adults reach various developmental milestones. Thus, there is always value in considering how a person's spirituality facilitates or complicates grief.

REFERENCES

Coles, R. (1990). *The spiritual life of children.* Boston: Houghton Mifflin.

Crenshaw, D. A. (1991). *Bereavement: Counseling the grieving throughout the lifecycle.* New York: Continuum.

Kastenbaum, R. (2000.) *The kingdom where nobody dies.* In K.J. Doka (Ed.), *Living with Grief: Children, Adolescents and Loss.* Washington, DC: Hospice Foundation of America.

Maurer, A. (1966). Maturation of the conception of death. *Journal of Medical Psychology, 39,* 35–41.

CHAPTER 1

Children's Emerging Awareness of Death

Charles A. Corr

A dults sometimes seem to believe that young children have no awareness of death. That is incorrect. To believe that children are unaware of death is self-serving—if it were true, adults would have no responsibility to explain a death to a child or teach a child about coping with loss. And even if this belief were true, it would pose a problem: If children have no awareness of loss and death when they are young, when does that awareness come into their lives? At what magical age does this awareness suddenly pop into a child's mind? What will cause that leap in awareness? Adults should be prepared to help even very young children understand death-related events and teach them about coping with loss.

This chapter describes our current state of knowledge about children's awareness and understandings of death. The chapter covers six major topics: (1) early inklings, or the beginning of awareness of themes and events related to loss and death; (2) direct encounters with loss and death during childhood; (3) a stage-based theory of the development of children's understandings of death; (4) some critical remarks about stage-based schemas; (5) the complexity of the concept of death; and (6) advice about listening actively and carefully to children's concerns about loss and death. Each section concludes with one or more lessons for parents, educators, counselors, and other interested adults. The chapter ends with 17 guidelines for adults who are interacting with or seeking to help children cope with sadness, loss, and death-related events.

EARLY INKLINGS

Children receive messages from the media, parents, family members, and other adults and children that certain topics, such as excretory functioning or sexual organs, are not considered suitable for open discussion. They also receive subtle or overt messages about whether or not death-related topics are acceptable for discussion. Unfortunately, these messages can be confusing and contradictory. Adults may talk freely among themselves (often within the hearing of a curious child) about the death of an elderly relative or a public figure but may try to suppress mention of someone who has committed suicide. Some adults deny that children are aware of death, even as television reports fatalities on the highway and casualties in Iraq, and entertainment programs are full of violent events.

The supposedly innocent environment of children's play is filled with death-related themes. For example, peek-a-boo is said to act out the sudden disappearance (death) of the external world and its equally sudden reappearance (Maurer, 1966). Other play activities involve acting out violent crashes and other forms of "killing" under the control of a child-master. In recent years, such play has come to include warlike situations in many video games.

Death-related themes are also prominent in the rhymes and songs of childhood. For example, everyone is familiar with the creepy song "the worms crawl in, the worms crawl out," but what about "Ring Around the Rosie"? This seemingly innocuous tune originated during the plague in England and describes the roseate skin pustules of the disease, as a result of which "we all fall down." "Rock-a-Bye, Baby" has a falling-cradle theme, and the child's prayer "Now I lay me down to sleep" is essentially a petition for safekeeping against death and other hazards of the night.

Many fairy tales also contain references to death (Lamers, 1995). For example, in the original version of the story, Little Red Riding Hood and her grandmother are eaten by the wicked wolf, not saved by a passing woodsman. In "The Three Little Pigs," the big bad wolf dies in a scalding pot of hot water when he falls down the chimney of the third pig's house. And Hansel and Gretel (who, by the way, were left to die in the forest by their parents because there was not enough food for them) ultimately shut the wicked witch up in her own hot oven. "The Goose Girl" has perhaps the most gruesome outcome—the false bride is put into a barrel lined with sharp nails and rolled until she is dead.

Play activities, rhymes, songs, and stories like these are not necessarily morbid or unhealthy for children. They can, in fact, allow children to work through fears and anxieties related to death in safe and distanced ways. We can take two lessons from these early involvements of children with death: (1) Most children are curious about death and death-related events, even when adults try to "protect" them from pursuing their curiosity; and (2) death is not absent from the fantasy world of childhood.

DIRECT ENCOUNTERS WITH LOSS AND DEATH DURING CHILDHOOD

Inklings of loss and death—along with experiences of separation and loss during early childhood—foreshadow later, more direct encounters with death-related events. Children are often tuned in to the events that take place around them. Even quite young babies notice when significant others leave their immediate surroundings. Their awareness is likely to increase as their cognitive abilities develop and as life events increasingly impinge on everyday activities. They may not always interpret the separations correctly, but understanding is grounded in early awareness.

Children also notice disruptions in the emotional currents of their families, so it is not unusual for them to sense that something important is happening when the adults around them are suffering grief. Children may not completely understand such emotional disruptions, but they are not likely to be oblivious. If they do not receive accurate information when they try to develop explanations for these disruptions, the demons of their imaginations may be far scarier than the truth about what is really happening.

Beginnings and endings, as well as separations and losses, are aspects of children's daily lives, and children are curious about these and other events that seem new or puzzling. In connection with death-related events, a child might ask: "Where did Grandpa go? Will he be here to read me a story at bedtime?" or "What happened to Fluffy? When will she come back?" This is part of a child's taking notice of life events and seeking to make sense of them.

Children encounter death in many ways. Grandparents, parents, and other important adults may die. Even siblings may die, particularly during infancy—nearly 30,000 babies and small children die each year in our society. And reports of the deaths of celebrities and public figures often appear in the media.

Pets are important sources of unconditional love and allow children to learn about the responsibilities involved in caring for a living creature. But pets typically have shorter—often much shorter—life spans than those of the children who love and care for them. An attachment to a childhood pet almost guarantees an eventual encounter with that pet's death.

The lesson in this section is that normal, healthy children do have thoughts, feelings, and encounters with death in various forms.

UNDERSTANDING DEATH: DEVELOPMENTAL STAGES

Children's understandings of death arise out of early inklings and direct encounters. The best-known and most frequently mentioned theory in this field is that of Maria Nagy, a Hungarian psychologist who examined 378 children living in Budapest just before World War II (Corr, 1996). Nagy published an account of her study shortly after the war and a slightly revised version later (1948, 1959).

In Nagy's study, children in the 7–10-year-old range were asked to "write down everything that comes into your mind about death" (1948, p. 4) and children in the 6–10-year-old range were asked to make drawings about death (many of the older children also wrote explanations of what they had drawn). Discussions were held with all the children, either about their compositions and drawings or (in the case of 3–5-year-olds) to encourage them to talk about their ideas and feelings about death.

According to Nagy, the children's understandings of death developed in three stages:

1. **There is no definitive death.** In this first stage, "The child does not know death as such" (Nagy, 1948, p. 7). The reason may be that the child has not fully distinguished the concept of death from other concepts or that he or she has not grasped its full implications. For example, a child might think of death in terms of departure or sleep. If death is thought of as departure, it involves some sort of continued life elsewhere; if death is like sleep, it involves a diminished form of life. In either case, life is not completely over and *death is not seen as final.*

2. **Death = a person.** In the second stage in their understandings of death, children may imagine death as a separate person (e.g., the grim reaper, a skeleton, a ghost, or a death angel). Or they may identify death with

dead persons. Nagy referred to this as *the personification of death*. If death is some sort of person external to the child, then those caught by that person die, but those who are sufficiently clever or quick can escape and need not die. Children with this understanding acknowledge the finality of death but still believe it can be avoided.

3. **The cessation of corporal life.** Children reach a third stage in their understandings of death when they recognize that death is a process that operates within us, a process in which bodily life ends. In this view, *death is both final and universal.*

Nagy saw a progression that moved from the idea that death is not final, to death is final but avoidable, to death is final and inevitable. She described her results as involving a developmental process, one that advances from an unrealistic to an ever more realistic and mature understanding of death.

Many later descriptions of children's understandings of death have followed this broad three-stage model, although some writers have argued that avoidability, not personification, is the key concept in stage 2. Perhaps using the device of an external figure is a child's concrete way of representing avoidability. Nagy's methods (asking children to make drawings of death) and her cultural context no doubt influenced her results. For example, her study involved pre-World War II Hungarian children who were familiar with oral tradition about death. These children differ in many ways from children in our society today, who are saturated with television and other media.

Nagy and other writers attached ages to the three developmental stages. She wrote, "The child of less than 5 years does not recognize death as an irreversible fact. In death, it sees life…. Between the ages of 5 and 9, death is most often personified and thought of as a contingency…. In general, only after the age of 9 is it recognized that death is a process happening in us according to certain laws" (1948, p. 7). In the later publication, Nagy added, "[I]t should be kept in mind that neither the stages nor the above-mentioned ages at which they occur are watertight compartments…. Overlapping does exist" (1959, p. 81).

The lesson in this section is that many adults approach children with a stage-based schema of their understandings of death at different ages in their development.

LET'S AVOID "STAGING" CHILDREN AND THEIR UNDERSTANDINGS OF DEATH

Research in the field of children's understanding of death has been plagued by methodological problems, such as lack of precision and agreement about the terms and definitions used for various components of the concept of death, as well as lack of reliable and valid standardized measures for these components. As a result, the literature on this subject has been said to offer a "confusing array of results" (Stambrook & Parker, 1987, p. 154). In particular, commentators have often applied their results uncritically, made them more rigid than they should be, and oversimplified their conclusions. The following paragraphs explore problems arising from each of these ways of misusing stage-based theories of the development of children's understandings of death.

In terms of how *critically* these schemas are applied, we might ask whether all children are alike. Should we expect the same results from children who have encountered war and genocide as from those who live in more peaceful areas of the world? What about the differences between children who have suffered tragic losses from epidemics such as AIDS or natural disasters compared with children who have lived far more innocent lives? Don't life experiences, cultural contexts, and messages from the adults and the society around them influence how children think or do not think about death?

In terms of how *rigidly* these schemas are employed, we might ask about the theoretical boundaries between the cognitive stages. For example, how valid is it to expect that a child who is 4 years and 11 months old will have a different concept of death than a child who is 5 years and 1 month old? What about children who are just under or just over 9 years of age? Are the chronological boundaries given for these stages absolute and inviolable? Are children no more complex than elevators—either at one level of understanding or at another, and that's all there is to it?

In terms of *oversimplifying* how we view children, two points can be made: (1) stage theories are appealing precisely because they put forward clear and undemanding progressions toward well-defined goals; and (2) broad generalizations gloss over the unique differences that make children distinct individuals. The staged portrait of children's understandings of death is attractive because it assumes a straightforward path toward a "mature" concept. We are easily seduced by this schema because it asks little of us beyond memorizing a few age ranges.

We might do better to ask questions like the following. Do children actually develop in this mechanical, step-by-step way, or is their cognitive development more complex? Isn't it true that children's cognitive development is likely to be closely related to other aspects of their lives, such as their feelings, the social contexts in which they find themselves, and their spirituality? And what about the distinctive features of each child's personality—how do they influence how the child thinks about difficult subjects like separation, loss, and death?

In brief, do all children at the same age (even in similar social and cultural contexts) think the same way about death? And does any given child think the same way about death at different points in the very broad stage/age categories described in this model? Is age alone an accurate indicator of cognitive development?

The lesson in this section is twofold: (1) We should be cautious in broadly applying a stage theory of the development of children's understandings of death; and (2) we should distinguish between a child's cognitive development and his or her chronological age.

THINKING ABOUT DEATH IS A COMPLEX MATTER

Stage-based accounts of the development of children's understandings of death assume that it is a process of working toward a mature concept of death. We might ask ourselves what a "mature" concept actually is. Do adults possess this concept, or are they constantly striving to gain an adequate concept of death? What are some of the components of a mature concept of death?

The two central components of most stage-based accounts of the concept of death—finality and universality—are neither simple nor uncomplicated (Corr, 1995; Speece & Brent, 1984, 1996). For example, *finality* embraces at least two elements: irreversibility and nonfunctionality.

Irreversibility means that the natural processes involved in the transition from being alive to being dead, as well as the state that results from those processes, cannot be reversed. Once the physical body of a living thing is dead, it can never be alive again. Apart from miracles or magical events, life is irreversibly absent from a dead body. (Medical resuscitation is not an exception here; it stimulates life in a body that is not fully dead but in a kind of boundary region between being alive and being dead.)

The other key element of finality is *nonfunctionality*. Children are often curious about what dead people might be doing in heaven or wherever else they are. But if death is truly final, that means the complete and absolute cessation of all the life-defining or functional capabilities (whether external and observable or internal and inferred) typically attributed to a living physical body.

Universality is an even more complex aspect of the concept of death. It brings together three closely related notions: all-inclusiveness, inevitability, and unpredictability. *All-inclusiveness* has to do with how broadly death applies to the group of living things. It responds to a familiar question: "Does everyone die?" The answer is yes. Apart again from miracles or supernatural intervention, no living thing is exempt from death.

Inevitability carries this one step further. To say that death is inevitable means that death is unavoidable for all living things. This relates not merely to the extent or number of those who will die, but to the fact that none of them can escape their deaths. A person may avoid this or that death-related event, but not death itself.

If death is all-inclusive and inevitable, one might think its timing would be certain and predictable, but that is not the case. In fact, death is *unpredictable*—anyone might die at any time.

These aspects of the finality and universality of death are important, but they are not the only subjects of concern to children, who often ask additional questions about death. One type of question has to do with the events or conditions that bring about the death of a living thing: "Why do living things die?" or "What makes living things die?" Questions like this are about the causes of death. Children (and others) try to understand the external and internal events or forces that can bring about death. For children, it is important to distinguish real causes from magical thinking, in which bad behavior or merely wishing could cause someone to die (Fogarty, 2000).

These three aspects of the concept of death—finality, universality, and causality—apply to the physical body, but they do not exhaust the death-related concerns of many children and adults. Those concerns lead to efforts to try to grasp or articulate what might be involved in some type of continued life apart from the physical body. For example, children often ask "What happens after death?" and "Where does your soul or spirit go when you die?" This indicates a conviction that some type of continued life exists after the death of the physical body. The conviction may be expressed in various ways, such as a belief in the ongoing life of a soul in heaven without the body or the reincarnation of a soul in a new and different body. Various religious, philosophical, and spiritual systems have attempted to provide frameworks for these questions. The important point here is that many children try to carry their understandings beyond the death of the physical body.

The lesson in this section is that death is not a simple and uncomplicated notion. It has many dimensions and implications, and children are not likely to grasp them all. In fact, they may have many different understandings of death at the same time or at different times. Adults who are aware of the complexity of the concept of death will be able to approach children and their understandings of death with a more sensitive ear than if they merely focus on undifferentiated concepts of finality and universality.

LISTEN TO THE INDIVIDUAL CHILD

It is probably obvious to anyone who has interacted with a young child that children usually do not think about death as adults do, but it would be wrong to conclude that children have no concept of death. Even when they incorrectly think of death as sleep, they are exhibiting an understanding of death. Trying to understand death as a type of sleep is an effort to explain something that is unknown or only partially grasped (death) through something else (sleep) that is a familiar part of a child's life.

Confusing death with sleep indicates that the two concepts have not been properly differentiated but shows that the child is trying to make sense of his or her experience. As Kastenbaum and Aisenberg (1972, p. 9) noted, "Between the extremes of 'no understanding' and explicit, integrated abstract thought, there are many ways by which the young mind can enter into relationship with death."

That leads us to a larger lesson about theories that seek to explain the development of children's understandings of death. Carl Jung, one of our greatest theoretical psychologists, said, "Theories in psychology are the very devil. It is true that we need certain points of view for their orienting and heuristic value; but they should always be regarded as mere auxiliary concepts that can be laid aside at any time" (Jung, 1954, p. 17). Jung does not advocate abandoning all theoretical frameworks. We need guidance from theoretical insights such as those set forth in this chapter. As long as we subject theories to critical analysis, appreciate their limits, and draw judicious lessons from them, they can help identify what we might otherwise have missed and point us in useful directions.

At the same time, Jung wanted us to recognize the limitations of psychological theories and insights. They are auxiliary concepts, tools meant to assist our comprehension and appreciation—in this case, of children's emerging awareness and understandings of death. Any tool has strengths and limitations. We should value it for its strengths and the help it can provide, but we should recognize its limitations and the ways in which it may become a hindrance. Jung advised us to set the tool aside when we touch the miracle of a living soul.

Nagy concluded her original article with these words of advice: "To conceal death from the child is not possible and is also not permissible. Natural behavior in the child's surroundings can greatly diminish the shock of its acquaintance with death" (1948, p. 27). Natural behavior involves active and sympathetic listening. We can only learn the causes of a child's shock and the nature of his or her acquaintance with death by listening. Active listening allows us to appreciate the child's concerns and questions and helps us respond in effective ways (Corr, 1995; 1996). More important, by allowing the child to become our teacher in this way, we can enrich each other's appreciation of death in life.

The basic lesson in this section is twofold: (1) Children do make an effort to grasp or understand death when it comes into their lives; and (2) a good way—perhaps the only effective way—to gain insight into a child's understandings of death is to establish a relationship of confidence and trust with the child, and to listen carefully to the child's comments, questions, and concerns about loss and death.

Some Guidelines for Helping Children Cope with Their Emerging Awareness and Understandings of Death

The lessons at the end of each of the six sections of this chapter suggest some useful guidelines for interacting with children and helping them cope with their emerging awareness and understandings of death.

- Don't assume that children, even young children, have no awareness of death.

- Accept that most children are curious about many aspects of life and death.

- Acknowledge that death and loss are not absent from the fantasy lives of children.

- Recognize that death-related themes and events are part of the ordinary environment of children's lives, such as play activities and fairy tales.

- Grant that healthy, normal children are likely to encounter death-related events in their own lives, as well as through the media and in the world around them.

- Appreciate that most children have thoughts and feelings about death, and that they make an effort to grasp or understand death when it comes into their lives.

- Be aware that many adults approach children with a stage-based schema in mind regarding the child's understanding of death at various ages.

- Acknowledge that stage-based theories of the development of children's understandings of death are not undesirable in themselves, but they can lead us astray when we apply them uncritically, too rigidly, or in oversimplified ways.

- Concede that any sound theory of the development of children's understandings of death is likely to be valid in a broad, general way.

- Know that any sound theory of the development of children's understandings of death must be applied in a careful and sensitive way to match the realities of a particular child's life.

- Recognize that chronological age is only a crude indicator of cognitive development; it may not be a precise indicator for many individual children.

- Appreciate that the concept of death is not a simple and uncomplicated notion; it has many dimensions and implications.

- Understand that children are not likely to grasp each of the central dimensions of the concept of death or all its implications at once. That is one reason they repeat their questions about death or ask them again in different ways.

- Understand that adults who are aware of the complexity of the concept of death will be able to approach children with a more sensitive ear than if they merely focus on undifferentiated concepts of finality and universality.

- Realize that one good way—perhaps the only effective way—to gain insight into a child's understanding of death is to establish a relationship of trust and confidence with the child and to listen carefully to the child's comments, questions, and concerns about death.

- Make an effort to answer a child's questions about death and to respond to the concerns that underlie such questions in an honest, accurate, and helpful way.

- Frame your answers and responses in ways that are suitable to the child's capacities and needs. Don't be afraid to say, "I don't know."

Charles A. Corr, Ph.D., CT, is a member of the Board of Directors of the Hospice Institute of the Florida Suncoast, the ChiPPS (Children's Project on Palliative/Hospice Services) Leadership Advisory Council of the National Hospice and Palliative Care Organization, the Executive Committee of the National Donor Family Council, the Association for Death Education and Counseling, and the International Work Group on Death, Dying, and Bereavement (Chairperson, 1989-93). He is also professor emeritus, Southern Illinois University Edwardsville. Dr. Corr's publications in the field of death, dying, and bereavement include 35 books and booklets, along with more than 100 chapters and articles in professional publications. His most recent publication is the sixth edition of *Death and Dying, Life and Living* (Thomson Wadsworth, 2009), co-authored with Clyde M. Nabe and Donna M. Corr.

REFERENCES

Corr, C. A. (1995). Children's understandings of death: Striving to understand death. In K. J. Doka (Ed.), *Children mourning, mourning children* (pp. 3–16). Washington, DC: Hospice Foundation of America.

Corr, C. A. (1996). Children and questions about death. In S. Strack (Ed.), *Death and the quest for meaning: Essays in honor of Herman Feifel* (pp. 217–238). Northvale, NJ: Jason Aronson.

Fogarty, J. A. (2000). *The magical thoughts of grieving children: Treating children with complicated mourning and advice for parents*. Amityville, NY: Baywood.

Jung, C. (1954). *The development of personality*. In H. Read, M. Fordham, & G. Adler (Eds.), *The collected works of Carl G. Jung* (2nd ed., Vol. 17). Princeton, NJ: Princeton University Press.

Kastenbaum, R., & Aisenberg, R. (1972). *The psychology of death*. New York: Springer.

Lamers, E. P. (1995). Children, death, and fairy tales. *Omega, Journal of Death and Dying, 31*, 151–167.

Maurer, A. (1966). Maturation of the conception of death. *Journal of Medical Psychology, 39*, 35–41.

Nagy, M. A. (1948/1959). The child's theories concerning death. *Journal of Genetic Psychology, 73*, 3–27. (Reprinted with some editorial changes as "The child's view of death," in H. Feifel (Ed.), 1959, *The meaning of death* (pp. 79–98). New York: McGraw-Hill.)

Speece, M. W., & Brent, S. B. (1984). Children's understanding of death: A review of three components of a death concept. *Child Development, 55*, 1671–1686.

Speece, M. W., & Brent, S. B. (1996). The development of children's understanding of death. In C. A. Corr & D. M. Corr (Eds.), *Handbook of childhood death and bereavement* (pp. 29–50). New York: Springer.

Stambrook, M., & Parker, K. C. (1987). The development of the concept of death in childhood: A review of the literature. *Merrill Palmer Quarterly, 33*, 133–157.

November 17th

Julia Marquez

The night my brother
Gabriel
died
I was at
a birthday party
which wasn't very fun
because the water in the pool was
murky and
hazy
and I couldn't see the bottom
and I didn't get in.

I got a green
balloon though.
It was tied to my wrist.

And later when I went to the hospital
and my mom and dad took me into a little
room with flowery furniture
and they told me Gabriel
died
I can't say I had a big moment of shock, or burst
into tears, or felt like I was falling — none of that,
none that I remember —
and I didn't really
do all those grieving things
you see in movies after someone dies, like
wear a black veil

and hover on the verge of tears all the time,
or hide away in my room.

In fact, I didn't think I really *grieved* at all.
How was I supposed to know how to grieve?
I was only
just turned six.

My parents didn't go to that
extent, but they were sad
and sometimes grumpy
or tired
and it seemed like the two of them
were floating aimlessly
in an shadowy, hazy world —
two dirt specks drifting
in that pool at the birthday party
where I got my green balloon.

The thing is, though — I didn't think I was really
with them.
They were floating — sad,
distant — in the pool
and I was sitting on its clammy edge, with cold toes
and my green balloon on my wrist
looking in, and not wanting to get in
because I couldn't see the bottom.

~

For a long time I thought that was how it was —
that I hadn't
grieved at all —
that I had only
sat on the edge of the pool
and peeked in, but

once I was sitting at the kitchen table and my mom
said
Oh no, you were a
scared
little kid.
You followed me everywhere.
You always had to have
someone else in the room with you —
even when you went to the bathroom.

And I remembered that —
that when I had to go
I would make Daddy come with me
and lean against the doorframe,
watching me.

And then she told me
that had I told her, once, after Gabriel died
about this dream I had

in it
someone rang the doorbell of our old house
and we peeked out the little window in the door
and there was a lady with black
scraggly hair covering her face
and we couldn't let her in, because if we did
she would grow bigger and bigger until she
broke the roof of our house
and we couldn't let that happen

Mom said that when you dream
about a house
you're dreaming about yourself, and she said
the lady with her face covered by black hair
was death, and that I was worried
and scared that since Gabriel died,

maybe I would too.

I had been grieving
in my own way
but I didn't know it
until maybe
six years later.

~

I never
ever told
anyone
that my brother Gabriel was
dead.
I always
told people
that my brother
Gabriel
died.

I always thought the word
dead
was such an awful word,
much too cold, too harsh
for such a delicate matter,
like someone who didn't *really* care
had said it.
It had a finality to it —
He's dead.
It was the period
at the end of a sentence.

If my brother
Gabriel
was dead, it meant he was gone

forever, his ashes
buried underneath a tree,

and he was never
coming back
ever
and I would never
see him again.

But if my brother
Gabriel
died —
maybe he hadn't gone
completely away.
Maybe
if my brother
Gabriel
wasn't dead, but he'd
died
he hadn't
disappeared forever, he'd only left this life
and gone on to someplace else
lovely.

The word
died
has a little bit of hopeful
something in it,
like a finger
trailed soft
across your cheek.

If my brother
Gabriel
Wasn't dead, but he had
died,

I had gotten up
from the side of the pool
and leaned down and put my hand inside it, and
pulled my parents out,
inch by
inch.

If my brother
Gabriel
wasn't dead, but had
died,
I had untied
the green balloon
from my wrist
and my parents and me, faces upturned,
had watched it
float hopefully
away
into the broad blue
sky.

Julia Marquez, *13, is an award-winning poet and short-story writer. She plays the piano and cello and loves to read and watch old movies. She lives in Overland Park, Kansas, with her parents and sister.*

CHAPTER 2

The Adolescent's Encounter with Death

David Balk

I
n discussing adolescent encounters with death, four primary questions arise: (1) How do adolescents understand death? (2) What experiences of death might adolescents have? (3) How might these experiences vary across class and culture? (4) What do educators and counselors need to understand to work with this population? Our starting point is a grim analysis from the World Health Organization.

A Starting Point

In a 1998 report, the World Health Organization (WHO) expressed grave concern for the health and lives of older children and adolescents around the world (WHO, 1998). For example, "The transition from childhood to adulthood will be marked for many in the coming years by such potentially deadly 'rites of passage' as violence, delinquency, drugs, alcohol, motor vehicle accidents and sexual hazards," such as HIV and other sexually transmitted diseases (p. 10).

Socioeconomic conditions play a significant part in the risks adolescents face—impoverished urban youth are at the greatest risk. In the United States, only the adolescent cohort has declined in life expectancy since the 1980s (WHO, 1998). This decline may be due to the staggeringly high homicide rates among 15-to-24-year-old African-American males (Pallone & Hennessy, 2000; Price, Thompson, & Drake, 2004; Slaby, 1994).

The Backstory: Adolescent Development

Actors commonly develop a "backstory" when they delve into a role; it includes aspects of the character's upbringing, conflicts, and values that inform the actor about the role but may never be verbalized in the performance. The crucible of adolescent development forms the backstory for exploring adolescent encounters with death. Scholars typically demarcate adolescent development into three phases: early, middle, and later adolescence. Peter Blos (1979) introduced this distinction, which has led to such practical outcomes as the development of middle schools, designed to ease the transition from elementary school to high school.

Early adolescence extends approximately from age 10 to age 14, and is marked by the onset of puberty. Middle adolescence extends from age 15 to age 17, and later adolescence extends from age 18 to age 22. These age ranges are conditioned by Western cultural biases in developed countries; in some cultures, coming of age cannot be delineated into three phases—boys and girls pass from childhood into adulthood when they reach puberty and can perform the tasks expected of an adult. Some examples are the rites of passage practiced in Colombian Indian tribes and among American Navajos (Correal, 1976; Markstrom & Iborra, 2003). Arnett and Taber (1994) noted that entrance to adulthood in most nonwestern cultures is socially defined and demarcated by a specific event, such as marriage.

In Western cultures, three specific developmental tasks mark the gradual transition from adolescence to adulthood. From early to later adolescence, it is expected that the person will gain skill and competency to (1) make career choices, (2) enter into and maintain intimate relationships, and (3) form an autonomous identity. In short, the developmental tasks adolescents are expected to master involve responsibility, interpersonal intimacy, and individuality.

Fleming and Adolph (1986; see also Fleming & Balmer, 1996) identified conflicts endemic to each phase of adolescent development: separation versus safety (the core conflict in early adolescence); independence versus dependence (middle adolescence); and closeness versus distance (later adolescence). Grappling with these conflicts and resolving their ambiguity and uncertainty is how people master the developmental tasks of responsibility, interpersonal intimacy, and individuality.

Reaching the age of 22 does not automatically propel one into adulthood. Some people remain ambivalent throughout their lives about accepting responsibility, sustaining interpersonal intimacy, and forging an autonomous identity. For later adolescents, failure to master the core issues around career, intimacy, and self-concept produces anxiety, because drifting through life is not an acceptable developmental outcome. Parents and faculty advisers are familiar with the anxiety felt by college undergraduates who have not found a direction.

David Elkind (1967) identified two self-reflective, egocentric thought processes that distinguish adolescence from other parts of the life cycle. Adolescents begin to think they are the center of everyone else's attention—that they are, in effect, always on stage. Elkind referred to this phenomenon as "the imaginary audience." In addition, adolescents may develop a notion that their uniqueness results from circumstances solely applicable to them; Elkind called this phenomenon "the personal fable."

In short, a paradoxical aspect marks adolescent cognitive development. Adolescents are more capable than children of reflecting on their experiences and distinguishing between what is and what is possible; at the same time, they become notoriously preoccupied with the self, convinced that no one else has ever endured what they must bear. Adolescent growth is at great risk of lapsing into solipsism—a state of extreme egocentrism in which one believes, consciously or not, that one is all that really exists or matters. Mastering the three fundamental developmental tasks moves a youth from self-absorption to mature involvement with the world. Such mastery is gradual (thus, the three phases), and not everyone successfully moves out of self-absorption.

Issues That Hinder an Adolescent's Understanding of Death

Thanatologists list four elements of a mature understanding of death: universality, finality, causality, and nonfunctionality. "Persons with a mature understanding know that (a) all living things eventually die, (b) death is irreversible, (c) both internal and external factors can lead to death, and (d) bodily functions cease with death" (Balk, 2007, 209–210). Before early adolescence, people attain a mature understanding of death and let go of the fuzzy or magical thinking about death characteristic of younger children, although magical thinking can reappear when cognitively mature persons are touched by a death. For eloquent evidence of this, see Joan Didion's reflective book (2005) written following the death of her husband. Adolescents' cognitive development does not necessarily prevent them from misunderstanding the reality of death.

The Noppes (1996) emphasized that ambiguity marks adolescent understanding of death, and it's easy to see that adolescents are at a distinct disadvantage when appraising death because of their belief in an imaginary audience and personal fable. Adolescents understand that death is irreversible and universal, and that it involves nonfunctionality (Koocher, 1974; Speece & Brent, 1996), but their solipsistic thinking eliminates their own death as a possibility. They believe, in effect, "It won't happen to me." Some scholars (e.g., Dolcini, Cohn, Adler, Millstein, Irwin, et al., 1989; Greene, Krcmar, Walters, Rubin, & Hale, 1997) consider adolescent risk-taking behavior an outgrowth of their egocentrism and perceptions of invulnerability. I am convinced that adolescents are no different than adults who intellectually understand death but engage in risky behaviors (e.g., drinking and driving or risky sexual activity), dismissing the fact that they are tempting fate.

Major Cause of Adolescent Death: Violence

In both developed and developing countries, adolescents and young adults typically die from some form of violence: homicide, suicide, or accident. Violent deaths account for over 50% of all deaths of 15-to-24-year-olds, regardless of country of residence (WHO, 2006). No other cause of death—for instance, heart disease, malignant neoplasms, leukemia, or circulatory system diseases—accounts for even 8% in this age group in any country.

In most cases, the likelihood of adolescent violent death correlates to the country's level of development, but not always. Consider the following data.

Adolescents in developed countries are half as likely to die as their peers in developing countries (Fingerhut, Cox, & Warner, 1998; WHO, 2006). However, 15-to-24-year-olds in the United States are six times more likely to be murdered than their peers in other developed countries—a rate that mimics that of developing countries.

Homicide is the leading cause of death for 15-to-24-year-old African-American males in the United States (National Center for Injury Prevention and Control, 2003; Price, Thompson, & Drake, 2004; U. S. Department of Justice, 2006); no other developed country comes even close to the incidence of firearm-related deaths of 15-to-24-year-olds in the United States.

Internationally, the adolescent suicide rate has increased 60% since the late 1950s (Befrienders, 2003). Females are more likely to make suicide attempts, but males are much more likely to take their own lives (Arias, Anderson, Hsiang-Chiong, Murphy, & Kochanek, 2003; WHO, 2003).

ADOLESCENT DEATH DUE TO LIFE-THREATENING ILLNESS

As noted earlier, WHO paints a gloomy picture for child and adolescent health around the world today. "One of the biggest 21st century hazards to children will be the continuing spread of HIV/AIDS. In 1997, 590,000 children under age 15 became infected with HIV. The disease could reverse some of the major gains in child health in the last 50 years" (WHO, 1998, p. 4).

Medical researchers have expressed concern at the growth of HIV infection among adolescents and young adults in both the developed and developing world (ReproWatch, 1999; Zha, 1998). For instance, researchers in the United States noted that a quarter of all new cases of HIV infection in this country occur in the 13-to 21-year-old group (Chabon & Futterman, 1999), and health professionals are alarmed at the spread of HIV infection among youth in Latin America and Africa (Snell, 1999; Weiss, Buvé, Robinson, Van Dyck, Kahindo, et al., 2001).

Adolescent Response to Life-Threatening Illness

Beliefs about human multidimensionality apply to adolescent responses to life-threatening illness—such an illness will require responses to physical, interpersonal, cognitive, emotional, behavioral, and spiritual issues.

Responding to physical issues

With invasive treatments, the adolescent may face major changes in energy and appearance (e.g., weight loss, hair loss, perhaps amputation), as well as the possibility of dying. As one adolescent with cancer said, "When I was first diagnosed, I thought I was going to die. There was no way I could be cured" (Rich, 2002, p. 571). Stevens and Dunsmore (1996) note that adolescents with cancer endure changes to body image at a point in life when appearance matters very much. Outsiders may not realize how upsetting these changes are to an adolescent "because many patients put on a brave front, but the pain of the experience is often felt for many years" (Stevens & Dunsmore, 1996, p. 110).

Responding to interpersonal issues

The adolescent will face challenges from peers, even friends, who do not understand the constraints imposed by the illness. Some peers who have their own anxiety and fear of death will shun the adolescent with a life-threatening illness. Noll and colleagues (1993) reported 2-year longitudinal findings indicating that adolescents with cancer were more socially isolated than healthy peers; however, they did not differ from their peers on a variety of measures of social acceptance and seemed psychosocially well-adjusted (see also Vance & Eiser, 2002).

Responding to cognitive issues

Adolescents will want to learn as much as possible about their illness and may become quite knowledgeable about symptoms, treatments, and prognosis. Another cognitive issue for adolescents with a life-threatening illness is determining the significance of their illness (for instance, determining the impact on career plans or assessing the prospects of death at an early age) (Burgess & Haaga, 1998; see Moos & Schaefer, 1986). Some researchers in Finland (Winqvist, Vainionpaeae, Kokkonen, & Lanning, 2001) have reported cognitive impairments in late adolescent and young adult cancer survivors who contracted cancer before age 5; these impairments typically involved short-term memory difficulties and were attributed to the effects of cranial radiation.

Responding to emotional issues

The adolescent will have to deal with a wide range of emotions, including anger and frustration over loss of independence (Stevens & Dunsmore, 1996). Rich (2002) noted that fear was a primary response of adolescents at a cancer camp. However, he questioned the opinion that adolescents with cancer constantly fear death. While fear of death was prominent at diagnosis among the adolescents he knew over a 5-year period at the camp, the fear dissipated over time for most of the youth: "The campers I have interviewed have been surprisingly open and comfortable discussing issues related to death and dying. It appears that having childhood cancer may actually make some of the campers…more comfortable with a topic that is taboo in western culture" (Rich, 2002, p. 573). Some campers seemed to have no fear of death, which Rich attributed to their having faced the real possibility of death.

Responding to behavioral issues

In addition to behavioral constraints that result from fatigue, a salient behavioral issue for adolescents involves depending on others for activities that persons typically do on their own; for example, dressing, eating, washing, making one's bed, and going to the toilet (Stevens & Dunsmore, 1996). Medical staff may add to the frustration adolescents feel by treating them like children.

Responding to spiritual issues

The adolescent will face questions of ultimate meaning and the future. "Hope becomes an essential ingredient for living successfully for these young people. Their hopes may not necessarily be for a cure or magical recovery, but more often for joy and success with the challenges of living" (Stevens & Dunsmore, 1996, p. 113). On her bedroom wall, one adolescent with cancer wrote, "Be realistic. Plan for a miracle" (Stevens & Dunsmore, 1996, p. 113).

Pamela Hinds and colleagues (1999) conducted a longitudinal study to determine the degree of hopefulness, and what was hoped for, among 78 adolescents (12 to 21 years of age) in the first 6 months of their cancer treatment. These adolescents were more hopeful than reported in other samples of adolescents with cancer; they hoped for many and varied things, such as regaining health and returning to normalcy. Only female research participants hoped for increased family closeness and economic independence. Only males hoped for public acclaim and success in athletics.

Adolescents Facing Illness and Death: Diagnosis Stage

At diagnosis, the most common reaction is denial, followed quickly by expectations that the worst will happen. The reported reactions reported by Stevens and Dunsmore seemed to be the same as those Kübler-Ross (1969) saw in adults dying of a terminal illness; however, Stevens and Dunsmore do not believe adolescents enter a progression of "stages of dying" when they discover they have cancer.

A key goal at diagnosis is to help adolescents and their parents appraise the situation realistically according to the adolescent's prospects. The quality and accuracy of communication at diagnosis sets the stage for the struggle to overcome the disease and has been shown to be instrumental in enabling terminally ill adolescents to accept palliative care if that becomes an option (Stevens & Dunsmore, 1996).

Communicating with the adolescent is a key factor. Adolescents want medical staff to talk with them about their illness; they resent being talked about by their parents and medical staff as if they weren't there. An extensive literature search conducted by researchers at the University of California at Berkeley found that very few efforts have been made to provide systematic information to adolescents about their cancer or to assess the effectiveness of such efforts (Scott, Harmsen, Prictor, Sowden, & Watt, 2003).

Adolescents Facing Illness and Death: Treatment Stage

During and following treatment, adolescents with cancer manifest remarkable resilience (Woodgate, 1999a; 1999b). For instance, because they have had to deal with terminal illness, they consider themselves to be more mature than their unaffected peers and better able to cope with difficult times (Stevens & Dunsmore, 1996). These adolescents seem to grow as a result of their difficult situation, much as researchers have reported is the case with bereaved adolescents (Balk, 1983; Offer, 1969). They are more sensitive to others' hardships, not afraid to be in the presence of people who are experiencing emotionally painful times, and more mature than their unaffected peers.

Research increasingly indicates that developmental factors are involved in the resilience of youth who battle cancer or cope with other traumatic experiences. The conclusion is that resilience in at-risk youth occurs when a set of basic human protective systems, including a supportive family, are present and active (Caffo & Belaise, 2003). These findings suggest directions and opportunities for the professionals who work with adolescents coping with cancer.

Adolescents Facing Illness and Death: Terminal Stage

Adolescents in the terminal stage of cancer have various reactions to dying. These variations are attributed to personality differences, disparities in the history of each adolescent's illness, different expectations about the kind of caregiving the adolescent will accept, and what is needed to provide adequate palliative care. The responses range from denial that death is imminent versus resigned acceptance of death, desire for peace and quiet versus preference for noise and bustle, wishing to be alone versus wishing to be surrounded by family and friends, and wanting to be alert to the end versus choosing to be heavily sedated (Stevens & Dunsmore, 1996).

There is a remarkable parallel between the needs expressed by older adults with a terminal illness and the needs expressed by adolescents in the later stages of cancer: the need to maintain a sense of identity, to remain active in decisions that affect them, to feel worthwhile and valued, and to receive appropriate, satisfactory care (Corr, Nabe, & Corr, 2005; Stevens & Dunsmore, 1996). Rather than fearing death, adolescents dread the loss of control they associate with the *process* of dying (Stevens & Dunsmore, 1996). While this equanimity is not true of all adolescents with cancer, some adolescents' views about death are captured in comments such as "Having cancer has changed my views about death. I realize that death is not something horrible but just another chapter in one's life" (Rich, 2002, p. 573).

It is important to remember, however, that not all adolescents reach such a state of equanimity—some remain in denial and others are very fearful at the end. It would be an injustice to impose on any adolescent with a terminal illness the expectation that becoming poised and composed about death is the norm. Equanimity in the face of dying is one possibility seen in some adolescents.

BEREAVEMENT DURING ADOLESCENCE: DEATHS OF OTHERS

So far, this chapter has focused on the adolescent's own death and dying, but most adolescent experiences of death will involve either the wrenching loss of someone the adolescent loves or the deaths of acquaintances, distant relatives, strangers in the news (e.g., soldiers in war or celebrities), and characters in TV shows and movies. Until death touches the adolescent personally, as in the death of someone loved or greatly admired, I believe it remains an abstraction, not an integrated part of the person's understanding of being human.

We know from surveys of American high school and college students that adolescents are familiar with bereavement (Balk, 1997; Ewalt & Perkins, 1979; LaGrand, 1985, 1986; Servaty-Seib & Hamilton, 2006; Zinner, 1985). Several surveys conducted with convenience samples (Balk, 1997) and supported by reports from educators and counselors indicate that, at any given time, 22–30% of college students are in the first 12 months of grieving a death. The most common death adolescents report is that of grandparents. Some deaths occur within the nuclear family; the most studied bereavement experiences of adolescents are the deaths of parents and siblings (Balk & Corr, 2001; Worden, 1996). More attention needs to be paid to the bereavement experiences of adolescents from minority cultures and from single-parent families.

We know that normal bereavement responses for adolescents (1) include distress of greater intensity and duration than the adolescent would have expected; (2) can produce interpersonal isolation (such as loss of friendship with persons who do not understand the grief); and (3) can involve transient cognitive difficulties such as trouble concentrating on schoolwork.

Implications for Those Who Work with Adolescents

Educators and counselors must understand the developmental tasks and issues that mark early, middle, and later adolescence. For example, a primary impetus in the lives of adolescents is making decisions. Dying or bereaved adolescents do not need well-meaning persons to rush in and rescue them and, in the process, disenfranchise them. At the same time, adolescents do not want to be left alone to deal with their confusion and fear.

Growing evidence in the bereavement literature (Balk, 1983; Saldinger, 2001; Saldinger, Cain, & Porterfield, 2003; Sandler, Ayers, Wolchik, Tein, Kwok, et al., 2003; Silverman, 2000; Worden, 1996) underscores the fact that consistent, engaged parenting helps bereaved adolescents cope effectively over time. Counselors and educators can design and deliver workshops that promote such parenting.

Adolescents who are experiencing normal bereavement are likely to be overwhelmed by the intensity of their feelings, the extended duration of these feelings, and the unexpected intervals of calm and then renewed distress. Educators and counselors can provide lucid explanations of what normal grieving entails. "Normalizing the normal" seems to be a freeing experience for the isolated, bereaved adolescent. As one grieving college student asked me some years ago, "Why are we left to go through this ordeal alone?"

Major complicating factors for bereaved adolescents are (1) the lack of accurate information about bereavement and (2) the lack of power to get such information (Ribbens McCarthy, 2006). Death educators need to disseminate, in understandable language, clinical and research knowledge that discloses what has been learned about the phenomenon of bereavement. Much has been written about the function of "meaning-making" in the grief process (Neimeyer, 2002; Ribbens McCarthy, 2006). Much should be written about the risks to bereaved youth who are forced to cope in a trial-and-error fashion because information that would help them construe meaning is not disseminated.

Interactions with peers are an important way for adolescents to move beyond the solipsism of the personal fable and the imaginary audience. Peer relationships help adolescents enter into and maintain interpersonal intimacy. Bereaved and dying adolescents are at great risk of losing contact with their peers, who prefer to avoid the distress of bereavement or of a life-threatening illness, or are afraid to be around someone who is dying or bereaved. Educators and counselors can design short modules of information to educate adolescents about the needs of their affected peers and to help them role-play ways of interacting with someone who is dying or bereaved.

The mission and activities of the student-initiated National Students of Ailing Mothers and Fathers (AMF) Support Network, established at Georgetown University, also has implications for educators and counselors. As of June 2007, the organization had chapters on 40 campuses. Its mission is to "support all college students with an ailing or deceased loved one, empower all college students to get involved in the fight against terminal illnesses, and raise awareness about the needs of grieving college students" (National Students of AMF, 2007). Among its activities are "developing Campus Chapters, providing interactive e-support online, awarding scholarships, distributing research grants to enhance the field of adolescent bereavement studies, conducting conferences on college student bereavement, and holding fundraising events—including the annual Boot Camp to Beat Cancer" (National Students of AMF, 2007). One response of educators and counselors involved with AFM chapters has been to ally themselves with students as facilitators and advisers rather than as primary decision makers.

We are not sure about the incidence and prevalence of prolonged grief disorder (formerly called "complicated bereavement") among adolescents. Given the gap in knowledge about this topic, the following would seem to be in order:

1. Well-designed research efforts using valid data-gathering procedures could identify the incidence and prevalence of prolonged grief disorder among early, middle, and later adolescents.

2. Adolescents who are experiencing prolonged grief disorder are at risk of not accomplishing the major developmental tasks. Interventions to help these adolescents—who might otherwise stop developing or even regress—are a social obligation of educators, counselors, and researchers.

3. Interventions should cover the whole person and take into account the conflicts and issues that mark early, middle, and later adolescent development. Covering the whole person means identifying the physical, behavioral, cognitive, emotional, interpersonal, and spiritual needs of adolescents who are experiencing prolonged grief disorder. For example, schoolwork may be imperiled while the adolescent struggles with grief; institutional policies should be in place that recognize the special academic circumstances of students who are temporarily unable to concentrate on their studies.

Concluding Comments

The focus of this chapter is on the adolescent's encounter with death. Such encounters encompass the causes of adolescents' deaths (primarily some form of violence) and bereavements produced by the deaths of family members and friends. Adolescent developmental tasks and transitions provide the backstory for understanding adolescent encounters with death, placing into developmental context adolescent reactions to terminal illness and to bereavement. A holistic template with its acknowledgement of multiple dimensions to human existence affords another important schema for appreciating the impact of terminal illness and of bereavement during adolescence. Developmental tasks and transitions along with a holistic template provide rich conceptual structure for intervening with dying and bereaved adolescents.

David E. Balk, Ph.D., is a Professor at Brooklyn College where he directs Graduate Studies in Thanatology. His research has examined adolescent bereavement over the death of family members and friends. Dr. Balk is collaborating with colleagues at different universities to establish the prevalence and severity of college student bereavement. With department colleagues and a Brooklyn physician, he is examining the psychological impact of early pregnancy losses. Dr. Balk is Associate Editor and Book Review Editor of the peer-reviewed journal *Death Studies*, and Editor-in-Chief of the 2007 publication *Handbook of Thanatology: The Essential Body of Knowledge for the Study of Death, Dying, and Bereavement.*

REFERENCES

Arias, W., Anderson, R. N., Hsiang-Chiong, K., Murphy, S. L., & Kochanek, M. A. (2003, September 18). Deaths: Final data for 2001. *National Vital Statistics Reports, 52*(3) 116 pp.

Arnett, J. J., & Taber, S. (1994). Adolescence terminable and interminable: When does adolescence end? *Journal of Youth and Adolescence, 23,* 517–537.

Balk, D. E. (1983). Adolescents' grief reactions and self-concept perceptions following sibling death: A case study of 33 teenagers. *Journal of Youth and Adolescence, 12,* 137–161.

Balk, D. E. (1997). Death, bereavement, and college students: A descriptive analysis. *Mortality, 2,* 207–220.

Balk, D. E. (2007). Working with children and adolescents: An overview of theoretical and practical issues. In K. J. Doka (Ed.), *Living with grief: Before and after the death* (pp. 209–227). Washington, DC: Hospice Foundation of America.

Balk, D. E., & Corr, C. A. (2001). Bereavement during adolescence: A review of research. In M. S. Stroebe, R. O. Hansson, W. Stroebe, & H. Schut (Eds.), *Handbook of bereavement research: Consequences, coping, and care* (pp. 199–218). Washington, DC: American Psychological Association.

Befrienders. (2003). Suicide statistics. Retrieved from www.befrienders.org/suicide/statistics.htm

Blos, P. (1979). *The adolescent passage: Developmental issues.* New York: International Universities Press.

Burgess, E. S., & Haaga, D. A. F. (1998). Appraisals, coping responses, and attributions as predictors of individual differences in negative emotions among pediatric cancer patients. *Cognitive Therapy and Research, 22,* 547–473.

Caffo, E., & Belaise, C. (2003). Psychological aspects of traumatic injury in children and adolescents. *Child and Adolescent Psychiatric Clinics of North America, 12,* 493–535.

Chabon, B., & Futterman, D. Adolescents and HIV. *AIDS Clinical Care, 11*(2), 9–11, 15–16.

Correal, G. S. (1976). Adolescence in tribal cultures. *Revista Colombiana de Psiquiatria, 5,* 76–84 [Original language Spanish].

Corr, C. A., Nabe, C. M., & Corr, D. M. (2005). *Death and dying, life and living* (5th ed.). Belmont, CA: Thomson Higher Education.

Creswell, J. W. *Educational research: Planning, conducting, and evaluating quantitative and qualitative research.* Upper Saddle, NJ: Merrill Prentice Hall.

Didion, J. (2005). *The year of magical thinking.* New York: Knopf.

Dolcini, M. M., Cohn, L. D., Adler, N. E., Millstein, S. G., Irtwin, C. E., Kegeles, S. M., & Stone, G. C. (1989). Adolescent egocentrism and feelings of invulnerability: Are they related? *Journal of Early Adolescence, 9,* 409–418.

Elkind, D. (1967). Egocentrism in adolescence. *Child Development, 38,* 1025–1034.

Ewalt, P. L., & Perkins, L. (1979). The real experience of death among adolescents: An empirical study. *Social Casework, 60,* 547–551.

Fingerhut, L. A., Cox, C. S., & Warner, M. (1998). *International comparative analysis of injury mortality.* Atlanta, GA: Centers for Disease Control and Prevention, National Center for Health Statistics.

Fleming. S. J., & Adolph, R. (1986). Helping bereaved adolescents: Needs and responses. In C. A. Corr & J. N. McNeil (Eds.), *Adolescence and death* (pp. 97–118). New York: Springer Publishing Company.

Fleming, S. J., & Balmer, L. E. (1996). Bereavement in adolescence. In C. A. Corr & D. E. Balk (Eds.), *Handbook of adolescent death and bereavement* (pp. 139–154). New York: Springer Publishing Company.

Greene, K., Krcmar, M., Walters, L. H., Rubin, D. H., & Hale, J. L. (1997). Targeting adolescent risk-taking behaviors: The contribution of egocentrism and sensation-seeking. *Journal of Adolescence, 23,* 439–461.

Hinds, P. S., Quargnenti, A., Fairclough, D., Bush, A. J., Betcher, D., Rissmiller, G., Pratt, C. B., & Gilchrist, G. S. (1999). Hopefulness and its characteristics in adolescents with cancer. *Western Journal of Nursing Research, 21,* 600–620.

Koocher, G. P. (1974). Talking with children about death. *American Journal of Orthopsychiatry, 44,* 405–411.

Kübler-Ross., E. (1969). *On death and dying.* New York: Macmillan.

LaGrand, L. E. (1985). College student loss and response. In E. S. Zinner (Ed.), *Coping with death on campus* (pp. 15–28). San Francisco: Jossey-Bass.

LaGrand, L. E. (1986). *Coping with separation and loss as a young adult: Theoretical and practical realities.* Springfield, IL: Charles C. Thomas.

Markstrom, C. A., & Iborra, A. (2003). Adolescent identity formation and rites of passage: The Navajo *kinaaldá* ceremony for girls. *Journal of Research on Adolescence, 13,* 399–425.

Moos, R. H., & Schaefer, J. A. (1986). Life transitions and crises: A conceptual overview. In R. H. Moos (Ed.), *Coping with life crises: An integrated approach* (pp. 1–28). New York: Plenum.

National Center for Injury Prevention and Control. (2003). *Fatal injuries: Leading causes of death reports.* Atlanta GA: Centers for Disease Control and Prevention.

National Students of Ailing Mothers and Fathers. (2007). Empowering the lives of grieving college students. Retrieved from www.studentsofamf.org/

Neimeyer, R. A. (2002). Making sense of loss. In K. J. Doka (Ed.), *Living with grief: Loss in later life*. Washington, DC: Hospice Foundation of America.

Noll, R. B., Bukowski, W. M., Davies, W. H., Koontz, K., & Kulkarni, R. (1993). Adjustment in the peer system of adolescents with cancer: A two-year study. *Journal of Pediatric Psychology, 18,* 351–364.

Noppe, L. D., & Noppe, I. C. (1996). Ambiguity in adolescent understandings of death. In C. A. Corr & D. E. Balk (Eds.), *Handbook of adolescent death and bereavement* (pp. 25–41). New York: Springer Publishing Company.

Offer, D. (1969). *The psychological world of the teenager.* New York: Basic Books.

Pallone, N. J., & Hennessy, J. J. (2000). Blacks and whites as victims and offenders in aggressive crime in the U.S.: Myths and realities. In N. J. Pallone (Ed.), *Race, ethnicity, sexual orientation, violent crime: The realities and the myths* (pp. 1–33). Binghamton, NY: Haworth Press.

Price, J. H., Thompson, A. J., & Drake, J. A. (2004). Factors associated with state variations in homicide, suicide, and unintentional firearm deaths. *Journal of Community Health: The Publication for Health Promotion and Disease Prevention, 29,* 271–283.

ReproWatch. (1999). More and more young people get HIV/AIDS. *ReproWatch (Youth Ed.), 5*(1), 1–2.

Ribbens McCarthy, J. (2006). *Young people's experiences of loss and bereavement: Towards an interdisciplinary approach.* Berkshire, England: Open University Press.

Rich, M. D. (2002). Memory circles: The implications of (not) grieving at cancer camps. *Journal of Contemporary Ethnography, 31,* 548–581.

Saldinger, A. L. (2001). *Anticipating parental death in families with school-aged children.* Unpublished doctoral dissertation, University of Michigan, Ann Arbor.

Saldinger, A., Cain, A., & Porterfield, K. (2003). Managing traumatic stress in children anticipating parental death. *Psychiatry, 66,* 168–181.

Sandler, I. W., Ayers, T. S., Wolchik, S. A., Tein, J.-Y., Kwok, O-M, Haine, R. A., et al. (2003). The Family Bereavement Program: Efficacy evaluation of a theory-based prevention program for parentally bereaved children and adolescents. *Journal of Consulting and Clinical Psychology, 71,* 587–600.

Scott, J. T., Harmsen, M., Prictor, M. J., Sowden, A. J., & Watt, I. (2003). Interventions for improving communication with children and adolescents about their cancer. *Cochrane Database of Systematic Reviews, 3,* 1–32.

Servaty-Seib, H., & Hamilton, L. A. (2006). Educational performance and persistence of bereaved college students. *Journal of College Student Development, 47,* 225–234.

Silverman, P. R. (2000). *Never too young to know: Death in children's lives.* New York: Oxford University Press.

Slaby, R. (1994). Reduction and prevention of violence. In L. Eron & J. Gentry (Eds.), *Violence and youth: Psychology's response Vol. II.* Papers of the American Psychological Association on Violence and Youth. Washington, DC: American Psychological Association.

Snell, J. (1999). The looming threat of AIDS and HIV in Latin America. *The Lancet, 354,* 1187.

Stevens, M. M., & Dunsmore, J. C. (1996). Adolescents who are living with a life-threatening illness. In C. A. Corr & D. E. Balk (Eds.), *Handbook of adolescent death and bereavement* (pp. 107–135). New York: Springer Publishing Company.

Speece, M. W., & Brent, S. B. (1996). The development of children's understanding of death. In C. A. Corr & D. M. Corr (Eds.), *Handbook of childhood death and bereavement* (pp. 29–50). New York: Springer Publishing Company.

U. S. Department of Justice Bureau of Justice Statistics. (2006, June 29). Homicide trends in the U.S. Retrieved from www.ojp.usdoj.gov/bjs/homicide/overview.htm

Vance, Y. H., & Eiser, C. (2002). The school experience of the child with cancer. *Child: Care, Health and Development, 28*, 5–19.

Weiss, H. A., Buvé, A., Robinson, N. J., Van Dyck, E., Kahindo, M., Anagonou, et al. (2001). The epidemiology of HSV-2 infection and its association with HIV infection in four urban African populations. *AIDS, 15* (Suppl. 4), S97–S108.

Winqvist, S., Vainionpaeae, L., Kokkonen, J., & Lanning, M. (2001). Cognitive functions of young adults who survived childhood cancer. *Applied Neuropsychology, 8*, 224–233.

Woodgate, R. L. (1999a). Conceptual understanding of resilience in the adolescent with cancer: Part I. *Journal of Pediatric Oncology Nursing, 16*, 35–43.

Woodgate, R. L. (1999b). A review of the literature on resilience in the adolescent with cancer: Part II. *Journal of Pediatric Oncology Nursing, 16*, 78–89.

Worden, J. W. (1996). *Children and grief: When a parent dies.* New York: Guilford Press.

World Health Organization. (1998). The world health report 1998. Life in the 21st century: A vision for all. Retrieved from http://ftp.who.int.gb/pdf_files?WHA51/ea3.pdf

World Health Organization. (2003). Suicide rates. Retrieved from www.who.int/mental_health/prevention/suicide/suiciderates/en

World Health Organization. (2006). Estimates of child and adult mortality and life expectancy by country. Retrieved from wwws.who.int/whosis/database/mort/table3.cfm

Zha, B. (1998, June). AIDS in China. *China Population Research Newsletter, 1*, 4–5.

Zinner, E. S. (Ed.). (1985). *Coping with death on campus. New Directions for Student Services*, No. 31. San Francisco: Jossey-Bass.

CHAPTER 3

Completing the Picture: Adult Perspectives on Death— Implications for Children and Adolescents

Kenneth J. Doka

> *"Doctor, doctor, will I die?*
> *Yes, my child, and so will I."*
>
> Nursery Rhyme

AWARENESS OF DEATH IN CHILDHOOD AND ADOLESCENCE

It is easy to take the position that, by early adolescence, children can understand the complex concept of death. However, the process of dealing with death continues throughout the life cycle, which means that the significant adults in the lives of grieving children and adolescents may also be struggling—perhaps not to understand death but to come to terms with their own loss, their own grief, and their own mortality. This process may limit their ability to be present for the child as he or she struggles with death, grief, and loss.

Between the two short lines of the nursery rhyme lies a complex developmental process. Very young children have a difficult time understanding an abstract term such as "death." As discussed in earlier chapters, children gradually master the concept and understand the universality of death—that it is inevitable, inclusive, unpredictable, and irreversible. Children begin to learn that the dead do not function in a corporal way. Yet, as they attempt to develop their own spiritual approach to death, they may believe that the dead continue in other ways, such as in memory, in some sort of afterlife, or in another conceptualization of symbolic immortality (see Lifton & Olson, 1976). Speece and Brent (1996) say that part of understanding death entails a greater comprehension of causality. Children move from magical thinking about death to understanding the reasons living things die.

But while older children are aware of death, the concept often is not personalized. The child recognizes that he or she, like all living creatures, will die, but that thought is pushed into a very abstract future. The issue of the inevitability of one's own death is not cogent unless it is provoked by a life-threatening illness (Bluebond-Langner, 1965). The cognitive comprehension of death does not necessarily entail the recognition of personal mortality. There is a great gap between "People die" and "I will die."

The recognition of death may begin in childhood as the understanding of the inevitability and universality of death increases, but developmental issues that arise in adolescence make the awareness of mortality more of a concern. Adolescents struggle with a number of issues that intersect with death. Primarily, they are striving to create an individual identity. As they struggle with this individuality, there can be a growing awareness that death/nonexistence represents a great threat to this emerging identity. In some cases, this awareness may lead to extensive denial of death or challenges to death—evident in the risky behaviors that often appear in this stage of life.

The threat of death can be exacerbated by the stress and isolation the adolescent experiences. In this time of critical reflection and reassessment, previous sources of support, such as religion, may no longer be as viable. With an emerging sense of individuality may come a growing sense of aloneness. "There is no one like me" easily becomes "No one understands me." There may be a sense of separation from parents and mourning for the loss of childhood. As Alexander, Colby, and Alderstein (1957) assert, death may become a more significant issue at times in which one's identity experiences psychological and social stress. Their projective testing techniques indicated that death is affect-laden for adolescents, albeit on a less conscious level.

While adolescents have a sharpened awareness of mortality, they are also defended against the awareness. One of the major defenses is that adolescents are very present-oriented. This is clear in Kastenbaum's (1965) work on the meaning of death in adolescence. Kastenbaum found that most of his adolescent participants had little sense of finality. In their present-oriented world, death was simply not a major issue. Only a small minority thought about death. These results were similar to a much earlier study that found college students to be relatively unconcerned about death (Middleton, 1963). In a review of literature, Newman (1987) found that while adolescents in that era feared nuclear war and environmental devastation, they had few concerns about personal death. Perhaps an illusion of invulnerability, emerging from the intense present orientation, contributes to the adolescent tendency to challenge death.

Thus, while adolescents may begin, perhaps subconsciously, to recognize their own mortality, their intense present orientation makes it unlikely that this awareness will become a significant issue for them.

Awareness of Mortality in Early Adulthood

Mortality can also be ignored in early adulthood. Erikson (1963), for example, saw young adults consumed by a quest to consolidate identity and establish intimacy. The young adult is concerned with the external world—establishing intimate relationships, beginning a family, and starting a career. However, some dimensions of early adult life do, at least in a remote way, raise issues of mortality. As young adults begin to accumulate assets and responsibilities—for a significant other, spouse, or child—they may begin to execute documents such as wills, advance health directives, and guardianships. Such documents involve an implicit recognition of mortality. Similarly, as adults begin to raise children, they consider the spiritual traditions, values, and beliefs they wish to share with their offspring. This may trigger thoughts about the afterlife that lead to a consideration or mortality. But these thoughts are usually remote and episodic.

We believe that adults in middle and later life feel the presence of death more keenly and that this understanding affects their orientation toward life and loss. Building on earlier work (Doka, 1988, 1995), we can say that people develop an *awareness of mortality* in midlife and an *awareness of finitude* (Marshall, 1980) in later life. This is the typical progression, but either awareness can occur earlier, especially if the person's life is marked by internal or external events such as war or catastrophe, unexpected losses, early onset of chronic illness, or the expectation of a limited life span.

It is important to understand this process and determine how these struggles might affect the ability of adults—such as parents, guardians, or grandparents—to help a child deal with death and loss. For example, when parents are deeply anxious about their own mortality, they may be unable or unavailable to help their child, and may even stifle conversations that would allow the child to make sense of his or her questions and anxieties about death or to be supported in his or her grief.

While some psychoanalytic theorists, such as Freud (1925) and Weisman (1972), assert that humans can never imagine their own deaths, development theorists have suggested that the full awareness of mortality begins to emerge in middle adulthood. This awareness is the recognition that one will die, although not necessarily in the immediate future. It is the understanding that the end to one's time is drawing inexorably closer. In short, it is the increasing perception that a person has only one life to live. Many theorists believe that mortality concerns become more internal and introspective in midlife. Erikson (1963) characterizes this stage of life as "generativity vs. stagnation." Implicit in his discussion is an increasing awareness of personal mortality that creates a desire in these adults to "pass the torch" to a younger generation. The middle adult wants to develop a legacy, a contribution that will establish the significance of his or her life. This desire is fueled by the increasing understanding that one's time is limited; if one does not use this time productively, there might not be an opportunity in the future.

Although the universality of the "midlife crisis" is debated, its adherents claim that the knowledge of future death provides the impetus for a major reevaluation of one's life (Brim, 1976; Jacques,1965; Levinson, 1978; Lifton, 1975; Neugarten, 1972; Zacks, 1980). Research by Rothstein (1967) supports the view that death becomes more of a concern in midlife. He interviewed 36 adults ages 30 to 48 years and found that the older respondents (43–48 years) tended to personalize death more than those in the 30–42 age group. Death becomes a more salient issue in midlife; the initial response is shock, followed by resigned accommodation.

MIDLIFE: DEVELOPING THE AWARENESS OF MORTALITY

A number of factors contribute to the awareness of mortality in middle adulthood. First, as adults reach their 30s, 40s, and 50s, they begin to experience various physiological and sensory declines that remind them of the inevitability of aging and dying.

In the late 30s and early 40s, a man falls below his earlier peak levels of functioning. He cannot run as fast or function on as little sleep as before. His vision and hearing are less acute; he remembers less well and finds it harder to learn masses of specific information (Levinson, 1978, p. 213). Women experience perimenopause, and both men and women may experience a gradual diminution of sexual prowess, which triggers thoughts of loss and aging. Kastenbaum and Aisenberg (1976) suggest the possibility of an inverse relationship between reproductive capability and the sense of terminus.

Second, the mortality rate increases dramatically in the 40s. For example, the mortality rate for men 45 to 64 years old is six times that of men 25 to 44 (Tamir, 1982). As one enters midlife, one begins to experience more often the deaths of peers from causes other than accident or suicide. Stephenson (1985) notes that these losses may trigger both reactive and existential grief. Reactive grief is a response to the loss of another person; existential grief is the recognition that I myself will suffer and die. The loss of others in one's cohort is a vivid reminder of personal vulnerability.

A third factor contributing to the awareness of mortality is the aging of one's parents and members of their cohort. The previously omnipotent parent seems increasingly weak and vulnerable. To Blenkner (1965), this is a significant factor in adult development. Not only does aging create a new relationship with the parent, it triggers thoughts of one's own aging and death. In addition, one's children typically are establishing their own families and careers, reinforcing the reality that the midlife cohort is advancing toward perhaps distant but definitely inescapable death. As Moss and Moss (1983, p. 73) state,

> The loss of a parent represents the removal of a buffer against death. As long as the parent was alive, the child could feel protected, since the parent by the rational order of things was expected to die first. Without this buffer, there is a

strong reminder that the child is now the older generation and cannot easily deny his or her own mortality.

Other factors in midlife may also increase awareness of mortality. Grandparenthood is often interpreted as a mark of age. Planning for retirement (although it may not be imminent) reminds adults of the passage of time. Certain birthdays (e.g., 40 or 50) may be felt as marks of age. A serious operation, health crisis, or onset of chronic illness is likely to increase awareness of mortality.

Awareness of mortality in adults can develop gradually over time as they become aware of physical declines and vulnerability. Or it may be a sudden insight in response to a crisis. The age at which a person achieves this awareness depends on the situations and circumstances of his or her life.

No matter how the awareness of mortality develops, it has certain implications for adult life. First, one's sense of time depends on one's age: The child primarily looks toward the future, while the elderly person may be more oriented toward the past. Neugarten (1972) theorizes that this restructuring of time occurs in middle age, when the increasing awareness of finiteness leads people to think in terms of both time since birth and time left to live.

The shift in time orientation has profound implications for the sense of self, and the recognition of personal mortality leads to a reassessment of one's identity. Middle-aged people consider what they have been, what they wished to be, and what they can still become. They begin to think about what they can leave behind. Using the terminology of Lifton and Olson (1974), there is a search for *symbolic immortality* in creations or progeny. According to Erikson (1963), *generativity* becomes a central issue. Generativity involves establishing and guiding the next generation; the concept includes productivity and creativity (p. 267). Levinson (1978) describes a similar phenomenon:

> Knowing that his own death is not far off, he is eager to affirm life for himself and for generations to come. He wants to be more creative. The creative impulse is not merely to "make" something. It is to bring something into being. To give birth; to generate life (p. 222).

The middle-aged person is not morbidly preoccupied with death—he or she is in the prime of life, with death likely to be decades away. But the recognition that it will come can create a desire to see that the remaining years are well spent.

Thus, the awareness of mortality can be considered to be life-enhancing. Neugarten (1968), for example, sees this awareness as a prod, adding zest to life. Koestenbaum (1971) believes that the knowledge of finiteness contributes to a renewed sense of vitality. If one comprehends personal mortality, one can appreciate—or at least tolerate—the tedious tasks that contribute to the completion of goals, and life takes on new meaning. Zacks (1980) believes that the recognition that time is limited creates an intensified quest for self-actualization. In addition, this awareness may cause a person to be more inner-directed—in the face of a finite life, constraints imposed by others may seem less important.

While the midlife reassessment symbolizes the beginning of long-term preparation for death, other preparations may take more mundane forms. The middle-aged person usually is concerned about such practical aspects of death as obtaining insurance, creating trusts, and writing a will. Preparation activities increase with age (Kalish & Reynolds, 1976).

While an awareness of mortality may in some ways enhance the quality of life and ease the impact of a future death, there are negative aspects as well. The full awareness tends to strike just as family responsibilities and financial constraints are at their peak. Career commitments may be at their apex. If life goals are reassessed, they may seem hopelessly incomplete. Under such conditions, the knowledge that one will die can provoke great anxiety. It could be expected, then, that death anxiety would be at its highest in midlife, as the adult becomes increasingly cognizant of the paradox of heightened responsibility and limited time (Marshall, 1980).

It is beyond the scope of this chapter to review the extensive and contradictory research on death anxiety, but support exists for the idea that it peaks in midlife (see Doka, 1988, 1995; Neimeyer, 1994). Older people in general seem to be less anxious about death. The relationship between age and death anxiety is a complex one that may have different explanations. This may be a statistical artifact, reflecting the greater religiosity of older cohorts that seems to reduce death anxiety (Kalish & Reynolds, 1981). Kalish and

Reynolds (1981) also suggest that the aged—suffering losses, disabilities, and pain—see life as having less value. Perhaps older persons believe that they have lived their lives and accept the fact that now, according to the natural state of the universe, they are approaching death. Or perhaps anticipating and preparing for one's own eventual death reduces overt anxiety about it.

Middle-aged persons have different concerns. They become acutely aware of death just as their commitments and opportunities are their most extensive. Death becomes the haunting specter that may rob them of the opportunity to achieve their goals and enjoy the fruits of their efforts. Death can be the great terror stalking midlife—threatening goals and plans, heralding incompleteness, and even, for some, suggesting the futility and meaninglessness of existence.

This crisis may result in a process of concession to eventual death. The process may include a reevaluation of one's life, renewed commitment to the achievement of critical goals, increased focus on health so as to forestall death, and attempts to reduce the uncertainty and impact of death by prudent preparation. There may also be an increased concern with spirituality. The issues of spirituality, religiosity, age, and death anxiety are too complex and contested to resolve here, but it is consistent with developmental approaches to posit that the recognition of eventual death may encourage spirituality, if not religiosity, in older cohorts. Perhaps the midlife crisis forces adults to confront life to find or construct meaning that will help them avoid the terror of death. Perhaps the longer one is aware of death, the less terrifying it becomes.

To summarize, the awareness of mortality may be the most significant psychological event in middle life. As discussed earlier in the chapter, this awareness has three major implications for adult life.

First, it changes the nature of time. Aware of their mortality, midlife adults struggle with the issue of time remaining. They can see both the starting line and the finish line. Their sense of future is now bounded.

Second, because awareness of mortality likely increases anxiety, adults may choose to deal with death through avoidance and denial. If they are parents, the strategy of avoidance may complicate their child's ability to understand death or deal with loss, especially if the avoidance takes the form of deflecting or forbidding conversations about death, discouraging questions and dialogue about death and loss, or trying to shield the child by limiting information about illness or death in the family or by not allowing the child to visit sick relatives or attend funerals.

Third, awareness of mortality leads to a quest for meaning in one's life. Aware of limited time, even if it is measured in decades, many midlife adults become deeply concerned about meaning in their lives. If one is generally content with one's past and present life and content with the direction life seems to be taking, the concern about meaning may not be overly troublesome. The person simply reaffirms the meaning he or she has already found and perhaps recommits to goals. Or perhaps the person will reprioritize goals; for example, deciding to spend more time with family. If one's past has been problematic, this may be the time to begin closure, perhaps by entering therapy or otherwise confronting past issues and demons. If one views the present as troubling or the future as frightening, the awareness of mortality can engender a sense of panic or terror. Perceiving the boundaries of life, a person may believe that not enough time is left to construct and live a meaningful life. Perhaps the midlife crisis is a manifestation of the frantic attempt to achieve meaning by rearranging one's present and future.

Not everyone, of course, struggles with the issue of meaning. To some, the awareness of mortality is simply too terrifying or the quest to find meaning too difficult to pursue. These persons may use various coping mechanisms, such as escapism or denial, to avoid confronting their mortality. Regarding the fear of nuclear holocaust, Lifton and Olson (1974) describe a process of "psychic numbing" in which the threat is so terrible yet pervasive that the person becomes psychologically incapable of considering it. Perhaps, for some, the threat of death holds so much terror that it can never truly be faced.

The awareness of mortality is the critical defining issue in adult life. It forces a person to find or construct significance and meaning in life, or to surrender to terror.

AWARENESS OF DEATH IN LATER LIFE

In time, the awareness of mortality (i.e., the awareness that one will eventually die) gives way to an awareness of finitude (see Marshall, 1980), in which death is perceived to be closer. The person does not expect to die immediately but realizes that he or she is in the latter part of life. People may become reluctant to think or plan too far into the future, and time is primarily viewed through the past (Neugarten, 1972). This awareness may mediate death anxiety (Neimeyer, 1994), which in turn may enable older adults, such as grandparents, to offer support to children and adolescents who are struggling with loss.

Consistent with the work of Erikson (1963) and Butler (1963), Marshall (1980) sees the awareness of finitude as prompting a life review process. Here one reviews one's life to affirm that it has had meaning and value. To Erikson, a successful life review means that the older person can view life with a sense of "ego integrity"; that is, a sense that he or she has lived a worthwhile life. Or, as Marshall says, that one's life has been "a good story." If the life review is not successful, the person may see a wasted life and may yield to a sense of despair.

Much like the awareness of mortality, the timing of the awareness of finitude is inexact. Illness, frailty, or institutionalization can accelerate it. In fact, a chronic illness or a condition that leads to the expectation of early death can trigger the awareness of finitude and the subsequent life review even in a very young person (Bluebond-Langner, 1965).

The awareness of finitude often engenders a concern for a "good death" (see Marshall, 1980; Weisman, 1972), in which the person will die in a manner consistent with his or her values, wishes, or earlier life. On a practical level, that might mean that the older person is intent on instructing adult children about the estate, advance directives, even wishes concerning funerals and other rituals. This may create a paradoxical situation: As older adults feel compelled to address issues surrounding death, their middle-aged children may be struggling with their own awareness of mortality. They may be deeply threatened by the idea of a parent's death and hence may avoid such discussions. This avoidance can also affect adult children's decision making when they confront the actual death of a parent.

CONCLUSION

There may, then, be three overlapping and related processes that occur as humans struggle with the concept of death. In the first process, *conceptualization*, the child must cognitively comprehend the reality of death. The second process, beginning in late childhood and culminating in middle adulthood, is one of *personalization*. In this process, the person becomes aware of his or her own mortality. In the final, *reconciliation*, a person concedes that death will occur soon—that life is near its end.

Awareness of mortality and of finitude may represent a significant process in adult life. And while such awareness increases the level of anxiety at first, one learns to live with the specter of death in midlife, and it becomes less frightening as we approach it. As Frank Herbert (1977) says in his epic novel *Children of Dune*:

> *To suspect your own mortality is the beginning of terror; to learn irrefutably that you are mortal is to know the end of terror (133–134).*

NOTE: *This chapter draws from the author's earlier published work. See K. Doka, "The awareness of mortality in mid-life: Implications for later life" (revised), in J. Kauffman (Ed.),* The awareness of mortality, *Amityville, NY: Baywood, 1995.*

Kenneth J. Doka, Ph.D., is a Professor of Gerontology at the Graduate School of The College of New Rochelle and Senior Consultant to the Hospice Foundation of America. A prolific editor and author, Dr. Doka's books include *Living with Grief: Before and After Death; Death, Dying and Bereavement: Major Themes in Health and Social Welfare; Pain Management at the End-of-Life: Bridging the Gap between Knowledge and Practice; Living with Grief: Ethical Dilemmas at the End of Life; Living with Grief: Alzheimer's Disease; Living with Grief: Coping with Public Tragedy; Men Don't Cry, Women Do: Transcending Gender Stereotypes of Grief; Living with Grief: Loss in Later Life; Disenfranchised Grief: Recognizing Hidden Sorrow; Living with Life Threatening Illness; Children Mourning, Mourning Children; Death and Spirituality; Living with Grief: After Sudden Loss; Living with Grief: When Illness is Prolonged; Living with Grief: Who We Are, How We Grieve; Living with Grief: At Work, School and Worship; Living with Grief: Children, Adolescents and Loss; Caregiving and Loss: Family Needs, Professional Responses; AIDS, Fear and Society; Aging and Developmental Disabilities;* and *Disenfranchised Grief: New Directions, Challenges, and Strategies for Practice.* In addition, Dr. Doka has published more than 60 articles and book chapters. Dr. Doka is editor of *Omega* and *Journeys: A newsletter to help in bereavement.*

Dr. Doka was elected President of the Association for Death Education and Counseling in 1993 and elected to the Board of Directors of the International Work Group on Dying, Death and Bereavement in 1995 and served as its chair from 1997–1999. He has received numerous awards for his work in thanatology and hospice. In 2006, Dr. Doka was grandfathered in as a mental health counselor under New York's first licensure of counselors. Dr. Doka is an ordained Lutheran minister.

REFERENCES

Alexander, I., Colby R., & Alderstein, A. (1957). Is death a matter of indifference? *Journal of Psychology, 43,* 277–283.

Blenkner, M. (1965). Social work and family relationships in late life, with some thoughts on filial maturity. In E. Shanas & G. Streib (Eds.), *Social structure and the family: Generations relations* (pp. 208–234). Englewood Cliffs, NJ: Prentice-Hall.

Bluebond-Langner, M. (1965). *The private worlds of dying children.* Princeton, NJ: Princeton University Press.

Brim, O. (1976). Theories of the male mid-life crisis. *Counseling Psychologist, 6,* 2–9.

Butler, R. (1963). The life review: An interpretation of reminiscence in the aged. *Psychiatry, 26,* 65–76.

Doka, K. (1988). The awareness of mortality in mid-life: Implications for later life. *Gerontology Review, 1,* 19–28.

Doka, K. (1995). The awareness of mortality in mid-life: Implications for later life (revised). In J. Kauffman (Ed.), *The awareness of mortality* (111–120). Amityville, NY: Baywood.

Erikson, E. (1963). *Childhood and society.* New York: MacMillan.

Freud, S. (1925). Thoughts for the times on war and death. In *Collected papers* (IV). London: Hogarth Press.

Herbert, F. (1977). *Children of Dune.* New York: Berkeley Books.

Jacques, E. (1965). Death and the mid-life crisis. *International Journal of Psychoanalysis, 46*, 502–514.

Kalish, R., & Reynolds, D. (1981). *Death and ethnicity: A psycho-cultural study*. New York: Baywood.

Kastenbaum, R., & Aisenberg, R. (1976). *The psychology of death*. New York: Springer.

Kastenbaum, R. (1965). Time and death in adolescence. In H. Feifel (Ed.), *The meaning of death* (pp. 99–113). New York: McGraw-Hill.

Koestenbaum, P. (1971). The vitality of death. *Omega: The Journal of Death and Dying, 2*, 253–271.

Levinson, D. J. (1978). *The seasons of a man's life*. New York: Alfred A. Knopf.

Lifton, R. J. (1975). On death and the continuity of life: A psycho-historical perspective. *Omega: The Journal of Death and Dying, 6*, 143–159.

Lifton, R., & Olson, E. (1974). *Living and dying*. New York: Bantam Books.

Marshall, V. (1980). *Last chapters: A sociology of aging and dying*. Monterrey, CA: Brooks/Cole.

Middleton, W. (1963). Some reactions toward death among college students. *Journal of Abnormal and Social Psychology, 31*, 155–173.

Moss, M., & Moss, S. (1983). The impact of parental death on middle-aged children. *Omega: The Journal of Death and Dying, 14*, 65–67.

Neimeyer, R. A. (Ed.). (1994). *Death anxiety handbook: Research, instrumentation and application*. Washington, DC: Taylor & Francis.

Newman, A. (1987). Planetary death. *Death Studies, 11*, 131–135.

Neugarten, B. (1972). Adaptation and the life cycle. *Counseling Psychologist, 6*, 16–20.

Neugarten, B. (1968). The awareness of middle age. In B. Neugarten (Ed.), *Middle age and aging* (93–99). Chicago: University of Chicago Press.

Rothstein, S. H. (1967). *Aging awareness and personalization of death in the young and middle adult years*. Ph.D. dissertation, University of Chicago.

Speece, M., & Brent, S. (1996). The development of children's understanding of death. In C. Corr & D. Corr (Eds.), *The handbook of childhood death and bereavement* (29–50). New York: Springer.

Stephenson, J. (1985). *Death, grief and mourning: Individual and social realities.* New York: Free Press.

Tamir, L. (1982). *Men in their forties: The transition to middle age.* New York: Springer.

Weisman, A. (1972). *On dying and denying: A psychiatric study of terminality.* New York: Behavioral Publications.

Zacks, H. (1980). Self-actualization: A mid-life problem. *Social Casework, 61*, 223–233.

The Dying Child

Not only do children cope with death at the earliest ages, sometimes they die. This brief but important section reaffirms this significant reality and offers sage discussion of the issues that may arise as a child dies.

Charles Corr offers an extensive review of the history and philosophy of children's hospice. Many forms of hospice care developed for adults do not have competency in pediatric pain management, proficiency in child and adolescent development, or expertise in the rare neurodegenerative and neuromuscular conditions that might affect children. For those reasons, he says, the development of children's hospice has been slow and uneven. Corr also acknowledges two key problems in offering hospice care for children. The first is that physicians cling to cure-oriented goals, even when those goals are no longer viable, if the patient is a child. Equally important, families are reluctant to admit that the care for their child has become palliative. Corr believes that many children would benefit from hospice and suggests that policies be changed so that any child who is not expected to live to adulthood be eligible for hospice care. He notes that many hospices serve bereaved children and adolescents even if they do not offer pediatric hospice care, and that children's hospices are emerging to fill the need.

These concerns are echoed in the chapter by Rebecca Selove, Dianne Cochran, and Ira Todd Cohen. These clinicians believe that a key factor inhibiting effective pain management in children and adolescents is the reluctance of both the medical team and the family to acknowledge that the goal of care is now palliative. The authors describe the different pain management issues at different ages, from the neonatal period through adolescence. They offer careful counsel on ways to assess and manage pain. The management of pain and symptoms is, of course, essential to providing palliative care to the child. In addition, it plays an essential role in the grief of survivors. The belief that a child died in pain can severely complicate the subsequent grief of parents, siblings, and significant others.

A final chapter, on ethics and children, concludes this section. Here Bruce Jennings suggests a paradigm shift to what he calls the "social ecology orientation," which considers the child in relationship to the family and the larger social world. Jennings acknowledges the tremendous conflicts parents face as they care for a dying child. In addition to offering an exceptional ethical analysis of the conflicts faced at the end of life, he suggests that hospices and other organizations that offer palliative care to children have an ethical responsibility to offer education, counseling, and support to parents and other surrogates who must make agonizing choices. To Jennings, the hospice philosophy is well-suited to the social ecology orientation because it acknowledges the reality of death and offers humane, holistic, and team-centered care.

An additional factor is implied throughout the chapters in this section and specifically addressed elsewhere in the book: The death of a child is a highly complicating factor in bereavement (Rando, 1993), and both the children and their caregivers need effective support as they grieve.

Reference

Rando, T. A. (1993). *The treatment of complicated mourning*. Champaign, IL: Research Press.

CHAPTER 4

Children's Hospice Care

Charles A. Corr

This chapter explores the development, achievements, challenges, and promise of children's hospice care. By first offering a sketch of the philosophy behind children's hospice care and tracing its form and development, discussion can continue on the services offered by such programs—services for dying children and their families as well as for bereaved children and their families. After a brief comparison between children's hospice care and pediatric palliative care, the chapter turns to some of the challenges encountered by children's hospice programs and to an outline of working principles from the Institute of Medicine that are intended to guide the future development of this care. Finally, advances in children's hospice care are illustrated by examples of organizational initiatives in the field, its publications, and other useful resources, as well as a short list of lessons for individuals to take home.

CHILDREN'S HOSPICE: A PHILOSOPHY OF CARE

The term "hospice" properly designates an approach to or a philosophy of care, not a facility. Sometimes the word is best understood as an adjective rather than as a noun. Hospice care need not refer to an inpatient facility, and hospice services can take many forms. The overriding goal of the hospice philosophy of care is to maximize present quality of life. In other words, the hospice philosophy affirms life, not death. That point is particularly important when someone is dying or living with a life-limiting or life-threatening condition.

Hospice care is essentially a form of palliative care or care aimed at managing and minimizing distressing symptoms. It falls within the mainstream of traditional medical care and (even more so) professional nursing care. In recent years, specialization in medical care has led to an increasing, sometimes single-minded focus on efforts to cure; that is, to delay, halt, or reverse the progress of diseases and other morbid conditions. But many diseases and life-threatening conditions cannot be cured.

Cure is a highly desirable goal that should be pursued whenever it is feasible. However, when cure is not possible, the obligation to care remains. Specific interventions may be withheld or withdrawn when they are no longer relevant to the person and the particular circumstances, but care must never be withheld or withdrawn from those who need it.

In order to maximize present quality in living, the hospice philosophy advocates holistic care, a fact that has two important implications. First, this care is offered to help people work on their physical, psychological, social, and spiritual tasks. Second, hospice care is offered not merely to individuals but to persons in the context of their family units. These twin aspects of holistic hospice care are especially relevant for children, because care offered to a child is usually not effective if it tries to separate one aspect of the child's life from another or if it isolates the child from his or her family unit.

Because hospice care addresses every dimension of a child's life, service provision typically involves an interdisciplinary team. No single care provider can be expected to address the full range of a child's physical, psychological, social, and spiritual needs and tasks at the same time. In addition, because hospice care for children is intended to serve both the child and the family, it must be structured to deliver care in the many and varied settings in which the child and the family may find themselves (e.g., hospital, clinic, hospice house, respite, or home) and to offer compassionate support to family members (and members of the care team) both before and after the child's death.

As a form of palliative care, hospice care has been seen as particularly appropriate for individuals with conditions whose natural outcome is death. For this reason, hospice care for adults has often been identified with or limited to care delivered during the last 6 months of life, when curative efforts have been halted. This understanding of hospice care poses special problems for situations involving children.

For example, it is often difficult to predict when a child will die. In addition, hospice care can have a beneficial effect on quality of life much earlier than just shortly before death. For these reasons, knowledgeable observers have proposed that hospice care should be made available to any child who is not expected to survive to adulthood. If that were done, it would enable children with life-threatening or life-limiting conditions and their family members to draw on the psychosocial and spiritual expertise of hospice programs without necessarily foregoing other types of interventions.

CHILDREN'S HOSPICE PROGRAMS AND THEIR DEVELOPMENT

Programs that offer one or more aspects of children's hospice care have developed in many different ways in different parts of the world. Some prominent examples demonstrate the variety and the breadth of services.

In England, children's hospice care began in the early 1980s as a result of the efforts of an Anglican nun who persuaded the parents of a girl named Helen to "lend" her their seriously ill child for short periods of time so they could have a break from the burdens involved in her care. That led to the creation of Helen House, an eight-bed facility with four family apartments built on the grounds of a convent in Oxford. Helen House began serving children with life-shortening conditions and their families in November 1982, offering a "home away from home" for respite and end-of-life care. In February 2004, Douglas House was established as a counterpart to Helen House. Douglas House was the world's first "respice," a seven-bed facility to serve people between 16 and 40 years of age. Helen House (Worswick, 2000) and many similar British programs specialize in respite care within inpatient facilities. In the United States, respite care was the initial focus of the Edmarc Hospice for Children program, established in 1978 in Virginia, which now also offers home health and hospice care, patient and family support, and bereavement support.

Earlier, in the 1970s, Ida Martinson, a nursing faculty member at the University of Minnesota, became involved in the care of a dying child. Martinson's work led to the development of a program of home care for dying children using volunteer nurses in Minnesota and parts of Wisconsin, with training and expert backup support. Martinson also led a research project to test the feasibility and desirability of such care. This and other programs have shown that many seriously ill children want to be at home with their families, even when their illness is far advanced, and that many family members (including the child's parents, siblings, and other relatives) can benefit from being involved in care when they are guided and supported by knowledgeable professionals. A recent article (Feudtner, Feinstein, Satchell, Zhao, & Kang, 2007) shows that, in the United States, children with complex chronic conditions are increasingly dying at home.

Another early initiative took place in the early 1980s at St. Mary's Hospital for Children in Bayside, New York, a long-term hospital for children that offers postacute medical care and rehabilitation therapy. Located in a major metropolitan area, St. Mary's currently offers a broad range of inpatient, home care, respite, and palliative services for children from birth through 18 years.

Two pioneering inpatient facilities have been established to offer hospice care to ill and dying children. They are Canuck Place Children's Hospice in Vancouver, Canada (the first freestanding hospice for children in North America, now supplemented by similar programs in other parts of Canada), and George Mark Children's House in San Leandro, California. Canuck Place opened its doors in November 1995; George Mark Children's House in April 2004. Both offer respite care, transitional care between home and hospital, and end-of-life care specially designed for children with progressive, life-limiting conditions.

Adult hospice programs have not been completely absent from children's hospice care. In the 1970s and 1980s in the United States, adult hospice programs—especially those in rural areas—sometimes were asked to care for ill children and their families who were being sent home from a children's hospital in a large metropolis. An adult program would receive such a request not because it had pediatric expertise, but because it was the only resource in the area that was familiar with the principles of hospice care and was willing to address psychosocial and spiritual issues.

More recently, children's hospice services have been sponsored by some large adult hospice programs in the United States, such as Daniel's Care at Hospice of the Bluegrass in Lexington, Kentucky, and the Child and Family Program at Hospice of the Florida Suncoast in Pinellas County, Florida (see Orloff, 2001). The willingness of programs such as these to devote hard-won funding and staff time to develop the expertise and the broad range of services involved in children's hospice care is a tribute to their commitment to their communities.

Two specialized forms of children's hospice care are found in neonatal and prenatal hospice programs. Neonatal hospice programs operate within the context of intensive care or special care units. In that context, these programs employ hospice and family-centered principles of care to address two types of situations: (1) conditions that can be diagnosed in the womb as incompatible with life even though they are not amenable to cure-oriented interventions; and (2) ramifications of the sudden, unexpected death of an infant in the unit. In both situations, parents, family members (e.g., siblings and grandparents), and healthcare providers need time, a quiet space, and support to cope with these death-related experiences at what should have been the beginning of a new life (Naulty, 2001; Whitfield et al., 1982). Similarly, prenatal hospice programs offer counseling services to parents and siblings when a fetus has died in the womb (Sumner, Kavanaugh, & Moro, 2006).

CHILDREN'S HOSPICE SERVICES

As we have seen, hospice programs focusing on children with life-threatening or life-limiting conditions and their family members have developed in many different ways. Sometimes, these programs have been initiated by a specific person or group of persons; at other times, children's hospice programs have had broad community or institutional backing. In each case, every program has had to define carefully the needs of its community, the populations it can serve, and the services it can best offer.

Two primary contexts for care for the care of ill and dying children (and their family members) suggest the challenges faced by children's hospice programs: (1) the child and family at home; and (2) the child in an inpatient facility. Home care for dying children is both feasible and desirable in many, although not all, instances. That is because the home is the primary health care center in all societies. It is where disease is first fought and quality of life (wellness) is enhanced. Home is the context most natural for children and families. In their homes, parents can carry on their fundamental parental roles and youngsters can most easily continue being their children. Being at home can minimize separation, enhance security, and promote realism in coping with adversity.

The goal of children's hospice home care is not for death to occur at home; it is to enable the child and family to function as well and as long as they can in the normal setting of their lives. Preparation and coordination are indispensable to achieve this goal. Family strengths must be mobilized and weaknesses minimized, both for routine care and to enable appropriate responses to emergency situations. Professional health care providers guide and prepare families to live with a dying child in the home, offer support and backup aid as needed, anticipate and plan for potential challenges, coordinate services among agencies and settings, and strive to minimize burdens imposed by well-meaning but sometimes discordant social and health care systems.

Inpatient care can occur in a variety of settings for a variety of reasons. It might involve a few days designed to bring pain or other distressing symptoms under control, a longer stay if the home situation is inappropriate or requires some relief, or an admission when the demands of a disease and the interventions it requires render any other setting impractical. A hospital, hospice residence, or other inpatient setting may offer important around-the-clock resources and expertise during the last days of a child's life. Simply having a choice as to whether care will be delivered at home or in an institution can contribute significantly to a child's and family's quality of life during a very difficult time.

Respite care can be a bridge between home and inpatient care, as well as a valued service in its own right. It can take the form of a trained "sitter" who comes into the home to provide relief to family caregivers. That person is often a registered or licensed practical nurse who can provide professional services. Respite care can also involve center-based day care or care through the night hours, or it can be offered for a short period in an inpatient facility.

Children's Hospice and Bereavement Care

In addition to ill and dying children, the hospice philosophy of care is also applicable to bereaved children and adolescents, as well as bereaved adults. Bereaved children and adolescents—youngsters coping with dying, death, and loss—include the dying child or adolescent and his or her siblings and peers, as well as the young offspring, relatives, and friends of adults who have died (both as hospice patients and as members of the local community). Adults who are bereaved in relation to the illness or death of a child can also be served by children's hospice care. For these adults and all others who are served by children's hospice care, bereavement care begins with the program's first contact with the individual or family member, not with the event of a death.

Hospice care for family members after the death of a child draws upon the well-established bereavement expertise of hospice programs. As a result, it can be offered in many of the same ways it is offered in adult bereavement follow-up programs. It may involve letters; telephone and personal contacts; provision of pamphlets, books, videos, and other resources; memorial services; support groups for children, adolescents, and adult relatives; and individual counseling. Services can also be offered to peers, classmates, and educators in school and other community settings both before and after a death. Some hospice bereavement services for children and their families can be carried out in conjunction with community agencies and resources, such as children's support groups or local chapters of the Compassionate Friends.

Two examples of community agencies illustrate services that can be offered for bereaved children, adolescents, and their family members. The Dougy Center in Portland, Oregon, founded in December 1982, sprang from the work of Beverly Chappell (2001) and her desire to help a boy named Dougy, while the Winston's Wish program in Cheltenham, England began in 1992 under the leadership of Julie Stokes (2004) and the auspices of a local hospital and hospice program. The Dougy Center (www.dougy.org) is perhaps best known for its bimonthly support groups for preschoolers through the late teens who have experienced the death of a parent or caregiver, a sibling or close friend, or a family member through suicide or homicide. Winston's Wish is distinguished by its residential weekend camps and telephone help line. Both programs rely heavily on trained volunteers. They also offer newsletters and other publications, workshops, and educational programs for lay persons and professionals; intervention programs for teachers and classmates of children who have died or those who are experiencing grief; community outreach programs; internships and practicums for students; and inservice programs for their own staffs. These stand-alone bereavement services are not "hospice" programs as such, but they clearly reflect hospice concerns and principles in helping bereaved children and their family members wherever they are and whatever losses they have suffered.

Children's Hospice and Pediatric Palliative Care

Children's hospice care is not alone in its concerns for minimizing sources of distress and improving quality of life for children and their families. It shares many of these concerns and some common principles with programs of pediatric palliative care. Recent years have witnessed the emergence of an increasing number of pediatric palliative care programs in our society, most often based in children's hospitals (Himelstein, Hilden, Boldt, & Weissman, 2004). These programs of pediatric palliative care have been inspired by the worldwide growth of the hospice movement in general and of children's hospice programs in particular. Another motivating factor has been the desire to move hospice/palliative principles "upstream" in order to apply them at earlier stages in a child's illness and treatment.

Pediatric palliative care recognizes that it may be difficult to know when cure-oriented interventions have reached their limits and should be discontinued. For some children, that time may not arrive until their deaths. Pediatric palliative care may overlap and work in tandem with efforts to prolong life and possibly deliver a cure. The two are not at odds since maximizing present quality of life is always a reasonable and desirable goal. However, pediatric palliative care takes on a special prominence when cure is no longer likely and when more attention should be paid to side effects of treatment, symptoms, and other sources of distress in the life of a child and his or her family. Children's hospice care and pediatric palliative care share many common goals.

Challenges Faced by Children's Hospice Care

In 2005, the National Hospice and Palliative Care Organization (NHPCO, 2006) estimated that approximately 18% of American hospice programs were already providing care for infants, children, and their families, with another 2% planning to do so. There are many reasons why only 20% of American hospice programs offer care for children and their families. For example:

- Many physicians are reluctant to offer a hospice option, perhaps viewing it as representing "giving up" on cure-oriented care.

- Many parents are reluctant to seek out hospice care for their youngsters for similar reasons.

- There is a general expectation in our society that children are not supposed to die, as a result of which we may be conditioned to avert our eyes and thoughts from dying children and their families.

- Public knowledge about hospice care—even after having had hospice programs in our society since the mid-1970s—still appears to be limited.
- Many American hospice programs continue to find it difficult to develop a willingness and the expertise needed to care for children with life-threatening conditions and their families.

Specific challenges to hospice programs that care for children, or might wish to do so, stem from many sources. For example, the "children" in question range widely from infants through adolescents, even including some fetuses prior to or at the time of birth. Only a small number of these children are afflicted with diseases and other life-threatening conditions that make them appropriate for hospice care. Also, their conditions are diverse, including relatively rare neurodegenerative and neuromuscular diseases.

These and other reasons led the Institute of Medicine to undertake a landmark study of pediatric palliative, hospice, end-of-life, and bereavement care (Field & Behrman, 2003). That study explored a wide range of issues, including patterns of childhood death in America; pathways to a child's death; communication, goal setting, and care planning; care and caring from diagnosis through death and bereavement; providing, organizing, and improving care; financing palliative and end-of-life care for children and their families; ethical and legal issues; educating health care professionals; and directions for research. The entire report is well worth reading; here, we can list its working principles (see Field & Behrman, 2003, p. 7):

1. Appropriate care for children with life-threatening medical conditions and for their families is designed to fit each child's physical, cognitive, emotional, and spiritual level of development.
2. Good care involves and respects both the child and the family.
3. Families are part of the care team.
4. Effective and compassionate care for children with life-threatening conditions and for their families is an integral and important part of care, from diagnosis through death and bereavement.

5. Professionals caring for children have a special responsibility to educate themselves and others about the identification, management, and discussion of the last phase of a child's fatal medical problem.

6. Both individual change and organizational change are needed to provide consistently excellent palliative, end-of-life, and bereavement care for children and their families.

7. More and better research is needed to increase our understanding of clinical, cultural, organizational, and other practices or perspectives that can improve palliative, end-of-life, and bereavement care for children and their families.

Implementing these praiseworthy principles so as to develop a full panorama of children's hospice and pediatric palliative care services has not yet been accomplished and will require a major effort on the part of researchers, clinicians, administrators, and ordinary citizens in our society. Still, many organizations' initiatives have been undertaken and numerous resources for this work are currently available.

ORGANIZATIONAL INITIATIVES

Several organizational initiatives illustrate the growing interest in children's hospice care. Since 1983, Children's Hospice International (CHI) has served as an advocate on behalf of hospice care for children and their families. CHI has sponsored national and international conferences while also developing a variety of helpful publications (e.g., Armstrong-Dailey & Zarbock, 2008; Huff & Orloff, 2004; Orloff & Huff, 2003). CHI also administers the Program for All-Inclusive Care for Children and Their Families (PAAC) (see Lowe et al., 2008; Zarbock, 2002), which develops, tests, and evaluates models of continuous, integrated, and comprehensive pediatric palliative and end-of-life care from the time of diagnosis by arranging waivers of certain federal or state Medicaid requirements to remove some financial and regulatory barriers to such care.

Another important organizational initiative is the ChiPPS (Children's Project on Palliative/Hospice Services) program of the National Hospice and Palliative Care Organization (NHPCO). Since its establishment in 1998, ChiPPS has helped sponsor conferences and produced several important publications: *Compendium of Pediatric Palliative Care* (NHPCO, 2000);

Education and Training Curriculum for Pediatric Palliative Care (NHPCO, 2003); and *Caring for Kids: How to Develop a Home-Based Support Program for Children and Adolescents with Life-Threatening Conditions* (NHPCO, 2004). ChiPPS also offers a free electronic newsletter through which expert contributors provide guidance and identify resources for those interested in children's hospice and palliative care.

In England, the Association for Children with Life-threatening or Terminal Conditions and their Families (ACT) has developed a charter (ACT, 2004) listing principles of care for these children and their families, as well as a *Guide to the Development of Children's Palliative Care Services* (ACT, 2003). Both the International Work Group on Death, Dying, and Bereavement (1993) and the American Academy of Pediatrics (AAP, 2000) have published statements on palliative care for children.

PUBLICATIONS AND RESOURCES

More than 20 years ago, Corr and Corr edited a book, *Hospice Approaches to Pediatric Care* (1985a), that reflected the state of the field at that time. They have also published journal articles about hospice care for children addressed to various audiences (1985b, 1988,1992). Many other publications have appeared, along with Internet-based resources. See, for example, books by Carter and Levetown (2004), Field and Behrman (2003), and Goldman, Hain, and Lieben (2005).

In addition to the NHPCO education and training curriculum, similar curricula have been published by the End-of-Life Nursing Education Consortium (ELNEC, 2003; directed to a nursing audience) and the Initiative for Pediatric Palliative Care (IPPC, 2003) specifically linked to hospital situations). The IPPC curriculum includes a number of useful training videos.

In the United States, the Children's Hospice and Palliative Care Coalition has established helpful online support sites for parents who are coping with challenges associated with a life-threatening illness in a child. The sites—in English and Spanish—offer support through diagnosis, treatment, death, and bereavement. (See www.PartnershipforParents.org or www.PadresCompadres. org.) A useful Internet resource for professionals in England is the Childhood Bereavement Network (www.ncb.org.uk/cbn).

LESSONS FOR INDIVIDUALS TO TAKE HOME

The Institute of Medicine report offers a series of complex recommendations for providing and organizing child and family-centered care, financing that care, educating health professionals, and conducting needed research. Readers of this chapter can work within their own agencies and organizations to implement those recommendations. But we do not have to wait until large organizations and health care systems have been stimulated into action. If the individuals and programs that pioneered this field (many of whom are mentioned in this chapter) had taken a wait-and-see attitude, many children and families would not have been served, and children's hospice/palliative care would not be where it is today. We can take the following lessons from these pioneers:

- There is great power in the hospice philosophy.

- There is a critical need for improvement in the implementation of hospice and palliative care principles, as well as for making these services more widely available to the children and families who need them.

- No single children's hospice or palliative care program will meet the needs of all children and adolescents with progressive life-limiting conditions, as well as the needs of their family members, in all settings and communities.

- Individuals must assess the specific needs of children and adolescents with life-threatening or life-limiting conditions in their particular communities, as well as the needs for child-related bereavement services, the resources that are already available in each community, and the initiatives that might be most promising.

- One of the most pressing needs is to break down barriers between service providers to achieve effective coordination of care.

- Opportunities abound for developing new services in the realm of children's hospice care and pediatric palliative care, as can be seen from the limited number of examples cited in this chapter.

- Consider what the situation of children with progressive life-limiting illnesses and their family members would be if these services were not available to them—and realize that this is often the case.

CONCLUDING THOUGHTS

In the preface to her well-known book *On Death and Dying* (1969), Elisabeth Kübler-Ross suggested three reasons why attention should be paid to dying persons (see also Corr, 1993). Each of these reasons can easily be adapted to children's hospice and the care it offers to ill and dying children and their family members.

First, a child who is seriously ill, dying, or bereaved, and his or her family members, are facing major stressors. During this time, they all have issues to face and unfinished business to address. To carry out these tasks, they need support and assistance from a caring community.

Second, providers will be more effective in offering care and support if they take the time to listen to those who are facing these difficulties, let them guide efforts to help, and learn about the application of hospice principles to these situations.

Third, children and their family members who are coping with the extraordinarily difficult experiences of dying and bereavement have much to teach others. All of us can learn about our own mortality, limitations, and vulnerability from the children and family members who are served by children's hospice care.

Charles A. Corr, Ph.D., CT, is a member of the Board of Directors of the Hospice Institute of the Florida Suncoast, the ChiPPS (Children's Project on Palliative/Hospice Services) Leadership Advisory Council of the National Hospice and Palliative Care Organization, the Executive Committee of the National Donor Family Council, the Association for Death Education and Counseling, and the International Work Group on Death, Dying, and Bereavement (Chairperson, 1989–93). He is also professor emeritus, Southern Illinois University Edwardsville. Dr. Corr's publications in the field of death, dying, and bereavement include 35 books and booklets, along with more than 100 chapters and articles in professional publications. His most recent publication is the sixth edition of *Death and Dying, Life and Living* (Thomson Wadsworth, 2009), co-authored with Clyde M. Nabe and Donna M. Corr.

REFERENCES

American Academy of Pediatrics, Committee on Bioethics and Committee on Hospital Care. (2000). Palliative care for children. *Pediatrics, 106,* 351–357.

Armstrong-Dailey, A., & Zarbock, Z. (Eds.). (2008). *Hospice care for children* (3rd ed.). New York: Oxford University Press.

Association for Children with Life-threatening or Terminal Conditions and Their Families (ACT). (2004). *The ACT charter for children with life-threatening conditions and their families* (4th ed.). Bristol, England: Author.

Association for Children with Life-threatening or Terminal Conditions and Their Families & the Royal College of Paediatrics and Child Health. (2003). *A guide to the development of children's palliative care services* (2nd ed.). Bristol & London, England: Authors.

Carter, B. S., & Levetown, M. (Eds.). (2004). *Palliative care for infants, children, and adolescents: A practical handbook.* Baltimore: Johns Hopkins University Press.

Chappell, B. J. (2001). My journey to the Dougy Center. In O. D. Weeks & C. Johnson (Eds.), *When all the friends have gone: A guide for aftercare providers* (pp. 141–154). Amityville, NY: Baywood.

Corr, C. A. (1993). Coping with dying: Lessons that we should and should not learn from the work of Elisabeth Kübler-Ross. *Death Studies, 17,* 69–83.

Corr, C. A., & Corr, D. M. (Eds.). (1985a). *Hospice approaches to pediatric care.* New York: Springer.

Corr, C. A., & Corr, D. M. (1985b). Pediatric hospice care. *Pediatrics, 76,* 774–780.

Corr, C. A., & Corr, D. M. (1988). What is pediatric hospice care? *Children's Health Care, 17,* 4–11.

Corr, C. A., & Corr, D. M. (1992). Children's hospice care. *Death Studies, 16,* 431–449.

End-of-Life Nursing Education Consortium (ELNEC). (2003). *Advancing palliative care in pediatric nursing: ELNEC—Pediatric palliative care.*

Duarte, CA: American Association of Colleges of Nursing and City of Hope National Medical Center.

Feudtner, C., Feinstein, J. A., Satchell, M., Zhao, H., & Kang, T. I. (2007). Shifting place of death among children with complex chronic conditions in the United States, 1989–2003. *Journal of the American Medical Association, 297*, 2725–2732.

Field, M. J., & Behrman, R. E. (Eds.). (2003). *When children die: Improving palliative and end-of-life care for children and their families.* Washington, DC: National Academies Press.

Goldman, A., Hain, R., & Lieben, S. (Eds.). (2005). *Oxford textbook on pediatric palliative care.* Oxford: Oxford University Press.

Himelstein, B. P., Hilden, J. M., Boldt, A. M., & Weissman, D. (2004). Pediatric palliative care. *New England Journal of Medicine, 350*, 1752–1762.

Huff, S. M., & Orloff, S. (Eds.). (2004). *Interdisciplinary clinical manual for pediatric hospice and palliative care.* Alexandria, VA: Children's Hospice International.

Initiative for Pediatric Palliative Care (IPPC). (2003). *The initiative for pediatric palliative care curriculum.* Newton, MA: Author.

International Work Group on Death, Dying, and Bereavement. (1993). Palliative care for children: Position statement. *Death Studies, 17*, 277–280.

Kübler-Ross, E. (1969). *On death and dying.* New York: Macmillan.

Lowe, P. A. et al. (2008). Children's Hospice International Program for All-Inclusive Care for Children and their Families® (CHI PACC®). In A. Armstrong-Dailey & S. Zarbock (Eds.), *Hospice care for children* (3rd ed.). New York: Oxford University Press.

National Hospice and Palliative Care Organization (NHPCO). (2000). *Compendium of pediatric palliative care.* Alexandria, VA: Author.

National Hospice and Palliative Care Organization (NHPCO). (2003). *Education and training curriculum for pediatric palliative care.* Alexandria, VA: Author.

National Hospice and Palliative Care Organization (NHPCO). (2004). *Caring for kids: How to develop a home-based support program for children and adolescents with life-threatening conditions.* Alexandria, VA: Author.

National Hospice and Palliative Care Organization (NHPCO). (2006). NHPCO's facts and figures—2005 findings. Alexandria, VA: Author. Retrieved from www.nhpco.org

Naulty, C. M. (2001). Neonatal death. In A. Armstrong-Dailey & S. Zarbock (Eds.), *Hospice care for children* (2nd ed.; pp. 110–112). New York: Oxford University Press.

Orloff, S. F. (2001). Incorporating children in an adult hospice program. In A. Armstrong-Dailey & S. Zarbock (Eds.), *Hospice care for children* (2nd ed.; pp. 353–377). New York: Oxford University Press.

Orloff, S., & Huff, S. M. (Eds.). (2003). *Home care for seriously ill children: A manual for parents* (3rd ed.). Alexandria, VA: Children's Hospice International.

Stokes, J. A. (2004). *Then, now and always—Supporting children as they journey through grief: A guide for practitioners.* Cheltenham, England: Winston's Wish.

Sumner, L., Kavanaugh, K., & Moro, T. (2006). Extending palliative care into pregnancy and the immediate newborn period. State of the practice of perinatal care. *Journal of Perinatal and Neonatal Nursing, 20*(1), 113–116.

Whitfield, J. M., Siegel, R. E., Glicken, A. D., Harmon, R. J., Powers, L. K., & Goldson, E. J. (1982). The application of hospice concepts to neonatal care. *American Journal of Diseases of Children, 136*, 421–424.

Worswick, J. (2000). *A house called Helen: The development of hospice care for children* (2nd ed.). New York: Oxford University Press.

Zarbock, S. (Ed.). (2002). *CHI PACC® implementation manual.* Alexandria, VA: Children's Hospice International.

CHAPTER 5

Management of End-of-Life Pain and Suffering in Children and Adolescents

Rebecca Selove, Dianne Cochran, and Ira Todd Cohen

INTRODUCTION

While many barriers remain to providing optimal quality of life for terminally ill children and adolescents, the need for an integrated and proactive approach to this painful reality has been widely recognized in the past decade. Sourkes, Frankel, Brown, Contro, Benitz, and colleagues (2005) contend that the Institute of Medicine's 2003 report *When Children Die* (Field & Berman, 2003) "significantly galvanized new initiatives" (p. 351) and that "an integrated vision…is emerging" (p. 350). Health care professionals can now easily find models and guidelines for providing comprehensive care for children and adolescents at the end of life (see, for example, the Initiative for Pediatric Palliative Care at www.ippcweb.org and the National Quality Forum (2006).

There are significant challenges to implementing these models (Liben, Papadatou, & Wolfe, 2007). For example, although providing optimal pain management must be considered early in a child's illness (Sourkes et al., 2005), family and staff are understandably reluctant to "give up hope" and sometimes delay palliative interventions until the last days or even hours of life. Another challenge arises from the involvement of health care professionals from multiple specialties and disciplines. Differences in philosophy and in coordinating communication among members of the team and with the family can be exacerbated by the hurried pace of medical care (Rushton, Reder, Harris, Comello, Sellers, et al., 2006). Third, the professionals dedicated to improving the quality of life of dying children must address and manage their own "strong emotional and professional tensions, psychological and emotional responses, and religious, spiritual and philosophical reactions" (Perilongo, Rigon, Sainati, Cesaro, Carli, et al., 2001, p. 59) to the impending death of a young person in order to provide high-quality, integrated care.

To provide adequate care for children and adolescents, the role and emotional needs of the family members must be considered (Bartell & Kissane, 2005). The child's comfort can be enhanced when parents experience support and guidance for their own grieving process, and for involving siblings in age-appropriate ways. Parents can then contribute more effectively to the plan for treating their child, have more confidence in its effectiveness, and sincerely reassure their child that relief is on the way.

In addition to considering these system-level variables, effective management of care for children and adolescents at the end of life requires taking into account the multitude of physiologic and psychological changes that occur from infancy through adolescence, including changes in relationships with parents (Thompson & Varni, 1986; Twycross, 1998). Physiologically and pharmacologically, neonates and infants exhibit renal, hepatic, and blood-brain barrier compromise. With maturation, these functions slowly approach those of healthy adults, but special considerations are still required in selecting analgesics, doses, and modalities for children. By assessing a child's conceptualization of what causes and eases pain, understanding of time, ability to implement behavioral and cognitive strategies for coping with pain, and psychosocial issues associated with stage of development, caregivers can gain crucial information to address the physical and emotional issues the child and the family face as death nears.

Neonates and Infants

> *Full acknowledgment of neonatal dignity and personhood is*
> *a prerequisite for an effective treatment of neonatal pain.*
> Belleini, 2005, p. 482

Death in children less than 1 year old, excluding perinatal mortality, most commonly arises from congenital malformations and complications of premature birth (Leunther, 2004; Pierucci, Kirby, & Leunther, 2001). Both of these broad categories of disorders frequently require multiple surgical interventions and ongoing invasive procedures. In addition, prolonged periods of mechanical ventilation and repeated diagnostic tests subject these infants to persistent and, at times, extreme pain. Many of these infants, if not severely compromised, may survive for weeks, even months, experiencing all the discomforts and complications of an intensive care setting (Carter, 2005).

An infant's ability to sense and respond to painful or noxious stimuli has been well documented over the past two decades (Fitzgerald, 2005; Wolf, 1999). By 20 weeks gestation, cerebral, spinal, and peripheral neurodevelopment has achieved thalamic-neocortical arborization, spinothalamic interconnections, and cutaneous sensory neuronal density equivalent to that found in adults. Myelination and inhibitory pathways are still developing after birth, allowing for slow but sustained nociception. In term infants, opioid-binding sites are found in greater numbers in the cerebellum than in adults, and measured brain activity is maximal in sensory areas.

Behavioral and physiological responses of infants strongly suggest that their response to pain is much more than reflexive. Reproducible facial expressions such as forehead bulging, eye closing, and nasolabial furrowing have been observed in both adults and infants with a variety of pain modalities. In the neonate, heart rate, blood pressure, intracranial pressure, and sweating all increase with painful stimuli. Persistent hypersensitivity has been documented in infants who have experienced heel sticks and circumcision without analgesia, demonstrated by increased withdrawal response, prolonged crying, sleep disturbance, and poor feeding. Older infants might exhibit physical resistance by pushing the stimulus away after it is applied, attempting to withdraw, opening the eyes with a look of anger, and crying loudly.

Effective pain management at the end of life starts with a complete pain assessment. Various observational pain assessment scales such as NIPS (the Neonatal Infant Pain Scale) (Lawrence et al., 1993) and CRIES (Crying, Requires increased oxygen, Increased vital signs, Expression, Sleeplessness) (Krechel & Bildner, 1995) provide professionals with standardized tools for evaluating and documenting pain. These instruments use the signs and symptoms described in the previous paragraph. Health professionals can maximize pain management through regular and frequent assessments, intervention planning, and administration of pharmacological treatments. It is imperative that clinicians provide ongoing family education regarding expected pain symptoms related to the trajectory of the disease and the necessity to report symptoms or changes as they are observed.

Compassionate care and symptom management by health professionals can help patients and their families transition from a curative model to a focus on palliative support. We can serve families best by acknowledging our limited ability to cure and at the same time assuring them that much can be done to ensure their child's comfort at the end of life. While they strive to manage symptoms, clinicians also should provide intimate, quiet time for the families to develop memories with their infant and to cope with the impending loss.

The immature physiology of infants often limits practitioners' choice and dosing of analgesic medications. Comparatively insufficient renal and hepatic function decreases clearance and metabolism of most medications, while lower serum protein levels decrease binding of medications and their metabolites. These factors increase drug serum levels in infants, necessitating lower doses, longer dosing intervals and, in some cases, total avoidance. In addition, the incomplete formation of the blood-brain barrier allows greater amounts of hydrophilic medication, such as morphine, to enter the central nervous system more rapidly (Nandi & Fitzgerald, 2005). Studies of analgesics in the infant population are limited, and medication use often falls outside the Food and Drug Administration's labeling recommendations.

Establishing a steady-state analgesic serum level—which minimizes the risk of undertreatment, side effects, and drug toxicity—is ideal for all patients but essential for infants. Around-the-clock dosing of oral and rectal medications and continuous infusions of intravenous drugs are strongly recommended (table 1). Morphine sulfate and fentanyl are often the opioids of choice, because data are available for this age group. Tolerance to fentanyl occurs within 2–3 days, making morphine a superior option (Suresh & Anand, 2001). Methadone, after optimal opioid dosing is determined, offers the advantages of its long half-life, availability in oral form, and antagonism of the NMDA receptors (Chana & Anand, 2001). Experience is limited for the use of adjunct medications in infants. Beh and Kearns (2001) reported on the efficacy of gabapentin in infants with chronic pain.

Regional anesthetic techniques should be considered for this age group (table 2). Epidural infusions via indwelling catheters can achieve remarkable relief of somatic, visceral, and neuropathic pain (Galloway & Yaster, 2000). In infants, many local anesthetics have narrow safety profiles in which therapeutic doses approach levels of toxicity. Ropivacaine has decreased cardio-depression, arrhythmogenicity, and serum free-fraction compared to bupivacaine, making its use relatively safer in this age group. If appropriate, peripheral nerve blocks can be considered for diagnostic purposes and limited treatment.

Because infants cannot verbalize the location and nature of their pain, caregivers rely on other sources of information to determine the cause of a baby's distress. The parents' beliefs and emotions related to their child—as well as the family's history, configuration, and dynamics—can affect their interpretation of their baby's fussiness, withdrawal, or lethargy. Understanding the parents' perspective is crucial, because treatment team members use parents' observations and perceptions to make decisions about pain management and because the treatment team should provide reassuring feedback to family members regarding the baby's behavior and mood. Asking family members about their observations demonstrates a welcoming interest in their involvement in the child's care.

Psychosocial interventions that focus on parents and other caregivers complement medical and pharmacological interventions for reducing pain and distress in neonates and infants. Parents and others who are close to the baby are usually most able to comfort him or her, and can provide blankets or favorite toys from home for the times when they can't be present. They may be able to recommend certain positions that have helped comfort their baby in the past and can provide music or recordings of themselves and other relatives talking or singing.

In many medical settings, chaplains, psychologists, and social workers provide compassionate listening so family members feel understood in their worry and grief. Sometimes these members of the team facilitate communication between the parents and various health care professionals, which can reduce parents' anxiety so they can focus more effectively on soothing their child.

Toddlers

A person's a person no matter how small.
Theodor Geisel (Dr. Seuss), 1954, p. 6

Beyond the first year of life, the most common cause of death during childhood is unintentional or inflicted trauma. In 2002, in the United States, trauma accounted for deaths in 42.5% of 1–4-year-olds (Anderson & Smith, 2005), with traumatic brain injury (TBI) accounting for the largest percentage of deaths. In the 1990s, the death rate due to TBI was 6.7 per 100,000 for children under 4 years (Adekoya, Thurman, White, & Webb, 2002). These children often require intracranial and intravascular monitoring, ventilatory support, and numerous diagnostic procedures. Cardiovascular function in these otherwise healthy trauma victims often remains stable until brain death is confirmed and supportive measures are withdrawn.

Assessing toddlers with a terminal illness should involve creativity on the part of the practitioner. Sick toddlers can still find pleasure and comfort in play activities. Games like "Simon Says," drawing, stacking blocks, singing, or playing with stuffed animals, dolls, or puppets provide a window into the patient while minimizing the disruption of family time. Participating in a toddler's play allows the professional to assess important aspects of the child's pain. Is it harder for a child to move from Mom's lap to color at a play table? Is the child no longer able to ride a tricycle up and down the hallway? Does it seem that the child cannot find a comfortable position on Dad's lap because of pain?

Most toddlers can report general information such as "It hurts a lot," can point to the part of their body that hurts, and can use pain tools such as FLACC (Face, Legs, Activity, Cry, and Consolability) (Merkel, Voepel-Lewis, Shayevitz, & Malviya, 1997) or the Wong-Baker FACES Pain Rating Scale (figure 1). However, they have not developed the ability to describe pain in detail, use qualitative descriptors, or accurately localize symptoms.

Toddlers and preschoolers might deny pain for fear of having another painful exam or to avoid taking bad-tasting medication. Children between the ages of 1 and 4 years might exhibit increased intensity of pain with hysterical crying or rigid body posture. A toddler may pat the body part that hurts. Toddlers may frown or grimace during physical exams, withdraw from beloved activities, or become disinterested in their surroundings as part of their response to increased pain. Parents can help with pain assessment by telling the professional what words are familiar to the child for describing pain.

Pain can provoke intense emotional distress in toddlers. Children ages 2 through 7 years generally do not understand pain as caused by illness or by efforts to treat them, and are prone to experiencing guilt because they think of illness and medical procedures as punishments. They may express anger at parents and at nursing and medical staff for allowing or causing pain to occur. Verbal expressions of pain by children in this age range (and older) can also reflect emotional distress, such as fear of separation from their parents. Emotional pain is sometimes more difficult to describe, even for older children and adolescents.

The toddler age group allows more options for pain intervention than infants, but limiting factors include their level of cognitive development, inability to swallow pills, and body weight too low for standardized medications and delivery systems. Around-the-clock use of oral elixirs and continuous infusions is indicated for these patients, who are unlikely to advocate for themselves (Hain, Miser, Devins & Wallace, 2005). The presence of concrete cognitive function and magical thinking makes toddlers poor candidates for patient-controlled analgesia (PCA), but nurse-assisted PCA has achieved successful pain management by dosing at more frequent intervals (Galloway & Yaster, 2000). As with infants, regional anesthetic techniques can offer alternative approaches (Dadure & Capdevila, 2005; Suresh & Wheeler, 2002).

Long-acting, sustained-released oral opioids depend on embedding the active agent in slowly digested matrixes. Crushing or compounding these medications is contraindicated. Capsules are not an option—they are typically formulated in doses too high for the weight of a toddler and are difficult to swallow. Methadone, as a tablet or an elixir, offers the advantage of a long half-life that increases with exposure to the medication. Dosing can be changed from every 6 hours to every 8 or 12 hours within days to weeks. Adjuncts such as gabapentin, lorazepam, and clonidine can be compounded as liquids (table 1). Transdermal patches do not exist in dose sizes for these patients, who typically weigh less than 20 kilograms. Intravenous lidocaine infusion is a viable alternative in toddlers with neuropathic or intractable pain (Massey, Pedigo, Dunn, Grossman, & Russell, 2002). Advances in topical anesthetic creams and transdermal delivery systems, such as electrophoresis, heat, and low-power laser (Berkowitz & Cohen, 2007; Sethna, Verghese, Hannallah, Solodiuk, Zurakowski, et al., 2005; Zempsky & Cravero, 2004), offer health care providers multiple modalities and the opportunity to select the technique best suited to the patient.

Psychosocial interventions for toddlers and young children include reinforcing cooperative behaviors with verbal praise and sticker charts. Explicit statements are important to emphasize the fact that illness is not a consequence of anything they did and that adults regret that some treatments are painful and will take steps, such as using topical anesthetics, to reduce discomfort.

Health care providers can help prepare children for procedures, transfers, and other aspects of care with simple, concrete explanations of what is planned and why. Child life specialists are trained in the use of medical toys and specially constructed dolls that enable children to see ahead of time a version of what they will experience. In the context of play, children sometimes can express their fear and anger, as well as develop a sense of mastery that helps them be more relaxed, which is associated with less pain and distress. Family members and child life specialists can also provide relaxing, distracting activities according to a child's interests, such as watching movies, drawing and coloring, or reading stories.

Situational factors not consistently associated with age, gender, or medical condition may modify the experience and expression of pain in children and adolescents (McGrath & Hillier, 2003). These factors may include staff behavior, parents' coping strategies, parent attitudes and behavior in relation to staff, and the impact of the child's illness on the family. The presence or absence of family members, as well as the mood and activity of those present, can contribute to or alleviate stress. While it may not be immediately apparent, stressful events in the patient's room may make relaxing and resting more difficult. Health care providers and psychosocial team members can model and coach staff and family members in the use of discretion regarding topics discussed in the child's presence, talking calmly and confidently about day-to-day and hour-to-hour plans, and validating the toddler's emotions.

CHILDREN

> *If children have the ability to ignore all odds and percentages, then maybe we can all learn from them. When you think about it, what other choice is there but to hope?*
>
> Lance Armstrong, 2000

Neoplasms account for approximately 20% of deaths that occur in children between 5 and 12 years (Bradshaw, Hinds, Lensing, Gattuso, & Razzouk, 2004). Childhood cancers are the diseases typically considered when health care providers discuss pediatric palliative care. Pain and discomfort can originate from the disease or as a result of medical or surgical intervention. In this patient population, it is not uncommon to encounter all three categories of pain: somatic (bone, muscle, and mucosa); visceral (hollow and solid internal organs); and neuropathic (nerve impingement, injury, and amputation). In addition, these patients can experience numerous hospital admissions, clinic visits, and diagnostic procedures that may further sensitize them to pain and other symptoms.

Children under age 10 may understand pain associated with trauma more easily than pain associated with disease, because they are operating at a more concrete cognitive level (Twycross, 1998). They may describe their pain in vague terms and may be better able to indicate the location of their pain by pointing to their body, on a drawn outline of a body, or on a simple doll rather than describing it in words. Children 10–12 years old can usually verbalize where they hurt and what has provided relief in the past. As they get older, children are more likely to associate pain with some kind of injury to their body, including illness and disease that has no external cause. They are also better able to collaborate with caregivers in considering various interventions.

Children can be exquisitely sensitive to their caregivers' reactions and moods, and their reports of pain may be affected by their efforts to cope with family dynamics. For instance, a child may deny pain even while grimacing if the parent seems anxious about pain as a sign that the child's condition is deteriorating. A child may complain of pain and ask for more comfort measures as a way of distracting parents who are arguing with each other or talking about other stresses in their lives. This is not to say that the child is not in pain; rather, because emotional stress has physiological repercussions, we could say that the child is attempting to change an interpersonal dynamic in an effort to reduce his or her pain.

In the context of a trusted relationship, children are more likely to describe their pain and express their feelings openly. In her groundbreaking book *The Private Lives of Dying Children*, Bluebond-Langner (1978) wrote, "[C]hildren…were faced with constant conflict. Even the decision to reveal one's awareness directly was fraught with questions of to whom and when. There were always risks involved. If the children used a distancing strategy that other people did not like, or if they attempted to reveal their knowledge and others did not accept it, they might be abandoned" (p. 228). Respectful attention and responses to a child's activities and words can help foster trust in a care provider.

School-aged children can be more actively involved than younger ones in their own pain assessment. Children who have been receiving medical care for ongoing health problems are usually familiar with standard pain tools such as the FACES pain scale or visual analog pain scales. It is common for children in this age group to seek information about why the pain is increasing. Being honest and involving the children and their families in determining the plan of care can lead to significantly better symptom management.

Children can have multiple pain sites and types of pain. It is important to address their concerns and those of their family members, and to continually reassess their pain after implementing treatment. Children should not be expected to make major decisions, but it is important to enable them to participate in their care planning.

Participation in care includes allowing school age children to use PCA and patient-controlled epidural anesthesia (PCEA). Because of their larger size and sometimes prolonged exposure to opioids, it may be possible to implement transdermal, transmucosal (Susman, 2005), and intraspinal (Saroyan, Schechter, Tresgallo, & Granowetter, 2005) delivery systems in these patients. Ideally, these modes of delivery should be reserved for patients who are unable to take (or whose pain is poorly controlled by) oral medications.

One of the greatest challenges in end-of-life pain management is the development of tolerance to and increased need for opioid analgesics. Rapidly escalating intravenous and oral opioid requirements can result in a multifold increase in milligram per kilogram doses (Chang, Chen, & Mao, 2007). Periodic rotation of opioid forms and the inclusion of NMDA receptor antagonists, such as methadone and ketamine, can slow this process (Subramaniam, Subramaniam, & Steinbrook, 2004). Ultra-low-dose ketamine infusions (0.1–0.7 mg/kg/hr) have been shown to have an opioid-sparing action as well as a tolerance-slowing response (Finkel, Pestieau & Quezado, 2007).

Adjuncts available in tablet form—such as gabapentin, nortriptyline, and mexiletine—should be considered for patients with neuropathic pain. Mexiletine is an oral antiarrhythmic that has a lidocaine-like effect in treating neuropathic and intractable pain (Galloway & Yaster, 2000). The medications and techniques discussed for infants and toddlers can also be used in the school-age child, especially when psychological regression and medical debilitation interfere with mental and psychomotor function. Doses of medications must be individualized to the intensity of pain being experienced and specific to the age-determined physiology, and health care providers must determine the correct delivery system for a particular child and that child's family.

Steroids, chemotherapy, radiation, and debulking procedures (which reduce tumors impinging on anatomical structures or nerves) may reduce pain in cancer patients. Regional techniques and nerve blocks can also be effective. If nerve blocks are successful, neurolysis should be offered, with the understanding that loss of associated function will be permanent (Table 2, page 98).

Children in the early elementary school years and younger may not be reassured when they are told that an unpleasant procedure or oral medication will make them feel better—at their level of cognitive development, the parent's kiss and the bandage have more comforting power.

Development of sleeping difficulties is not unusual in children nearing the end of life. They may become anxious about being alone at night, fearing that they will die while they are asleep or worried that their parents will be unable to cope with their death. Preparing parents for the possibility of nighttime fears and helping them create a plan for supporting their child is an important part of care. Parents can model and support bedtime rituals such as reading or telling stories, sharing relaxing images, and focusing on slow, rhythmic breathing. At all stages of a young person's life, a parent's physical contact can be of tremendous comfort. It may take the form of hand-holding, cuddling, and rubbing feet for younger children, and more elaborate massage techniques for older children and teenagers.

By the later elementary school years, most children can benefit from additional behavioral and cognitive interventions. Many children can help plan for distracting activities, practice relaxation techniques such as focusing on their breath and using imagery, and talk about relationships among factors such as worrisome thoughts, difficulty sleeping, and increased pain and distress. Some children like to be asked questions to elicit a detailed description of what is in a favorite room at home or what they did on their Make-a-Wish trip. Parents can enhance the effectiveness of relaxation techniques by practicing them at times when their child is relatively comfortable and better able to concentrate on the activity.

Children and adolescents may need help expressing their thoughts, desires, and grief for the dreams they are unable to fulfill. One should consider what goals a child may want to achieve as his or her life is ending. Children this age and older may be soothed by reviewing family photographs with their parents. Experiencing the meaningfulness of their lives through the voices and memories of their parents can be reassuring to children facing the end of life.

Some young people who feel secure with their caregivers may ask questions about what it will be like to die and what their families will do after their death. A counselor from the family's faith community or a hospital chaplain who has been trained to work with young people may be able to help them express their preferences for memorial services and disposition of their personal belongings.

When home hospice is being discussed as an option, children and families might fear giving up the "safety" of the hospital and losing established professional relationships. Parents may be anxious about living in the house after their child has died there. It can be helpful to have hospice staff meet the child and family in the hospital, to answer questions and begin the process of becoming familiar to the family.

ADOLESCENTS

> *Chances, chances are some might not hold out.*
> *Chances are, hang on right now.*
> *Though my days are filled with sorrow*
> *I see years of bright tomorrows.*
>
> "Chances Are," Bob Marley

Teenage patients can experience death from trauma, neoplasms, and other less frequent causes. Genetic and acquired disorders such as cystic fibrosis, sickle cell anemia, and AIDS can become lethal in the second decade of life. Pain can arise from chronic conditions such as pancreatitis, sinusitis, and aseptic necrosis. Although physiologically similar to adults, these patients require special consideration because they are at a time of life during which intense development in many areas is the norm (Freyer, 2004).

Teens often want to be involved with their pain assessment and care plan, and to be respected by having their questions answered truthfully. They can verbalize their level of pain using the visual analog scale, the numeric scale, or the FACES pain scale. A teenager can be asked to describe the intensity, quality, and patterns of pain he or she has noticed, as well as aggravating factors and anything that has helped alleviate pain. A pain diary can be useful for some adolescents to keep track of changes in pain in relation to activities, mood, and pain interventions. Asking what the adolescent thinks the pain means and how it affects activities of daily living can yield key information.

Adolescents can be supported with explicit messages that they are an important part of the team and their thoughts and ideas will be integrated into the care plan. Sensitivity regarding the pace at which they process information and find words to express themselves increases their comfort with the assessment process, as does respect for their physical privacy.

Adolescents may be "grown up" in physical appearance, vocabulary, and demeanor, but we must be aware of aspects of cognitive and emotional development that distinguish them from adults. Furthermore, considering the social and medical history of each adolescent patient will allow us to be more in sync with what that person needs to be more comfortable. The perspective of a child with a chronic illness, many years of treatment, or an earlier history of treatment followed by remission and then relapse will be quite different from that of a child with a recent, sudden onset of a life-threatening condition.

Adolescents tend to think they are old enough to make many significant decisions for themselves, and they want to be seen as competent. At the same time, they may feel anxious about making mistakes and may know that they don't have the knowledge and experience to make decisions in complex situations. Ideally, health care providers will honor both sides of the seesaw—the wish to be consulted and the wish to involve supportive adults who provide input and reassurance. It can be very important to engage the adolescent in the process of assessing and treating pain while recognizing that parental input, judiciously timed and phrased, can enhance a teenager's sense of control in treatment decisions. Health care professionals can model respectful inclusion of the teenager's attitudes and feelings during conversations with parents. This is a way of proactively addressing the teenager's yearning to be respected as an autonomous individual.

Some adolescents will appreciate education about the team's approach to pain management, perhaps with ABCDE (Assess, Believe, Choose, Deliver, Empower) and PQRST (Precipitating factors, Quality, Radiation, Severity/site, Time) (Hoff & Jensen, 2003). Adolescents may need clarification of the differences between drug tolerance, physical dependence, and addiction. Health care providers should address and dispel the myth that the strongest medications are always saved for last.

Journaling can be useful for some adolescents during this challenging time as a way to reflect on their experience and life. Their goals and priorities may change as they grapple with the realization that their life is ending; writing about their thoughts can help them clarify what they want to communicate to others. Adolescents who are facing the end of life may obtain significant relief by creating tangible expressions of their values, feelings, and memories. Paintings and sculptures, poetry, musical compositions and recordings, scrapbooks, and other crafts can be means for teenagers to "leave a legacy" (Carter & Levetown, 2004, p. 192). Such activities can help a teenager relax during their creation and can provide spiritual comfort because the teenager experiences a sense that his or her impact on the world will continue after death.

Regression, depression, and "normal" adolescent opposition can interfere with a teenage patient's participation in pain management. Both assessment and treatment can be disrupted. By being patient and respectfully listening to an adolescent who is complaining or arguing, the practitioner may be able to convey acceptance of a range of thoughts and emotions and help the young person see the practitioner as an ally.

Although the medications and modalities used for adults are available to this age group, they may not be appropriate or acceptable to individual patients. The effects of a particular therapy may be more intrusive or uncomfortable than the symptoms it is designed to address. For example, an additional intravenous line or epidural catheter, or the disturbance of a preferred routine, may be unwelcome. Prevention or reduction of medication side effects is important in all age groups. Pruritis, nausea, vomiting, constipation, lethargy, and altered sensorium can be as distressing as pain to patients and their families. Antihistamines, serotonin antagonists, laxatives, and stimulants, as well as different medication schedules, should be considered. Wolfe and colleagues (2000) reported that although pain was the number one concern of end-of-life patients and their families, oversedation was also a major concern and was typically not recognized or addressed by the health care team. The children and their parents wanted wakeful periods so that life could be lived before death arrived.

Hyperalgesia—a state of increased sensitivity to noxious and non-noxious stimuli—can develop in patients who receive long-term and high-dose opioids (Chang et al., 2007). This paradoxical response, which can be difficult to distinguish from opioid tolerance, may necessitate a rapid opioid wean supported by analgesic alternatives such as regional anesthesia, behavior interventions, and adjunct therapies. Adjuncts such as NMDA receptor antagonists (methadone, ketamine) and alpha 2-adrenoceptor agonists (clonidine, dexmedetomidine) are especially useful owing to their analgesic properties and ability to prevent or control symptoms of opioid withdrawal (Axelrod & Reville, 2007; Tobias, 2007). Dexmedetomidine, which requires careful titration and monitoring for hypotension and bradycardia, may also be useful in the treatment of end-of-life distress (Jackson, Wohlt, & Fine, 2006).

CONCLUSION

The "multimodal approach" (Chafee, 2001) to alleviating end-of-life pain and suffering for children and adolescents includes integrating pharmacological and psychosocial care with consideration of each patient's physical, cognitive, emotional, and spiritual level of development. Quality care depends on clear and ongoing communication among members of the medical team and with the patient and family. Across the developmental spectrum, optimal care for pediatric patients at the end of life involves integrating respect for their emotional needs as well as those of their family members and the health care professionals. Those who care for children with life-threatening medical conditions must use effective systems of communication and sometimes address complex ethical dilemmas, which can be very challenging when busy providers from multiple departments are involved in a patient's care (see Bearison, 2006). It may be helpful to identify a team member who will take responsibility for coordinating and monitoring each participant's satisfaction with the flow and timeliness of information.

Addressing the emotional well-being of pediatric palliative care staff can improve patients' pain management at the end of life (Burns, Mitchell, Griffith,

& Truog, 2001; Perilongo et al., 2001; Sahler, Frager, Levetown, Cohn, & Lipson, 2000). Professional education and support for staff can lead to improvements in the coordination of services and in staff members' "confidence and ability to manage personal grief" (Rushton et al., 2006, p. 922). When staff members trust their colleagues and feel supported by them, and understand and practice good self-care, they will function better as an integrated team. They will be able to stay in the professional field longer, contributing their collective wisdom to the improvement of systems of care, which ultimately benefits junior practitioners as well as patients and their families.

Each system in which end-of-life care is provided can establish "an array of highly visible and readily available options" (Dixon, Vodde, Freeman, Higdon, & Mathieson, 2005, p. 87) that fit the dynamics of the caregivers and the pace of care, so caregivers will not have to search out a time and place to talk about a patient who is dying or has died. By developing debriefing (Serwint, 2004) or memory-sharing opportunities, staff can design a supportive program that fits the character of their particular group. In this way, they can enhance the quality of their work together, which will translate into better care for patients and their families. Kane (2006) noted that in pediatric palliative care, "[W]e have an opportunity to become co-creators of a health care system that allows us to find meaning in our profession by addressing the needs of the individual as a whole person, and as a community of caring professionals" (p. 849).

Rebecca Selove, Ph.D., M.P.H., is the Clinical Psychologist for the Department of Hematology/Oncology at Children's National Medical Center (CNMC) in Washington, D.C. She received her graduate training at George Peabody College of Vanderbilt University and the Child Study Center at Yale University. She has worked with children and families in hospitals as well as in public schools and community mental health centers. Her research interests include disseminating evidence-based practice in psychosocial care for children with cancer and sickle cell disease and their families, as well as quality of life for long-term survivors of pediatric cancers. She is Primary Investigator for the Palliative Care Improvement Project which obtained information from surveys and focus groups with bereaved parents to develop recommendations for improving end-of-life care at CNMC.

Dianne Cochran, B.S.R.N., received her Bachelor of Science of Nursing from West Virginia Wesleyan College. She has specialized in pediatrics for 22 years and maintained her certification of pediatrics nurse since 1995. Dianne has spent her clinical years at Children's National Medical Center Burn ICU/Burn step-down for five years, eleven years in Post Anesthesia Care and the past six years with the Anesthesia Pain Service. She is actively involved with Pain PI, sickle cell committee and the PANDA (Pediatric Advanced Needs Assessment and Care team) committee.

Ira Todd Cohen is an Associate Professor of Anesthesiology and Pediatrics. He completed his residency in Pediatrics at the Albert Einstein Affiliate Hospitals and in Anesthesiology at the New York University Medical Center. He received further training during his fellowship in Pediatric Anesthesiology at Children's National Medical Center (CNMC) and in pain management at the Pittsburgh Pain Evaluation Treatment Institute. Dr. Cohen received a Masters of Art in Education from the George Washington University. He is an active member of Acute Pain Team and a founding member of the Palliative and End-of-Life Care Committee at CNMC.

REFERENCES

Adekoya, N., Thurman, D. J., White, D. D., & Webb, K. (2002). Surveillance for traumatic brain injury deaths–United States, 1989–1998. *Morbidity and Mortality Weekly Report, 51,* 1–14.

Anderson, R. N., & Smith, B. L. (2005). Deaths: Leading causes for 2002. *National Vital Statistics Report, 53,* 1–89.

Armstrong, L. (2000). *It's not about the bike: My journey back to life.* London: Yellow Jersey.

Axelrod, D. J., & Reville, B. (2007). Using methadone to treat opioid-induced hyperalgesia and refractory pain. *Journal of Opioid Management, 3,* 113–114.

Bartell, A. S., & Kissane, D. W. (2005). Issues in pediatric palliative care: Understanding families. *Journal of Palliative Care, 21,* 165–172.

Bearison, D. J. (2006). *When treatment fails: How medicine cares for dying children.* New York: Oxford University Press.

Beh, M. O., & Kearns, G. L. (2001). Treatment of pain with gabapentin in a neonate. *Pediatrics, 108,* 482–484.

Belleini, C. (2005). Pain definitions revised: Newborns not only feel pain, they also suffer. *Ethics Medical, 21,* 5–9.

Berkowitz, D., & Cohen, I. T. (2007). Laser-assisted anesthesia prior to intravenous cannulation: Acceptability and effectiveness in children. Pediatric Academic Societies, 7125, 4.

Bluebond-Langner, M. (1978). *The private worlds of dying children.* Princeton, NJ: Princeton University Press.

Bradshaw, G., Hinds, P. S., Lensing, S., Gattuso, J. S., & Razzouk, B. I. (2004). Cancer-related deaths in children and adolescents. *Journal of Palliative Medicine, 8,* 86–95.

Burns, J. P., Mitchell, C., Griffith, J. L., & Truog, R. D. (2001). End-of-life care in the pediatric intensive care unit: Attitudes and practices of pediatric critical care physicians and nurses. *Critical Care Medicine, 29*(3), 658–664.

Carter, B. S. (2005). Providing palliative care for newborns. *Pediatric Annals, 33,* 770–777.

Carter, B. S., & Levetown, M. (Eds.). (2004). *Palliative care for infants, children, and adolescents.* Baltimore: Johns Hopkins University Press.

Chaffee, S. (2001). Pediatric palliative care. *Primary Care Clinics in Office Practice, 28,* 365–390.

Chana, S. K., & Anand, K. J. (2001). Can we use methadone for analgesia in neonates? *Archives of Disease of Children, 85,* 79–81.

Chang, G., Chen, L., & Mao, J. (2007). Opioid tolerance and hyperalgesia. *Medical Clinics of North America, 91,* 199–211.

Dadure, C., & Capdevila, X. (2005). Continuous peripheral nerve blocks in children. *Clinical Anaesthesiology, 19,* 309–321.

Dixon, D., Vodde, R., Freeman, M., Higdon, T., & Mathieson, S. G. (2005). Mechanisms of support: Coping with loss in a major children's hospital. *Social Work in Health Care, 41*(1), 73–89.

Field, M. J., & Berman, R. E. (Eds.). (2003). *When children die: Improving end-of-life care for children and their families.* Washington, DC: Institute of Medicine of the National Academies.

Finkel, J. C., Pestieau, S. R., & Quezado, Z. M. (2007). Ketamine as an adjuvant for treatment of cancer pain in children and adolescents. *Journal of Pain, 8,* 515–521.

Fitzgerald, M. (2005). The development of nociceptive circuits. *National Review of Neuroscience, 6,* 507–520.

Freyer, D. R. (2004). Care of the dying adolescent: Special considerations. *Pediatrics, 113,* 381–388.

Galloway, K. S., & Yaster, M. (2000). Pain and symptom control in terminally ill children. *Pediatric Clinics of North America, 47,* 711–746.

Geisel, T. S. (a.k.a. Dr. Seuss). (1954). *Horton hears a who!* New York: Random House.

Hain, R. D., Miser, A., Devins, M., & Wallace, W. H. (2005). Strong opioids in pediatric palliative medicine. *Paediatric Drugs, 7,* 1–9.

Hoff, D. S., & Jensen, P. D. (2003). Pediatric pharmacotherapy. In *Pharmacotherapy self-assessment program* (book 9, pp. 1–24). Kansas City: American College of Clinical Pharmacology.

Jackson, K. C., Wohlt P., & Fine, P. G. (2006). Dexmedetomidine: A novel analgesic with palliative medicine potential. *Journal of Pain Palliative Care Pharmacotherapy, 20,* 23–27.

Kane, J. R. (2006). Pediatric palliative care moving forward: Empathy, competence, quality, and the need for systematic change. *Journal of Palliative Medicine, 9,* 847–849.

Krechel, S. W., & Bildner, J. (1995). CRIES: A new neonatal postoperative pain measurement score. Initial testing of validity and reliability. *Paediatric Anaesthesia, 5*, 53–61.

Lawrence, J., Alcock, D., McGrath, P., Kay, J., MacMurray, S. B., & Dulberg, C. (1993).The development of a tool to assess neonatal pain. *Journal of Neonatal Nursing, 12*, 59–66.

Leunther, S. R. (2004). Palliative care of the infant with lethal anomalies. *Pediatric Clinics of North America, 51*, 747–759.

Liben, S., Papadatou, D., & Wolfe, J. (2007). Paediatric palliative care: Challenges and emerging ideas. www.thelancet.com. Published online August 16, 2007.

Massey, G. V., Pedigo, S., Dunn, N. L., Grossman, N. J., & Russell, E. C. (2002). Continuous lidocaine infusion for the relief of refractory malignant pain in a terminally ill pediatric cancer patient. *Journal of Pediatric Hematology and Oncology, 24*, 566–568.

McGrath, P.A., & Hillier, L. M. (2003). Modifying the psychologic factors that intensify children's pain and prolong disability. In N. L. Schechter, C. B. Berde, & M. Yaster (Eds.), *Pain in infants, children, and adolescents* (pp. 85–104). Philadelphia: Lippincott, Williams & Wilkins.

Merkel, S. I., Voepel-Lewis, T., Shayevitz, J. R., & Malviya, S. (1997). The FLACC: A behavioral scale for scoring postoperative pain in young children. *Pediatric Nursing, 23*, 293–297.

Nandi, R., & Fitzgerald, M. (2005). Opioid analgesia in the newborn. *European Journal of Pain, 9*, 105–108.

National Quality Forum (2006). A national framework and preferred practices for palliative and hospice care quality. Retrieved from http://www.qualityforum.org/publications/reports/palliative.asp

Perilongo, G., Rigon, L., Sainati, L., Cesaro, S., Carli, M., & Zanesco, L. (2001). Palliative and terminal care for dying children: Proposals for better care. *Medical and Pediatric Oncology, 37*, 59–61.

Pierucci, R. L., Kirby, R. S., & Leunther, S. R. (2001). End-of-life care for neonates and infants: The experience and effects of a palliative care consultation service. *Pediatrics, 108*, 653–660.

Rushton, C. H., Reder, E., Hall, B., Comello, K., Sellers, D., & Hutton, N. (2006). Interdisciplinary interventions to improve pediatric palliative care and reduce health care professional suffering. *Journal of Palliative Medicine, 9*, 922–933.

Sahler, O. J., Frager, G., Levetown, M., Cohn, F. G., & Lipson, M. (2000). Medical education about end-of-life care in the pediatric setting. *Pediatrics, 104*, 575–584.

Saroyan, J. M., Schechter, W. S., Tresgallo, M. E., & Granowetter, L. (2005). Role of intraspinal analgesia in terminal pediatric malignancy. *Journal of Clinical Oncology, 23*, 1318–1321.

Serwint, J. R. (2004). One method of coping: Resident debriefing after the death of a patient. *Emergency Department, 145*, 229–234.

Sethna, N. F., Verghese, S. T., Hannallah, R. S., Solodiuk, J. C., Zurakowski, D., & Berde, C. B. (2005). A randomized controlled trial to evaluate S-Caine patch for reducing pain associated with vascular access in children. *Anesthesiology, 102*, 403–408.

Sourkes, B., Frankel, L., Brown, M., Contro, N., Benitz, W., Case, C., et al (2005). Food, toys, and love: Pediatric palliative care. *Current Problems in Pediatric and Adolescent Health Care, 35*, 350–386.

Subramaniam, K., Subramaniam, B., & Steinbrook, R. A. (2004). Ketamine as adjuvant analgesic to opioids: A quantitative and qualitative systematic review. *Anesthesia and Analgesia, 99*, 482–495.

Suresh, S., & Anand, K. J. (2001). Opioid tolerance in neonates: A state-of-the-art review. *Paediatric Anaesthesia, 11*, 511–521.

Suresh, S., & Wheeler, M. (2002). Practical pediatric regional anesthesia. *Anesthesiology Clinics of North America, 20*, 83–113.

Susman, E. (2005). Cancer pain management guidelines issued for children; adult guidelines updated. *Journal of the National Cancer Institute, 97,* 711–712.

Thompson, K. L., & Varni, J. W. (1986). A developmental cognitive-biobehavioral approach to pediatric pain assessment. *Pain, 25,* 283–296.

Tobias, J. D. (2007). Dexmedetomidine: applications in pediatric critical care and pediatric anesthesiology. *Pediatric Critical Care Medicine, 8,* 115–131.

Twycross, A. (1998). Children's cognitive level and perception of pain. *Professional Nurse, 14,* 35–37.

Wolf, A. R. (1999). Pain, nociception and the developing infant. *Paediatric Anaesthesia, 9,* 7–17.

Wolfe, J., Grier, H. E., Klar, N., Levin, S. B., Ellenbogen, J. M., Salem-Schatz, S., et al. (2000). Symptoms and suffering at the end of life in children with cancer. *New England Journal of Medicine, 342,* 326–333.

Zempsky, W., & Cravero, J. (2004). Relief of pain and anxiety in pediatric patients in emergency medical systems. *Pediatrics, 114,* 1348–1353.

TABLE 1. PEDIATRIC ANALGESIC MEDICATIONS FOR END-OF-LIFE PAIN

Medication	Route	Dose/kg (q 4–6h)	Nota Bene
Nonopioids			
Acetaminophen	Oral	10–15 mg/kg	Infant: 5–8 mg/kg q 6h
	Rectal	Load: 30–40 mg/kg → 20 mg/kg q 6h	(–) Immunodeficiency
Ibuprofen	Oral	10 mg/kg/	(–) Coagulopathy, Oncology patients
Ketoralac	Oral, IV	Load: 0.5 mg/kg → 0.25–0.5 mg/kg q 6h	(–) Renal insufficiency; use limited to 5 days
Tramadol	Oral	1–2 mg/kg	(–) Use of Selective serotonin reuptake inhibitor
Opioids			
Codeine	Oral	0.5–1 mg/kg	Ineffective for 20% of patients
Oxycodone	Oral	0.05–0.15 mg/kg	
Morphine sulfate	Oral	0.2–0.5 mg/kg	Morphine sulfate immediate release
	IV, SQ	0.1 mg/kg	
	IV Infusion	0.02 mg/kg/h	Patient-controlled analgesia (PCA) (self or nurse-assist)
Hydromorphone	Oral	0.03–0.08 mg/kg	
	IV	0.015 mg/kg	
	IV Infusion	0.003 mg/kg/h	PCA (self or nurse-assist)
Methadone	Oral, IV	0.1 mg/kg q 6h	↑ Half-life with exposure
Fentanyl	IV Infusion	1 microgram/kg/h	Rapid onset of tolerance
• Patch	Transdermal	1 microgram/kg q 3d	(–) Opioid naïve patient
• Oralet	Transmucosal	5–15 micrograms/kg	(–) Infants < 15 kg
Adjuncts			
Gabapentin	Oral	5 mg/kg; Day 1 q hs Day 2 q 12h, Day 3 q 8h	(+) Neuropathic pain; advance gradually
Nortriptyline	Oral	0.1–0.5 mg q hs	(+) Neuropathic pain; advance gradually
Mexiletine	Oral	2–3 mg/kg q 6–8h; increase very slowly	(+) Neuropathic pain; (–) Seizure, cardiac
Lorazepam	Oral, IV	0.02–0.1 mg/kg q 8h	(+) Spasm, anxiety
Ketamine	IV Infusion	0.1–0.5 mg/kg/h	↓ Opioid tolerance
Dexmedetomidine	IV Infusion	0.1–0.7 microgram/kg/h	Monitor for hypotension and bradycardia
Lidocaine	IV Infusion	2–5 mg/kg/h	Monitor for toxicity
Clonidine	Oral	2–4 micrograms/kg	(+) Neuro/visceral pain
• Patch	Transdermal	0.1–0.2 mg/kg q 7d	(–) Hypotension

All doses q 4–6h unless otherwise noted; PO = by mouth; IV = intravenous;
SQ = subcutaneous; q = every; h = hour; d = day; →= then; hs = hour of sleep;
(–) = contraindicated; (+) = therapeutic

The information in this table is drawn from the multiple sources cited in the text.

TABLE 2. PEDIATRIC REGIONAL ANALGESIA FOR END-OF-LIFE PAIN

Technique	Rate/Dose	Risk/Benefit	Possible Side Effects
Epidural	0.2–0.4 ml/kg/h	Infection, hematoma, urinary retention, weakness	
• Morphine	20 micrograms/ml	Rostral spread	Sedation, ↓ RR, pruritis
• Hydromorphone	10 micrograms/ml	Rostral spread	Sedation, ↓ RR, pruritis
• Fentanyl	1–2 micrograms/ml	Systemic absorption	Pruritis, sedation, ↓ RR
• Clonidine	0.1 microgram/ml	↓ Blood pressure	Sedation, hypotension
• Bupivacaine	0.1 %	Toxic > 0.4 ml/kg/h	Tinnitus, disinhibition,
• Ropivacaine	0.1 %	Safer toxicity profile	Seizures, dysrhythmias
Nerve Block		**Administration**	
• Bupivacaine	0.5 ml/kg (0.25%)	Single dose only	See above
• Lidocaine	0.5 ml/kg (0.1%)	Single dose only	See above
• Ropivacaine	0.1–0.3 ml/kg/h (0.2%)	Catheter for infusion	Infection, signs of toxicity
• Levobupivacaine	0.1 ml/kg/h (0.25%)	Catheter for infusion	Infection, signs of toxicity
• Neurolysis	Alcohol or phenol	Ablation of nerve	Loss of function
Cutaneous		**Penetration**	
• EMLA®	Lidocaine/prilocaine (2.5%)	After 90 min, 5 mm	Methemoglobin, blenching
• LMX4®	Liposomal Lidocaine 4 %	After 30 min, 5 mm	Lidocaine toxicity
• S-Caine Patch®	Eutectic mixture of lidocaine/ tetracaine	After 20 min, 5 mm	(Uses a self-contained heating system)
• Lidoderm® Patch	12 hours on/off (5%)	Dermal analgesia	Only approved for PHN

RR = respiratory rate; EMLA = eutectic mixture of lidocaine and prilocaine; PHN = post-herpetic neuralgia

The information in this table is drawn from the multiple sources cited in the text.

FIGURE 1. WONG-BAKER FACES PAIN RATING SCALE

	0	1	2	3	4	5
	NO HURT	HURTS LITTLE BIT	HURTS LITTLE MORE	HURTS EVEN MORE	HURTS WHOLE LOT	HURTS WORST
alternate coding	0	2	4	6	8	10

From Hockenberry, M. J., Wilson, D., Winkerstein, M. L. (2005). Wong's essential pediatric nursing, *ed. 7. (p. 1259). St. Louis, MO: Mosby. Used with permission.*

CHAPTER 6

Dying at an Early Age: Ethical Issues in Pediatric Palliative Care

Bruce Jennings

INTRODUCTION

Approximately 53,000 children die each year in the United States. About half of them die suddenly of acute trauma or other lethal conditions; the others die as a result of chronic, incurable conditions. At any given time, some 400,000 American children are living with life-threatening conditions (Himmelstein, Hilden, Boldt, & Weissman, 2004). Yet, in 2001, only 5,000 children received hospice care near the end of their lives, and often for only a very short period. The number has increased since then, but in 2005, pediatric patients still accounted for less than 1% of hospice patients (National Hospice and Palliative Care Organization [NHPCO], 2006). Palliative care for children during the course of treatment for life-threatening conditions remains inadequate and has only slowly been incorporated into the services offered at pediatric cancer centers (Feudtner et al., 2002; Initiative for Pediatric Palliative Care, 2003; Postovsky & Ben Arush, 2004).

End-of-life care for children is not ethically straightforward, and the ethical challenges it poses for society and for health care professionals are complex and difficult. Relating to dying children with justice, respect, and compassion is not simply a case of ethical conduct toward human beings in general. It requires special knowledge, skill, and sensitivity. Ethical obligation in health care grows out of need and vulnerability, and is usually proportional to them. With dying children and their families, vulnerability is at a peak for emotional and cultural reasons.[†]

Children are not small adults and should not be treated as such. They are not merely future adults either; they must be respected and treated for who they are and the situation they are in here and now, not on the basis of an imagined future that adults (including their parents) project on them. Dying is a chapter of living, even at an early age. If dying can be prevented, ethical prompting is not required. (In some parts of the world, where children die in staggeringly large numbers from easily treatable and preventable causes, that is obviously not the case.) But when it cannot be prevented, dying needs to be honored and incorporated into our understanding of who children are and what their present demands.

In the past few years, many professional and bioethical groups have directed concerted attention to the domain of pediatric palliative care and hospice (Field & Behrman, 2003). In some cases, there has been an understandable tendency to start with existing ethical guidelines and rules for medical decision making (which have been developed mainly with adult patients in mind) and try to adapt them to the special circumstances of end-of-life care for children. This work has concentrated principally on the following topics:

- Problems of informed consent and "informed assent" with children of various ages, especially adolescents (Alderson, Sutcliffe, & Curtis, 2006).

- Problems with surrogate decision making, when no guidance can be obtained from the patient's advance directive and no firm inferences can be made from the patient's past identity, preferences, and values (with children, those aspects are not yet formed), and therefore, the standard of "best interest" must be used (Rhoden, 1988).

- Problems with the special authority of parents as surrogate decision makers and concerns about the capacity of these "natural" and customarily recognized surrogates to fulfill the obligations of their role, given circumstances of emotional distress, family tensions and conflict, the concurrent needs and interests of other children in the family, and the like.

[†] *In keeping with the usage of the American Academy of Pediatrics, in this chapter I use the terms "child" and "children" to refer to infants, children, adolescents, and young adults up to age 21.*

The move from the ethics of adult dying to the ethics of childhood dying requires more than simply adapting general ethical rules of decision making to the specific qualifications presented by the age, capacities, and potentialities of the child patient. What is needed is not merely an adaptation, but a more complex shift in orientation—a movement of tectonic plates in our moral imagination and caring practices, so to speak, to produce a new conceptual foundation for end-of-life decisions at an early age. This shift is happening implicitly in the ethics of pediatric end-of-life care, because it is fully consonant with the values, perspectives, and demonstrated efficacy of the hospice and palliative care movement. It also dovetails with reform efforts and changing thinking in pediatrics and family medicine.

In this chapter, I suggest a way of thinking about this paradigm shift and reflect on its implications for ethical decision making. I do this by describing three basic orientations through which we perceive the reality of the dying child and our appropriate response to him or her. I call these (1) the rescue orientation, (2) the individualistic interests orientation, and (3) the social ecology orientation. Each of these orientations has a corresponding model of the provider-patient-family relationship, which I label medical treatment, medical services, and health caring.

The medical treatment model and the rescue orientation perceive the person confronted with a life-limiting illness as the victim of an attack; this model enlists medicine as the defender and rescuer of the endangered victim. The medical services model and its individualistic interests orientation see the dying person as an unencumbered self, still planning and directing his or her life right up to the end, and as a consumer, enlisting medicine in the quest to control the dying process in accordance with preferences and values. The health-caring model and its social ecology orientation place the situation of the dying person in relational terms; that is, dying is a process that takes place within a system of interrelationships and a network of shared meanings. To be spared death is to navigate those relationships and meanings intact through the shoals of a crisis and to attain survival; to die well is to preserve, and perhaps repair, those relationships right up until the end, and even beyond in the memory of those who survive.

I distinguish these orientations not to conclude that one is appropriate and the others misguided. This is not a question of right and wrong ways of perceiving, thinking, and feeling. Human life and experience are multifaceted and complex: Each of these orientations survives because it helps in some way to make sense of that experience. Most parents and society as a whole cling to the medical treatment model and the rescue orientation, but often at great cost to the child—who experiences the ordeal of aggressive but futile life-sustaining treatment—and to the loving parents, other adults, and siblings who watch. When it comes to childhood death, the individualistic interests orientation has its limits and must be applied indirectly and awkwardly. The social ecology orientation draws on the tradition of hospice and palliative care and on the perspectives of family practice medicine and pediatrics. It combines respect for developmental personhood; for the inherent dignity of all human beings regardless of age; and for their need for care, presence, and relief of suffering. It is based on the insight that human beings are not isolated atoms but relational and interdependent selves.

I believe the social ecology orientation holds the greatest promise to guide the ethical treatment of children with incurable, irreversible terminal illness and their families. Pediatric palliative care requires a countervailing vision to offset the medical orientation and the will to power in the face of death. It also requires a fundamentally different way of conceiving the personhood of the patient, the context of communication and caregiving, and the goals of care. Ultimately, ethical issues will have to be handled in the clinical setting on the basis of the uniqueness of each child and each family. Ethical decision making must be sensitive to the child's age and the developmental maturity and to family dynamics.

First, I describe the medical orientation and its embrace of the will to power in the face of death. Next, I consider how the individualistic interests orientation has developed in law, in the health professions, and in bioethics over the past 30 years, and how it shifts the balance back in the direction of dignity and respect for the person against power and rescue. I discuss the shortcomings of the latter framework when it is applied to the care of dying children.

Numerous ethical frameworks and guidelines have been developed recently in the fields of family medicine, pediatrics, and palliative hospice care. They suggest a convergence toward the approaches and practices of the social ecology orientation (American Academy of Pediatrics, 2000, 2003; Field & Behrman, 2003; Himmelstein et al., 2004; NHPCO, 2001). I conclude with a discussion of the social ecological perspective, pointing out the modifications that it makes in the individualistic interests orientation, which is the standard ethical framework for decisions near the end of life.

MEDICAL TREATMENT MODEL AND THE RULE OF RESCUE

People tend to value medical treatment because it gives them power rather than because it respects their dignity. A patient's power derives from the physician's power and from the power of medical science and technology to rescue the patient from illness and to preserve and prolong life.

The emphasis on the principle of patient autonomy in the field of bioethics in recent years seems intended to protect dignity, but autonomy also involves the will to power. Indeed, power is so basic to the way we have come to think about medical care that we don't often state it explicitly. It exercises an enormous influence over the way we think and feel about illness, disability, hope, and about what we must accept and what we can try to change. It influences our attitude toward death and dying because it defines—largely, if not entirely—the value of life. Power shapes medical decision making throughout the lifespan and even in the terminal phase of chronic degenerative disease. It is a profound obstacle to the acceptance of biological limits, life limits, and palliative and hospice care, which ease dying but do not attempt to prolong life.

Asserting, through medical assistance, our power over death redoubles its cultural and emotional strength when injury or disease threatens the life of a child. Those who love and care for a child turn to medicine with an overwhelming hope and desire for power and a virtual disregard for dignity. That is perhaps the key moral pitfall in the care of critically and terminally ill children—all other ethical, communication, and decision-making issues revolve around the gravitational pull of this black hole at the center of pediatric end-of-life care.

Medicine is granted tremendous resources and deference because it saves lives. Our predominant image of disease or illness is that of a foreign invader, something that attacks us and against which we must defend. This enemy will deprive us of what is supremely valuable to us, either life itself or life as we ideally wish to live it. Disease may kill us, or it may render us so ill and impaired that life loses its quality and meaning. There is never a time when this attack is "natural" or should be accepted. Medicine rescues us from disease in this sense; it gives us power and control by staving off death and helping us avoid a fundamental transformation and limitation of our lives.

It is generally recognized that serious acute illness poses a threat to the individual and morally requires others to help that person counteract that threat. In life-threatening emergencies and most cases of acute care medicine—even when the condition is not immediately life-threatening—the person's needs, the proper actions for the physician to take in response to those needs, and the moral rights and responsibilities of the parties involved are all reasonably clear. By and large, with acute illness (for example, pneumococcal pneumonia) the source of the threat can be singled out and identified—the invading organism, the disease process, the biochemical malfunction. In acute care, establishing the correct diagnosis is more than half the battle, for it is on that basis that the course of treatment usually proceeds.

When we identify the threat, it is easy to identify what is threatened—life, health, a level of "normal" functioning that can be restored. Moreover, the threat is viewed as evil because life, health, and function are intrinsic values or primary human goods. Finally, physicians know how to respond to the threat—the range of appropriate medical treatments is determined by the current state of medical knowledge, and perhaps there will be one specific intervention that will eliminate the threat once and for all.

The fact that the desire to have power and control over death often takes precedence over dignity and quality of life is shown by people's willingness to submit to temporary pain, suffering, and loss of control in return for access to the scientific knowledge and technological power that may rescue them. How else to explain the willingness to undergo the significant risks of major surgery and difficult rehabilitation? How else to explain the willingness to put up with the side effects of powerful cancer treatments, and even to clamor for acceptance into experimental treatment programs?

The medical treatment model is a perspective that supports the military metaphors commonplace in our cultural ideology of medicine. Disease is the enemy within. The patient and physician enter an "alliance" in which the technical "armamentarium" of medicine is used to defend the patient and attack the invader. The objective of the campaign is restoration to the status prior to the illness (cure). Such metaphors tend to rationalize any pain, suffering, or disruption of personal life that the patient and those around him or her are asked to endure. The more deadly the enemy, the greater the sacrifice that may be required to win the war. The body becomes a battleground, and patients go to war on themselves.

Seeing the illness as a threatening intruder allows us to externalize and objectify it, and makes the illness extrinsic and foreign to the person, even though it is inside the body. Illness represents a temporary identity imposed on the person by an alien source, a heteronomy that thwarts self-determination and the pursuit of life's "normal" goals. Similarly, illness undermines well-being because well-being is taken to mean a state of being well without—not in spite of—illness; a state of being for which illness is an Other.

As difficult as this perspective is for many adults to comprehend and accommodate, the adult patient at least retains some residual sense of free will. Children, on the other hand, may go through this emotionally disruptive experience without conceptual rationalizations and metaphorical constructs to fall back on (Doka, 1995). And while the adult patient *volunteers* to "go to war" (the ethical requirement of informed consent), the child is *drafted* by his or her parents and by physicians (strangers with charismatic and mysterious authority).

This draft into aggressive care at the end of life is especially problematic for adolescents, because they occupy the gray zone between those who have a right to volunteer and conscripts who are subject to their parents' will. Ethical standards generally recommend that the decision-making process be set up to involve the child to the greatest extent possible, given his or her capacity to understand and emotionally process medical information. Failing full informed consent, adolescents and prescient older children should at least be given the opportunity to "assent"; that is, even though they do not have the power to refuse treatment that their parents and physicians have decided is in their best interest, they should be treated with age-appropriate respect. Decisions made by others on their behalf should be transparent to them. They should be given information and an opportunity to ask questions. They should be encouraged to voice their hopes, fears, preferences, and values, and adult decision makers should take this expression into consideration, although the young person's preferences are not dispositive.

This attempt to sustain the agency and personhood of the child is laudable, but it is destined to fail, because the medical orientation renders patients of all ages passive, submissive, and reactive. The tacit contract of the medical perspective is roughly as follows. The physician says to the patient, 'You suspend your normal activities and expectations for a while, give me your body (which I may use roughly, but out of care and concern, not out of malice), and I will give you back your life, your healthy function restored as much as humanly possible, and extra time."

Undergoing treatment for a serious illness is very much like entering what sociologists call a "total institution," in which one must suspend one's normal rights, freedoms, expectations, and routines and must submit to physical and emotional treatment that under other circumstances would surely be condemned as abuse (Goffman, 1961). Acute medical treatment is also akin to social transformation—leaving one's normal social space and entering an alien world—because it involves the abandonment of one's personal identity and everyday roles and the assumption of a very different persona and role. The so-called "patient role" or "sick role" is a condition of passivity and temporary exemption from ordinary social norms and expectations. While you undergo the suffering, exposure, and helplessness of submitting to treatment, you are socially and morally indulged by those to whom you have entrusted your life.

This experience can precipitate a feeling of loss of self-identity. It can cause an alienation from one's past—and perhaps even from what one fears will be the future—when it is that past that one is desperate to regain and that future on which the entire treatment enterprise is predicated. It can involve a detachment from one's family and closest loved ones who, still healthy and whole, reside on the other side of the looking glass.

The medical treatment orientation remains alluring, even irresistible, in the social imagination. We deny death at any age, but we are unwilling to accept what we call "premature" death, and we resist most strongly death in childhood, including the neonatal period, where extremely large expenditures have been made on intensive care and life-sustaining technologies, and where many remarkable advances have occurred (Jennings, 1988). However, in the law and in ethics, the medical treatment orientation has been gradually replaced by a very different way of viewing the situation of the critically or terminally ill patient, the nature and goals of medical care, and the structure of treatment decision making.

Medical Services Model and Patient Interests

The shift has been from defeating death to providing services that are in keeping with the interests, preferences, and values of the patient as a separate and unique individual—an "unencumbered self." Power and authority in the decision-making process are shifting from the expert physician to the sovereign consumer of that expertise. Depending on the patient's personal goals, this arrangement may lead to an attempt to defeat death through aggressive life-sustaining treatment or to its acceptance through decisions to forgo life-sustaining treatment and shift to a system of palliative care. In this orientation, the main concern about the power of medical technology is not that it may be unsuccessful and ineffective, but that it may be wrongly used (or forgone) and that it will fall into the wrong hands (e.g., the physician, a malevolent or uncaring family member, the state).

In addition to these concerns about power, the emergence of a new orientation in end-of-life decision making focuses on respect for the dignity and self-sovereignty of the patient. Lethal illness is still the enemy, but the patient's body is no longer a battlefield commanded by physician-generals; it is now the private property of the patient. The physician who imposes unwanted or nonbeneficial treatments is a trespasser; the one who fails to provide wanted and beneficial treatment is a poor steward; and both are accountable to the landlord. This is true for adult patients—for whom the protection of "autonomy" is essentially equivalent to protecting their interests—and for children, for whom, lacking autonomy, the question of protecting their best interest must be addressed directly.

Although important legal rulings exist dating back to the early part of the 20th century on a patient's right to give or withhold consent to medical treatment (*Scholendorf v. Society of New York Hospital*, 1914), the legal and ethical framework that I call the individualistic interests orientation began in the mid-1970s with the case of Karen Ann Quinlan, a woman in her early 20s who suffered irreversible anoxic brain injury and fell into a state of permanent unconsciousness now known as permanent vegetative state (PVS). In a landmark decision in 1976, the New Jersey Supreme Court ruled that Quinlan had a constitutional right to refuse life-sustaining treatment (in this case a ventilator) and that, since she could not exercise that right herself, it could be exercised by her legal guardian, who was her father (*In re Quinlan*, 1976).

This ruling set the pattern for more than 100 appellate-level state court rulings in similar cases over the next 15 years. There are two legal bases for these rulings. The first is the common law right to bodily integrity, also developed in the body of law on informed consent. Invasive, life-extending treatments and technologies cannot be imposed upon a person without consent and must be withdrawn if refused. The second legal basis is a constitutional right to privacy (later called a "liberty interest") found by the court in both the New Jersey and the United States constitutions.

In the mid-1980s, a remarkably similar case unfolded in Missouri involving Nancy Beth Cruzan, who also fell into PVS after a devastating anoxic brain injury. Cruzan was not on a ventilator; it was the artificial nutrition and hydration that her family wanted to withdraw. Litigation first in the Missouri Supreme Court (*Cruzan v. Harmon*, 1988) and then in the U.S. Supreme Court (*Cruzan v. Director*, 1990) clarified and eventually reaffirmed this autonomy and best-interest-oriented end-of-life decision-making consensus (Hastings Center, 1987; Meisel, 1993; National Center for State Courts, 1992).

However, this framework has two related problems. First, it has not led to the desired behavioral change either among ordinary citizens (who have failed in large numbers to execute advance directives) or among physicians and health care facilities (which continue to practice aggressive forms of life-extending treatment and are often very reluctant to agree to more conservative or palliative treatment plans) (Wolfe et al., 2000). The second problem with this framework is that it is out of step with the experiences and values of most dying patients and their families. In a word, the law has created a decision-making process that very few people (aside, perhaps, from lawyers) can understand, successfully navigate during times of extreme illness and emotional turmoil, or embrace wholeheartedly. When our deepest experience at crucial transitions in life is at odds with the public vocabularies of value and meaning available to us, we have a crisis of thought and spirit too unsettling to ignore.

Obviously, end-of-life treatment decisions for minors entail a form of surrogate decision making, but the way of thinking about surrogate decision making provided in the individualistic interests orientation is difficult or impossible to apply to the care of children. With infants and, presumably, younger children, "the basis for deciding as the patient would decide if he or she were able" does not make sense, because the patient has never yet been able; there is as yet no autonomous self to respect and obey. With older children and adolescents, the absence of a previous authentic and autonomous self is not as clear-cut. Different children may differ in this regard. Legally, however, advance directives and the full autonomy orientation do not apply until age 18. (The category of *emancipated minor*—a person under 18 years who is residing and making a living independently or who is married—is an exception.) In most cases of pediatric care, including end-of-life care, parents are generally recognized as the appropriate decision makers, and the standard to which their decisions must adhere is the best interest of the child (New York State Task Force on Life and the Law, 1992).

The notion of "best interest" functions as the equivalent of the voice of the patient in adult medical decision making in the autonomy orientation. In situations in which families break down and children must be removed from the custody of their parents, the state becomes their guardian, and all adults are then in the category of strangers who have potentially conflicting interests concerning the child and no presumed bonds of natural affection. At such times, the concept of best interest acts as a shield and a protection, isolating and individuating the child in a heartless or hostile world.

But should the notion of best interest be interpreted that way in the context of end-of-life care and medical decisions made by committed parents in a functional family system? Best interest can be made protective and individuating for a child much in the same way that patient autonomy protects and insulates an adult patient. Both best interest and autonomy can be used to build fences. There are two ways of talking about the child whose best interest we are trying to determine. One is as an unencumbered self—a self outside any social context, socially unembedded, and considered dualistically apart from its own (malfunctioning, dying) body; ontologically unembodied. The other is as a relational, interdependent self who is socially embedded and physically embodied.

To move from the child as unencumbered to the child as relational self is to move from the orientation of health services for the promotion of patient interests to a health-caring and social ecology orientation. I believe that this is a shift in the right direction. No human being, especially not one who is very sick or dying, is really an unencumbered self. The image is even more implausible and morally inadequate when it is applied to children (Murray, 1996). Being protected behind fences is neither what children primarily need nor what rights and justice require, especially not when children are faced with an incurable terminal illness and a radically foreshortened life. Properly understood in end-of-life and palliative care settings, the notion of best interest should be interpreted as authorizing a reaffirmation of bonds, not a loosening of them. We need to shore up and reaffirm the family as the appropriate environment for good communication and caring, ethically responsible stewardship of the life of a child (that is to say, the quality of life, as well as its duration), and the quality of living while dying at an early age.

Social Ecology Orientation: Pediatric Ethics in a New Key

The notion of social ecology is an essential element of the reorientation shift that I have analyzed in this chapter. Understanding the ethical dimension of pediatric hospice and palliative care requires more than a traditionally individualistic conception of best interest; it requires that we shift our focus from the individual interests orientation to a social ecology orientation. In biology and environmental science, ecology is the study of the systemic interaction and interdependency of various organisms among themselves and with their inorganic environment. Social ecology applies the same systems approach to the complex nexus of social and cultural relations among human beings, with their extraordinarily diverse and powerful cognitive, affective, and communicative capacities.

This orientation is particularly apt with regard to the human experience of dying and death (Morrissey & Jennings, 2006). Here the law seeks to intervene and regulate one of the most intense, highly charged, and delicate moments in human affairs. Invested with meanings that are at once intimately personal or private and necessarily social and public, dying (or, better, living near the end of life) is a particularly complex ecology. In the past 40 years or so, life near the end of life has been invaded and colonized by hard medical technologies. Their benefit in prolonging life can be great, but their destructive potential is alarming. They can destroy the delicate social ecology of families and the tissue of meaning that dying children, their parents, and families need in order to get a grip on the terrible thing that has befallen them. When it was technologically impotent, medicine (together with religion) presided over social rituals and cultural meaning during the dying process. Relationships and identities were repaired and renewed—with family and friends at hand, with an opportunity to reconcile with those estranged, to forgive and to ask forgiveness. Today, medicine and medical treatment decisions set up a dynamic that makes that ecology unstable at best, impossible at worst (Kaufman, 2005).

To improve end-of-life care, liberation of the patient from the paternalism of the medical orientation is necessary but far from sufficient. Law, ethics, and policy must also come to grips with fundamentally communal and public—not private—issues of mortality and meaning. We sometimes seem to act as though dying were solely the concern of the dying person. This vision is too narrow. What happens in dying—like what happens in life—is shaped by and shapes social relationships. This is one of the key insights of the social ecology model.

Central to the task of expanding our vision in the care of children are the notions of personhood and relationships—or, more precisely, *personhood in and through relationships*. These notions have been profoundly shaped and defined by the individualistic notions of patient interests and the best interest of the child now governing treatment decision making at the end of life.

In making autonomy central to our understanding of the ethics of medical care for the dying and in interpreting the notion of the best interest of the child in a strongly individualistic way, we create some blind spots that are particularly instructive. One blind spot is the gap between the regulative ideals of ethics and the law and the lived moral experience of the actual persons—physicians, family members, and patients themselves—who make decisions near the end of life. This gap is a warning sign of something amiss in our moral thinking and imagination. The quotidian moral experience of our familial and relational lives as selves—our social embeddedness as persons—serves as an essential corrective to the aspiration for power and the dignity of isolated independence; the will to power and the will to self-affirmation and self-expression.

It is often said that our denial of death leads us to shy away from palliative care and hospice as alternatives to aggressive treatments without reasonable hope of success. Nowhere is this denial stronger than among parents of dying children. But perhaps it is less our desire to hold on to life than our desire to hold on to *control* that leads to demands for futile overtreatment and the undertreatment of pain and suffering. That might explain why the shift in law and ethics from the rescue orientation to the patient's interests orientation has made so little difference in the actual conduct of decision making at the bedside by physicians and family surrogates. And why it is more than fear of death alone that keeps the rescue orientation so powerful at the emotional level in our culture.

The challenge facing us is to rebuild, reinforce, and reinterpret our laws, institutions, and practices around the acknowledgment that dying is interpersonal, not strictly individualistic. Hospice has long done this, creating space for families and intimate friends to be close to the dying person. Hospice also recognizes the emotional needs of those same people (Corr & Corr, 1985). Parents as surrogate decision makers and guardians of the best interest of their children can and should take into account the dying child's concerns for those whose lives will be affected by his or her death. Note that when we understand selfhood from a social ecology perspective, as embedded and embodied, for children to have concerns of this kind does not require advanced cognitive abilities or development.

Some may question the plausibility of this view. The ideology of childhood in American society may overestimate the narcissism of children and fail to realize at how young an age they actually achieve a rather complex social awareness. Is it necessarily the case that children experience their own illness and the prospect of their own death simply through their own eyes rather than through the eyes of their parents and perhaps siblings? I see no justification for interpreting the best interest of a child as a protective fence that separates his interests from the interests, concerns, and feelings of his family (Murray, 1996). Adults worry about what their medical care and dying process will do to their families; young children cannot express this idea, but that does not mean that they cannot experience it. Adolescents clearly do (Nelson, 1992).

From the perspective of both the medical treatment model and the medical services model, family-centered care is merely an add-on, not the essential purpose of the enterprise. In the social ecology model, the notion of caring for the family in caring for the patient—and caring for the patient in caring also for the family—is central. In pediatric community practice ethics, this is now the established norm (American Academy of Pediatrics, 2003); in pediatric palliative care and hospice, it is emerging rapidly as the norm (American Academy of Pediatrics, 2000). Only in neonatology does the medical model still dominate and the social ecology orientation lag behind, except in the most progressive neonatal intensive care units (Jennings, 1990).

CONCLUSION: TOWARD BEST PRACTICES FROM A SOCIAL ECOLOGY PERSPECTIVE

Moving from the medical treatment and medical services models to a health-caring and social ecology model involves a number of steps to build on and improve the current system of pediatric end-of-life care. I believe that pediatric palliative and hospice care can be the central agents of change in this regard, through professional leadership and advocacy and through institutional and policy reform to improve access to these models of care (Jennings, Ryndes, D'Onofrio, & Baily, 2003).

A number of recommendations follow from the social ecology orientation that apply to pediatric end-of-life decision making and to adult and geriatric cases as well. In the following discussion, I will highlight the pediatric applications.

Primarily, we must focus on improving communication, both horizontally within families and vertically with physicians.

The appropriate role of family members in such cases should be more easily accommodated. Here pediatrics has something to learn from discussion and debate in the adult end-of-life arena. For adult cases, the weakest link in the medical services end-of-life decision-making framework has always been the problem of how to translate the right of a competent person to refuse life-extending treatment into a right exercised by someone else on behalf of a person who no longer has decision-making capacity. Many are now challenging not only the practicality of advance directives but also their validity. Should a healthy or able-bodied person at a time before suffering impairment or disability be permitted to make a decision that will be binding at a later time in his or her life? Is there sufficient continuity of values and preferences over time to be confident about a decision made by the earlier self? What do the notions of "substituted judgment" and "best interest" really mean in practice? Many of the advance directive statutes and legal standards articulated by the courts appeal to these concepts without sufficiently examining how problematic they can be in actual end-of-life situations (Dresser, 1986).

These fundamental ethical and philosophical issues do not lend themselves well to new court decisions and legislation. Before we get more law, we need more deliberation, debate, and moral wisdom coming from the mechanisms of communication in family contexts. Learning how to analyze in a substantive way what the best interests of the dying patient, at any age, actually are in a given case requires fuller inclusion and participation of family members in the decision-making process.

There is an ongoing need to develop more extensive professional education for all professionals involved in end-of-life care, both in terms of legal and ethical content, and skills for working with patients and families. The process should engage educators in a meaningful dialogue about how to infuse this content into curricula at every level of professional education.

Research should be funded and conducted that will give us more insight into how we can improve end-of-life care and outcomes for patients and families. An evidence base for informing policy decisions regarding end-of-life care will enhance our knowledge of the relationship between policy and outcomes.

Interdisciplinary collaboration across the professions should be fostered both informally and formally. Structures and methodologies of care delivery may require study and reform to permit a fundamental change in systems orientation from a product-driven approach to a social ecology model when it comes to end-of-life decision making.

Surrogates—whether those named in advance directives executed by once-capacious adults or parents serving as the guardians of a child—should receive adequate information, counseling, and support. We need to place more emphasis on education, counseling, and support for all health care agents, including parents of dying children, to improve their capacity to play this role and to improve the quality of the decisions they make (Contro, Larson, Scofield, Sourkes, & Cohen, 2002). A surrogate on the scene has the flexibility to exercise judgment and to interpret the patient's wishes and values in light of specific (and sometimes rapidly changing) medical information about the patient's condition, treatment options, and prognosis. But while we seem to expect surrogates to have these skills, we have done little or nothing to study the environmental conditions in the health care setting that are most conducive to them, nor have we developed protocols of education, counseling, and support aimed at enabling surrogates to engage in good decision making. Improvement and reform in end-of-life care have focused almost exclusively on how to *empower* agents to make decisions, or we have taken the customary legal empowerment of parents as medical decision makers for their child as a given. We must also begin to address how to *enable* these agents and parents to make good decisions.

Hospitals and other health care facilities have an institutional and systemic responsibility and role to play in enhancing the quality of parental and surrogate decision making. Of course, individuals and families also have a responsibility to prepare for these decisions on their own initiative, but the institutional side of the equation has been relatively neglected. More research and assessment tools are needed to assess and improve current institutional practices. Health care professionals must become more knowledgeable about and sensitive to the special needs of surrogates and the burdens of the surrogacy role. We must draw on many disciplines to improve the quality of support that parents and other surrogates receive, including medicine and nursing but also ethics, pastoral counseling, social work, and other sources of expertise about the full range of cognitive and emotional work surrogate decision making entails.

Families and surrogates need to have a framework within which information has meaning and validates their past relationship with the patient. This framework should also validate the surrogates' sense of themselves as loving, caring, responsible people faced with life-and-death decisions in the midst of shock, loss, possibly guilt, and grief. Surrogacy is both a cognitive and an affective task. It involves scientific facts, normative ideas, and deep-seated emotions. While surrogacy is—and should be—primarily focused on the wishes, values, and best interests of the patient, the decisions a surrogate makes affect the surrogate him- or herself and the entire family as well. To see surrogacy, especially the surrogacy of parents with a dying child, as simply an information-processing task is to miss most of its human angst and drama. And yet that is the approach that many health care facilities have taken, implicitly or explicitly, by the paucity of resources they provide to agents and surrogates, by the nature and style of the communication they offer, and by the low priority they give to multidisciplinary counseling and support.

When conflicts and disagreements arise in families, independent media-tion and conflict resolution services, including pastoral counseling, should be readily available in health care institutions. No form of surrogate decision making is immune to dispute. Instructions must be interpreted; relationships evolve. Family members sometimes adhere to the rule of rescue and the medical treatment model not because their sense of the child's best interest dictates it, but because it seems the best way to avoid family conflict, since it reduces the agency and explicit choice of the parents and family and places them in a passive role. Support services and mediation efforts informed by an understanding of family dynamics and ecological orientations toward dying as a family experience can give parents an alternative to falling back on aggressive treatment as the path of least resistance.

Erring on the side of aggressive, life-prolonging treatment is not cost-free in terms of child and family suffering. It should not be allowed to take its toll unless it is genuinely the best available and freely chosen plan of care.

Bruce Jennings is director of the Center for Humans and Nature, a private foundation that supports work on environmental and public health policy and planning. He is also senior consultant to the Hastings Center and teaches at the Yale School of Public Health. He has written and edited 20 books and has published more than 100 articles on bioethics and public policy issues. He is currently completing a book on dementia, self-identity, and the ethics of long-term care. Future projects include a study of public health ethics and political theory.

REFERENCES

Alderson, P., Sutcliffe, K., & Curtis, K. (2006, November–December). Children's competence to consent to medical treatment. *Hastings Center Report 36*(6), 25–34.

American Academy of Pediatrics, Committee on Bioethics and Committee on Hospital Care. (2000, August). Palliative care for children. *Pediatrics, 106*(2), 351–357.

American Academy of Pediatrics, Committee on Hospital Care. (2003, September). Family-centered care and the pediatrician's role. *Pediatrics, 112*, 3.

Contro, N., Larsen, J., Scofield, S., Sourkes, B., & Cohen, H. (2002, January). Family perspectives on the quality of pediatric palliative care. *Archives of Pediatric Adolescent Medicine, 156,* 14–19.

Corr, C. A., & Corr, D. M. (1985). Hospice approaches to pediatric care. New York: Springer.

Cruzan v. Harmon. (1988). 760 S.W.2d 408.

Cruzan v. Director, Missouri Department of Health. (1990). 497 U.S. 261.

Doka, K. (1995). *Children mourning, mourning children.* New York: Routledge.

Dresser, R. (1986). Life, death, and incompetent patients: Conceptual infirmities and hidden values in the law. *Arizona Law Review, 28,* 373–405.

Field, M. J., & Behrman, R. E. (Eds.). (2003). *When children die: Improving palliative and end of life care for children and their families.* Washington, DC: Institute of Medicine, National Academies Press.

Feudtner, C., Christakis, D. A., Zimmerman, F. J., Muldoon, J. H., Neff, J. M., & Koepsell, T. D. (2002). Characteristics of deaths occurring in children's hospitals: Implication for supportive care services. *Pediatrics, 109*(5), 887–893.

Goffman, E. (1961). *Asylums.* Garden City, NY: Anchor Books.

Hastings Center. (1987). *Guidelines on the termination of life-sustaining treatment and the care of the dying.* Bloomington: Indiana University Press.

Himmelstein, B., Hilden, J. M., Boldt, A. M., & Weissman, D. (2004, April 22). Pediatric palliative care. *New England Journal of Medicine, 350*(17), 1752–1762.

Initiative for Pediatric Palliative Care (IPPC). (2003). IPPC Curriculum. Newton, MA.: Education Development Center. Retrieved October 26, 2007, from www.ippcweb.org/index.asp

In re Quinlan. (1976). 70 N.J. 10, 355 A.2d 647 (N.J.).

Jennings, B. (1988, Winter). Beyond the rights of the newborn. *Raritan: A Quarterly Review, 7*(3), 79-93.

Jennings, B. (1990). Ethics and ethnography in neonatal intensive care. In G. Weisz (Ed.), *Social science perspectives on medical ethics* (pp. 261–272). Dordrecht, Netherlands: Kluwer.

Jennings, B., Ryndes, T., D'Onofrio, C., & Baily, M. A. (2003). Access to hospice care: Expanding boundaries, overcoming barriers. *Hastings Center Report, Special Supplement, 33*(2). S1–S60.

Kaufman, S. R. (2005). *And a time to die: How American hospitals shape the end of life.* New York: Scribner.

Meisel, A. (1993). The legal consensus about forgoing life-sustaining treatment: Its status and its prospects, *Kennedy Institute of Ethics Journal, 2,* 309–345.

Morrissey, M. B., & Jennings, B. (2006, Winter). A social ecology of health model in end of life decision making: Is the law therapeutic? *New York State Bar Association Health Law Journal, 11*(1), 51–60.

Murray, T. H. (1996). *The worth of a child.* Berkeley: University of California Press.

Murray T. H., & Jennings, B. (2005). The quest to reform end of life care: Rethinking assumptions and setting new directions. In B. Jennings, G. Kaebnick, & T. H. Murray (Eds.), Improving end of life care: Why has it been so difficult? *Hastings Center Report, Special Supplement, 35*(6), S52–S57.

National Hospice and Palliative Care Organization (NHPCO). (2001). *A call for change: Recommendations to improve the care of children living with life-threatening conditions.* Alexandria, VA.

NHPCO. (2006). NHPCO's Facts and Figures—2005 Findings. Retrieved October 26, 2007, from www.nhpco.org/i4a/pages/index.cfm?pageid=3274

National Center for State Courts. (1992). *Guidelines for state court decision making in life-sustaining medical treatment cases* (2nd ed.). Williamsburg, VA.

New York State Task Force on Life and the Law. (1992). *When others must choose: Deciding for patients without capacity.* Albany, NY: Health Research.

Nelson, J. L. (1992). Taking families seriously. *Hastings Center Report 22*(4), 6–12.

Postovsky, S., & Ben Arush, M. W. (2004). Care of a child dying of cancer: The role of the palliative care team in pediatric oncology. *Pediatric Hematology and Oncology, 21*, 67–76.

Rhoden, N. (1988). Litigating life and death. *Harvard Law Review, 102*, 375–446.

Scholendorf v. Society of New York Hospital. (1914). 211 N.Y. 125, 105 N.E. 92 (N.Y.).

Wolfe, J., Grier, H., Klar, N., Levin, S., Ellenbogen, J. M., Salem-Schatz, S., Emanuel, E. J., & Weeks, J. C. (2000, February 3). Symptoms and suffering at the end of life in children with cancer. *New England Journal of Medicine, 342*(5), 326–333.

Children, Adolescents, Grief, and Loss

T his section explores significant loss in the life of a child or adolescent. The chapters by William Worden and by Rachel Haines, Tim Ayers, Irwin Sandler, and Sharlene Wolchik both describe the effects of the death of a parent on the surviving children, including how the family functions and how it offers opportunities for the expression of grief and validates grieving. An essential intervention strategy is to buttress the family unit through emotional education and support of both informal and formal networks. Sam Jensen's *Voices* piece rounds out this section by powerfully recounting the ongoing impact of his father's death in a deeply personal way.

Nancy Hogan's chapter describes the effects of sibling loss. The sibling relationship is unique in the family system. Siblings share experiences, perceptions, and memories that are held by no one else. These are often the longest relationships people sustain throughout their lives. Without minimizing the horrendous impact the death of a sibling may have, Hogan suggests possibilities for transformation and for maintaining a continuing bond with the deceased sister or brother.

The final chapter in this section reminds readers of the importance of acknowledging the grief a child or adolescent feels at the death of a friend. Far too often, these losses are disenfranchised—unrecognized and unsupported by others—so the child experiences a loss but does not feel entitled to grieve it. Ilene and Lloyd Noppe describe the critical importance of friendships to children and adolescents. Friendship is a full-time job—adolescents in particular spend a large proportion of their time building and sustaining friendships. The Noppes explain the importance of supporting adolescents and children as they cope with the loss of a friend. They also remind readers of the many non-kin losses—pets, teachers, coaches, and even celebrities—that children and adolescents mourn.

The chapters in this section reaffirm that the child must be viewed in a larger context. The family and the friendship network are the most immediate aspects of that larger milieu, but they are not the only ones. The child also needs to be understood in the context of his or her culture. Culture influences the experience of grief in both obvious and subtle ways. Culture can frame attachments—determining which attachments are closest and most important, and which are more formal or distant. For example, in many African-American families, fictive kin (often given honorary titles of "aunt" or "uncle") play important roles in the child's life. In many Hispanic families, *compadre* and *comadre* (godfather and godmother) may have a very significant role in the life of a child, particularly if a parent is dead or absent.

Culture can also influence the expression of grief. Every culture has norms that suggest what types of behavior are acceptable as an expression of grief. In some cultures, intense emotional displays are considered appropriate; in others, stoicism is encouraged. These norms may differ by gender and age. For example, in some cultures, women and children may be accorded more freedom than men to express strong emotion.

Cultures also offer different methods for adapting to or coping with a loss, beginning with the rituals that surround dying and the immediate period after the death. Cultural norms may include the types of support traditionally given to the bereaved, the expectations placed on the bereaved, the understanding of grief prevalent in the culture, rituals to mark or recognize anniversaries or other milestones in the grieving process, and receptiveness to interventions such as counseling or support groups.

Children whose parents come from two different cultural backgrounds can find themselves in a confusing situation. When cultural patterns differ between the parents, the child may receive mixed messages about what is appropriate. It is crucial to assess the child's cultural context and how it facilitates or complicates his or her grief.

Social class is another important aspect of grieving. It is more than simply economic standing; it can be a culture or a way of life in and of itself, and is defined by a host of objective and subjective variables, from family income and residence to values and beliefs. Social class frames many aspects of loss. It may influence the kind of care that one receives or the type of death that is experienced.

Moreover, social classes differentially access resources, including grief resources. Lower income children may not have the same access to support groups or counseling, perhaps because of limited services in the area, expectations of parental involvement, or direct or indirect costs, such as transportation. Even when grief programs and support groups are offered, they may inadvertently include activities that highlight class differences and serve to isolate a poor child. For example, lower income families may not have many photographs, either because they are an expensive luxury or because they have been misplaced or lost, especially if the family has moved often. Thus, activities that use a lot of photographs—such as montages and memory books—may not always be suitable.

But each social class has its unique strengths as well. Children from a lower class background may have been less sheltered from knowledge or exposure to death and may have developed strong survival skills. The family may have developed supportive networks of relatives and friends. As with culture, it is important to assess both the limitations and strengths inherent in the child's social class.

CHAPTER 7

Grieving Children and Adolescents: Lessons from the Harvard Child Bereavement Study

J. William Worden

The Harvard Child Bereavement Study is a unique longitudinal investigation of the impact of parental death on families with school-age children (Worden & Silverman, 1996). The study looked at 125 children ages 6–17 years following the death of one of their parents. Families were recruited from communities in the greater Boston area representing a varied demography. Matched nonbereaved control children were also followed and assessed to identify consequences that were the result of bereavement rather than age, gender, or developmental differences. Information was gathered from both the child and the surviving parent.

Children in the study came from 70 families. The average age of the child was 12; the average age of the surviving parent was 42. Other demographic characteristics were as follows: gender (boys 52%, girls 48%); age group (preteen 50%, teen 50%); type of death (sudden 40%, expected 60%); religion (Protestant 23%, Catholic 70%, Jewish 6%, other 1%).

Assessments were done 3 months after the death and at 13 and 25 months post-loss. In addition to an extensive interview, the children's emotional/behavioral problems were assessed using the Achenbach Child Behavior Checklist (CBCL); their self-efficacy using the Locus of Control Scale for Children; their self-esteem using the Perceived Competence Scale for Children; and their understanding of death using the Smilansky Death Questionnaire.

Families were assessed by looking at family structure (FACES III), family coping (F-Copes), and family life changes (Family Inventory of Life Events, or FILE). For the surviving parent, depression was assessed using the Center for Epidemiological Studies—Depression Inventory (CES-D) and trauma using the Impact of Events Scale (IES).

In this chapter, I will discuss eight key findings from this study and the clinical implications of these findings.

FINDING 1. THE MAJORITY OF CHILDREN (80%) WERE COPING WELL BY THE FIRST AND SECOND ANNIVERSARY FOLLOWING THE DEATH OF A PARENT.

However, some children (20%) were not doing well 1 and 2 years after the death. They had clinically significant levels of emotional and behavioral problems on the CBCL. The percentage of bereaved children who fell into the risk group exceeded the percentage of children from the matched nonbereaved control group who were not doing well during the same time periods (1 year 10%, 2 years 7%).

Children who were doing well tended to come from more cohesive families, where communication about the dead parent was easy and where fewer changes and disruptions in daily life activities helped them feel safer. They came from families that tended to cope actively rather than passively and that could reframe and find something positive in a difficult situation. Active coping helped the children experience higher levels of self-efficacy and believe that they could affect what was happening in their lives. Children who were doing well also participated in more social activities than children who were doing less well.

The children who did not do as well (those in the risk group of 20%) tended to come from families in which the surviving parent was young, depressed, and not coping well, and from families that experienced numerous stressors and changes resulting from the death. These children showed lower self-esteem and felt less able to control what was happening to them, especially 2 years after the death.

Gender was an important aspect of risk group membership. At 2 years, there were more girls than boys in the risk group. This was especially true for teen girls, whose membership in this group had risen to 28%. Risk group membership was particularly high for teen girls who had lost a mother and were living with their father. High levels of aggressive and delinquent behavior were found in these teen girls.

Clinical Implications

Teen girls whose mothers die are a particularly vulnerable group and should receive special attention. There are several possible explanations for this phenomenon. One is the oedipal effect, which reemerges in the early teens. The child wants a special, close relationship with the parent of the opposite gender, but these preconscious wishes are ameliorated by identification with the parent of the same gender. When the same-gender parent is missing, emotional ambivalence toward the opposite-gender parent can be high—both wanting and not wanting that parent.

A more observable explanation is that many of the teen girls in the study were oldest daughters and were likely to be assigned tasks of meal preparation, child care, and the like. They accepted these tasks in the early months after the death of the mother but came to resent them 1 and 2 years later. If the father had brought a new woman into the home, the daughter's special relationship with him was significantly disrupted—high levels of aggressive and acting-out behavior were seen in these girls.

FINDING 2. THE MOST POWERFUL PREDICTOR OF A CHILD'S ADJUSTMENT TO THE DEATH OF A PARENT IS THE FUNCTIONING LEVEL OF THE SURVIVING PARENT.

Parental functioning was assessed by looking at levels of depression (CED-D), trauma response (IES), and a self-rated assessment scale of current stress and coping (Worden & Silverman, 1993). Parents who were particularly vulnerable to poor functioning were those who reported more concurrent stresses and changes in the family, were experiencing financial struggles, reported more ongoing tension with the children, and perceived less support from family and friends. Their coping was marked by high levels of passivity and little ability to find something positive in a bad situation.

Children with a single parent who was not functioning well showed more anxiety and depression, along with more sleep and health problems, than children whose parent was functioning better.

Clinical Implications

This is not the only study to show the impact of parental functioning on the adjustment of bereaved children. Irwin Sandler's group in Arizona has shown similar findings (Haine, et al., 2006) and it is logical that this should be true. Because parental functioning accounts for so much of the variance in child adjustment, intervening with the at-risk parent may make more sense than merely intervening with the children. Although some bereavement programs target both the child and the parent, many address only the needs of the bereaved child. In the Harvard study, we developed a screening scale to identify the at-risk child (described under Finding 8). Perhaps we should also develop a screening scale to identify high-risk parents and then target interventions toward them. The assumption behind this approach is that helping high-risk parents adjust to the death of their spouse would redound to the benefit of the children. Sandler's group developed a time-limited family intervention for bereaved children and parents and is looking at its short- and long-term effects (Sandler et al., 2003).

Finding 3. The loss of a mother was worse for most children than the loss of a father.

This was especially true during the second year of bereavement. When the death of a father leaves the mother as a single parent, many families experience financial stresses. But these financial difficulties do not affect the children (with the exception of adolescents) as much as the daily life changes that occur when the mother dies. Fathers can fulfill the role of single parent, but not as easily as most mothers. The ability to keep the household functioning, including meal preparation, was a real difficulty for most of the men in the study.

The death of a mother often means the loss of the emotional caretaker of the family. Again, this is a role that the father can pick up, but it is not easy and is another adaptation facing a father who is trying to adapt to the loss of his spouse. In the Harvard study, the loss of the mother was associated with more emotional/behavioral problems among children, including higher levels of anxiety, more acting-out behavior, lower self-esteem, and less belief in self-efficacy.

One key variable of adjustment after parental death is the number of daily life changes the child faces. This does not mean major changes—such as changing houses or schools—but rather small but important changes in such things as bedtime, discipline, homework expectations, or on-time meals. Children who experienced fewer of these daily life changes did better than children who experienced more of them. Children experienced more daily life changes if it was the mother who died.

Clinical Implications

Those of us who conduct bereavement groups often talk about how few men attend these groups. When the purpose of a bereavement group is primarily emotional support, women participate in much larger numbers. It occurred to us that men are basically problem solvers, and many would probably want to learn how to be better single parents. So we established a group for bereaved dads that focused on learning how to be a better single parent. In no time, men were coming to the group because it met a need that was more important to them than emotional support. I would encourage others who offer bereavement groups to try this approach. The emotional support will rub off while the men discuss the tasks of discipline, meal preparation, listening to kids, and so on.

FINDING 4. ATTACHMENT IS IMPORTANT, AND MANY CHILDREN REMAIN "CONNECTED" TO THE DEAD PARENT LONG AFTER THE DEATH.

Earlier psychodynamic understanding of mourning suggested that bereaved persons needed to emotionally detach from lost loved ones so they would have the emotional energy to make new attachments. We now know that continuing bonds and ongoing connections to the deceased are normative and beneficial. Findings from the Harvard study contributed to our rethinking of the earlier psychodynamic position (Silverman, Nickman, & Worden, 1992). Many children in this study stayed connected to their dead parents—talking to them, feeling watched by them, thinking about them, dreaming about them, and locating the parent in a specific place, often heaven.

Children who were highly connected to the deceased parent were more likely to have lost a parent of the same gender. They came from more cohesive families and were better able to talk with others about the death and show their emotional pain. They were more able to accept support from their families and friends than children who were less connected. They also saw themselves as very much like the deceased parent in terms of personal characteristics.

Clinical Implications

A surprising number of the children were afraid that they were going to forget their dead parent. This fear can be addressed in several ways. One of the easiest ways is to help the children create a memory book—a scrapbook in which they can write stories and poems about the dead parent, draw pictures of activities they remember doing with the parent, cut and paste family photographs, and include things that remind them of the lost parent. This may be best done as a family activity. Instead of a book, some children create a memory box, in which they can store memorabilia of the lost parent. In my experience, children who make such a book or box revisit it at various transitional times in their lives. As children age, they ask themselves, "What would my parent be like now if he/she had lived?" Revisiting these memory treasures can often help them with this query.

Another way to remember the dead parent is to include the parent in daily conversations in a natural way. "Do you remember how proud your dad was of you the day you finished a whole rack of ribs at the steakhouse?" a mother asked her young teen son. "No one can make an apple pie like your mother could," said a dad at the dinner table. Including remembrances of the parent in an easy way can help the whole family keep memories alive.

FINDING 5. PARENTAL DATING WAS A MIXED BLESSING FOR THESE CHILDREN.

Parental dating in the first year of bereavement was associated with withdrawn behavior, acting out, and somatic symptoms among children, especially if the surviving parent was a father. On the other hand, an engagement or remarriage after a suitable bereavement period had a positive effect on the children, leading to less anxiety, less depression, and less worry about the safety of the surviving parent.

In the first 4 months after the death, few parents (9%) dated. Those who did were more likely to be men, particularly those with high levels of depression and lower self-esteem. These parents seemed to be reaching out for some kind of replacement for the spouse who had been their primary source of support. They had less cohesive families that were experiencing a lot of chaos, and they tended to come from lower socioeconomic levels (Worden & Silverman, 1992).

By the end of the first year of bereavement, 37% of the surviving parents had dated. Many of the children resisted parental dating. "I wouldn't want him to remarry. I don't like the idea of remarriage. I just don't want him to," said a 9-year-old girl. "I really don't want another mother, although I know that I cannot have another mother—no one else would be the same as my mother was," insisted a 12-year-old girl. She resisted her father's idea of inviting his girlfriend to spend the first Christmas with them after the mother's death.

Not all children were upset by parental dating; some welcomed it. One teen girl signed her mother up for a Jewish dating service with the hope that she would meet a nice man to help assuage her extreme loneliness after the death of her husband. A preschool boy asked his mother if they could go to the Daddy Store and find a new daddy—a touching but upsetting comment to the mother. "I think it's neat that she's dating," said an 11-year-old boy, "Cause she doesn't want to be lonely for the rest of her life."

During the second year of bereavement, there were fewer behavioral differences between the children whose parents were dating and those who were not. But the resistance to dating did not go away for some children. A 17-year-old girl who struggled with her ambivalence said, "Sometimes I have to hide my feelings 'cause she's going out with some guy I don't like. I know she really likes him, and I have to say, 'Yeah, he's okay.'"

By the end of year 2, 17% of the children had a parent who was either engaged or remarried. This had a positive effect on the parents, who reported lower levels of depression, less intrusive and avoidant thinking, and more optimism about their coping abilities. Children benefited from remarriage—they reported lower levels of anxiety and depression and fewer concerns about the safety of their surviving parent. The family as a whole also benefited—there was less tension between the parents and the children.

Clinical Implications

Accepting a new person into the family system is difficult for many children, whether in bereaved families or families of divorce. In some ways, it is easier for bereaved children than for children of divorce. It is common for children to hope for the return of the divorced parent, and this hope may persist for some time, until it is dashed by the remarriage of one of the parents. After the death of a parent, the bereaved children long for the parent to return, but they soon accept that this is impossible. Therefore, in general, they are more open to a "replacement" parent, especially when they see how the new person addresses their surviving parent's loneliness—something that is difficult for the child to do. This openness grows as children move out to 2 years after the death. Having a "new parent" allows the children to be less concerned about the safety of their surviving parent.

FINDING 6. MOST CHILDREN WERE GIVEN THE CHOICE OF PARTICIPATING IN THE FUNERAL AND OPTED TO DO SO.

Bereaved parents often wonder if they should include children in funeral activities and rituals. In general, children should be given the choice of participating or not, although adults should make the decision for pre-school children. However, when giving children a choice, it should be an informed choice. Better outcomes were observed in the children who were prepared for the service. Many bereaved children have never participated in funeral activities, so they need information about what they might see or hear. Otherwise, they might experience things at the funeral that they are not expecting and that have a traumatic effect. Most of the children in the Harvard study chose to participate in the various services and rituals. Including children in planning the funeral had a positive effect, helping them feel important and useful at a time when many were feeling overwhelmed (Silverman & Worden, 1992).

Over time, the children recaptured memories of the funeral and were increasingly able to talk about it. When we interviewed the children 4 months after the death, their memories of the funeral were vague and often focused on one image, such as the adult who was kind to them and took them to the bathroom. On the first anniversary of the death, most children's memories of the funeral events were clearer. By the second anniversary, they could remember most things about the service. More than half of the children said they would have made some changes to the service. Some wished it had been larger, so more people could have honored and celebrated the life of their parent. Other children wished it had been smaller and more intimate, which would have served their needs better. Several children mentioned specific changes, such as an oak casket for a father whose hobby was woodworking or a beach location for a mother who spent most warm days at the ocean. To the children, these changes in the funeral would have better reflected who the parent was and made the event more of a memorial.

Clinical Implications

Children should be given the choice to participate in funerals and memorial services, but it should be an informed choice. Adults should describe what the children will see and hear, then let the children decide. Most children will decide to participate.

If younger children are participating, designate an adult (not an immediate family member) who can sit with the child and take him or her outside or to the bathroom if needed.

Children should be included in the planning for memorial remembrances on the anniversaries of the death, and on birthdays and other family holidays. This helps them keep the memory of their dead parent alive and is an important part of the continuing bond.

FINDING 7. THERE ARE LONG-TERM EFFECTS FROM THE LOSS.

We found that some of the important effects from the death did not show up until 2 years later. Some children who appeared to be doing well at 1 year postdeath were not doing as well at 2 years postdeath. Among the long-term consequences were lower self-esteem and a lower sense of self-efficacy in the bereaved children compared with the nonbereaved controls. At 2 years, the bereaved children saw themselves as doing less well in school and having more depression and anxiety than the control group.

Clinical Implications

This finding has two important clinical implications. First, bereaved children should be followed longer than just 1 year. Many bereavement follow-up programs, including many hospice programs, follow families for 1 year. The Harvard study suggests that some children and families should be followed for a longer time because of late consequences of losing a parent. Second, it is possible to identify at 4 to 6 months the children who will be at risk 2 years later and to single them out for intervention. Using longitudinal data from the study, we have developed a screening instrument (see Finding 8) that predicts with a high degree of accuracy which children are more at risk for poor adaptation to loss. Identifying these children and offering intervention may preclude the negative sequelae of parental loss.

A debate is ongoing in the field as to whether grief counseling is effective for children; in fact, some people think it can be harmful. There is more universal agreement (Stroebe, 2005; Currier et al, 2007), that grief counseling can be beneficial if it is targeted to the children who really need it.

FINDING 8. PREDICTION OF AT-RISK CHILDREN IS POSSIBLE.

There are three basic approaches to intervention with bereaved children. The first is to intervene with all children who lose a parent to death. It is true that it is difficult for a child to lose a parent; however, evidence from the Harvard study and similar investigations shows that not all bereaved children need intervention. Most do well over the first 2 years after loss without a special intervention.

The second approach is to wait and see which bereaved children have emotional or behavioral problems and refer those children to professional resources. This approach is followed in many communities. The downside is that one must wait until the child is experiencing difficulty before reaching out to him or her. It is important to note that many of the children in the Harvard study did not experience emotional/behavioral difficulties until 2 years after the death of a parent.

The third approach is to develop an instrument that can predict which children will have difficulty at some point in the future and offer interventions to these children. This philosophy of screening and early intervention is espoused by the Department of Psychiatry at the Harvard Medical School, where preventive mental health has long been a major focus. We used information we collected on the children and their families 4 months after the death to develop a screening scale that would predict which children would be in the risk group 2 years later. A number of these children were already showing emotional/behavioral difficulties 4 months after the loss, but not all of them were. If this screening approach is used, we can be sure that we are reaching the children most in need of intervention. It is not a problem if low-risk children receive interventions—presumably, they will be helped by being in some type of bereavement program. However, the main benefit of screening is to make sure that intervention is offered to those who are most needy—those who are predicted to be in the at-risk group. The assumption is that intervention will lessen the negative sequelae of parental loss.

Clinical Implications

The clinical implication is clear. If not all bereaved children need intervention, our resources are best used treating the children who are most in need. Using a well-crafted screening instrument is a good approach.

ADDITIONAL FINDINGS

Donna Schuurman is director of the Dougy Center in Portland, Oregon, the premier center for treating bereaved children. We used the screening instrument to see which children this center was reaching. Were they mostly children who didn't need an intervention but wouldn't be hurt by it, or were they those predicted to be in the at-risk group 2 years after the death? We found that a large majority of the children being served by the program fell into the at-risk group, which meant that the Dougy Center was treating children most in need, at least according to the Harvard screening instrument.

Currier, Holland, and Neimeyer (2007) recently studied the effectiveness of bereavement interventions with children. After looking at 13 controlled-outcome studies, they concluded that bereavement groups for children were not very effective compared with the effect size of general psychotherapy with children. They concluded that the children most helped by intervention were those who were at high risk or already showing signs of difficulty. In their investigation, only one study screened for problems and selected children who were displaying adjustment difficulties at the start of treatment. The authors make a strong case for the use of assessment before beginning childhood bereavement intervention.

Also supporting this notion of treating the most needy children is a very well-crafted family intervention study by Sandler and colleagues in Arizona

(Sandler et al., 2003). These investigators found that children who had higher problem scores when they entered the intervention program had been most helped by the intervention a year later.

The Harvard Child Bereavement Study has produced many other findings of interest. These findings, along with the screening instrument and its scoring instructions, can be found in *Children and Grief: When a Parent Dies* by J. William Worden (1996, New York: Guilford). More findings from the study appear in *Never Too Young* by Phyllis R. Silverman (2000, New York: Oxford).

J. William Worden, Ph.D., ABPP, is a Fellow of the American Psychological Association and holds academic appointments at Harvard Medical School and the Rosemead Graduate School of Psychology in California. He is also co-principal investigator for Harvard's Child Bereavement Study, based at Massachusetts General Hospital. His research and clinical work over 30 years has centered on issues of life-threatening illness and life-threatening behavior. Dr. Worden has lectured and written on topics related to terminal illness, cancer care, and bereavement. He is the author of *Personal Death Awareness; Children & Grief: When a Parent Dies*; and is co-author of *Helping Cancer Patients Cope*. His book *Grief Counseling & Grief Therapy: A Handbook for the Mental Health Practitioner*, now in its third edition, has been translated into 12 languages and is widely used around the world as the standard reference on the subject. Dr. Worden's clinical practice is in Laguna Niguel, California.

REFERENCES

Currier, J., Holland, J., & Neimeyer, R. (2007). The effectiveness of bereavement interventions with children: A meta-analytic review of controlled outcome research. *Journal of Clinical Child & Adolescent Psychology, 36*, 253–259.

Haine, R. A., Wolchik, S. A., Sandler, I. N., Millsap, R. E., & Ayers, T. S. (2006). Positive parenting as a protective resource for parentally bereaved children. *Death Studies, 30,* 1–28.

Sandler, I. N., Ayers, T. S., Wolchik, S. A., Tein, J.-Y., et al. (2003). The family bereavement program: Efficacy evaluation of a theory-based prevention program for parentally bereaved children and adolescents. *Journal of Consulting and Clinical Psychology, 71*, 587–600.

Silverman, P. R., & Worden, J. W. (1992). Children's understanding of funeral ritual. *Omega, 25*, 319–331.

Silverman, P. R., Nickman, S., & Worden, J. W. (1992). Detachment revisited: The child's reconstruction of a dead parent. *American Journal of Orthopsychiatry, 62*, 494–503.

Stroebe, W., Schut, H., & Stroebe, M. S. (2005). Grief work, disclosure, and counseling: Do they help the bereaved? *Clinical Psychology Review, 25*, 395–414.

Worden, J. W. (1996) paperback edition (2001). *Children & grief: When a parent dies*. New York: Guilford.

Worden, J. W., & Silverman, P. R. (1992). The challenge of single parenting. *The Director, 63*, 30–32.

Worden, J. W., & Silverman, P. R. (1993). Grief and depression in newly widowed parents with school-age children. *Omega, 27*, 251–260.

Worden, J. W., & Silverman, P. R. (1996). Parental death and the adjustment of school-age children. *Omega, 35*, 95–102.

Too Much Death at Age Eleven

By Sam Jensen

A cough. That rasping sound forced through the throat. That damning little sound changed my life forever. Dad had a nasty little cough. Mom took him to the doctor to check it out, like any sane person would. Have a cough, go see a doctor. Another routine. Well, all routines and schedules were about to go out the window.

I don't know if the cancer caused the cough; I guess it doesn't really matter now. I can't remember when they broke the news to us. I'm not even sure if my little brother was with me. I don't think they ever told us outright. Not "Daddy has cancer" or something like that. They only hinted at it. But I knew.

For the first month or so, I thought he would make it. Like that one afternoon when he got out of his chair, oxygenator (as I thought of it) attached, came out into the backyard, and played catch with me. His son. Little ol' Sam. That moment shines very brightly in my murky memories. For him to do that, my 11-year-old mind reasoned, meant he was going to get better. That's one of the last good memories I have of my father.

From the time he was diagnosed to the time he died, all seems like a gray haze now. There are little blips, like dots on a number line from school. I hate those things. The little points are bits of clear space in my memory where the gray steps back. A couple moments. The announcement that Dad was going to have chemotherapy, and their talk with me and my little bro. We were in his room. Doing a puzzle, I think. Someone was staying in my room, and we were lying on an air mattress Mom had set up. "The therapy isn't working," she says. "'Kay," we say. What else is there to say? I remember not crying. I didn't cry much through the whole ordeal. Don't know why.

I remember Dad's situation worsening in little stages. He's fine. He can't do much physical stuff. He never leaves his chair. He never leaves his bed. He never leaves the hospital bed we brought home for him. He's getting worse. We're pulling the plug. He's dying. He's dead.

I remember the hospice nurse who helped us. She was an angel. Her name escapes me. But perhaps angels have no names, only beautiful hearts. I don't exactly remember her job, but she was great nonetheless.

My father died on December 24, 2003—Christmas Eve. Jesus, that sounds bad now. I was 11 years old. My little brother, Elliot, was 6. We were watching "Clifford," of all things, when Mom came in, shouting, "The nurse thinks your dad is dying, come here!" So, we run in. He's there, breathing, but not healthily. We all sit together in one chair—me, Mom, and Elliot. His last breath I remember very clearly. His head kind of raised itself up, and he opened his mouth like he was trying to eat a cherry inches above his lips. Then he was gone. I only cried a little.

Then two men in suits came. They carried dad out into their truck. They had trouble moving the stretcher through the hallway. The sight of my dad's body almost sliding off the stretcher scarred me for life.

Ah, but the horrors were not over yet.

On Christmas, a day after my father died, my Mom's and my friend Yvonne had a heart attack and died in our driveway. I saw her in the entryway, gasping for air. "Go get Fred, *miho.*" Fred was her husband. I ran and told Fred, then told everyone else. We didn't know she had died until we got a call from the hospital. I cried then. I exploded. My life had just turned into freakin' hell. Everyone bawled. We went to see her in the hospital, but I didn't want to see the body. I was too scared, I suppose.

I went to both funerals. I cried more at Yvonne's than at my dad's. I guess I knew Dad was going to die, so the grief was spread out over time. Yvonne's death messed me up, messed me up bad.

Then we go to this place, this Children's Grief Center. I hated the idea at first, but it ended up saving me. If we had never gone, my family and I would be way worse off than we are now. I thank them for everything. I met many great friends: Matthew, Amanda, Melissa, Franky, Gali, the twins. I love them all. And I love the counselors— guides from heaven itself. They are eternally my family.

So there's my story. So here I am. Since then, I've had one grandpa and one dog ripped away from me. And my best friend's dad was diagnosed with cancer. Damned cancer. I've cursed God once or twice since my dad's death. I don't know if I've forgiven Him yet. I don't know if He even cares. All I know is that I've got to protect those whom I love.

There's a line from one of my favorite movies, *A Knight's Tale*, which describes where I am now: "So, I leave you all with hope. It is what gets me through the day and especially the night. The hope that tomorrow, when I wake up, I'll be in a better place, in a better time."

Till that better time.

Sam Jensen *is a 15-year-old student at Canutillo High School in Canutillo, Texas. His interests include anime, Scouting, Japanese culture, reading, and video gaming.*

CHAPTER 8

When a Parent Dies: Helping Grieving Children and Adolescents

Rachel A. Haine, Tim S. Ayers, Irwin N. Sandler, and Sharlene A. Wolchik

T he death of a parent is one of the most traumatic events that can occur in childhood. In the United States, the yearly prevalence rate for experiencing the death of a parent or primary caregiver based on the U.S. Census is approximately 3.5% (2.5 million) of children under age 18 (Social Security Administration, 2000). The death of a parent increases the risk of many negative outcomes, including mental health problems such as depression, anxiety, somatic complaints, posttraumatic stress symptoms, traumatic grief, reduced academic success and self-esteem, and a maladaptive sense of control (e.g., Dowdney, 2000; Lutzke, Ayers, Sandler, & Barr, 1997).

This chapter draws from observational and intervention research to provide bereavement counselors with both general knowledge and specific strategies to apply in working with children and adolescents following the death of a parent or primary caregiver. The term "child" in this chapter refers to the child and adolescent age ranges. The chapter is divided into sections on the basis of common questions posed by bereavement counselors. We highlight strategies from the Family Bereavement Program conducted by our research team at Arizona State University (ASU) (Ayers et al., 1996; Sandler, Ayers, Twohey, Lutzke, & Kriege, 1996) to illustrate how bereavement counseling can focus on multiple target areas and use various approaches in working with children and families. We refer to our experience with the Family Bereavement Program because it is directed at families that have experienced various causes of death and it has been evaluated using highly rigorous research methods (Sandler et al., 2003).

1. WHAT DEMOGRAPHIC FACTORS SHOULD I CONSIDER IN WORKING WITH CHILDREN FOLLOWING THE DEATH OF A PARENT?

Developmental level, gender, and cultural background all have implications for children's adjustment to parental death.

Developmental level. Children vary in their understanding of death, depending on developmental level (Worden, 1996). Speece and Brent (1996) defined four components of children's concept of death. They define *universality* as children's understanding that death is inevitable and will happen to everyone, including themselves. *Nonfunctionality* refers to the understanding that all life-defining functions (e.g., eating, sleeping, thinking) cease at death. *Irreversibility* refers to the understanding that when things die they do not come back to life. *Causality* refers to a child's ability to understand the objective and biological causes of death. Children tend to understand universality and irreversibility before they understand nonfunctionality and causality (Lazar & Torney-Purta, 1991). Counselors must consider developmental differences in responses to and experiences following the death of a parent. For example, descriptive studies have found that younger children are more likely to feel watched by the deceased parent and to dream about that parent, and are generally more expressive than older children (Silverman & Worden, 1993; Worden, 1996). Researchers have noted that older children are significantly more likely than younger children to be told that they should act more grown up, and are more likely to talk to their friends about the deceased parent (Silverman & Worden, 1993; Worden, 1996). Additional information about differences in responses to the death of a parent across childhood can be found in Christ and Christ (2006).

Gender. Research indicates that among children (as in the general population), females typically exhibit more depression, anxiety, and somatic symptoms following the death of a parent, while males exhibit more disruptive behavior (e.g., Dowdney, 2000; Saler & Skolnik, 1992; Worden, 1996). Studies have found that girls are more vulnerable to anxiety and depressive symptoms following the death of a parent—a state that continues over time (e.g.,

Schmiege, Khoo, Sandler, Ayers, & Wolchik, 2006)—and that the experience of parental death in childhood is a vulnerability factor for depression in early adulthood for females (Reinherz et al., 1999). Some recent research indicates that the increased vulnerability for girls is in part due to higher sensitivity to interpersonal stressors and a lower sense of internal control (Little, Sandler, Wolchik & Ayers, 2007). It is interesting to note that, contrary to intuitive beliefs, gender match between the deceased parent and child is not associated with the child's adaptation (Worden, 1996).

Cultural background. Minimal research has been conducted regarding cultural differences in child bereavement experiences, and no study has examined the role of culture in adaptation to the death of a parent during childhood. Cross-cultural comparisons of the development of death concepts have found both similarities and differences between cultures (e.g., Schonfeld & Smilansky, 1989). For example, one study that compared Israeli and American school-age children found that Israeli children scored higher in terms of ability to understand irreversibility and finality, indicating a more mature understanding of these concepts (Schonfeld & Smilansky, 1989). Conceptualizations of grief in adults have included discussions of the culture-bound assumptions of the normal course of bereavement. Some have argued that U.S. mainstream culture tends to focus on individuals rather than relationships, to deny the notion that important attachments endure following a death, and to pathologize atypical grief reactions (Shapiro, 1996). While these assumptions may be prevalent in the dominant U.S. culture, it is important to recognize that ethnic minority families in the United States (and even families from the majority) may not subscribe to these assumptions, and their needs may differ. Counselors can help families examine the match between cultural expectations and their own beliefs and needs in coping with the death of a parent.

2. WHAT IS THE ROLE OF THE CAUSE OF DEATH IN COUNSELING CHILDREN?

Although studies have indicated that cause of death alone is not a major predictor of negative outcomes in children (Brown, Sandler, Tein, Liu, & Haine, 2007; Worden, 1996), addressing children's concerns about the cause of death is an important focus of treatment. Counselors can draw from several interventions that have been designed to address specific causes of death, including cancer, HIV/AIDS, suicide, and other traumatic deaths.

HIV/AIDS and cancer. Anticipatory interventions have been developed for children and families experiencing the terminal illness of a parent due to HIV/AIDS or cancer. One intervention for families with a parent in the terminal stages of HIV/AIDS focuses on helping the parents discuss their disease with their children, facilitating child coping, establishing positive daily family routines, and preparing the child for the transition to a new caregiver (Rotheram-Borus, Lee, Gwadz, & Draimin, 2001). An anticipatory intervention for families with a parental diagnosis of terminal cancer has been developed to enhance the healthy parent's ability to provide support for the children, to ensure consistency and stability in the children's environment before and after the death, and to create an environment in which the children feel comfortable expressing their feelings about the loss (Christ, Raveis, Siegel, & Karus, 2005).

Suicide and other traumatic deaths. Recently, attention has focused on supporting children who have experienced the suicide or other traumatic death of a parent, such as the World Trade Center and Pentagon attacks of 2001 or Hurricane Katrina in 2005. Traumatic parental death has been associated with child posttraumatic stress disorder (PTSD) (Dowdney, 2000). One intervention designed specifically for families in which a parent or sibling has committed suicide includes explicit discussions of suicide (e.g., reasons people choose to commit suicide and prevention of children's own suicidal ideation) and activities intended to help children manage traumatic thoughts and stigma-related concerns about suicide (Pfeffer, Jiang, Kakuma, Hwang, & Metsch, 2002). Trauma-focused cognitive-behavioral therapy (TF-CBT) has been proposed as an effective treatment for children who experience the traumatic death of a parent (Cohen, Mannarino, & Deblinger, 2006; Saltzman, Pynoos, Layne, Steinberg & Aisenberg, 2001). The basic principles of TF-CBT include focusing on exposure and direct discussion of the traumatic experience, challenging and correcting cognitive distortions and harmful automatic thoughts, and teaching stress management and relaxation techniques (Cohen, Mannarino, Berliner, & Deblinger, 2000).

3. HOW CAN I SUPPORT HEALTHY GRIEF REACTIONS IN CHILDREN FOLLOWING THE DEATH OF A PARENT?

Counselors can focus on several areas to support healthy grief reactions, including educating children about the grief process, encouraging a healthy continuing bond with the deceased, and supporting the expression of emotions.

Educating children about the grief process. Counselors can help children adapt to the death of a parent by providing information about the grief process (Corr, 1995). Such information can normalize children's experience and help reduce anxieties about the future. Counselors can make these important points: (a) the death is not the child's fault; (b) the child may feel a wide range of emotions; (c) it is okay to talk about the parent who died; (d) it is not unusual for children to think they see or to dream about the deceased parent; and (e) children never forget their deceased parent (e.g., Lohnes & Kalter, 1994; Sandler et al., 1996, 2003; Silverman & Worden, 1993; Tonkins & Lambert, 1996).

Helping children maintain a connection with the deceased parent. Counselors can support children in understanding that the deceased parent is indeed gone but that they can maintain a relationship with that parent (Silverman & Worden, 1993). Strategies to maintain a connection include talking to the parent who died; sharing memories of the deceased; symbolic communication, such as attaching a message to a balloon and releasing the balloon or writing a letter to the deceased parent; and memorial activities, such as visiting the grave or attending memorial services or rituals (Lohnes & Kalter, 1994; Sandler et al., 1996; Tonkins & Lambert, 1996).

Supporting adaptive expression of emotions. Grieving children may experience a range of emotions following the death, such as sadness, guilt, anger, and anxiety (e.g., Silverman & Worden, 1993; Worden, 1996). Overt affective responses such as crying and sleep disturbances are common soon after the death, but they decrease over time (Silverman & Worden, 1993). There is little evidence that cathartic expression of emotion is necessary for all children; however, children who believe they must inhibit the expression of negative emotions are more likely to experience mental health problems (Ayers, Sandler, Wolchik, & Haine, 2000; Tein, Sandler, Ayers, & Wolchik, 2006). Counselors can support the child in expressing emotions and can encourage significant others, such as surviving parents, to show that they understand the child's feelings (Ayers et al., 1996; Sandler et al., 1996). Activities that can be used to support children's desired emotional expression include using sentence stems (e.g., "When I think about the death of my parent, I sometimes feel angry because…") (Sandler et al., 1996) and discussing topics such as a favorite time the child had with the deceased parent, a favorite gift from the deceased parent, or the child's favorite characteristic of the deceased parent (Black & Urbanowicz, 1987; Sandler et al., 1996; Zambelli & DeRosa, 1992). It is important to note that these techniques must be used sensitively without attempting to deepen the child's level of emotional expression; the adult should follow the child's lead and comfort level in expressing feelings. Counselors should avoid conveying the message that children *must* express negative feelings to move forward in their grief work.

4. How can I help a child build skills to cope with the death?

Counselors can facilitate several skills associated with positive outcomes for children following the death of a parent, including self-esteem, adaptive sense of control, positive coping skills, and a sense of coping efficacy.

Promoting self-esteem. Grieving children often experience negative events following the death of a parent that reduce their self-esteem, such as less positive interactions with significant others or an increase in harsh parenting by the surviving parent (Haine, Ayers, Sandler, Wolchik, & Weyer, 2003; Wolchik, Tein, Sandler, & Ayers, 2006). One strategy counselors can use to promote self-esteem in grieving children is to identify and reframe negative self-statements (e.g., "Things will never get better") into positive self-talk (e.g., "Things may be bad now, but they will get better") (Sandler et al., 1996). Through exercises and role-plays, counselors can demonstrate how these negative self-statements create additional problems and how positive reframes can help the children feel better (Sandler et al., 1996). Counselors can encourage parents to provide increased positive feedback and opportunities for esteem-enhancing activities outside the therapy context, such as one-on-one time with the surviving parent or activities that provide opportunities to experience mastery (Ayers et al., 1996; Zambelli & DeRosa, 1992).

Increasing adaptive control beliefs. Grieving children can feel helpless and believe that they have little control over events (Worden & Silverman, 1996). A faulty belief that one can or should control negative events can lead to negative self-evaluations (e.g., "I've got to fix it" or "I'm no good if I don't fix it") (Sandler et al., 1996). Healthy control beliefs involve using emotion-focused coping strategies to manage uncontrollable events. Bereavement counselors can promote an adaptive sense of control by distinguishing the problems that are the child's "job" to fix from the problems that are adult responsibilities (e.g., financial concerns, a parent's depression) (Sandler et al., 1996). Grieving children sometimes believe it is their job to care for and protect their surviving parent and to make the parent feel less sad (Sandler et al., 1996). Counselors can communicate to children and their surviving parents that although the children can let their parents know they are there for them and hope they feel better soon, children are not responsible for making their parents feel less distressed or for addressing issues such as having less money. Counselors can encourage surviving parents to communicate reassuring messages to their children about the parents' ability to cope with their emotions and challenges, even though they may be struggling. Counselors can work with parents to ensure that they are not entangling children in the problems of the family, encouraging parents to find "adult ears" to listen to their problems (Ayers et al., 1996).

Improving coping skills. Children's use of active coping strategies and possession of high levels of coping efficacy have been associated with positive outcomes following the death of a parent (Wolchik et al., 2006). Specific coping strategies that can be taught include problem-solving coping, positive reframing coping (optimism and focusing on the positive aspects of a situation), and support-seeking coping (seeking support for stressful situations) (see Sandler et al., 1996). Coping efficacy refers to the sense that one has a set of tools that can be used to manage stressful events and situations (Sandler, Tein, Metha, Wolchik, & Ayers, 2000). To enhance children's sense of efficacy, the counselor can have them create their own "coping toolbox," select their own goals, and use their coping tools to work on these goals. Counselors can help children evaluate the effectiveness of their coping efforts and help them express an ongoing belief in their efficacy to deal with problems (Sandler et al., 1996).

5. How can I work with the surviving parent or primary caregiver to improve child adaptation following the death?

Counselors can work with surviving parents to facilitate a positive parent-child relationship, reduce the parent's own distress and grief, minimize children's exposure to stressful life events, and increase positive family interactions.

Promoting a positive parent-child relationship. Positive parenting by the surviving parent is strongly associated with positive adjustment in grieving children (Haine, Wolchik, Sandler, Millsap, & Ayers, 2006; Kwok et al., 2005; Raveis, Siegel, & Karus, 1999; Saler & Skolnik, 1992; West, Sandler, Pillow, Baca, & Gersten, 1991). A positive parent-child relationship reflects the parent's creation of a supportive and structured environment that allows for open communication and includes a balance of warmth and effective discipline.

Elements of *parental warmth* include having general positive regard for the child, conveying acceptance, expressing affection, and providing emotional support (e.g., Lamborn, Mounts, Steinberg, & Dornbusch, 1991; Maccoby & Martin, 1983). Strategies to improve warmth can include teaching parents to listen (e.g., to reflect content and feelings, and summarize what they hear); to establish regular (daily) periods of unstructured, one-on-one time in which the child has the parent's undivided attention and all judgment is withheld; and to increase positive exchanges with the child by reinforcing positive behaviors (Ayers et al., 1996).

Open parent-child communication is important in bereaved families (e.g., Raveis et al., 1999; Saler & Skolnik, 1992) and can be encouraged by teaching complementary expression skills to children (e.g., use of "I-messages" to express feelings) and listening skills to parents (e.g., appropriate body language and eye contact, identifying underlying feelings) (Ayers et al., 1996; Sandler et al., 1996). Parents can communicate that they are open to hearing about their child's experience and can normalize the range of feelings the child might be experiencing.

The few existing studies indicate that *effective discipline* is associated with reduced mental health problems in children following the death of a parent (Lin, Sandler, Ayers, Wolchik, & Leuken, 2004; Worden, 1996). Parents often have difficulties with discipline following the death of a spouse, including not being familiar with the role of disciplinarian, lacking a partner to share the discipline responsibility, not wanting to act negatively toward the grieving child, and feeling overly busy, tired, or depressed. Counselors can support parents by identifying positive self-statements around effective discipline (e.g., "I'm being a good parent—my child will learn from this") (Ayers et al., 1996; Sandler et al., 2003). Counselors can encourage parents to be clear, calm, and consistent in communicating their expectations and consequences for misbehavior; to increase their use of positive reinforcement for desirable behaviors; to implement the least punitive consequences; and to be calm and consistent in implementing those consequences (Ayers et al., 1996). Parents can practice these skills by creating a plan to change problem behaviors and then measuring the behavior before and after the plan is implemented.

Increasing positive family interactions. Stable positive events and family cohesion decrease following the death of a parent, and such decreases have been associated with increased mental health problems for children (e.g., Sandler et al., 1992; West et al., 1991; Worden, 1996). Counselors can promote family-related positive events through an activity called "Family Time," which is used in the ASU Family Bereavement Program (Ayers et al., 1996; Sandler et al., 1996). Family Time consists of a weekly scheduled activity in which the entire family participates. The activities are active (e.g., having a picnic, going for a walk or bike ride, playing board games) rather than passive (e.g., watching TV or a movie), and family members agree to abide by rules such as "no fighting or problem solving." Family Time provides a "break" from grief and helps strengthen the family. A regularly scheduled positive activity can improve mood, increase warmth and open communication among family members, and help develop consistency and structure in the family. Families can brainstorm ideas for activities with the counselor and then allow one of the children to choose an activity each week. Counselors can work with parents to identify and address any obstacles to a weekly Family Time. Counselors also can encourage families to read books together—this can offer emotionally and financially overwhelmed surviving parents a quick and inexpensive way to bond with their children and create a positive routine (e.g., Moody & Moody, 1991).

Reducing the parent's own distress and grief. High distress and intense grief in the surviving parent are associated with negative outcomes for children following the death of a parent (e.g., Lutzke et al., 1997). Counselors can support the mental health of parents by teaching positive reframing of negative thoughts, encouraging parents to seek support and engage in self-care, acknowledging and reinforcing parents' efforts to change their parenting practices, and supporting them in achieving personal goals associated with the death (e.g., maintain/improve relationships with in-laws and extended family) (Ayers et al., 1996).

Reducing the child's exposure to stressful life events. A consistent association has been found between increases in stressful life events following the death of a parent and child mental health problems (e.g., West et al., 1991). Counselors can work with parents to reduce the occurrence of stressful events and can encourage them to shield children as much as possible from the deleterious consequences of events that cannot be prevented. For example, grieving children often are concerned when their surviving parent begins to date and develop a new long-term love interest. Parents can be encouraged to introduce a new partner slowly and to talk with their children openly and in an age-appropriate manner about the relationship (Ayers et al., 1996). Counselors can help parents shield children from being overly involved in other family stressors, such as financial strains, over which they have little control. While parents cannot and should not *hide* these stressors from children, they can reassure the children about the strength of the family with messages such as "We'll make it through these tough times." Counselors can encourage parents to use listening and problem-solving skills, and to send reassuring messages in response to other types of stressors (e.g., extended-family conflict, holidays).

Summary

The death of a parent during childhood is a traumatic event that can result in negative outcomes for children. Research has identified several areas for effective bereavement counseling, including attending to characteristics of the child and of the cause of death. Bereavement counselors can work with the child to support healthy grief reactions as well as to build skills to manage thoughts, feelings, and events that occur following the death. In addition, counselors can work with the surviving parent to increase the warmth and structure of the post death environment, including promoting positive family interactions, helping parents manage their own distress, and helping them shield their children from being overly involved in family stressors.

Rachel A. Haine, Ph.D., earned her Ph.D. in clinical psychology from Arizona State University, where she was trained in the design, implementation, and evaluation of prevention programs for parentally bereaved children and children from divorced homes. She is an assistant research scientist at the Child and Adolescent Services Research Center, which is part of Rady Children's Hospital–San Diego. Her current research interests include the study of usual care in youth mental health services, issues in implementing family-based interventions in existing service settings, and the evaluation of services for young children with mild to moderate developmental delays. Dr. Haine is also a licensed clinical psychologist in private practice in San Diego, with a focus on supporting children and families following the death of a parent or during a parent's terminal illness.

Tim S. Ayers received his Ph.D. in clinical psychology from Arizona State University and completed a postdoctoral fellowship at Yale University. He is an associate research scientist and the assistant director of the Prevention Research Center for Families in Stress at Arizona State University. His substantive research interests include the assessment of coping and competence in children and adolescents and the evaluation of prevention programs for children. For the past 14 years, he has been involved in the evaluation of interventions for families in which there has been a parental death. His interests include the assessment of complicated grief and how to improve services for the bereaved. He is a licensed clinical psychologist.

Irwin N. Sandler received his Ph.D. in clinical psychology from the University of Rochester. He is a Regents' professor in the Department of Psychology and director of the Prevention Research Center for Families in Stress at Arizona State University. His research has focused mainly on understanding child resilience following major stressful situations such as parental divorce and bereavement, and on developing, testing, and disseminating programs that promote resilience in these populations. His work has emphasized linking theory and research with program development, evaluation, and dissemination. His most recent research has focused on developing models for the effective implementation of evidence-based prevention and resilience-promotion programs in natural community service delivery systems.

Sharlene A. Wolchik received her Ph.D. in clinical psychology from Rutgers University in 1981. Dr. Wolchik has been a member of the Psychology Department at Arizona State University since 1980. For the past 20 years, her research has focused on at-risk children and their families. She has conducted research on identifying malleable risk and protective factors for children in divorced homes and for parentally bereaved youth. She has combined this research with the larger literature to design empirically based interventions for these two at-risk groups. Rigorous short-term and long-term evaluations of these programs have shown positive program effects on multiple domains of functioning. Currently, she is using concepts and methods from business models to redesign the intervention for children from divorced homes so it can be implemented with high quality and fidelity in real-world settings.

The authors would like to acknowledge grants R01MH49155 and P30MH068685 from the National Institute of Mental Health, which have supported their ongoing research on parentally bereaved children.

REFERENCES

Ayers, T. S., Sandler, I. N., Wolchik, S. A., & Haine, R. A. (2000, June). *Emotional expression and mental health problems of bereaved children.* Poster presented at the annual meeting of the Society for Prevention Research, Montréal, Canada.

Ayers, T. S., Wolchik, S. A., Weiss, L., Sandler, I. N., Jones, S., Cole, E., et al. (1996). *Family Bereavement Program group leader intervention manual for parent program.* Tempe, AZ: Arizona State University Program for Prevention Research.

Black, D., & Urbanowicz, M. A. (1987). Family intervention with bereaved children. *Journal of Child Psychology and Psychiatry, 28*, 467–476.

Brown, A. C., Sandler, I. N., Tein, J.-Y., Liu, X., & Haine, R. A. (2007). Implications of parental suicide and violent death for promotion of resilience of parentally bereaved children. *Death Studies, 31*, 301–335.

Christ, G. H., & Christ, A. E. (2006). Current approaches to helping children cope with a parent's terminal illness. *CA: A Cancer Journal for Clinicians, 56*, 197–212.

Christ, G. H., Raveis, V., Siegel, K., & Karus, D. (2005). Evaluation of a preventive intervention for bereaved children. *Journal of Social Work in End of Life & Palliative Care, 1*, 57–82.

Cohen, J. A., Mannarino, A. P., Berliner, L., & Deblinger, E. (2000). Trauma-focused cognitive behavioral therapy for children and adolescents: An empirical update. *Journal of Interpersonal Violence, 15*, 1202–1223.

Cohen, J. A., Mannarino, A. P., & Deblinger, E. (2006). *Treating trauma and traumatic grief in children and adolescents*. New York: Guilford Press.

Corr, C. A. (1995). Children's understandings of death: Striving to understand. In K. J. Doka (Ed.), *Children mourning: Mourning children* (pp. 3–16). Washington, DC: Hospice Foundation of America.

Dowdney, L. (2000). Annotation: Childhood bereavement following parental death. *Journal of Child Psychology and Psychiatry and Allied Disciplines, 41*, 819–830.

Haine, R. A., Ayers, T. S., Sandler, I. N., Wolchik, S. A., & Weyer, J. L. (2003). Locus of control and self-esteem as stress-moderators or stress-mediators in parentally bereaved children. *Death Studies, 27*, 619–640.

Haine, R. A., Wolchik, S. A., Sandler, I. N., Millsap, R., & Ayers, T. (2006). Positive parenting as a protective resource for parentally bereaved children. *Death Studies, 30*, 1–28.

Kwok, O.-M., Haine, R. A., Sandler, I. N., Ayers, T. S., Wolchik, S. A., & Tein, J.-Y. (2005). Positive parenting as a mediator of the relations between caregivers' psychological distress and children's mental health problems following the death of a parent. *Journal of Clinical Child and Adolescent Psychology, 34,* 261–272.

Lamborn, S. D., Mounts, N. S., Steinberg, L., & Dornbusch, S. M. (1991). Patterns of competence and adjustment among adolescents from authoritative, authoritarian, indulgent, and neglectful families. *Child Development, 62,* 1049–1065.

Lazar, A., & Torney-Purta, J. (1991). The development of the subconcepts of death in young children: A short-term longitudinal study. *Child Development, 62,* 1321–1333.

Lin, K., Sandler, I., Ayers, T., Wolchik, S., & Leucken, L. (2004). Parentally bereaved children and adolescents seeking mental health services: Family, child, and stress variables that predict resilience. *Journal of Clinical Child and Adolescent Psychology, 33,* 673–683.

Little, M., Sandler, I., Wolchik, S., Tein, J.-Y., & Ayers, T. (2007). Gender differences in internalizing problems and the development of depression after parental loss. Manuscript under review.

Lohnes, K. L., & Kalter, N. (1994). Preventive intervention groups for parentally bereaved children. *American Journal of Orthopsychiatry, 64,* 594–603.

Lutzke, J. R., Ayers, T. S., Sandler, I. N., & Barr, A. (1997). Risks and interventions for the parentally bereaved child. In S. A. Wolchik & I. N. Sandler (Eds.), *Handbook of children's coping with common life stressors: Linking theory, research and interventions* (pp. 215–243). New York: Plenum Publishers.

Maccoby, E., & Martin, J. (1983). Socialization in the context of the family: Parent-child interaction. In E. M. Hetherington (Ed.), *Handbook of child psychology: Socialization, personality, and social development* (Vol. 4, pp. 1–101). New York: Wiley.

Moody, R. A., & Moody, C. P. (1991). A family perspective: Helping children acknowledge and express grief following the death of a parent. *Death Studies, 15,* 587–602.

Pfeffer, C., Jiang, H., Kakuma, T., Hwang, J., & Metsch, M. (2002). Group intervention for children bereaved by the suicide of a relative. *Journal of the American Academy of Child and Adolescent Psychiatry, 41*, 505–513.

Raveis, V. H., Siegel, K., & Karus, D. (1999). Children's psychological distress following the death of a parent. *Journal of Youth and Adolescence, 28*, 165–180.

Reinherz, H. Z., Giaconia, R. M., Carmola Hauf, A. M., Wasserman, M. S., & Silverman, A. B. (1999). Major depression in the transition to adulthood: Risks and impairments. *Journal of Abnormal Psychology, 108*, 500–510.

Rotheram-Borus, M. J., Lee, M. B., Gwadz, M., & Draimin, B. (2001). An intervention for parents with AIDS and their adolescent children. *American Journal of Public Health, 91*, 1294–1302.

Saler, L., & Skolnick, N. (1992). Childhood parental death and depression in adulthood: Roles of surviving parent and family environment. *American Journal of Orthopsychiatry, 62*, 504–516.

Saltzman, W. R., Pynoos, R. S., Layne, C. M., Steinberg, A. M., & Aisenberg, E. (2001). Trauma- and grief-focused intervention for adolescents exposed to community violence: Results of a school-based screening and group treatment protocol. *Group Dynamics: Theory, Research, and Practice. Special Issue: Group-Based Interventions for Trauma Survivors, 5*, 291–303.

Sandler, I. N., Ayers, T. S., Twohey, J. L., Lutzke, J. R., Li, S., & Kriege, G. (1996). *Family Bereavement Program group leader intervention manual for child program.* Tempe, AZ: Arizona State University Program for Prevention Research.

Sandler, I. N., Ayers, T. A., Wolchik, S. A., Tein, J.-Y., Kwok, O.-M., Haine, R. A., et al. (2003). The Family Bereavement Program: Efficacy evaluation of a theory-based prevention program for parentally bereaved children and adolescents. *Journal of Consulting and Clinical Psychology, 71*, 587–600.

Sandler, I. N., Tein, J.-Y., Metha, P., Wolchik, S. A., & Ayers, T. S. (2000). Coping efficacy and psychological problems of children of divorce. *Child Development, 71*, 1099–1118.

Sandler, I. N., West, S. G., Baca, L., Pillow, D. R., Gersten, J. C., Rogosch, F., et al. (1992). Linking empirically based theory and evaluation: The Family Bereavement Program. *American Journal of Community Psychology, 20*, 491–521.

Schmiege, S. J., Khoo, S. T., Sandler, I. N., Ayers, T. S., & Wolchik, S. A. (2006). Symptoms of internalizing and externalizing problems: Modeling recovery curves after the death of a parent. *American Journal of Preventive Medicine, 31*, 152–160.

Schonfeld, D. J., & Smilansky, S. (1989). A cross-cultural comparison of Israeli and American children's death concepts. *Death Studies, 13*, 593–604.

Shapiro, E. R. (1996). Family bereavement and cultural diversity: A social developmental perspective. *Family Process, 35*, 313–332.

Silverman, P. R., & Worden, J. W. (1993). Children's reactions to the death of a parent. In M. S. Stroebe, W. Stroebe, & R. O. Hansson (Eds.), *Handbook of bereavement: Theory, research, and intervention* (pp. 300–316). New York: Cambridge University Press.

Social Security Administration. (2000). *Intermediate assumptions of the 2000 trustees report*. Washington, DC: Office of the Chief Actuary of the Social Security Administration.

Speece, M. W., & Brent, S. B. (1996). The development of children's understanding of death. In C. A. Corr & D M. Corr (Eds.), *Handbook of childhood death and bereavement* (pp. 29–50). New York: Springer Publishing.

Stroebe, M., & Schut, H. (1999). The dual process model of coping with bereavement: Rationale and description. *Death Studies, 23*, 197–224.

Tein, J.-Y., Sandler, I. N., Ayers, T. S., & Wolchik, S. A. (2006). Mediation of the effects of the Family Bereavement Program on mental health problems of bereaved children and adolescents. *Prevention Science, 7*, 179–195.

Tonkins, S. A. M., & Lambert, M. J. (1996). A treatment outcome study of bereavement groups for children. *Child and Adolescent Social Work Journal, 13*, 3–21.

West, S. G., Sandler, I. N., Pillow, D. R., Baca, L., & Gersten, J. C. (1991). The use of structural equation modeling in generative research: Toward the design of a preventive intervention for bereaved children. *American Journal of Community Psychology, 19*, 459–480.

Wolchik, S., Tein, J.-Y., Sandler, I., & Ayers, T. (2006). Stressors, quality of the child-caregiver relationship, and children's mental health problems after parental death: The mediating role of self-system beliefs. *Journal of Abnormal Child Psychology, 34*, 221–238.

Worden, J. W., & Silverman, P. R. (1996). Parental death and the adjustment of school-age children. *Omega: Journal of Death and Dying, 29*, 219–230.

Worden, J. W. (1996). *Children and grief: When a parent dies.* New York: Guilford Press.

Zambelli, G. C., & DeRosa, A. P. (1992). Bereavement support groups for school-age children: Theory, intervention, and case example. *American Journal of Orthopsychiatry, 62*, 484–493.

CHAPTER 9

Sibling Loss: Issues for Children and Adolescents

Nancy Hogan

Approximately 1.8 million children from birth to 18 years old are bereaved sibling in the United States at any given time. A small number of these children and adolescents are fortunate enough to attend bereavement support groups, where they can learn from others their age about the characteristics, intensity, and enduring nature of the bereavement process. They learn that others have similar thoughts and feelings related to grieving a sibling's death and its aftermath. They also learn various ways that bereaved siblings can cope with grieving. They learn to anticipate times and circumstances that may initiate regrieving episodes, such as holidays and special family occasions. They learn that adapting to a world in which their sibling is physically missing is a slow and painful process, and that healing will likely never be complete. They may also come to realize that their parents will be permanently changed by their own suffering and that living in a grieving family is difficult. They learn from bereaved siblings who are further along in their grief that it is possible to finding meaning and purpose in life. They hear others in the group talk about a new kind of "normal" that is different than the normal life they had before the death but that includes fun and laughter. Finally, they learn that they may have matured in some ways beyond their same-age peers; for example, they may find that they can ease the pain of others who suffer. However, the vast majority of bereaved siblings do not attend a grief support group; on the contrary, they are left to grieve alone, without effective support from adults or peers.

The purpose of this chapter is to describe a sibling bereavement theory derived from children's and teenagers' stories of living with grief, their ideas about what helps or hinders their efforts to cope and adapt, how they maintain an ongoing attachment to their dead sibling, and their personal growth as an outcome of the bereavement process. The pathway through grief described here represents the child or adolescent who successfully copes and adapts following the death of a sibling. This framework for understanding sibling bereavement is used as a background to delineate factors that might facilitate or complicate the healing process.

Before the 1980s, most bereavement studies were conducted with psychiatric populations of varying age groups, relied on retrospective case studies and interviews, and focused on identifying the pathology of grief (Hogan & DeSantis, 1996a). The bonds between parents and children and between husbands and wives have long been recognized and studied, but the term "sibling bond" didn't appear in the literature until the seminal book *The Sibling Bond* was published in 1982 (Bank & Kahn). The book focused on the vital nature of this bond and included a chapter on the impact of the death of a sibling on the lives of children and adolescents. Researchers began to study the impact of bereavement on children and adolescents.

Throughout the 1980s, research attempted to identify and describe the variables and conditions of bereavement as a process. Most research was conducted by nurses who used community-based samples and studied the effects of sibling death on self-concept, depression, and academic performance (Balk, 1983a, 1983b, 1983c; Davies, 1983, 1988, 1991; Demi & Gilbert, 1987; Demi & Howel, 1991; Hogan, 1987; Martinson, Davies, & McClowry, 1987; McCown & Pratt, 1985; Michael & Lansdown, 1986). Researchers studied child and adolescent sibling bereavement using indirect measures such as depression, self-esteem, self-concept, and stress reactions, as no instrument was available to directly measure sibling bereavement.

The Hogan Sibling Inventory of Bereavement (HSIB)—an instrument designed specifically to study the multidimensional nature of the child and adolescent sibling bereavement process—allowed researchers to study the impact of sibling death and its aftermath directly rather than by using proxy measures (Charles & Charles, 2006; Hogan, 1987; Hogan & Balk, 1990; Hogan & Greenfield 1991; Neimeyer & Hogan, 2001; Neimeyer, Hogan, & Laurie, 2008). [See Table 1.]

TABLE 1. HOGAN SIBLING INVENTORY OF BEREAVEMENT (HSIB)
GRIEF ITEMS AND PROPERTIES

Increased Vulnerability

Fears
- I worry about everything
- I am afraid that more people I love will die
- I am afraid to get close to people
- I have panic attacks over nothing
- I believe I am going crazy

Guilt
- I am uncomfortable when I am feeling happy
- I am uncomfortable when I am having fun
- I should have died and he/she should have lived
- I don't believe I will ever be happy again
- I feel uncomfortable when I am having fun

Loss of Control
- I believe I will lose control when I think about him/her
- I believe I have little control over my life
- I have no control over my sadness

Sadness
- I feel depressed when I think about him/her
- I do not think I will ever be happy again
- I don't believe I will ever get over his/her death
- Family holidays such as Christmas are sad times for my family
- I have nightmares about his/her death
- I have difficulty sleeping at night
- I don't care what happens to me
- I do not sleep well at night

Loneliness
- People don't know what I am going through

Physical Effects
- I am sick more often

Permanently Changed Reality of Self/Family
- My family will always be incomplete

Cognitive Interference
- I have trouble concentrating

Desire for Reunion with Sibling
- I want to die to be with him/her

Coping Behavior
- I take risks to help me forget that he/she is dead

In the 1990s, research on adolescent sibling bereavement focused on clarifying and further delineating its characteristics, intensity, and duration (Balk, 1990; Balk & Hogan, 1995; Davies, 1994, 1998; Hogan & DeSantis, 1992, 1994, 1996b; Hogan & Greenfield, 1991; Walker, 1993). Bereavement researchers studied the impact of childhood death on religion and spirituality in the lives of bereaved adolescents; they found that the majority of the bereaved adolescents believed that their faith had become more important to them and that faith helped them cope with bereavement (Balk & Hogan, 1995). The role of social support in adolescent sibling bereavement was identified and described, as were other social system factors that helped or hindered bereaved siblings in becoming resilient survivors (Hogan & DeSantis, 1994). One study investigated the congruence between the adolescents' appraisal of their own grief and their parents' ability to accurately perceive the adolescents' grieving following the death of a brother or sister. The findings were counterintuitive: The fathers' perception of their children's scores on the HSIB were congruent, while the mothers' scores were significantly different, suggesting that fathers were better able than mothers to correctly perceive the intensity of their children's grief (Hogan & Balk, 1990).

In sibling bereavement support group meetings, children and adolescents frequently express the sentiment, "If I could only see him/her one more time." This plea was turned into the research question, "If you could ask or tell your dead sibling something, what would it be?" Bereaved siblings (n = 157) provided written answers to the question. The most common response was "I miss you and I love you." The data revealed empirically that bereaved siblings maintained an ongoing attachment to their dead sibling and that the sibling bond transcends time and space (Hogan & DeSantis, 1992, 1996b).

Recent sibling bereavement studies have investigated how the death of a sibling during childhood affects adult attachment style (Charles & Charles, 2006); the effectiveness of parental guidance intervention on communication among adolescents whose sibling has died (Horsley & Patterson, 2006); and the value of weekend retreats for bereaved children, their parents, and hospital staff who cared for a child at the end of life (Kramer & Sodickson, 2002).

The death of a sibling changes childhood, and thus life, forever. The event is so powerful that bereaved siblings refer to events in their lives as "before it happened" and "after it happened." They compare their family's life when the family was whole with the current family—smaller and different. Most children and adolescents are able to meet the challenges of coping and adapting following a sibling's death. The grief-to-personal-growth theory provides a framework for understanding the sibling bereavement process.

GRIEF TO PERSONAL GROWTH

This section describes the key factors that constitute the grief-to-personal-growth theory as it applies to sibling bereavement. The studies cited above are used to generate a framework for understanding how siblings perceive their grief, social support, ongoing attachment, and personal growth.

Multidimensional Characteristics of Sibling Grief

The initial reaction to bereavement is typically acute grief. The intensity of this grief may soften over time, but grief has no defined end-point. The death of a brother or sister leaves the surviving siblings feeling that their lives and their family have been irrevocably altered and will never be the same again. They are faced prematurely with the harsh reality that all people die; unfortunately, that may include young people. As individuals and as families, they are diminished quantitatively and qualitatively by the death of a sibling. Bereaved children and adolescents grieve for their dead sibling and for the family that existed before their sibling's death.

Bereaved adolescents may feel a general loss of well-being, including feeling less physically well. Younger children may express their stress as headaches, stomachaches, jumpiness, or being clingy and fearful when their parents are not present. Many bereaved siblings report experiencing sleep difficulties, including nightmares. Some nightmares may reach the intensity of night terrors, especially if the sibling died a violent death. Bereaved siblings may experience attention deficit and have trouble concentrating on day-to-day tasks. Such cognitive problems can directly affect their ability to keep up with schoolwork. Socially, they may feel lonely and isolated because no one understands what they are going through, and they may avoid becoming close to others for fear that "bad things" will befall them. These children may experience feelings of hopelessness, anger, guilt, fear, and profound sadness. They may feel guilty about being alive when their sibling is dead. They may feel that they are dishonoring their deceased sibling if they enjoy any degree of happiness, laughter, or fun. The home life of bereaved siblings is often enveloped in a shroud of sadness, and they may feel the need to escape the intensity of the grief. Younger children are limited in their ability to find relief, but adolescents often seek out activities that keep them busy and away from the sadness that pervades their home.

In time, the intensity of the suffering begins to soften and the grief becomes less all-consuming. However, grief is periodically reintensified when developmental markers and thoughts about the deceased preoccupy the bereaved siblings. Such reintensification can be precipitated by the absence of the dead sibling at family reunions, births, marriages, graduations, and other rites of passage. Intrusive thoughts can occur when the bereaved sibling relives events surrounding the death. Regrieving episodes can be stimulated by hearing the dead sibling's favorite music, seeing pictures of the deceased sibling, or going past the place where the sibling died. Media events and other incidents that stimulate intrusive thoughts and feelings are particularly distressing and likely to precipitate reintensification of grief if the sibling died by homicide or suicide. Anticipated and unanticipated episodes of regrieving persist, but they become less intense, less preoccupying, and shorter in duration. At some point, there are more good days than bad days; eventually, there are mostly good days.

Ongoing Attachment to the Dead Sibling

Ongoing attachment is a phenomenon in which the surviving sibling maintains a continuing bond with the deceased brother or sister. The sibling learns to live simultaneously with the physical absence and the emotional/spiritual presence of the deceased sibling, describing the sibling as "my guardian angel" or "my confidant."

During childhood and adolescence, sibling relationships are typically fraught with conflicting feelings that ebb and flow. The death of a sibling freezes the relationship as it existed at that moment. In time, many children and adolescents learn to forgive themselves for perceived past transgressions related to their interactions with the dead sibling. For example, bereaved siblings often wish they had been nicer to their dead sibling and spent more time with him or her. They express regret that they cannot continue sharing their lives on a daily basis with their dead brother or sister—talking, hugging, teasing, playing, or hanging out together. They also express regret at the loss of their deceased sibling as confidant, friend, and companion, and are sorry that the sibling relationship was not closer during life.

Children and adolescents who lose their only sibling have a particularly keen sense of loss. They are often left alone, with no companion to grow up with and have a lifelong sibling relationship with. One bereaved child lamented, "My parents have each other, but now I have no one."

Bereaved siblings endeavor to make sense of the death of their brother or sister by trying to understand how and why they died. They want answers to unanswerable questions and may ask over and over precisely how the death occurred. Children may find it difficult to accept that the death couldn't have been prevented and may ask, "How did it really happen?" Adolescents sometimes ask for details that cannot be known; "How did you get in the center divider? Were you sleeping, or did someone run you off the road?" Regardless of how the sibling died, surviving children and adolescents ruminate on how the death could have been prevented.

Bereaved children and adolescents often express a desire to keep in touch spiritually with the dead brother or sister to assure themselves that the sibling is happy, comfortable, and at peace in the afterlife. They seek information about how and what the deceased sibling is doing: "How's life in the other world?" "Did you see Granny?" They may want to keep the deceased sibling caught up on current events: "I'm doing all right with life." And they may want to help the dead brother or sister: "Are there any messages I can deliver to others?"

Bereaved adolescent siblings may reaffirm an ongoing emotional and spiritual relationship with the dead brother or sister by declaring how much they love them and miss them: "I love her very much, and I know she loves me. I miss her." "I would tell him how much I love him and ask him not to leave me." They express loving and missing their sibling in the present tense, regardless of the time that has elapsed since death. They ask the deceased sibling to help them be strong: "I would ask him to watch over me and guide me to be more like him and strong for my family." They vow to keep the dead sibling's memories and dreams alive: "Her dreams won't die." "He will always live in my heart, no matter what." "He will always be my shining star." And many bereaved children and adolescents strongly believe that they will join their dead sibling in the afterlife: "I'll see you again someday." "I know someday we'll be together again."

The Impact of Social Support on Coping with Grief

The bereavement process is a profoundly personal experience that occurs in a public context. Ideally, bereaved children and adolescents are helped through their grief by parents and family members who care for and comfort them, friends who are there for them, and other members of their social systems who help them cope with their loss. From the perspective of a bereaved adolescent, social support can help normalize the intensity, characteristics, and duration of their grief.

The social world of a bereaved child or adolescent changes after the death of a sibling. They talk about living in two worlds: the public world, in which they must "appear normal" to their friends in order to fit in, and the private world, where they grieve and let their feelings out. Navigating these two worlds successfully is a major struggle. They must deal with difficult questions from others, such as "How many brothers and sisters do you have?" Some siblings include the dead sibling in the answer without an explanation, some provide the information that a brother or sister is dead, and some bereaved siblings do not account for the dead sibling in their answer. The way such questions are answered may depend on the bereaved sibling's assessment of the ability of the person to handle the answer.

The bereaved sibling may experience social support that either helps or hinders efforts to cope. Family members, especially parents, are perceived as supportive when they comfort their bereaved child and share memories of and grief for the dead sibling/child with them. Such support helps the bereaved sibling accept and express despair about the death of the brother or sister. Conversely, family bickering and discord make coping more difficult, and upset and anger the bereaved child or adolescent. The child's distress is intensified if parents are openly distraught over the sibling's death—crying, withdrawing from family members, and being openly sad and distant with the surviving children. Many actions bereaved siblings find distressing occur early in the bereavement process, as the parents attempt to cope with the catastrophic loss of their child. Bereaved siblings recognize their parents' need to grieve, but they may feel deprived because their parents are unable to give them the same amount of nurturance after their brother's or sister's death as before. Some bereaved siblings in support groups questioned whether their parents would grieve as much if it had been they who died instead of their sibling.

When peers are unwilling or incapable of letting bereaved adolescents grieve in their own way and on their own timetable, they cease to be considered friends. They are perceived as not "being there" for them. Other people— including adults in their social system—may hinder the bereaved adolescents' coping abilities by being insensitive, presumptuous, and judgmental about their needs; for example, telling them when, where, how, and to what extent they should grieve. Adolescents in support groups said they learned to avoid people who gave advice about how much and how long they should grieve. They talked about how their friendship system had changed after their sibling's death—they no longer had time for classmates who wanted them to forget about the death and quickly get back to normal.

Bereaved siblings cited a number of things that helped them cope with the death and its aftermath. Friends were considered supportive by just "being there." "Friends let me do it my way and just stood by me." They said the people who were most helpful were those who took the time to listen to how they felt and let them express their thoughts and feelings openly and honestly, without judgment. Also supportive were some professionals and peers in organized groups (e.g., Boy Scouts, Compassionate Friends, and church groups) who had experienced a death or another type of significant loss and had recovered. These people helped them grasp the complexities of life and death, and realize that others have coped with similar thoughts, feelings, and experiences. Few bereaved children or adolescents in support group meetings mentioned teachers as persons who helped them cope after a sibling's death.

PERSONAL GROWTH AS AN OUTCOME OF SUFFERING

Personal growth can evolve from suffering and pain. Bereaved siblings are aware that they are different in substantial ways from how they were before the sibling's death. Often, they believe they have matured more rapidly than many of their peers and can cope more effectively with life problems. They may reassess their priorities and put more emphasis on family and friends, and they may feel closer to loved ones. Bereaved siblings perceive themselves as more sensitive to others and more tolerant of other people's feelings and actions. They believe that they have an increased sense of responsibility for and concern about others. They try to be kinder to others (Table 2).

TABLE 2. HOGAN SIBLING INVENTORY OF BEREAVEMENT (HSIB) PERSONAL GROWTH ITEMS AND PROPERTIES

Permanently Changed Reality
- I know how fragile life is
- I have learned that all people die
- I don't take people for granted
- I have changed my priorities

Maturity
- I have grown up faster than my friends
- I have learned to cope better with my problems
- I have learned to cope better with my life
- I am more tolerant of myself

Increased Sensitivity to Others

Attachment to Others
- I am a more caring person
- I care more deeply for my family

Sensitivity to Others
- I am more tolerant of others
- I am more understanding of others
- I am more aware of others' feelings
- I try to be kinder to others
- I have more compassion for others

Ability to Give and Receive Help
- I can give help to others who are grieving
- I can get help for my grief when I need it

Optimism
- I have a better outlook on life

Self-Worth
- I believe I am stronger because of the grief I have had to cope with
- I believe I am a better person
- I am more creative

Sense of Faith
- Religion has become more important to me

They sense that they can help others who have suffered a loss or been through difficult times. In addition to helping others, they have learned to seek help when they need it. They tend to know who is approachable and truly helpful, and they avoid people who are unable or unwilling to be supportive.

The pathway through grief can result in the surviving sibling becoming resilient or vulnerable. Vulnerable survivors remain mired in the despair and misery of grieving. Resilient survivors find new meaning in life; they transcend the loss of their sibling by keeping his or her memory alive through deeds and thoughts, and by persevering in spite of the death.

Resilient survivors develop an outlook on life that is optimistic. They are grateful for things that their peers take for granted. They have a renewed sense of being hopeful about the future. They sense that they have survived the worst and are better able to cope with difficult times. In essence, they believe that in coping with their sibling's death, they learned to trust their ability and inner strength to cope with future traumatic life events.

PROVIDING EFFECTIVE COUNSELING FOR THE GRIEVING CHILD OR ADOLESCENT

This chapter is based on the written or spoken words of bereaved siblings who told what it feels like to grieve the death of a sibling and what helped or hindered in coping and adapting after the death.

There are many different pathways through the bereavement process; they vary in reactions (characteristics), time (duration), and preoccupation with grieving and regrieving (intensity). Each child or adolescent will be on his or her personal journey through grief. While there is no empirical evidence that counseling can shorten the normal trajectory of grief; by normalizing the process, counselors can help bereaved siblings anticipate difficult times and have faith that their grief will soften and they will find relief from the thoughts, feelings, and images associated with the early, acute period of grief.

Counselors can ask parents to inform school personnel that their child is grieving a sibling's death. School counselors and nurses can be encouraged to offers a quiet place for the child to retreat to for a few moments if a grief reaction occurs.

Tables 1 and 2 provide a quick reference to the language bereaved siblings use to talk about grief and personal growth. The sentences on the tables are the items on the HSIB. These items have been tested for reliability and validity in representing sibling bereavement. Counselors can share these items with bereaved siblings to educate them about common grief reactions that others have experienced and as the basis for discussion. "Here are some concerns that other bereaved siblings have experienced. You may have some of the same concerns and might like to talk about them."

- "I worry about everything."
- "I am afraid that more people I love will die."
- "I am afraid to get close to people."
- "I have panic attacks over nothing."
- "I believe I am going crazy."

Bereaved siblings often find relief in knowing that others have had some of the same grief reactions they are having.

The purpose of providing bereaved siblings with the personal growth content (table 2) is to help them see that things do get better and positive change is possible. Bereaved siblings need to have their victories on the path to becoming resilient survivors celebrated. Acknowledging that they are reaching new milestones of growth and maturity helps them find the energy to continue the commitment to work through the bad days.

Counselors may need to recommend that children or adolescents be referred for professional care if they are stuck in sadness and distressing feelings of blaming themselves and others; they continue to be angry at themselves, others, and the world; they express ongoing feelings of guilt; or they have unrelenting fears that preoccupy their emotional life. Children and adolescents should be referred for professional counseling if they express a lack of will to live, indicate a desire to harm themselves, or are preoccupied with the belief that they are responsible for their sibling's death. These danger signals must be taken seriously. Worden's handbook on grief counseling for mental health practitioners (Worden, 2002) is an invaluable resource for health care professionals and others who work with bereaved children and adolescents.

Fortunately, most bereaved siblings do not succumb to grief. Instead, they suffer through the painful work of grieving the death of their sibling and learn to create new ways of living happy, fulfilling lives. Counselors can help children and adolescents understand that they are not alone as they make this journey of grief and recovery.

Nancy S. Hogan, Ph.D., RN, FAAN, is a researcher and scholar whose body of work includes the generation and testing of instruments to measure adolescent and adult grief and personal growth, social support and continuing bonds. The Grief to Personal Growth Theory and adolescent and adult bereavement questionnaires have undergone rigorous testing, and are used nationally and internationally to guide research and practice. The theory and measures are the foundation of several federally funded longitudinal studies of parent, child, and grandparent bereavement, for which she provides consultative services. She has published over 50 peer-reviewed bereavement and end-of-life works in the national and international literature. Over the past 25 years, she has undertaken more than 80 presentations to local, regional, national, and international audiences. She was awarded the Association of Death Education and Counseling 2007 Research Award.

REFERENCES

Balk, D. E. (1983a). Adolescents' grief reactions and self-concept perceptions following sibling death: A study of 33 teenagers. *Journal of Youth and Adolescence, 12,* 137–159.

Balk, D. E. (1983b). Effects of sibling death on teenagers. *Journal of School Health, 15,* 14–18.

Balk, D. E. (1983c). How teenagers cope with sibling death: Some implications for school counselors. *The School Counselor, 31,* 151–159.

Balk, D. E. (1990). The self-concept of bereaved adolescents: Sibling death and its aftermath. *Journal of Adolescent Research, 5,* 112–132.

Balk, D. B., & Hogan, N. S. (1995). Religion, spirituality, and bereaved adolescents. In D. W. Adams & E. Deveau (Eds.), *Loss, threat to life, and bereavement* (pp. 61–85). Amityville, NY: Baywood.

Bank, S., & Kahn, M. (1982). *The sibling bond.* New York: Basic Books.

Charles, D. R., & Charles, M. (2006). Sibling loss and attachment styles: An exploratory study, *Psychoanalytic Psychology, 23,* 72–90.

Davies, E. B. (1983). Behavioral responses of children to the death of a sibling. Doctoral dissertation, University of Washington. *Dissertation Abstracts International, 44,* 1060–B.

Davies, B. (1988). Shared life space and sibling bereavement responses. *Cancer Nursing, 11,* 339–347.

Davies, E. B. (1991). Long-term outcomes of adolescent sibling bereavement. *Journal of Adolescent Research, 6,* 83–96.

Davies, B. (1994). Sibling bereavement research: State of the art. In I. B. Corless, B. Germino, & M. Pittmen (Eds.), *A challenge for living: Dying, death, and bereavement* (pp. 173–201). Boston: Jones & Bartlett.

Davies, B. (1998). *Shadows in the sun: The experience of sibling bereavement in childhood.* Philadelphia: Brunner/Mazel.

Demi, A., & Gilbert, C. (1987). Relationship of parental grief to sibling grief. *Archives of Psychiatric Nursing, 6,* 385–391.

Demi, A. S., & Howel C. (1991). Hiding and healing: Resolving the suicide of a parent or sibling. *Archives of Psychiatric Nursing, 5,* 350–356.

Hogan, N. S. (1987). An investigation of adolescent sibling bereavement and adaptation Doctoral dissertation, Loyola University Chicago. *Dissertation Abstracts International, 48,* 741.

Hogan, N. S., & Balk, D. E. (1990). Adolescent reactions to sibling death: Perceptions of mothers, fathers, and teenagers. *Nursing Research, 39,* 103–105.

Hogan, N. S., & DeSantis, L. (1992). Adolescent sibling bereavement: An ongoing attachment. *Qualitative Health Research, 2,* 159–177.

Hogan, N. S., & DeSantis, L. (1994). Things that help and hinder adolescent sibling bereavement. *Western Journal of Nursing Research, 16,* 132–153.

Hogan, N. S., & DeSantis, L. (1996a). Adolescent sibling bereavement: Toward a new theory. In C. A. Corr & D. E. Balk (Eds.), *Handbook of adolescent death and bereavement* (pp. 173–195). New York: Springer.

Hogan, N. S., & DeSantis, L. (1996b). Basic constructs of a theory of adolescent sibling bereavement. In R. Silverman, S. Nickman, & D. Class (Eds.). *Continuing bonds: New understandings of grief* (pp. 235–253). Bristol, PA: Taylor & Francis.

Hogan, N. S., & Greenfield, D. B. (1991). Adolescent sibling bereavement. Symptomatology in a large community sample. *Journal of Adolescent Research, 6,* 97–112.

Horsley, H., & Patterson, T. (2006). The effects of a parental guidance intervention on communication among adolescents who have experienced the sudden death of a sibling. *American Journal of Family Therapy, 34,* 119–137.

Kramer, R., & Sodickson, S. L. (2002). A weekend retreat for parents and siblings of children who have died. *Journal of Palliative Medicine, 5,* 455–464.

Martinson, I. M., Davies, E. B., & McClowry, S. G. (1987). The long-term effects of sibling death on self-concept. *Journal of Pediatric Nursing, 2,* 227–235.

McClowry, S. G., Davies, E. B., Kulenkamp, E. J., & Martinson, I. M. (1987). The empty space phenomenon: The process of grief in the bereaved family. *Death Studies, 11,* 361–374.

McCown, D. E., & Pratt, C. (1985). Impact of sibling death on children's behavior. *Death Studies, 9,* 323–335.

Michael, S., & Lansdown, R. (1986). Adjustment to the death of a sibling. *Archives of Disease in Childhood, 61,* 278–283.

Neimeyer, R. A., & Hogan, N. (2001). Quantitative or qualitative? Measurement issues in the study of grief. In H.S.M. Stroebe, R. Hansson, & W. Stroebe (Eds.), *Handbook of bereavement research* (pp. 89–118). Washington, DC: American Psychological Association.

Neimeyer, R. A., Hogan, N. S., & Laurie, A. (in press). The measurement of mourning: Psychometric considerations in the assessment of grief. In M. Stroebe, R. O. Hansson, H. Schut, & W. Stroebe (Eds.). *Handbook of bereavement research: 21st century perspective*. Washington, DC: American Psychological Association.

Walker, C. L. (1993). Sibling bereavement and grief responses. *Journal of Pediatric Nursing, 8*, 325–334.

Worden, J. W. (2002). *Grief counseling and grief therapy: A handbook for mental health practitioners* (3rd edition). New York: Springer.

CHAPTER 10

When a Friend Dies

Illene C. Noppe and Lloyd D. Noppe

G iven the importance of friendship to children and adolescents, the death of a friend can have a profound impact that may persist throughout development. Children's and adolescents' reactions to death and loss have been extensively studied in the past few decades. We have learned that understanding of death and dying is influenced by cognitive development as well as actual loss (Oltjenbruns, 2007). Children's concept of death tends to start with the belief that it is temporary and then evolves (usually in middle childhood) to the understanding that it is permanent, universal, and due to a cessation of physical functioning (Corr, 1995). We recognize that children's concept of death differs from that of adults, but we tend to think that adolescents share the adult concept. However, adolescents' understanding and beliefs about death are affected by their own developmental issues (Noppe & Noppe, 1997).

The literature reveals that while children do mourn, they do so according to their level of emotional and cognitive maturity, so that grief tends to occur in spurts and to manifest in regressive behaviors and, sometimes, hyperactivity (Webb, 2002; Wolfelt, 1996). Adolescents, on the other hand, tend to grieve privately and intensely, holding on to their sadness for a long time (Noppe & Noppe, 1997). The research on children's and adolescents' responses to death has primarily been with regard to the loss of a parent (Lieberman, Compton, Van Horn & Ippen, 2003; Silverman, 2000; Worden, 1996). However, it is widely recognized that the social interactions, emotional satisfaction, cognitive enhancement, and self-esteem resulting from friendship during childhood and adolescence set the stage for mental health and satisfying intimate relationships in adulthood. There is no reason to believe that children would not also grieve the loss of these important relationships.

In this chapter, we discuss the significance of children's and adolescents' responses to the loss of a friend and how that kind of loss is unique. We describe friendship and peer development during childhood; how children respond to the death of a friend; the functions and characteristics of adolescent friendships; and how the special nature of these relationships affects the bereavement experience. Although many aspects of friendship are similar across development, the meaning, functions, and interactions among friends differ for children and teenagers. Thus, we distinguish how grief responses to the death of a friend may be the same or different between children and adolescents.

CHILDHOOD FRIENDSHIP

Peer relationships, along with family, school, and community, are an essential cornerstone of child and adolescent development (Rubin, Bukowski, & Parker, 1998). As children grow—especially through the adolescent years—friendships play an ever more significant role in healthy or maladjusted socialization. The study of social development in children and adolescents is complicated by their individual backgrounds and the various levels of friendship, from casual interaction to close friendship to group membership (Hinde, 1987). In addition, the literature addresses gender differences, cultural variations, and romantic relationships. In the context of our discussion, we can hardly do justice to the burgeoning research and theory on peer dynamics.

Buhrmester (1996) has argued, based on Harry Stack Sullivan's interpersonal perspective, that friendships are important for the social development of children and adolescents because they fulfill (a) communal needs relating to nurturance, intimacy, support, companionship, and affection and (b) agentic needs for status, power, self-esteem, achievement, identity, and approval. Friendships among girls tend to emphasize the former needs, and friendships among boys focus more on the latter needs, but both boys and girls desire friends for all these reasons. The developmental pattern of peer relationships transcends gender differences, and, as Selman (1980) indicates, children are increasingly aware of the importance of friends in their lives.

Even during the first year of life, play partners direct gestures and expressions toward each other (Hay, Pedersen, & Nash, 1982); are enthusiastic and interested in playing with other infants (Howes, 1996); carefully observe what their peers are doing (Eckerman, 1979); and may respond to them with appropriate behaviors (Mueller & Brenner, 1977). During the second year of life, toddler games become more interactive and increasingly vocal. They may include complex imitation, coordinated play sequences, and sharing behaviors. Rubin and colleagues (1998) concluded that toddler friendships exist, while Ross, Conant, Cheyne, and Alevizos (1992) identified specific play partner recognition and differential reactions to familiar versus unfamiliar peers. So how might such a young human being interpret the loss of a friend?

A major development in social interaction during the preschool years is the evolution of sociodramatic (pretend) play, in which the coordination of symbolic activities allows imagination to flourish and cooperation to become more complex (Garvey, 1990). Pretend play provides the arena for communicating meaning to peers, for learning to negotiate and compromise, and for exploring intimacy in a relatively safe context (Howes, 1992). The more sophisticated nature of these interactions fosters genuine friendships and clear preferences for certain peers. Rubin and colleagues (1998) note that preschoolers are more likely to engage in prosocial behavior when they are playing with friends, more likely to have conflicts with nonfriends, and better able to reconcile difficulties with friends than nonfriends. Outside of dyadic relationships, dominance hierarchies begin to emerge in the group, but the children are unlikely to recognize them. It is interesting to speculate (although empirical studies have yet to be conducted) about how the loss of a friend would affect the group interactions of preschool children.

In middle childhood, an increasing proportion of time is spent with peers rather than family members, and peer interaction moves from the home and the child care setting to the school and the neighborhood. Peer groups become larger, especially for boys, and unstructured play is replaced by "hanging out"; talking on the phone (more so for girls); instant messaging on computers or text messaging on cell phones; and organized sports (particularly for boys). Rubin and colleagues (1998) point out that verbal aggression (especially for girls) starts to replace physical aggression, bullying behavior becomes more evident, and hostility is generally directed at another person rather than an object. In middle childhood, the death of a friend may trigger an external grief reaction toward one or more peers because of immaturity in dealing with emotions.

Broad patterns develop in middle childhood friendships (Rubin et al., 1998), including stability over time and an increasing number of close friendships (a number that tends to peak at the end of middle childhood). Children also develop an ability to change perspective when interacting with their peers, which allows them to appreciate how their friends think and feel, particularly when conflict arises in the relationship. Friends begin to think of each other in terms of trust, intimacy, and loyalty, not merely as companions in an activity or the source of some tangible reward. Reciprocity exists at a higher level, although it does not always survive a serious argument. The notion of a "fair-weather" friend derives from middle childhood fickleness, and a particular friendship may compete with issues affecting popularity in the larger peer group.

Newcomb and colleagues (1993) summarize patterns of popularity among peers in several categories on the basis of membership in formal (e.g., class, team, club) or informal (e.g., clique, crowd) groups. They describe popular children, who are outgoing and cognitively advanced; rejected children, who tend to be less cognitively skilled and more aggressive and withdrawn; neglected children, who are withdrawn but not particularly disruptive; controversial children, who demonstrate qualities of both popular and rejected children; and average children, who exhibit moderate behaviors. These emerging characteristics in middle childhood—typically fueled by extraversion and athleticism in boys and physical attractiveness and family background in girls—presage the emergence of more clearly structured peer networks in adolescence (McHale, Dariotis, & Kauh, 2003).

DEATH OF A FRIEND

Thus, from infancy until adolescence, friends change from being interesting and familiar playthings to subjects of reciprocal mutual interaction. These relationships are voluntary and mostly pleasurable. Because friends tend to share many characteristics in common—such as cohort, gender, social class, interests, and abilities—they are sources of self-definition and affirmation of self-worth. Sociologists have long held that the concept of "self" arises from social interaction (Kegan, 1994; Mead, 1934). A friend is a basis of comparison; this form of self-reference is lost when the friend dies (deVries, 2001). The routines that friends develop and the familiarity of their temperamental styles, idiosyncrasies (such as food preferences and tastes in movies), and even their possessions ("my friend has a dog and an Xbox") make the lives of children predictable and secure. When this relationship is disrupted by death, the consequences for the surviving friends can be devastating.

The death of a young person is a tragic event. Fortunately, such deaths have become relatively rare in the United States. In 2004, the death rate per 100,000 for children ages 1–4 years was 29.9 and for children ages 5–14 years was 16.8. For adolescents and young adults (15–24 years), the rate rose to 80.1 (National Center for Health Statistics, 2007). In comparison, the overall death rate for 2004 was 816.5 (NCHS, 2007). These rates differ according to gender (higher for males at all ages) and race (highest at all ages for Blacks and American Indian/Alaska Natives). It is not unreasonable to think that by the time a person reaches young adulthood, he or she is likely to have experienced the death of at least one friend (McNeil, Silliman, & Swihart, 1991). In a classic study that surveyed death experiences of high school juniors and seniors, 40% (591 teenagers) said a close friend had died (Ewalt & Perkins, 1979). For children younger than 15 years, the leading cause of death is unintentional injury (primarily in motor vehicle accidents), followed by drowning, fire, and choking (Federal Interagency Forum on Child and Family Statistics, 2006). For adolescents in the 15–19 year age range, death is most likely to be due to motor vehicle accidents or guns. The Institute of Medicine (2003) reported that with increasing age through adolescence, there is an eightfold increase in death due to homicide and a sevenfold increased in death due to suicide. Thus, children and adolescents may experience the sudden, tragic, and perhaps violent loss of a peer. And although the death of a child or adolescent is relatively rare, the impact is tsunami-like.

DEATH OF A FRIEND IN CHILDHOOD

Although we know it is a myth that "childhood is the kingdom where nobody ever dies," the literature suggests that "childhood is the kingdom where nobody's *friend* ever dies." What little has been published on the topic typically relates to adolescence (e.g., Oltjenbruns, 1996); less is known about how children younger than age 12 process and cope with the loss of a friend. Work on sibling grief (Bluebond-Langer, 1989; Davies, 1999) can be extrapolated, but the experience must differ when the loss is a voluntary, intimate relationship in which family rivalries are not present and the child's role in the family is not left in an ambiguous state. Bereavement associated with the loss of a pet (often the first major loss in childhood) (Dickinson, 1992) may bear some similarities to the loss of a childhood friend, although the latter is likely to be much more profound and may trigger the same kind of developmental transformation that has been seen as a result of friendship loss in adolescence (Oltjenbruns, 1996). In addition, as Silverman (2000) notes, mourning friends receive minimal support and guidance, and there are few rituals to commemorate the loss of a friend in childhood. American culture is impatient with adult grief; children are expected to recover even more quickly from the loss of a friend.

For young children, the first major challenge in the death of a friend is to understand the circumstances of the death and the long-term implications of the loss. Children need to understand that their friend will not come back to play with them; that the friend is not functioning in a limited fashion somewhere else; and that neither they nor any fantastical entity was the cause of death (Corr, 1995). Because friends share so many common characteristics, the death of a friend may shake a child out of his or her sense of immortality. Whatever happened to the friend who died enters the realm of possibility for the grieving child.

Even for infants and toddlers, the loss of a friend may trigger secondary losses, such as no longer going to that child's house or playing with his or her toys, and no longer seeing this child at the day care center or babysitter's house. One of the first intellectual puzzles for young children is solving the mystery of appearance and disappearance (the concept of object permanence). How can these children understand the mysterious disappearance of another child? How do established groups of children, in day care and preschool classrooms, dynamically change when a member dies?

Unlike adolescents, who may seek solace in their surviving friends, children typically turn to their families for support, information, and comfort during times of major stress. However, with the best of intentions, adults may not offer much information; may provide euphemistic explanations ("sleeping with the angels"); or may fail to recognize symptoms of grief in their child. The death of the child's friend is a stark reminder to the parents of their own potential vulnerability to loss. Because the death did not occur within the family, it may be easier for the parents to downplay the loss in a misguided desire to protect their child. The desire to protect may also be operative when a child's friend is dying from an illness such as cancer. In this case, parents may forbid their child to visit or interact with the sick peer. In the case of a tragic, violent loss or one that is associated with stigma, children may be exposed to graphic media reports or rumors that conflict with what their parents have told them. Many children respond to death by asking questions—the communication channel must be open for them to do so. If the adults in their home, school, or community are uncomfortable about their own beliefs and feelings, the child quickly learns not to ask questions or talk about the death.

Attending a friend's funeral may be a difficult task for children during the early and middle childhood years. Many of the issues regarding funeral attendance (e.g., receiving information about what to expect, being given the choice to participate partially or fully, handling the intense emotions of others) apply to the funeral of a young friend. The sight of a playmate in an open casket can trigger heightened fears and anxieties.

ADOLESCENT FRIENDSHIP

Many aspects of the loss of a friend during early or middle childhood also apply to the adolescent years. However, given the developmental tasks of this period and the changing nature of friendships, the loss of a friend in adolescence places its own stamp on the bereavement process.

Peer relationships evolve considerably during adolescence with respect to the amount of time spent with friends, the diversity of friends, the increasing intimacy of shared feelings, and the overall significance of closeness to a friend (Savin-Williams & Berndt, 1990). Interactions occur with same-sex friends, opposite-sex friends, and romantic partners (heterosexual and homosexual), and in the context of larger groups. These interactions are coupled with the biological transformation of puberty, the educational transitions to middle school and high school, and the cognitive and emotional development associated with this stage of life. Exclusive clique membership (small groups of closely knit peers) tends to peak in late middle school and early high school, then decline into a looser and less hierarchical crowd, defined through broad and stereotyped attitudes reflected in the common labels of jocks, brains, populars, loners, nerds, druggies, greasers, and the like (Brown, 1990). A sense of well-being and resilience to stress has been linked to group identification (Hansell, 1981).

The maturation of such relationships factors into the development of personal identity. Rubin and colleagues (1998) observed that "adolescents recognize an obligation to grant friends a certain degree of autonomy and independence" and, compared with younger children, "show fewer elements of possessiveness and jealousy and more concern with how the relationship helps the partners" (p. 642). Adolescent friendships also tend to become increasingly more stable than those in middle childhood (Berndt, Hawkins, & Hoyle, 1986); begin to compete in time and significance with parental support and advice (Buhrmester, 1996; Csikszentmihalyi & Larson, 1984); and are usually fewer in number than during middle childhood (Urberg, Degirmencioglu, Tolson, & Halliday-Scher, 1995). The potential value of having one or more good friends has both a short-term and a long-term impact. Romantic relationships are considered to be the closest forms of friendship for adolescent boys and girls (Laursen, 1996).

Mixed-sex and dating interactions emerge in the context of transitions from same-sex cliques to crowd membership. The power of such relationships is a relatively recent topic of study in the scientific literature. Connolly, Furman, and Konarski (2000) demonstrated that having close friends of both sexes is predictive of the later formation of romantic relationships, and the attachment theory of Bowlby (1988) has been used to explore the purposes of romantic relationships in adolescence. These relationships include attachment or maintaining proximity, affiliative behaviors such as hugging or flirting, caretaking (seeking and providing comfort when stressed), and reproductive or sexual goals. The nature of these attachments may differ from one couple to another, may change over time, and can have both positive and negative consequences for development. Romantic relationships during adolescence have the potential to be extremely emotional and all-consuming, and their ending through death can be particularly difficult.

DEATH OF A FRIEND IN ADOLESCENCE

Compared with childhood friendships, the enhanced reciprocity, intimacy, and psychological basis (as opposed to activity basis) of the adolescent friendship make the death of a friend a major challenge for a teenager's coping abilities. Adolescent friendships are characterized by stability—adolescents believe they will be "friends forever"—and death disrupts their assumptive model of their future. Complicating the grieving process may be the tensions, contradictory feelings, and ambivalent quality of the relationship, which may have vacillated between the need for intimacy and interpersonal emotional conflicts (Oltjenbruns, 1996). Adding to the complexity are the shocking, tragic ways in which many adolescents die, which shake friends, families, schools, and communities to the core. Even if the adolescent dies from an illness, people are shocked because of their assumptions about the power of medical cures and their belief that death occurs only in later years.

Although most adults recognize the importance of peers in adolescent development, the loss of a friendship from death typically is not the focus of grief support. Rather, community and individual support rallies around the bereaved family. Sometimes adults do not even know that the relationship existed or the significance of the relationship to the teenager. This can be especially true in romantic relationships. Raphael (1983) describes Steve, whose girlfriend Jenny was killed in a bicycle accident. Not only did he find out about her death secondhand, from one of his friends, but his parents were unsympathetic:

> That night his parents casually remarked that they were sorry to hear of Jenny's death—she'd been a "nice little thing." His father said he was sorry, he supposed Steve must be a bit upset, but at least now his mind might be off girls for a bit, and his work at school might improve (p. 168).

How sad for Steve, who was not even allowed to attend the funeral.

In addition to the unique quality of the adolescent friendship, whether romantic or not, the developmental tasks of adolescence color the grief experience (Noppe & Noppe, 1997; Oltjenbruns, 1996). For adolescents, friends are significant sources of feedback in the evolving sense of self. Not only is this resource lost when a friend dies, but the "fragile ego" (McNeil et al., 1991) of the adolescent must incorporate the loss in his or her identity formation, which is a crucial task in the continued development of this young person (Erikson, 1994). The surviving friend may engage in a temporary identification with the one who died and may lose his or her own sense of self in the process (Raphael, 1983). Furthermore, surviving teens may experience survivor guilt and think of themselves as "bad" persons. Grieving adolescents may suspend their evolution into thinking about themselves in a complex, multidimensional manner, and view themselves primarily in a perpetual state of loss and grief. Such identification, if not redirected through gentle support, may lead to long-term grieving (McNeil et al., 1996; O'Brien & Goodenow, 1991).

Studies of cognitive development (e.g., Inhelder & Piaget, 1958) have emphasized the advent of formal hypothetical thinking that leads to the capacity to think abstractly in a "what-if?" way. This inversion of the real with the possible makes death even more threatening to one's sense of immortality when a friend's death occurs during adolescence. Additionally, hypothetical thinking can lead to recursive thoughts by the surviving friend about how the death could have been prevented. Such rumination—or emotion-focused coping—may lead to depression if it is not tempered by a focus on problem-solving in the grief process (Stroebe & Schut, 1999). Such emotion-focused grief might be more characteristic of adolescent grief over the loss of a friend, although this has not been empirically tested. The feeling that one is unique ("the personal fable") and the social paranoia of these years heighten the adolescents' sense of isolation and the need to hide emotions and grief (Oltjenbruns, 1996).

The significance of the peer group during adolescence may keep teens from turning to parents or school counselors for support during the tumultuous period after the death of a friend. Instead, the peer group may become the source of solace. McNeil and colleagues (1991) found that adolescents who were relatively close to a teenager who died of leukemia leaned on one another for emotional support and coping activities. On the other hand, adolescents may become socially disengaged when they are bereaved (Noppe, Noppe, Servaty-Seib, VandeVoorde, & Wisneski, 2007), Sometimes, particularly in the school setting, shared grief over the loss of a peer can become so intense that it overshadows any possible benefits (McNeil et al., 1991).

Adolescent grief over the loss of a friend can have a spiritual aspect. Religious education typically begins in the elementary school years or earlier, and these teachings are usually accepted without question until adolescence, when it seems that all previously held beliefs are questioned, examined, and turned inside-out. Religious faith supplies a system that organizes our understanding of the world and our place in it. At a time—such as adolescence—when perspectives on life and death are changing anyway, a death can precipitate a spiritual crisis. When a friend dies, adolescents may seek comfort and solace through their faith, or they may feel that faith is hypocrisy and God is unjust. They may direct their anger (an emotion that is common to grief) toward clergy and God. An eighth-grader, reflecting on the freakish death of a classmate who was hit by a playground slide during a windstorm, said,

> *I thought it was unfair. I was angry with the priest…I couldn't*
> *understand how he (God) could do this to A. I felt that God*
> *had taken the slide and just thrown it toward A.* (Dyregrov,
> Wikander, & Vigerust, 1999, p. 198).

Belief systems may affect how an adolescent grieves the death of a friend by suicide. As Doka (2007) notes, suicide may be particularly complicating in the grief process if it leads to the bereaved's anxiety and concern over eternal damnation of the deceased.

WHAT WE KNOW AND HOW WE CAN HELP

The glow of friendship reflects across age, gender, culture, and country. In this chapter, we pondered the significance of friendship from the earliest years of life through adolescence. In our review of the implications of the loss of a friend, we acknowledge the variety of ways in which these losses constitute painful marker events for children and adolescents. In spite of the continued lack of specific research on the loss of friends through death during these years, it is possible to extrapolate from what we have learned about bereavement and grief to suggest several ways parents, teachers, counselors, and others who work with children and adolescents can help.

Each grief experience is unique to the relationship and the situation. In addition to understanding the developmental level of friend-grievers and their past histories with death, adults who want to help must consider factors such as how the death occurred and the closeness of the friendship. The grief process also will be affected by the extent to which the child or adolescent receives support over an extended period. Friend-grievers frequently are disenfranchised grievers. Children and adolescents who lose friends may not be considered legitimate grievers, and they are frequently neglected in the rituals, support, and consolation that accompany the death of a child (Deck & Folta, 1989; Silverman, 2000). Thus, one of the ways adults can help children and adolescents is to simply acknowledge the loss and validate their grief, without pressuring them to display emotions that they may not feel or are not comfortable exhibiting. Adults must strike a delicate balance between acknowledging grief and pathologizing normal child and adolescent behavior. Children and adolescents, in particular, need to have their privacy respected.

Racial and ethnic background may affect the grief process for children and adolescents who lose a friend through death. In some ethnic groups, community involvement includes children and adolescents; rituals and traditions provide guidance and solace; and friendship is valued even for the youngest. In these communities, the child or adolescent's grief is less likely to be disenfranchised. In communities and cultures where sudden violent death is a frequent occurrence, special care must be taken to attend to the needs of children and adolescents. How the child or adolescent learns about the death is a crucial factor (O'Brien & Goodenow, 1991). Many adults avoid discussing death with children, but children require education, guidance, support, and open dialogue about this topic. Children and adolescents can see through insincerity; they crave honesty and an opportunity to ask questions about what happened. In the aftermath of September 11, 2001, adolescents were asked what they needed from adults to help them cope with the events of that tragic day. The highest percentage of responses affirmed the desire for adults to be open and honest with them (Noppe, Noppe, & Bartell, 2006). This must also be the case when a child or adolescent loses a friend through death.

The successful resolution of grief does not necessarily entail relinquishing the relationship, as was believed in the past. Rather, people tend to maintain their link to the deceased loved one in a variety of ways, such as keeping cherished objects, talking to the deceased and using him or her as a guide, dreaming about the deceased, and recognizing that this person is still an important part of one's life (Silverman, 2000). This "continuing bond" may occur when a friend dies. As Silverman (2000) points out, surviving friends become a "living legacy" of the person who has died, which can be growth-enhancing for them (Oltjenbruns, 1996).

There is one final aspect of friendship lost during childhood and adolescence that frequently is overlooked. In reaction to the emphasis on the potential long-term damage of negative life experiences during childhood and adolescence, a growing literature has demonstrated that children and adolescents can also be incredibly resilient in the face of tragedy (Masten, 2001; Werner, 1989). Social support appears to be a crucial factor for such resilience; thus, it is incumbent on adults to provide that support or to facilitate support from friends and others to whom the child or adolescent may turn.

For children and adolescents who have lost a friend, the experience with death and grief is a part of who they are and what they will become. A part of their identities will be forged out of sadness and pain from the death of their friend. But the outcome can be a life-affirming road map for their future, an appreciation of their loved ones, and a new definition of the meaning of friendship and its value to their existence.

Illene C. Noppe, Ph.D., a graduate of Temple University, is a professor of human development at the University of Wisconsin-Green Bay. She developed the "Dying, Death, and Loss" course on her campus more than 20 years ago and is the founder of the Death, Dying, and Bereavement Institute, which provides outreach education for professionals in northeast Wisconsin. Her research has involved the study of attachment and grief, death in child care centers, and adolescent grief. She is currently interested in developing an evidence-based model for death education based on the scholarship of teaching and learning and is participating in a national study of college student bereavement. In partnership with a local hospice, she founded Camp Lloyd, a day camp for grieving children. She is a member of the Association for Death Education and Counseling, and currently serves as editor of its quarterly newsletter/journalette, The Forum.

Lloyd D. Noppe, Ph.D., is a graduate of Temple University and a professor of human development at the University of Wisconsin-Green Bay. He recently stepped down after chairing the program for 12 years. Since 1980, he has taught the course on middle childhood and adolescence, as well as

"Development of Creative and Critical Thinking" and the human development interdisciplinary senior seminar. He served for a year as interim dean of liberal arts and sciences. He has coauthored several textbooks on life span and child development, and has published research on creative thinking, adolescence and death, and other aspects of development. He is a member of the Society for Research in Adolescence, the Society for Research in Child Development, the American Psychological Association, and the American Educational Research Association.

References

Berndt, T. J., Hawkins, J. A., & Hoyle, S. G. (1986). Changes in friendship during a school year: Effects on children's and adolescents' impressions of friendship and sharing with friends. *Child Development, 57,* 1284–1297.

Bluebond-Langner, M. (1989). Worlds of dying children and their well siblings. *Death Studies, 13,* 1–16.

Bowlby, J. (1988). *A secure base: Parent-child attachment and healthy human development.* New York: Basic Books.

Brown, B. B. (1990). Peer groups and peer cultures. In S. S. Feldman & G. R. Elliott (Eds.), *At the threshold: The developing adolescent* (pp. 171–196). Cambridge, MA: Harvard University Press.

Buhrmester, D. (1996). Need fulfillment, interpersonal competence, and the developmental contexts of friendship. In W. M. Bukowski, A. F. Newcomb, & W. W. Hartup (Eds.), *The company they keep: Friendship during childhood and adolescence* (pp. 158–185). New York: Cambridge University Press.

Connolly, J., Furman, W., & Konarski, R. (2000). The role of peers in the emergence of heterosexual romantic relationships in adolescence. *Child Development, 71,* 1395–1408.

Corr, C. A. (1995). Children's understandings of death—striving to understand death. In K. J. Doka (Ed.), *Children mourning. Mourning children* (pp. 3–16). Washington, DC: Hospice Foundation of America.

Csikszentmihalyi, M., & Larson, R. (1984). *Being adolescent.* New York: Basic Books.

Davies, B. (1999). *Shadows in the sun. The experiences of sibling bereavement in childhood.* Philadelphia: Brunner/Mazel.

Deck, E. S., & Folta, J. R. (1989). *The friend-griever.* In K. J. Doka (Ed.), *Disenfranchised grief. Recognizing hidden sorrow* (pp. 77–89). Lexington, MA: Lexington Books.

Dickinson, G. E. (1992). First childhood death experiences. *Omega, 25,* 169–182.

Doka, K. (2007). Religion, spirituality, and assessment and intervention. In D. Balk (Ed.), *Handbook of thanatology* (pp. 203–225). Northbrook, IL: Association for Death Education and Counseling.

de Vries, B. (2001). Grief. Intimacy's reflection. *Generations, 25,* 75–80.

Dyregrov, A., Wikander, A. M. B., & Vigerust, S. (1999). Sudden death of a classmate and friend. *School Psychology International, 20,* 191–208.

Eckerman, C. O. (1979). The human infant in social interaction. In R. Cairns (Ed.), *The analysis of social interactions: Methods, issues, and illustrations* (pp. 163–178). Hillsdale, NJ: Erlbaum.

Erikson, E. H. (1994). *Identity, youth, and crisis.* New York: W. W. Norton.

Ewalt, P. L., & Perkins, L. (1979). The real experience of death among adolescents: An empirical study. *Social Casework, 60,* 547–551.

Federal Interagency Forum on Child and Family Statistics (2006). America's children in brief: Key national indicators of well-being, 2006. Retrieved August 15, 2007, from www.childstats.gov/americaschildren06

Garvey, C. (1990). *Play.* Cambridge, MA: Harvard University Press.

Hansell, S. (1981). Ego development and peer friendship networks. *Sociology of Education, 54,* 51–63.

Hinde, R. A. (1987). *Individuals, relationships, and culture.* Cambridge, England: Cambridge University Press.

Hay, D. F., Pedersen, J., & Nash, A. (1982). Dyadic interaction in the first year of life. In K. H. Rubin & H. S. Ross (Eds.), *Peer relationships and social skills in childhood* (pp. 11–40). New York: Springer-Verlag.

Howes, C. (1992). *The collaborative construction of pretend.* Albany: State University of New York Press.

Howes, C. (1996). The earliest friendships. In W. M. Bukowski, A. F. Newcomb, & W. W. Hartup (Eds.), *The company they keep: Friendship in childhood and adolescence* (pp. 66–86). New York: Cambridge University Press.

Inhelder, B., & Piaget, J. (1958). *The growth of logical thinking from childhood to adolescence.* New York: Basic Books.

Institute of Medicine (2003). *When children die: Improving palliative and end-of-life care for children and their families.* Washington, DC: National Academies Press.

Kegan, R. (1994). *In over our heads. The mental demands of modern life.* Cambridge, MA: Harvard University Press.

Laursen, B. (1996). Closeness and conflict in adolescent peer relationships: Interdependence with friends and romantic partners. In W. M. Bukowski, A. F. Newcomb, & W. W. Hartup (Eds.), *The company they keep: Friendship in childhood and adolescence* (pp. 186–210). New York: Cambridge University Press.

Lieberman, A. F., Compton, N. C., Van Horn, P., & Ippen, C. G. (2003). *Losing a parent to death in the early years: Guidelines for the treatment of traumatic bereavement in infancy and early childhood.* Washington, DC: Zero to Three Press.

Masten, A. (2001). Ordinary magic. Resilience processes in development. *American Psychologist, 56,* 227–238.

McHale, S. M., Dariotis, J. K., & Kauh, T. J. (2003). Social development and social relationships in middle childhood. In R. M. Lerner & M. A. Easterbrook (Eds.), *Handbook of psychology:* Vol. 6. *Developmental psychology* (pp. 241–265). New York: Wiley.

McNeil, J. N., Silliman, B., & Swihart, J. J. (1991). Helping adolescents cope with the death of a peer: A high school case study. *Journal of Adolescent Research, 6,* 132–145.

Mead, G. H. (1934). *Mind, self, and society: From the standpoint of a social behaviorist.* Chicago: University of Chicago Press.

Mueller, E., & Brenner, J. (1977). The origins of social skills and interaction among playgroup toddlers. *Child Development, 48,* 854–861.

National Center for Health Statistics (2007). Deaths/mortality. Retrieved August 15, 2007, from www.cdc.gov/nchs/fastats/death.htm

Newcomb, A. F., Bukowski, W. M., & Pattee, L. (1993). Children's peer relations: A meta-analytic review of popular, rejected, neglected, controversial, and average sociometric status. *Psychological Bulletin, 113,* 99–128.

Noppe, I. C., & Noppe, L. D. (1997). Evolving meanings of death during early, middle, and later adolescence. *Death Studies, 21,* 253–275.

Noppe, I. C., Noppe, L. D., & Bartell, D. (2006). Terrorism and resilience: Adolescents' and teachers' responses to September 11, 2001. *Death Studies, 30,* 41–60.

Noppe, I. C., Noppe, L. D., Servaty-Seib, H. L., VandeVoorde, E., & Wisneski, M. P. (2007, April). *Using electronic event sampling method to assess adolescent grief.* Presented to the 29th Annual Conference of the Association for Death Education and Counseling, Indianapolis, IN.

O'Brien, J. M., & Goodenow, C. (1991). Adolescents' reactions to the death of a peer. *Adolescence, 26,* 431–440.

Oltjenbruns, K. A. (2007). Life span issues and loss, grief, and mourning. Part 1: The importance of a development context: Childhood and adolescence as an example. In D. Balk (Ed.), *Handbook of thanatology* (pp. 143–149). Northbrook, IL: Association for Death Education and Counseling.

Oltjenbruns, K. A. (1996). Death of a friend during adolescence: Issues and impacts. In C. A. Corr & D. E. Balk (Eds.), *Handbook of adolescent death and bereavement* (pp. 196–215). New York: Springer.

Raphael, B. (1983). *The anatomy of bereavement.* New York: Basic Books.

Ross, H. S., Conant, C., Cheyne, J. A., & Alevizos, E. (1992). Relationships and alliances in the social interactions of kibbutz toddlers. *Social Development, 1,* 1–17.

Rubin, K. H., Bukowski, W., & Parker, J. G. (1998). Peer interactions, relationships, and groups. In W. Damon (Series Ed.) & N. Eisenberg (Vol. Ed.), *Handbook of child psychology.* Vol. 3. *Social, emotional, and personality development* (5th ed.) (pp. 619–695). New York: Wiley.

Savin-Williams, R. C., & Berndt, T. J. (1990). Friendship and peer relations. In S. S. Feldman & G. R. Elliott (Eds.), *At the threshold: The developing adolescent* (pp. 277–307). Cambridge, MA: Harvard University Press.

Selman, R. L. (1980). *The growth of interpersonal understanding: Developmental and clinical analyses.* New York: Academic Press.

Silverman, P. R. (2000). *Never too young to know. Death in children's lives.* New York: Oxford University Press.

Stroebe, M., & Schut, H. (1999). The dual process model of coping with bereavement: Rationale and description. *Death Studies, 23,* 197–224.

Urberg, K. A., Degirmencioglu, S. M., Tolson, J. M., & Halliday-Scher, K. (1995). The structure of adolescent peer networks. *Developmental Psychology, 31,* 540–547.

Webb, N. B. (2002). The child and death. In N. B. Webb (Ed.), *Helping bereaved children* (2nd ed.) (pp. 3–18). New York: Guilford Press.

Werner, E. E. (1989). Children of the Garden Island. *Scientific American, 210,* 106–111.

Wolfelt, A. (1996). *Healing the bereaved child.* Fort Collins, CO: Companion Press.

Worden, J. W. (1996). *Children and grief: When a parent dies.* New York: Guilford Press.

CHAPTER 11

Military Children and Grief

Betsy Beard, with Judith Mathewson,
Tina Saari, and Heather Campagna

INTRODUCTION

Thousands of American deaths have resulted from U.S. military participation in Operation Iraqi Freedom and Operation Enduring Freedom in Afghanistan. Many military deaths are front-page news in local newspapers or the lead stories on local television stations. Occasionally, there is a follow-up report on the funeral. Americans are saddened by these losses, but after a brief cathartic surge of sympathy and patriotic support for the bereaved family, they move on to other topics.

But what becomes of the family? After the flag is folded and the last echoing notes of "Taps" have sounded, the burden of grief is on the shoulders of those who loved the fallen soldier. Often those shoulders are too small, too fragile, and too young to bear this burden alone. They are the shoulders of the surviving children of the military men and women who have given, in the words of Abraham Lincoln, their "last full measure of devotion" in service to our country.

Although the service member's death is reported publicly, the continuing grief and persistent courage of surviving military families is usually hidden from the media and, in general, from public view. Privacy is the standard, and each branch of service is careful to protect grieving families from unwanted intrusions by the media. However, away from the spotlight, the grief following a military death continues for months and years: horrendous, traumatic, and complicated by a number of factors. Effective support for this kind of bereavement requires some background and understanding of the culture and customs of the military.

Unlike many children growing up in the United States today, the children of military parents are more likely to realize that the world is not safe and that, with multiple deployments, there is a chance that the outcome of their parents' military service may be death. Although at this time most military deaths occur in a combat zone, death can also occur as the result of noncombat injuries, accidents, or suicide, even after the deployment is over and the soldier is home.

Not all the issues discussed here will be relevant to every situation. The problems that arise when someone dies by suicide at home differ greatly from those related to a combat-related death. Regardless of the cause of death, however, many customs and traditions of military culture differ greatly from civilian experience. Recognizing how different a military death is for the surviving children is an important step in helping them cope with grief. In this chapter, we look at some of the specific factors that affect the grieving process for children of the military and some of the coping strategies that have helped.

MILITARY FACTORS THAT COMPLICATE GRIEF

Absence of the Deployed Parent

> *[It's hard] because I don't get to give him a good-night kiss.*
> Katie Staats, 8-year-old military survivor.
> KKTV News, Colorado Springs, August 17, 2007

The deployment of a member of the armed forces creates a single-parent family overnight. In addition to the financial difficulties, the long absence of one parent, and the extra strain on the remaining parent, there is the constant worry about injury or death. Family dynamics are altered by deployment. Recent studies of U.S. Army databases suggest that the incidence of maltreatment of children in military families rises significantly during a combat deployment (Gibbs , Martin, Kupper, Johnson, 2007). If this has occurred, the family's grief journey will be even more difficult.

During a long deployment, a child may feel responsible for his or her siblings or the remaining parent. Additional stress may be unwittingly placed on a child when Dad says; "Take care of Mom and your sisters while I'm gone" or "Be good until I get home, and don't give Mom a hard time." If the father doesn't return from war, the child may feel that the mandate remains in effect forever. Acting "like a kid" again seems like a betrayal of Dad's trust.

Another aspect of deployment is that the families become accustomed to their loved ones being gone for long periods. This makes it harder, especially for a younger child, to realize or acknowledge that the parent is gone forever this time. And if a death occurs during deployment, a long time may have elapsed since the child last saw or spoke to the now-deceased parent.

Death Notification

> We thought when we heard the doorbell it was the pizza man.
> I went to the door and I told my mom it wasn't...and the next
> thing I knew, she came inside starting to cry.
> Angel Van Dusen, 11-year-old military survivor
> (Berkes, 2007)

The death notification itself can be highly traumatic. A child raised on a military base knows the significance of a government vehicle coming to a house with a chaplain and a notifying officer, both in Class A dress uniform. One 6-year-old girl looked out the window and, when she saw the chaplain and the casualty notification officer approaching the house, screamed, "No! Not my house! You have the wrong house!" Another young child said, "Daddy promised that the chaplain would not knock on our front door. When Mommy saw the car pull up in the driveway, she knew right away what had happened. So she walked out to the driveway. She made sure that Daddy kept his promise."

The Loved One's Remains

> We're getting him back in pieces....
> Jocelyn Burns, mother of LCPL Kyle Burns
> (Weller, 2007)

Because of the nature of combat injuries and training accidents resulting in death, the physical remains of the deceased may not be viewable. This can be traumatic for several reasons. First, children are often haunted by images of what may have happened to their loved one. These thoughts can be extremely disturbing and frightening. Second, the family will have unanswerable questions regarding what was left of the body. And finally, the children are prevented from verifying the identification of their parent for themselves and from saying a final goodbye by sight or touch.

Another disturbing aspect of a combat death is that more of the loved one's remains may be discovered on the field of battle and subsequently identified. Each time, the family is contacted regarding the disposition of these remains. One mother said, "We're getting him back in pieces…I'll be crying for the rest of my life." A military widow said, "I want every piece of him back home. I don't want that country to have any part of him." Yet another family, after three of these notifications, authorized the army to handle any further remains without contacting them.

Military Funerals

> We salute the flag. We serve under it. And some come home beneath it. It should be presented with the utmost honor and respect.
>
> Lt. Col. Steve Beck, as he presented a service flag to
> 10-year-old Taylor Heldt (McCrimmon, 2007)

The military does a wonderful job of memorializing those who die in service to the nation. But an added complication of a military death in a combat zone is the lengthy process of recovering and transporting the body home before the burial can take place. The body must be repatriated through the Dover Air Force Base mortuary in Delaware, and it is autopsied before being released to the family. The family has no control over this process and receives very little information about the time frame. The family's grief is agonizingly prolonged by this process, during which they have no access to their loved one. The deceased's remains belong to the military until it releases the body to the family.

As the family waits, the first memorial ceremony takes place in the combat zone. The deployed unit honors its military member in a remembrance ceremony on the field of battle. This service includes eulogies by the soldier's friends and commanders; the symbolic representation of the deceased using his or her dog tags, helmet, and boots; the rifle volley; the rendering of "Taps" by a lone bugler; and farewell salutes by each person in attendance. Often, the ceremony is taped and sent to the soldier's family.

Meanwhile, the family must plan a funeral service in the soldier's hometown and possibly a second service, if the deceased is to be buried in a national cemetery such as Arlington National Cemetery. Travel arrangements must be made. And all this time, the children really have no functioning parent—one has died and the other is consumed by grief and the pressure to complete the funeral arrangements.

If the family wishes, military honors are performed at the burial site, regardless of whether it is a private or national cemetery. Military pallbearers are supplied, medals earned posthumously are presented to the next of kin, the flag that has draped the casket is ceremoniously folded and presented to the family, a rifle volley is sounded consisting of seven rifles fired three times, and the notes of "Taps" echo solemnly through the cemetery.

These ceremonial observances may be repeated when the deployed unit of the deceased service member returns to the United States. The family is invited to attend yet another memorial service, sometimes many months after their loved one has been buried.

Sometimes individual family members are not in agreement about funeral and burial arrangements, details of the disposal of personal effects, and receipt of military mementoes and honors. A soldier may be survived by a very young spouse who may not be well acquainted with the soldier's family of origin. Financial benefits (which can be considerable) are distributed according to the soldier's wishes and predetermined military policy. Before deployment, the soldier designates a person who will make funeral arrangements and decisions. Preexisting family conflicts may be significantly exacerbated if, for example, an ex-spouse receives the life insurance or a young girlfriend makes the funeral arrangements.

Media Attention and Political Protesters

> *It's hard enough losing someone, but losing them to a situation as politically charged as this? I'm not going to let anything take away from [my children's] father. They will know he wanted to go to Iraq and wanted to jump out of airplanes because he loved his country, but he loved us so much, too.*
>
> Crystal Becker
(Brown, 2007)

Because of the sometimes public nature of a combat death and the political nature of war, some families have been subjected to vindictive protests at their loved one's funeral and interment. Picketers have displayed extreme insensitivity by shouting at the bereaved family and waving signs telling the children and surviving spouse that God hates their country in general and their loved one in particular. The grieving family is subjected to this behavior at a time when they are least able to cope with the additional trauma.

> *I wonder how long this war is going to be in [my child's] face?*
>
> Mother of 11-year-old military survivor

After the funeral, the family is faced with images that can intensify their grief. Newscasts are filled with reports of death and descriptions of destruction. In an ongoing war, scenes from the combat zone are aired repeatedly. Children may be subjected to extensive media coverage not only of their loved one's death but of subsequent deaths as they occur.

Isolation from Peers in the Military Community

> *The American culture (which in reality is an umbrella for many different cultures within our borders) has a great reluctance to talk openly about death. We are one of the most "death-denying" cultures today. We simply do not like discussing death in any form. In fact, we don't even like to use the word "died"* (Sims, 2006b).

Children who have been raised on military bases and have lost a parent are surrounded by other children whose parents are at risk. These other children may avoid the bereaved child because of their fear that their own parent may die. Mirroring the adults around them, they don't want to talk to the bereaved child.

A bereaved military child feels especially isolated when the deceased parent's unit returns home from a combat deployment. The child bears the pain of watching the joyful homecoming ceremonies and reunions of children with parents who are returning home alive and well. This painful and difficult event increases the child's feeling of isolation on the grief journey.

Isolation from the Military Community

If you are living in government housing as an authorized
dependent, you are eligible to continue living in government
housing for a year from the date of your loved one's death
(Department of Defense, 2007,13).

Families that have suffered the tragic loss of a parent on active duty often move off base to be closer to remaining extended family. They are *required* to move off base within one year of the death. (Previously, such families had to move within the first month; the requirement was later extended to nine months.) Regardless of the timing, this is a drastic change for children who are accustomed to military life and the sense of pride and community that comes with it. This secondary loss greatly affects the military child—the stress of adapting to a new neighborhood and a new school adds to the stress of the grieving process.

One boy could not have been prouder when his father was named Army Aviator of the Year. Two months later, his dad was killed in a helicopter crash, and his family moved—away from the army he had grown up with, away from the sound of rotor blades, and away from the other kids who appreciated his father's national distinction. No one in his new school understood. The loss of identity, on top of the loss of a parent, is considered a secondary loss and the ongoing effects can be overwhelming (Gurian, Kamboukas, Levine,Pearlman, Wasser, 2006, 33). Just when they need familiarity and support the most, many of these children are taken away from everything familiar, from all their friends and the world they have grown up in. Many discover that they are grieving not only the loss of someone they love but also the loss of friendships, self-esteem, and self-identity (Sims, 2006a).

Civilian Reactions to Military Death

The bullies at my school would pick on me all the time and
say, "Your dad was a pussy. He died for no reason."
Dakota Givens, 10-year-old military survivor
(Berkes, 2007)

Military children say that the civilian children in their schools don't understand the military culture and may torment them about not having a dad or mom. One 12-year-old told of being taunted by another boy in his class who said, "If your dad had done his job right, he wouldn't be dead." The bereaved boy was humiliated and deeply hurt. At school, he had no one to turn to, and he didn't want to worry his mother, who was already struggling as the surviving parent.

Other military youth have shared how difficult it is to deal with these hurtful comments. They may try to talk to teachers and counselors, but support in the school setting isn't as prevalent as it should be to assist active duty, National Guard, and Reserve families. Children need to feel that they have allies in their schools, churches, and communities while they grieve for their dead parent. External support is vital, since support is not always available from the surviving parent or a sibling who is also grieving.

Tension between Pride in Service and the Emotions of Grief

Most military survivors experience a dichotomy between the devastating negative emotions of grief and a feeling of immense pride in the accomplishments of the loved one. It is uncomfortable to speak of the pride outside the military context, because many civilians can't identify with it or mistake it for a lack of sorrow.

But despite the pride, all the usual emotions of grief are in evidence. Children often express guilt that they didn't write enough letters while their parent was deployed and remorse about not behaving well while Mom or Dad was away at war. They may feel anger toward the opposing combatants who caused the death, the government and its officials, or even the military itself, which sent their mother or father to war.

SPECIALIZED HELP FOR MILITARY GRIEF

The Tragedy Assistance Program for Survivors (TAPS) is the only nonprofit veterans service organization chartered solely to help those affected by the death of a loved one serving in the U.S. armed forces or in support of the military mission. The organization had its beginning in November 1992, as a result of a tragic military airplane accident over the skies of Juneau, Alaska. Brigadier General Tom Carroll and seven of his Army National Guard team perished in the crash of a C-12 military aircraft, leaving behind eight widows and 14 children.

In the months and years following the loss of their loved ones, the survivors turned to various grief support organizations; but when they turned to each other for comfort and to share common fears and problems, they found new strength and the beginning of healing. They realized that the tragedy they shared was different from other types of losses: They shared pride in their spouses' service to the United States, as well as tremendous sadness at the ultimate sacrifice their loved ones had made (TAPS, 2007).

Because there was no national equivalent to this informal local support group for military survivors, TAPS was created. Over the years, it has grown from its modest beginnings to its current status as a national organization offering hope, healing, comfort, and care to thousands of U.S. armed forces families facing the death of a loved one. A significant part of the TAPS mission is to minister to the mental, emotional, and spiritual welfare of children who are part of a military family and have suffered the traumatic death of a parent.

Surviving parents have indicated that the most critical need for their families is an organized program of assistance for the children. TAPS has responded by creating the Good Grief Camp for Young Survivors. Each year, TAPS holds a grief support camp in Washington, D.C., over Memorial Day weekend. In addition to the national camp, regional camps are hosted at military bases and posts throughout the year. TAPS and its efforts on behalf of surviving children are known throughout the Department of Defense.

The Good Grief Camp

The Good Grief Camp for Young Survivors is the only national program focused on children who have lost a parent, sibling, or loved one in military service to the country. The camp gives youngsters a solid foundation on which to build a healthy future following the tragic loss of a parent in the military. The youth learn to rebuild their shattered lives and look to the future with hope. In the words of the TAPS motto, they "Remember the love, celebrate the life, share the journey."

Young survivors learn coping skills and discover that the feelings they are experiencing are normal reactions to an abnormal event—the untimely death of a parent. At the Good Grief Camp, children find the courage to face the unthinkable together. TAPS uses four major elements to accomplish its mission:

- Age-based peer support groups
- Individual military mentors who partner with each child
- Coping strategies learned through activities and education (grief work)
- Ceremonies and rituals that honor the sacrifice of the military loved one

Age-based Peer Support Groups

> Peer support groups provide opportunities for expression that helps grieving children and adolescents to understand their day-to-day needs for healing during the grieving process. Peer support groups offer children and teens a safe place to talk about similar feelings, thoughts, and experiences; provide emotional, physical, spiritual, and mental support in a nonjudgmental environment; and provide a forum to search for meaning about life and death as [they] find normalcy and commonality in their lives (Parga, 2007, 8).

At the Good Grief Camp, children are grouped according to age with others who have suffered a similar loss. This may be the first time they have met anyone else whose parent died in service to the country. Each child is also paired with an adult mentor. (This component of the program is discussed in the next section.) In addition to individual mentors, each age-based peer group has two group leaders. Generally, one is a person who works in the mental health field and the other has a background in the military culture. Both are experienced, qualified, mature, and trained in facilitating group interactions. With the help of the individual mentors, the group leaders encourage the children to talk freely about their losses.

The age-based support group provides a safe environment for the children to grieve together and share their loss in a way they may not have experienced before. Sharing and expressions of grief are encouraged in Circle Time. Children are greatly relieved to realize that they are not alone in their grief, and to be with other children who understand them without ridiculing, teasing, or harassing them. A surprising number of children admit that they have never told anyone that their parent died. In fact, sometimes they tell people that he or she is still in Iraq and will be home later. At these camps they finally feel safe enough to talk about the loss. They know they are not alone as they tell their story to others who have lost a loved one in the armed forces.

At one of the regional camps, a 10-year-old girl said, "I have never told even my best friends about my dad's death because if I say it out loud or talk about it to anyone else, it means he is really not coming home. But I can talk about it here, because people understand and don't say they know what I am going through when they have no idea." She shared her story for the first time 11 months after her father was killed in Iraq.

Numerous teens have spoken about the feelings of anger, sadness, and guilt that surface each day as they try to find their place in the world. One said, "I don't know what to tell people about my dad. There are days that I feel like I'm in a fog. Other days, I feel that nothing is right. I'm worried that Mom is spending all our money and we won't have a place to live." Another teen shared that although she was 18 years old, she had never learned how to drive, because her dad promised that he would teach her when he returned from Iraq. When he didn't return, she didn't want to learn without him. Some teens talked about how painful it is for them to listen when their friends complain about their dads being hard on them or embarrassing them.

Therapy dogs trained in grief work are in attendance at the national camp in Washington, D.C. They give children a feeling of support, understanding, and acceptance. It is not uncommon to find children lying on the floor, petting the Labrador retrievers and telling the dogs about their sorrow. One young boy who was having difficulty participating in the peer group was allowed to go out into the hallway. He sat with two of the comfort dogs and told them the story of how his father had died. At the end of the story, he said to the dogs, "I don't want anyone else to know that I really miss my dad. But I know that you won't tell, right?" Talking to a dog is a start toward being able to share his feelings with a person.

The participants in each age-based support group share contact information. This helps to create a network of support and comfort that can carry the children far into the future. The young survivors can keep in touch for birthdays, holidays, and the extremely difficult anniversaries of the deaths of their loved ones.

TAPS also networks with chaplains and other supportive peer mentors to allow the families to receive added assistance when they return home. In larger cities, Vet Centers (Readjustment Counseling Services of the Department of Veterans Affairs) provide bereavement support sessions for the families of deceased military members.

> *Through age-appropriate peer support groups, children and teens find what is lost, what is left, and what is possible. Through this process, children and adolescents bond, in a safe and secure climate in which information and self-confidence turns adversity into opportunity, as they learn about themselves and others. At most, friendships are made, and even in the difficult time of grief, tears and laughter are shared* (Parga, 2007, 8).

Individual Military Mentors

> *Grieving children need to feel that they are being heard and understood…. Many young people will experience grief and trauma…. They need caring adults to create an oasis of safety to explore these sensitive experiences* (Goldman, 2007,12).

At the Good Grief Camp, each child is paired with a volunteer military mentor. Most mentors at the annual Washington, D.C., camp come from the ranks of the Honor Guard, which is stationed nearby. These are the people who serve at Arlington National Cemetery as pallbearers or members of the firing party, or who present the service flag to the surviving spouse, child, or parent. Additional mentors come from the ranks of military spouses and retired military. A background check is performed, and the mentors attend a training event each year before the camp.

The mentors understand military culture and can explain all the military customs and courtesies to the children, to help them realize how highly the military values their sacrifice. The mentors allow the children to share whatever they are able to about their loved one—likes and dislikes, the fun they had with him or her, and the hurt and sorrow they are experiencing with their loss. For four days, the mentor accompanies his or her buddy to all activities and on all field trips.

A concept that is familiar to military personnel but little known in the civilian world is the "battle buddy." Each soldier who deploys to a distant location has a battle buddy—someone who will watch out for him and make sure he is doing well, both mentally and physically. A battle buddy understands that his partner will be there for him in difficult times, just as he will pick up the slack for his buddy when the need arises. The experience of caring for a battle buddy helps TAPS mentors as they work with their young charges.

Coping with Grief through Activities and Education

> Children need age-appropriate information, skills to identify their emotions, and ways to express them in order to appropriately cope with death and grief. Size has nothing to do with the hurt in one's heart (Sims, 2006b).

Lesson plans for the camp incorporate accepted psychological strategies for coping with grief. Each child receives a copy of the official TAPS edition of *A Kid's Journey of Grief*, by Susan K. Beeney and Jo Anne Chung. This book is "a coloring and activity book for children of military families who never chose to travel down the path of grief, but, nevertheless, find themselves on the road" (Beeney, 2005, title page). The book uses the grief model of Dr. J. William Worden, which involves four tasks of mourning. The first task is to acknowledge the reality of the death of your loved one and understand that the grieving process will be difficult. The second is to experience, rather than avoid, the pain of loss. The third is to adjust to an environment that no longer includes your loved one. The fourth task is to devise ways to emotionally relocate your loved one in your heart, since the relationship can no longer be interactive (Beeney, 2005, 1).

The children learn to work through the pain of their grief as they express it in words, artwork, music, and with animals. They discover that they "feel some relief from expressing their inward thoughts outwardly" (Goldman, 2007, 12). The mentors and group leaders accompany the children on this journey by listening and being present for them. Younger children may be led in a guided discussion as they work through *A Kid's Journey of Grief*. In the teen group, journaling, artwork, and music therapy are used.

Recently, camp activities have revolved around specific themes, such as "Seasons of Grief," "Remembering Our Loved Ones," and "The Circus of Grief and Loss." Age-appropriate activities are developed to address why the child or teen is attending the camp, to explore the emotions of grief, and to create a memorial or tribute to the loved one.

Some activities allow the children to use their creativity to connect with and honor their loved one with stories, artwork, and poems. The poems and stories can be incorporated into songs that are sung in memory of the deceased. Other activities allow them to explore emotions. In one project, the children made stress balls using Play-Doh and balloons to cope with anxiety. In another, they cut out words from magazines and glued them to both the inside and outside of paper bags, expressing how they felt on the inside compared with what they showed to the world. Circus-themed activities were developed for the 2007 Good Grief Camp in conjunction with the Ringling Brothers Barnum and Bailey Circus. In a metaphoric journey through grief, the circus team helped children learn about keeping everything going in their lives by learning to spin plates; handling the many life challenges they were facing by learning to juggle; painting their face with a clown's smile while they feel sad on the inside; and walking a tightrope to learn to have balance in their life.

Ceremonies and Rituals that Honor the Sacrifice

> *Dear Dad, What is it like in heaven? What are you doing?*
> *Does it really hurt when you die? Do you miss me? I LOVE*
> *YOU! From Ryan.*
>
> Message on a helium balloon
> from a young military survivor

At the national Good Grief Camp, field trips are designed to show the young military survivors how much the country honors those who have died in service. They learn that their family is now a part of a national legacy, and that their loved ones will not be forgotten. The mentors help the children understand the history and significance of the war monuments. Recent camps have toured the Vietnam Wall, the World War II Memorial, the Korean War

Memorial, and Arlington National Cemetery. While on field trips with their mentors, the young survivors explore the importance of the funeral traditions that honored their loved ones: the rifle volley, the ceremonious folding of the flag, and the playing of "Taps."

The field trips are designed to be interactive and participatory, allowing the children to join other Americans in honoring fallen war heroes. One year, roses were placed at the base of the Vietnam Wall. Each year, several children are chosen to lay a wreath at the Tomb of the Unknowns in Arlington National Cemetery on Memorial Day. The wreath is made of red, white, and blue paper cutouts of each child's handprint, on which they have written a message to their loved one. A trip to the Caisson Stables in Arlington National Cemetery allows young military survivors the experience of sitting on or hugging the specially trained horses that draw the caissons carrying the caskets in military funerals.

Senior military leaders spend time with the children during the course of the weekend. The chairman of the Joint Chiefs of Staff often visits. Other senior leaders host the group at nearby military installations, such as the Marine Barracks or Ft. Myer. The children come to understand the extent to which their loved one's sacrifice is honored throughout the ranks.

A final ceremony at the camp is the launching of helium balloons containing messages to the loved one who has died. Children tie handwritten messages to their balloons and take them outdoors to release, accompanied by their mentors. In Washington, TAPS works with the air traffic control tower at Reagan National Airport. The messages to heaven are given priority for departure airspace: All air traffic is halted until the balloons are safely airborne. A 7-year-old survivor asked, "Do these balloons really go to heaven?" Her mentor said, "Well, they go pretty high" (Meadow, 2007, 27).

Self-care

No discussion about helping bereaved people would be complete without a few words on self-care. Often, the mentors who are chosen to be buddies for grieving children are combat veterans who are grieving their own losses. Members of the Honor Guard have experienced many funerals and provided military honors for many grieving families. Becoming TAPS mentors allows them to relate on a personal level to the children of fallen soldiers, sailors, marines, airmen, and Coast Guard personnel. Many mentors say that in volunteering, they feel that they are fulfilling a commitment to their fallen battle buddies. Part of the U.S. Army Warrior Ethos states, "I will never leave a fallen comrade" (United States Army, 2007). Helping the family of a fallen comrade is a significant part of "never leaving."

However, the volunteer work can take its toll on these young men and women. They are with the children all day and evening for four consecutive days. They are touched by the grief and pain they witness. At the end of the Good Grief Camp, a closing circle for mentors allows them to express their own sorrows and losses. They are given the support and resources they need for continuing the connection with "their" child.

In the words of Ralph Waldo Emerson, "It is one of the most beautiful compensations in life that no man can sincerely try to help another without helping himself." Many of the mentors return year after year. As one said, "These children give me the courage and strength to do my job each day with pride and respect. They are the real heroes."

Summary

The average American doesn't understand the immense sacrifices military families make for the country. Being a military family requires a certain kind of commitment and dedication. When a parent in that family dies in service to his or her country, the rest of the family deserves the very best care possible. The military child, in particular, needs a caring adult to be present for him or her as the surviving parent struggles to regain some balance amid the grief and the added complications of a military death.

The military death requires a special type of grieving, allowing room for the customs and courtesies of the branch of service, the military honors, the assignment of a casualty assistance officer, and the certainty of relocation at some point. Hospices, school counselors, hospitals, and outpatient settings often need guidance to successfully help these military families and children. TAPS is a ready resource. Its mission statement includes helping all who have been affected by a death in the military.

Much can be learned from the U.S. military culture, including honoring the lives that were lived and taking pride in their accomplishments. The ceremony of a military burial service, with its history and traditions, provides a tangible and visible symbol of honor, dignity, and respect. It also provides a fitting final salute that signals the end of one chapter and, with the help of programs like TAPS, the beginning of a new chapter of comfort and healing. That is the message—that we can survive the pain, cherish the memories, and gain strength from walking side by side down this painful journey of grief, alongside those who understand and care.

The children of the men and women who have died in service to the country are proud of their family members' military service. They are among the most worthy recipients of our help as they face the fears and struggles that may lie ahead for years to come. Listen to their stories so that they, too, can begin to heal. Help them as they strive to:

Remember the love, celebrate the life, share the journey.

Betsy Beard is a TAPS peer mentor and frequent contributor to *TAPS Magazine*. In her writing, she draws freely on her own experience of traumatic grief following the death of her only son, SPC Bradley S. Beard, who was killed in action during combat operations in Ar Ramadi, Iraq, on October 14, 2004. She lives in Chapel Hill, North Carolina, with her husband Randy and their daughter Staci. Before Brad's death, she worked in various fields, including banking, substitute teaching, and medical laboratory technology.

For their invaluable contributions of background and anecdotal information in this chapter, as well as in its initial development, the author wishes to thank **Judith Mathewson, Heather Campagna**, and **Tina Saari**, who tirelessly and selflessly give of themselves to the bereaved military children of TAPS throughout the year and especially during the Good Grief Camps. Judith Mathewson, M.Ed., M.S., is a lieutenant colonel in the Air National Guard. She was instrumental in the conception of the TAPS Good Grief Camp and continues to serve as its director. Tina Saari, wife of an Army Blackhawk pilot with a background in education, and Heather Campagna, an Army spouse and school psychologist, serve as co-directors of the Regional TAPS Good Grief Camps and provide daily support to the children of America's military.

REFERENCES

Beeney, S. K., & Chung, J. A. (2005). *A Kid's Journey of Grief.* Long Beach: Vision Unlimited Publishers.

Berkes, H. (2007). Grief camp helps children cope with war losses. *NPR All Things Considered.* Retrieved August 22, 2007 from www.npr.org/templates/story/story.php?storyId=13863193

Brown, A. K. (2007). Camp offers comfort to children of war victims. *Army Times.* Retrieved August 19, 2007 from http://www.armytimes.com/news/2007/08/ap_griefcamp_070818/

Department of Defense. (2007, July). *A survivor's guide to benefits: Taking care of our own.* Retrieved October 22, 2007 from https://cs.mhf.dod.mil/content/dav/mhf/QOL-Library/Project%20Documents/MilitaryHOMEFRONT/Service%20Providers/Casualty%20Assistance/Survivors%20Guide.pdf

Emerson, R. Retrieved October 22, 2007 from http://www.quoteworld.org/quotes/4507

Gibbs, D. A., Martin, S., Kupper, L., Johnson, R. (2007). Child maltreatment in enlisted soldiers' families during combat-related deployment. *JAMA, 298,* 528–535.

Goldman, L. (2007). Common signs of grief. *TAPS Magazine, 13*(3), 10–13.

Gurian, A., Kamboukas, D., Levine, E., Pearlman, M., Wasser, R. (2006). *Caring for kids after trauma Disaster, and death: A guide for parents and professionals, revised September 2006.* New York: Institute for Trauma and Stress, New York University Child Study Center.

McCrimmon, K. K. (2007). Living fellowship honors the fallen. *Rocky Mountain News.* Retrieved August 18, 2007 from www.rockymountainnews.com/drmn/local/article/0,1299,DRMN_15_5676729,00.html

Meadow, R. (2007). Sharing the journey. *Rocky Mountain News.* August 18, 2007, News, p. 27.

Parga, E. B. (2007). *No child should grieve alone.* Reno, NV: The Solace Tree.

Sims, D. (2006a). Issues of grieving children. *Touchstones on Grief.* Retrieved September 18, 2007 from www.touchstonesongrief.com/touchstones/articles/ISSUES%20OF%20GRIEVING%20CHILDREN.pdf

Sims, D. (2006b). Myths about children and grief. *Touchstones on Grief.* Retrieved September 18, 2007 from www.touchstonesongrief.com/touch-stones/articles/MYTHS%20About%20Children%20and%20Grief.pdf

TAPS (Tragedy Assistance Program for Survivors, Inc.). (2007). Our mission. Retrieved September 20, 2007 from www.taps.org/mission

United States Army. (2007, April 27). *Warrior Ethos.* Retrieved December 6, 2007 from http://www.army.mil/warriorethos/

Weller, R. (2007). Families share grief, comfort over loved ones lost in Iraq. *AP, Fort Carson, CO.* August 17, 2007. Retrieved September 15, 2007 from www.examiner.com/a-887085~Families_ share_ grief__comfort_over_loved_ones_lost_in_Iraq.html

Therapeutic Interventions with Children and Adolescents

T he final section of the book considers a crucial question: How can we develop therapeutic interventions for grieving children and adolescents? David Crenshaw differentiates grief support and counseling (where the goal is to help children deal with the normal, albeit painful, process of grief) from grief therapy (which attempts to help children deal with more complicated or traumatic losses). Assessment is a key skill to determine the most helpful approach, but Crenshaw acknowledges the importance of support even when grief is neither traumatic nor complicated. This point is reaffirmed in Rebecca Wayne's *Voices* piece.

The next three chapters explore specific modalities. Sherry Schachter and Maria Georgopoulos describe Calvary Hospital's (a palliative care hospital in New York) Camp Courageous. They offer an extensive review of camp programs and explain the need for such programs to deal with the wide range of reactions and issues experienced by grieving children. Donna Schuurman touches on some of the same points in her chapter on grief groups. Both chapters emphasize that interventions should be evidence-based, theoretically grounded, and constantly evaluated. Nancy Boyd Webb's chapter describes play therapy, which is an effective strategy for children to explore and explain, at least symbolically, the meaning of their loss.

These three chapters reaffirm the importance of expressive therapies with children. Such therapies—which can include modalities such as art, music, play, storytelling, dance, sculpture, photography, and film, to name a few (see Bertman, 1999)—are valuable in a number of ways. First, they are *natural* activities that children often do on their own and with others. Few children find it natural to speak with an adult in a therapeutic setting. Second, expressive therapies are *cathartic* in that they allow children to act on their feelings and thoughts. Finally, such modalities are *reflective* and *projective*. They allow the therapist and the child to reflect on the activity, and the child may project latent thoughts and emotions onto the work.

Kenneth Doka's chapter offers another modality—that of ritual. Doka emphasizes two points. First, rituals are historic methods for handling loss. Because they are so powerful, children benefit from opportunities for inclusion. Second, rituals can be adapted and used as an effective intervention with grieving children and adolescents.

Libba James, Kevin Ann Oltjenbruns, and Peggy Whiting provide an important reminder in their chapter of the role of the Internet as a source of grief support for adolescents and children. Contemporary adolescents and children are *digital natives*—they have grown up with computers and the Internet. Most adults, on the other hand, are *digital immigrants*, having migrated to that world. It is natural for adolescents and children to look toward the Internet as a source of support, information, and memorialization as they cope with loss. The chapter is a reminder that adults are limited in their ability to control the information and support children receive, and that they should be asking questions about the ways adolescents and children are using technology as they grieve.

Robert Stevenson's chapter reminds us that children grieve not only at home but at school, where they are likely to spend a lot of time. He offers suggestions for ways schools can provide support for their students. Mike Santoro reiterates that need in the *Voices* piece.

The last two chapters illustrate the problems inherent in particular types of losses. Lillian Range discusses the complicating factors of adolescent suicide, and Marcia Lattanzi Licht reviews the ways schools and other organizations can respond to public tragedy. These chapters remind us that interventive strategies must be sensitively designed for different circumstances of loss. In addition to strategies to deal with adolescent suicide or public tragedy, specialized approaches are required to work with children or adolescents who have experienced trauma (Cohen, Mannarino, & Deblinger, 2006) or specific types of death such as from AIDS (Geballe, Gruendel, & Andiman, 1995).

The book concludes with appendices that offer additional print and organizational resources.

REFERENCES

Bertman, S. (Ed.). (1999). *Grief and the healing arts: Creativity as therapy.* Amityville, NY: Baywood Publishing.

Cohen, J. A., Mannarino, A., & Deblinger, E. (2006). *Treating trauma and traumatic grief in children and adolescents.* New York: Guilford Press.

Geballe, S., Gruendel, J., & Andiman, W. (Eds.). (1995). *Forgotten children of the AIDS epidemic.* New York: Guilford Press.

CHAPTER 12

Grief Therapy with Children and Adolescents: An Overview

David A. Crenshaw

Not every child or adolescent who experiences the death of a loved one will need grief therapy. Even though the death of loved ones, family members, and close friends can be devastating and acutely painful, to avoid self-fulfilling prophecies we should never assume trauma. Throughout human history, the love and support of surviving family members, the concern and caring of the community, and the guidance and help offered by spiritual advisers have been the primary sources of solace. Grief is inevitable in the course of a life journey, because death is as natural a part of it as birth. It is a mistake to pathologize a child's normal—although painful—response to the death of someone close. (For ease of communication in this chapter, "child" or "children" will include adolescents unless otherwise noted)

WHO NEEDS INTERVENTION?

Worden (1996) summarized the findings of the Harvard Child Bereavement Study that most bereaved children don't need special counseling, but about a third of children exhibit emotional or behavioral difficulties serious enough to justify some type of counseling intervention during the first two years of bereavement.

Bonanno (2004) argued that we underestimate the resilience of people in coping with adversity in life. He discussed the trait of "hardiness," which helps to buffer exposure to extreme stress (Kobasa, Maddi, & Kahn, 1982). Bonanno said that hardiness consists of three dimensions: (1) a commitment to finding a meaningful purpose in life; (2) the belief that one can influence one's surroundings and the outcome of events (internal locus of control); and (3) the belief that one can learn and grow from both positive and negative life experiences. Buffered by these beliefs, "hardy individuals" appraise potentially stressful situations as less threatening than others do, thus minimizing the experience of distress. Hardy individuals also are more confident and better able to use positive coping mechanisms, such as problem solving, and to find support to help them deal with the distress they do experience (Florian, Mikulincer, & Taubman, 1995).

Bonanno (2004) observes that clinicians who provide critical incident debriefing and grief work in the aftermath of exposure to a potentially traumatic event ignore the hardiness inherent in people. Providing services, according to Bonanno, is usually unnecessary and, in some cases, can have a deleterious effect, at least for those capable of normal grieving. Bonanno asserts that critical incident debriefing, grief therapy, or any form of treatment should be offered only after a thorough assessment of the clinical needs of exposed individuals. He makes the point that chronic posttraumatic stress disorder (PTSD) is of great concern but stresses that "the vast majority of individuals exposed to violent or life-threatening events do not go on to develop the disorder" (p. 24).

Not all stressful experiences are traumatizing. Searching for pathology and ignoring healthy responses to adversity is an ill-advised practice. Bonanno's writings bring a more balanced view to the topic, but they should not cloud our vision about those who—after careful assessment—are in genuine need of treatment. It would be a sad mistake if the concept of resilience were taken to mean that everyone can be resilient or hardy. Neimeyer (2000) reported in a meta-analytic study of grief therapies that 38% of participants got worse after treatment compared with no-treatment controls. Clear benefits were seen, however, when services were provided to bereaved persons who were experiencing chronic grief.

Recently, the negative effects of grief counseling cited by Neimeyer have been challenged in a review by Larson and Hoyt (2007). After a critical examination of Neimeyer's methodology and analysis, they say that such a negative characterization has little or no empirical foundation. These authors take strong issue with the wave of pessimism about the efficacy of grief counseling, which they believe has been based on faulty conclusions and studies with serious methodological and statistical flaws.

Larson and Hoyt summarize their critical review of the literature as follows: "In conclusion, let us emphasize the good news growing out of our investigation of the basis for pessimistic claims about the efficacy of grief counseling: There is no empirical or statistical foundation for these claims. There is no evidence that bereaved clients are harmed by counseling or that clients who are 'normally' bereaved are at special risk. There is not even any strong evidence that grief counseling, as typically practiced, is less efficacious than other forms of counseling and psychotherapy [which have been shown to have strong positive outcomes for many forms of psychological distress—see Lipsey & Wilson, 1993; Wampold, 2001]" (Larson & Hoyt, 2007, p. 354).

While this controversy is far from resolved, it behooves grief counselors and therapists to carefully examine the scientific basis of the claims on both sides and to be careful in drawing conclusions that are not backed by consistent and solid empirical support.

THE CRUCIAL TASK OF ASSESSING NEEDS

To make an informed decision about whether children require (1) no intervention, (2) bereavement counseling or support, or (3) grief therapy, an evaluation must consider what Worden (1996) called "red flags"—the indicators that children or adolescents may require referral to a child therapist. Careful consideration needs to be given to those who may be at greater risk because of an ambivalent or highly conflicted relationship with the deceased and those who are exposed to a sudden death or a death under traumagenic circumstances.

Current research on childhood bereavement suggests that two important conditions should be recognized as requiring intervention by licensed mental health professionals specializing in child therapy and experienced in treating childhood bereavement. The first condition is childhood traumatic grief (CTG), which Cohen and Mannarino (2004) define as a condition in which trauma symptoms impinge on the ability of a child to undertake the normal grieving process. Brown and Goodman (2005) elaborate as follows: "According to our current understanding of CTG and normal grief, thoughts and images of a traumatic nature are so terrifying, horrific, and anxiety provoking that they cause the child to avoid and shut out these thoughts and images that would be comforting reminders of the person who died…. In contrast, a child who does not have intrusive reminders, or who did not experience the death as traumatic, is able to access the person in memory in a manner that is positive and beneficial to integrating the death in his or her total life experience" (pp. 255, 257).

Distressing and intrusive images, reminders, and thoughts of the traumatic circumstances of the death, along with the physiological hyperarousal associated with such re-experiencing, prevent the child from proceeding in an adaptive way with the grieving process. CTG is understood to overlap with but remain distinct from uncomplicated bereavement, adult complicated grief, and PTSD (Cohen, Mannarino, Greenburg, Padlo, & Shipley, 2003).

The second condition that needs to be assessed carefully and requires referral to a child therapist is complicated grief. Webb (2002) describes complicated grief as mourning in which the griever attempts to deny, repress, or avoid the loss and tries to avoid relinquishing the lost loved one. Webb says that complicated grief is more likely to occur after multiple losses or after a sudden or traumatic death. In a preliminary report on a 5-year longitudinal study (Melhem, Moritz, Walker, Shear, & Brent, 2007), complicated grief was significantly related to functional impairment, even after controlling for depression, anxiety, and PTSD. It was also associated with other measures of psychopathology, including suicidal ideation. In this preliminary analysis, complicated grief appears to be a clinically significant syndrome in children and adolescents.

Longitudinal data will help clarify the prognostic significance of complicated grief and its relationship to other psychopathologies. Recently there has been increased interest in complicated grief reactions as a possible new diagnostic category. Empirical support exists for a cluster of diagnostic criteria for complicated grief, marked by efforts to avoid reminders of the deceased, purposelessness and futility, a shattered worldview, and clinically significant disruption in life functioning (Jacobs, Mazure, & Prigerson, 2000). The diagnosis of complicated grief 6 months after a loss has been associated with a range of negative long-term outcomes, both psychological and medical (Prigerson et al., 1997). A recent study determined that complicated grief has independent validity apart from other grief-related psychopathologies such as depression and PTSD (Bonanno et al., 2007).

Among the issues that should be considered in the evaluation process are both risk and protective factors discerned from empirical research. Numerous contributing factors in complex interaction with each other influence the development of trauma in a given child, including hardiness and resilience (Bonanno, 2004; Maddi, 2005) or, conversely, unusual vulnerability (Roe-Burning & Straker, 1997); cognitive processing of the event (Kindt & Engelhard, 2005); concurrent or lifespan trauma exposure and interpersonal factors (Neria & Litz, 2004); gender and ethnicity (Elklit, 2002; Flett, Kazantzis, Long, MacDonald, & Millar, 2004); nature of the traumatic event (Derluyn, Broekaert, Schuyten, & Temmerman, 2004; Elklit, 2002; Heptinstall, Sethna, & Taylor, 2004; McCloskey & Walker, 2000; Roussos et al., 2005); social context in which the grief arises (Parkes, 2002); and nature of the attachments that precede and influence the reaction to bereavement and traumatic life events (Parkes, 2002). To complicate matters further, traumatic death may be superimposed on a history of multiple losses or sociocultural trauma, or a major psychiatric disorder in the child or family. Webb's (2002) comprehensive tripartite assessment of traumatic grief considers the nature of the child, the nature of the traumatic event, and the family and social context.

Children and adolescents undertake grieving in a developmentally sequenced manner (James, 1989). The younger the children, the more they will need to grieve in small steps. A child may grieve minimally at age 5. At age 9, as he develops more advanced cognitive and emotional resources, the loss may trigger further grief as he understands it in a new way. In adolescence, reminders may trigger a period of profound grieving, because he can appreciate the magnitude of his loss in a manner more akin to that of an adult.

It is important for counselors and therapists to approach grief according to developmental constraints and progressions, so they do not pathologize the normal process of child grieving. Also, the assessment process in the acute stages of grief must take into account the wide range of possible responses in the aftermath of loss, especially after a sudden, unexpected death. It is not unusual even for adults in the acute period of grief to express the fear that they are losing their minds. It is a mistake to quickly jump to the conclusion that this is a manifestation of pathological grief, although adequate support and close monitoring should be offered.

Sometimes children or adolescents are brought to therapy at a later time for a symptom that may or may not be related to the death. Careful assessment is needed to evaluate whether blocked, delayed, or distorted grief is contributing to the symptom. It is not unusual for both the child and the family to minimize such a connection, especially if a few years have passed since the death; but often when the symptom is explored, it does originate at least partly in unresolved grief. Sometimes the symptom has symbolic significance. For example, I provided counseling to a 16-year-old after he was arrested for shoplifting. In exploring the origin of the symptom of stealing, I discovered that he was enraged that his childhood had been "stolen" from him by the suicide of his father when he was 8 years old.

Perry and Szalavitz (2006) articulate the danger of improper assessment or intervention in their report on a study conducted at the Child Trauma Academy. The study found that children with supportive families who were assigned to therapy to focus on trauma were more likely to develop PTSD than children whose parents were told to bring them to the clinic only if they noticed specific symptoms. The authors say the weekly therapy focused on their symptoms had the effect of worsening rather than relieving the children's suffering. The children would think about their trauma each week in the days leading up to the therapy session in order to have something to talk about in the session. In addition, some children missed school or their normal extracurricular activities to attend the therapy session at the clinic. The authors note that the therapy disrupted the children's lives instead of relieving their distress.

Another finding of this study was that children who did not have a strong social support network were more likely to benefit from therapy. Thus, the strength of the family and the social support system must be factored into the equation in deciding whether intervention will help or hinder. Comprehensive evaluation of the needs of children and careful treatment planning informed by clinical experience and research can mitigate the iatrogenic effects of intervention.

GRIEF THERAPY VERSUS GRIEF SUPPORT SERVICES AND COUNSELING

It is important to distinguish between bereavement support and counseling services and grief therapy for children. Worden (1996) argues that those who write about intervention with bereaved children frequently fail to make an important distinction between the needs of children who exhibit serious adjustment problems and those who are simply struggling to adapt to the normal process of loss. The appropriate interventions, Worden says, are quite different for the two groups, so careful diagnosis and evaluation are critical.

Bereavement support or counseling services can be offered in an individual, group, or family context. Counseling and support groups are intended to bolster the bereaved person's coping resources and defense mechanisms and to reduce feelings of isolation and disconnection. Because of the reluctance of many bereaved children and adolescents to engage in formal counseling sessions, some community-based programs and school-based programs provide outreach services to those identified as being at risk. The supportive context of individual counseling, a bereavement group, or family counseling can help at a time of painful separation and loss. The implicit message in these forms of counseling is "You are not alone, and we will get through this painful time together."

The cultural landscape has changed greatly in recent decades; in fact, certain major shifts in the lives of extended families date back to the Industrial Revolution. In the agricultural society that prevailed before the development of factories, several generations of a family typically lived in the same house or in separate houses on the family farm. If a death occurred, the family grieved together and helped one another through the painful process of reconciling the loss and moving on with life. Today, families are far more likely to be scattered over a wide geographical area. Children may travel across the country to attend the funeral of a grandparent they barely knew; in previous generations, children might have lived in the same town or even the same house with a grandparent. The gaps in support caused by the fragmentation and geographical scattering of the extended family are felt most deeply at times of family crisis, and the death of a family member is often the most stressful of all life crises. This void has been partially filled by support groups offered by churches, schools, and hospice.

Grief therapy uses specialized techniques to address abnormal or complicated grief reactions. Worden (1991) believed that grief therapy was needed when grief takes the following forms: (1) The complicated grief reaction is manifested as prolonged grief; (2) the grief reaction manifests itself through some masked somatic or behavioral symptom; or (3) the reaction is manifested by an exaggerated grief response.

Grief therapy is a process required by a small minority of grievers; for example, in certain forms of traumatic grief or complicated bereavement syndromes, or when a recent loss is superimposed on a history of multiple losses. Grief therapy may also be required in some instances of disenfranchised grief, such as the suicide of a family member, which may be traumatic and also carries with it stigma, guilt, and shame, so that the surviving family may not receive an outpouring of comfort and support from the community. Grief therapy is sometimes needed when the recent encounter with loss and grief activates unresolved intrapsychic conflicts or old wounds that never healed, with the "unfinished business" being at least partially outside of awareness.

Cohen, Mannarino, Berliner, and Deblinger (2000) reviewed four major components of trauma-focused cognitive behavioral therapy (CBT) for children and adolescents who were exposed to traumatic events. The components described were exposure, cognitive processing and reframing, stress management, and parental treatment. The most recent update of the trauma-focused CBT model, which has garnered increasing empirical support (Cohen, Mannarino, & Deblinger, 2006), delineates both the grief and trauma components of the treatment, along with parent and parent-child interventions. The model is designed as a relatively brief 16-week intervention. The authors clearly state that the treatment is not adequate for all cases of traumatic grief; they stress the need for flexibility and the importance of clinical judgment in the use of the protocol. An even briefer 12-week protocol is undergoing testing (Cohen, Mannarino, & Staron, 2006). An expansion of their model to meet the needs of children who have complicated grief reactions or exposure to repeated trauma was proposed (Crenshaw, 2007). This model is also informed by neurobiological research and interpersonal neurobiological/attachment theory. It includes 12 tasks to address grief and traumatic grief in children and adolescents.

TRAINING FOR THOSE WORKING WITH GRIEVING CHILDREN

Worden (1996) pointed out that bereavement support groups may be led by people with minimal or no training in child therapy. To improve the level of training of those providing grief counseling, the Association for

Death Education and Counseling has established standards for obtaining a Certification in Thanatology. The requirements include a bachelor's degree and 2 years of verified related experience, or a master's or doctorate and 1 year of verified related experience. In addition, 60 documented contact hours in thanatology and related topics are required. The training contact hours consist of course work or workshops in grief counseling.

Licensed child therapists who offer treatment for traumatic grief or complicated grief conditions need solid training in assessment. Skills in intervention—including individual, group, and family therapy—are essential, as is training in bereavement issues, grief therapy, and trauma-informed therapy, whether delivered in the context of individual, group, or family therapy, or a combination thereof.

Perry and Szalavitz (2006) emphasize that grief therapists need to stay abreast of research and evidence-based informed clinical practice. They take issue with the widely held belief that one cannot recover from trauma unless one remembers the specific details of a past trauma. They caution that this can easily become a self-fulfilling prophecy. The authors believe the needs of child trauma survivors vary widely and that no one should be pushed to discuss trauma if they are not ready to do so. They challenge the wisdom of seeking out that one elusive memory that will release the person from suffering, explaining that this is not how the memory system works: "The problem with traumatic memories tends to be their intrusion into the present, not an inability to recall them. When they intrude, discussing them and understanding how they may unconsciously influence our behavior can be extraordinarily helpful" (p. 165).

Another example of how empirical research informs practice is the longitudinal research on guilt and shame (Tangney & Dearing, 2002). These researchers define guilt as "condemnation of a specific act" in contrast to shame, which they define as "condemnation of self." Guilt is a prosocial and constructive emotion that was associated in the longitudinal research with positive social adjustment; shame, on the other hand, was associated with a wide range of psychopathology. Clinicians have not always distinguished between the two and have failed to realize that appropriate guilt simply needs to be validated, whereas shame requires vigorous therapeutic challenge and disputation.

Traits and Core Attributes Required to Work with Grieving Children

Grief therapy with children and adolescents is emotionally taxing work, but it is potentially very rewarding in terms of making a difference in the lives of children and their families. Those who do this work must recognize their vulnerability to "compassion fatigue" (Figley, 1995) and vicarious traumatization. Clinicians need to develop a "self-care package" that includes the support of colleagues, training programs, supervision, consultation with more experienced colleagues, connections with family and close friends, recreation, exercise, and rest. Child clinicians often put themselves second, to the detriment not only of their own well-being but also those they are trying to help.

Grief therapy with children can activate countertransference issues. It is difficult to witness the devastating pain of children during an important loss. The therapist may feel a sense of impotence because he or she cannot remove the child's pain in the acute period of grief. The therapist must be able to accompany children through the acute stage without feeling the need to "move them along" before they are ready to move. If the therapist—out of a sense of powerlessness—seeks to move children quickly to a more hopeful, less despairing place, significant problems may develop in the therapeutic relationship, because the children feel that their grief is being minimized, trivialized, or devalued.

John Bowlby (1979) said many years ago that those who help grieving children are strongly tempted to serve as a "representative of reality" when, in fact, it is far more helpful to simply be a reliable companion on the rough road of grief. The desire to do more can cause problems in the therapeutic process. These countertransference issues make supervision for unseasoned therapists and consultation with colleagues for all therapists essential.

Grief therapists who work with children or adolescents are not exempt from their own losses and grief as they go through life. The self-care package that therapists need to develop should include provision for adequate attention to their own grief as losses arise. A study on countertransference issues in grief work (Hayes, Yeh, & Eisenberg, 2007) and a personal account of the therapist's own grief and its effects on working with grieving clients

(Rappaport, 2000) should be required reading for all therapists who are doing this kind of work.

In the end, what each of us brings to the healing process is that most sensitive of all instruments: our self. It is our ability to make ourselves emotionally available in a sensitive, empathic way without becoming overwhelmed that provides the essential therapeutic context of healing. We cannot afford to neglect the care of that vital healing instrument, our self.

David A. Crenshaw, Ph.D., is a licensed psychologist, Board Certified in Clinical Psychology by the American Board of Professional Psychology (ABPP), and Fellow of the Academy of Clinical Psychology. He is a Registered Play Therapist-Supervisor by the Association of Play Therapy and Co-Founder and current President of the New York Association for Play Therapy. He is author of *Bereavement; A Guidebook for Engaging Resistant Children in Therapy: A Projective Drawing and Storytelling Series* (2004), and two books he co-authored with John B. Mordock, Ph.D., ABP , *Understanding and Treating Aggressive Children: Fawns in Gorilla Suits* and *A Handbook of Play Therapy with Aggressive Children.* His newest book, *Evocative Strategies in Child and Adolescent Psychotherapy,* was published by Rowman & Littlefield Publishers in September 2006. Two forthcoming books, *Therapeutic Engagement with Children and Adolescents: Play, Symbol, Drawing, and Storytelling Strategies* and *Child and Adolescent Psychotherapy: Wounded Spirits and Healing Paths* will be published in the coming year by Rowman & Littlefield. He worked in residential treatment with children for 30 years and was Clinical Director of the Astor Home for Children Residential Treatment Center from 1986-2001. Dr. Crenshaw is currently on the Board of Directors of the Astor Home for Children and a Member of its Governance Committee. He is the Founder and Director of the Rhinebeck Child and Family Center, LLC, which offers training and consultation to clinicians and agencies working with at-risk youth.

REFERENCES

Bonanno, G. A. (2004). Loss, trauma, and human resilience: Have we underestimated the human capacity to thrive after extremely aversive events? *American Psychologist, 59,* 20–28.

Bonanno, G. A., Neria, Y., Mancini, A., Coifman, K. G., Litz, B., & Insel, B. (2007). Is there more to complicated grief than depression and posttraumatic stress disorder? A test of incremental validity. *Journal of Abnormal Psychology, 116,* 342–351.

Bowlby, J. (1979). *The making and breaking of affectional bonds.* London: Tavistock Publications.

Brown, E. J., & Goodman, R. F. (2005). Childhood traumatic grief: An exploration of the construct in children bereaved on September 11. *Journal of Clinical Child and Adolescent Psychology, 34,* 248–259.

Cohen, J., & Mannarino, A. (2004). Treatment of childhood traumatic grief. *Journal of Clinical Child and Adolescent Psychology, 33,* 819–831.

Cohen, J., Mannarino, A., Berliner, L., & Deblinger, E. (2000). Trauma-focused cognitive behavioral therapy for children and adolescents: An empirical update. *Journal of Interpersonal Violence, 15,* 1202–1223.

Cohen, J., Mannarino, A., & Deblinger, E. (2006). *Treating trauma and traumatic grief in children and adolescents.* New York: Guilford Press.

Cohen, J., Mannarino, A., Greenberg, T., Padlo, S., & Shipley, C. (2003). Childhood traumatic grief: Concepts and controversies. *Biological Psychiatry, 53,* 827–833.

Cohen, J. A., Mannarino, A. P., & Staron, V. R. (2006). A pilot study of modified cognitive-behavioral therapy for childhood traumatic grief (CBT-CTG). *Journal of the American Academy of Child and Adolescent Psychiatry, 45,* 1465–1473.

Crenshaw, D. A. (2007). An interpersonal neurobiological-informed treatment model for childhood traumatic grief. *Omega, 54,* 315–332.

Derluyn, L., Broekaert, E., Schuyten, G., & Temmerman, E. D. (2004). Post-traumatic stress in former Ugandan child soldiers. *Lancet, 363,* 861–863.

Elklit, A. (2002). Victimization and PTSD in a Danish national youth probability sample. *Journal of the American Academy of Child and Adolescent Psychiatry, 41,* 174–181.

Figley, C. R. (Ed.) (1995). *Compassion fatigue: Coping with secondary traumatic stress disorder in those who treat the traumatized.* New York: Brunner/Mazel.

Flett, R. A., Kazantzis, N., Long, N. R., MacDonald, C., & Millar, M. (2004). Gender and ethnicity differences in the prevalence of traumatic events: Evidence from a New Zealand community sample. *Stress and Health: Journal of the International Society for the Investigation of Stress, 20,* 149–157.

Florian, V., Mikulincer, M., & Taubman, O. (1995). Does hardiness contribute to mental health during a stressful real-life situation? The role of appraisal and coping. *Journal of Personality and Social Psychology, 68,* 687–695.

Hayes, J. A., Yeh, Y.-J., & Eisenberg, A. (2007). Good grief and not-so-good grief: Countertransference in bereavement therapy. *Journal of Clinical Psychology, 63,* 345–355.

Heptinstall, E., Sethna, V., & Taylor, E. (2004). PTSD and depression in refugee children: Associations with pre-migration trauma and post-migration stress. *European Child and Adolescent Psychiatry, 13,* 373–380.

Jacobs, D., Mazure, C., & Prigerson, H. (2000). Diagnostic criteria for traumatic grief. *Death Studies, 24,* 185–199.

James, B. (1989). *Treating traumatized children: New insights and creative interventions.* Lexington, MA: Lexington Books.

Kindt, M., & Engelhard, I. M. (2005). Trauma processing and the development of posttraumatic stress disorder. *Journal of Behavior Therapy and Experimental Psychiatry, 36,* 69–76.

Kobasa, S. C., Maddi, S. R., & Kahn, S. (1982). Hardiness and health: A prospective study. *Journal of Personality and Social Psychology, 42,* 168–177.

Larson, D. G., & Hoyt, W. T. (2007). What has become of grief counseling? An evaluation of the empirical foundations of the new pessimism. *Professional Psychology: Research and Practice, 38,* 347–355.

Lipsey, M. W., & Wilson, D. B. (1993). The efficacy of psychological, educational, and behavioral treatment: Confirmation from meta-analysis. *American Psychologist, 48,* 1181–1209.

Maddi, S. R. (2005). On hardiness and other pathways to resilience. *American Psychologist, 60,* 261–262.

McCloskey, L. A., & Walker, M. (2000). Posttraumatic stress in children exposed to family violence and single event trauma. *Journal of the American Academy of Child and Adolescent Psychiatry, 39,* 108–115.

Melhem, N. M., Moritz, G., Walker, M., Shear, M. K., & Brent, D. (2007). Phenomenology and correlates of complicated grief in children and adolescents. *Journal of the American Academy of Child and Adolescent Psychiatry, 46,* 493–499.

Neria, Y., & Litz, B. T. (2004). Bereavement by traumatic means: The complex synergy of trauma and grief. *Journal of Loss and Trauma, 9,* 73–78.

Neimeyer, R. A. (2000). Searching for the meaning of meaning: Grief therapy and the process of reconstruction. *Death Studies, 24,* 541–548.

Parkes, C. M. (2002). Grief: Lessons from the past, visions for the future. *Death Studies, 26,* 367–385.

Perry, B. D., & Szalavitz, M. (2006). *The boy who was raised as a dog and other stories from a child psychiatrist's notebook.* New York: Basic Books.

Prigerson, H. G., Beirhals, A. J., Kasl, S. V., Reynolds, C. F., Shear, M. K., et al. (1997). Traumatic grief as a risk factor for mental and physical morbidity. *American Journal of Psychiatry, 154,* 616–623.

Rappaport, J. (2000). Traumatic time: The therapist's mourning. *Psychoanalysis and Psychotherapy. 17,* 55–64.

Roe-Burning, S., & Staker, G. (1997). The association between illusions of invulnerability and exposure to trauma. *Journal of Traumatic Stress. 10,* 319–327.

Roussos, A., Goenjian, A. K., Steinberg, A. M., Sotriopoulou, C., Kakaki, M., Kabakos, et al. (2005). Posttraumatic stress and depressive reactions among children and adolescents after the 1999 earthquake in Ano Liosia, Greece. *American Journal of Psychiatry, 162,* 530–537.

Tangney, J. P., & Dearing, R. L. (2002). *Shame and guilt.* New York: Guilford Press.

Wampold, B. E. (2001). *The great psychotherapy debate: Models, methods, and findings.* Mahwah, NJ: Erlbaum.

Webb, N. B. (2002). Complicated grief—Dual losses of godfather's death and parents' separation: Case of the Martini family. In N. B. Webb (Ed.), *Helping bereaved children: A handbook for practitioners* (2nd ed.) (pp.70–93). New York: Guilford Press.

Worden, J. W. (1991). *Grief counseling and grief therapy: A handbook for the mental health practitioner* (2nd ed.). New York: Springer.

Worden, J. W. (1996). *Children and grief: When a parent dies.* New York: Guilford Press.

CHAPTER 13

Camps for Grieving Children: Lessons from the Field

Sherry R. Schachter and Maria Georgopoulos

INTRODUCTION

Bereaved children have unique needs that may go unnoticed because of their inability to fully understand and express their feelings as readily or openly as adults. Therapeutic interventions with children must be creative and unique to tap into the well of inner resources that each child possesses. It is widely accepted that children respond well to play and artful expression because these mediums help them give voice to their inner worlds much more effectively than talk therapy. Therapeutic interventions such as bereavement camps incorporate both artwork and play to draw children into grief work.

NEEDS OF BEREAVED CHILDREN

Approximately 4% of children in the United States under the age of 18 years have experienced the death of a parent (Sandler, Ayers, & Wolchik, 2003; Wolchik, Tein, Sandler, & Ayers, 2006). U.S. Census Bureau data from 2002 indicate that about 857,000 children in the United States live in a single-parent household because of the death of the other parent (Lohan, 2006). This is significant, because "a parent's death is perceived as a loss of security, nurture, and affection" (DeSpelder & Strickland, 2002, p. 363). The death of a parent is a highly stressful event for children that can leave them at risk for complicated grief (Cerel, Fristad, Verducci, Weller, & Weller, 2006; Christ & Christ, 2006; Kirwin & Hamrin, 2005). Bereaved children exhibit symptoms of distress that frequently include pain, sadness, anger, confusion, sleep disturbances, and an inability to focus on schoolwork (Corr, 2000; Dowdney,

2000; Lohan, 2006). In addition, about 20% of bereaved children exhibit a wide range of emotional and behavioral symptoms that can persist for 2 years after a parent's death (Dowdney, 2000; Worden, 1996).

One of the variables that can affect the grieving process is the support systems available to bereaved children (Charkow, 1998). Studies have shown that with adequate family resources and competent substitute care, including enhanced parenting skills and emotional support, bereaved children are better able to return to their previous level of functioning (Christ & Christ, 2006). Studies have shown a higher rate of psychological symptoms and distress is found in children who have less stable home environments and those from families that have few resources or supports (Dowdney et al., 1999; Sanders, 1998; Worden, 1996; Zambelli & DeRosa, 1992). Open communication and shared information between the surviving parent and the child are associated with better psychological outcomes for bereaved children (Christ, 2000).

The insecurity and loss of affection that children experience when they lose a parent is typically not seen after the death of a sibling (DeSpelder & Strickland 2002). However, children who experience a sibling's death often have an increased sense of their own vulnerability to death. This may be even more prevalent when the deceased sibling is close in age to the surviving child. A recent study of healthy siblings' experiences with cancer (Woodgate, 2006) was conducted with 30 children between the ages of 6 and 21 years (mean age = 12 years). The author noted that healthy siblings were at risk for many behavioral problems, including poor school performance, increased anger, feelings of guilt, isolation, loneliness, and increased anxiety. The study concluded that healthy siblings reported sadness, stress, and an increase in family disruption. Children who experience the death of a sibling may have a profound sense of loss as their roles within the family change (Creed, Ruffin, & Ward, 2001; DeSpelder & Strickland 2002; Worden, 1996) and their assumptions and expectations about the future are challenged. Not infrequently, parents are so engulfed in their own grief over the loss of a child that they are not able to "parent" their surviving child(ren), thus creating further loss for the bereaved child(ren). The need is great to facilitate a healthy response to bereavement, as children who experience these losses can suffer long-lasting deleterious effects (Mitchell et al., 2007; Rando, 1984; Zambelli & DeRosa, 1992).

In her comprehensive article on bereavement interventions that facilitate the normal grief process, Steen (1998) describes the importance of identifying, assessing, and mitigating risks for bereavement complications and health deterioration. She notes the importance of intervening with bereaved children in a timely manner, quoting one counselor who said, "[A]ll children and adolescents need a grief support group of peers within 3 to 6 months of their loss" (p. 67). Children who are not supported in the early phases of their grief are at high risk for complicated grief and major psychiatric disorders (Kirwin & Hamrin, 2005).

A variety of psycho-educational and psycho-social programs are available for bereaved children and adolescents. These include individual therapy, support groups, and opportunities to attend bereavement camps or retreats. Children who are supported after a significant death can grow emotionally without becoming maladjusted. Studies have shown that attendance at bereavement support groups and bereavement camps is helpful for children (Christ & Christ 2006; Creed et al., 2001; Mitchell et al., 2007; Steen, 1998) and teens (Geis, Whittlesey, McDonald, Smith, & Pfefferbaum, 1998).

LITERATURE REVIEW—BEREAVEMENT CAMPS

Although more programs exist today than in the past, their effectiveness has not been fully explored or documented, nor are they readily available to all who could benefit from participating. A recent Internet search for "bereavement camps" produced 721,000 hits. Included were weekend camps, summer camps, year-round camps, sleepover camps, and day camps. However, a review of the literature on camps for bereaved children and adolescents indicates a paucity of information. Theoretical and clinical implications for such programs are limited, despite the positive anecdotal experience of many clinicians.

Camp Sunrise

In 1995, Summers described Camp Sunrise, a 4-day sleepover camp initiated in 1985 by Bannock Regional Medical Center and Geriatric Center in Idaho, whose goal is to support healthy grieving for children. In 1992, 34 children between the ages of 8 and 16 years attended the camp. Summers identified three major objectives of the camp: giving children permission to grieve; exposing them to others who also had experienced the death of a significant family member or friend; and creating an environment that supports friendship and play as a way of showing them that loss is a part of life while affirming that they can find meaning in continuing to live their own lives.

Campers were recruited through advertisements in local newspapers and brochures sent to hospitals and pediatricians in the community. Telephone interviews were conducted with interested parents to describe the program. Parents completed a fact sheet and children completed an information form. To gain a clearer understanding of the loss, the forms included questions about who died and whether the child attended the funeral service. Two weeks before the camp, parents and family members met with participating health professionals (nurses, pediatricians, clergy, social workers, and counselors) and received general information relating to children's grief process as well as information about the program.

Children were assigned to cabins according to age and gender. The camp experience included both bereavement and recreational activities. Bereavement activities focused on helping the children identify and express their feelings of loss; they included a candle ceremony, a tree planting, making friendship bracelets, and painting T-shirts. These activities were broken into large and small group sessions to encourage communication and the expression of feelings. Recreational activities were geared toward teamwork and included basketball and water volleyball.

A week after the end of the camp, evaluations were sent to parents and children; a month later, a pizza party was held at which participants could share memories of the experience and view photographs taken during the camp. Parents were provided with additional literature about children's grief, to promote healthy communication among family members.

Summers noted that Camp Sunrise met its stated goals in that the children formed new friendships and shared their feelings of loss with one another. The comments in the evaluations were very positive, indicating that the camp inspired the children to learn how to cope with their loss and hold on to their memories. From the article, it appears that Camp Sunrise is a one-time experience for bereaved children; there is no indication of follow-up with the children or families to further facilitate or evaluate their grieving process.

Camp Carousel

Camp Carousel—a weekend retreat for bereaved children, teens, and adults—was started in 1991 by the Hospice of Winston-Salem in North Carolina (LoCicero, Burkhart, & Gray, 1998). The model includes not only grieving children and teens but their family members as well. The retreat aims to equip parents and other adults with the tools they need to experience their own grief and to help children with theirs. Recently, the camp was opened to any adult who is grieving a loss, not only those who have a child attending. Campers fill out evaluations at the end of the weekend and receive information about resources for assistance with their grief process, including written material and referrals for individual counseling.

The founders of the camp used Worden's Four Tasks of Mourning (Worden, 1991) and Wolfelt's Six Reconciliation Needs of Mourning (Wolfelt, 1996) as their theoretical model. Staff members include a combination of professionals and volunteers; they attend 10 hours of training focusing on communication skills, group process, and developmental differences in children as they relate to the grief process. During the weekend, peer group activities help the campers build support networks and normalize their grief process, while cabin group activities address grief issues related to gender and focus on building trust and providing positive role modeling. All the participants of the camp come together for certain activities.

In the weekend described by LoCicero and colleagues (1998), the children were grouped according to age and type of loss for five distinct sessions. In Session I, the children acknowledged the reality of the death by sharing details of the death and what they remembered about this difficult time. In Session II, they shared memories and explored their relationship with their loved one through art activities (e.g., making memorial candles that were later used in a remembrance ritual). In Session III, they explored coping skills and support systems, and discussed self-identity. Session IV initiated the process of closure for the campers. During this session, children were given a certificate for their courage in expressing themselves. The closing ceremony in Session V included a balloon release. Throughout the weekend, the adults participated in parenting classes to help them learn how to deal with their children's grief. Bereaved adults also participated in art activities, such as making a memorial candle. Adults participated in their own groups, with the exception of the closing ceremony at which everyone came together. The authors suggest that a follow-up group session or phone calls would be beneficial to assess how the campers are coping and whether additional resources are needed.

Comfort Zone Camp

Comfort Zone Camp (McDonald, 2006) was initiated in 1998 and currently operates in three locations. In the Richmond, Virginia, area, it facilitates children's support groups and a weekend camp program for grieving children and adolescents. After the terrorist attacks of September 11, 2001, sites in New York and New Jersey were added for children who lost a loved one at the Twin Towers or the Pentagon. The camp serves bereaved children ages 7–17 years and is limited to 35 campers per session.

Each child is paired with a trained volunteer (a Big Buddy), who spends the weekend providing support and encouragement. Licensed counselors facilitate the programs and teach techniques and coping skills that will help the grieving child. At the conclusion of the weekend, parents/guardians attend a closing memorial session. Children may return to camp for reunion events as friendships continue over time.

A unique quality of this program is that the camps are run throughout the year, which increases the number of children who can be helped in their grieving process. Comfort Zone Camp has helped more than 2,000 children and claims to be the largest independent bereavement camp in the United States. The camp is free; it is supported by donations from individuals, corporations, and civic groups.

Camp New Horizons

Creed and colleagues (2001) describe Camp New Horizons, a weekend camp for bereaved siblings. In the study period, 19 children attended the camp; they were separated into two groups: ages 6–11 and 12–15 years. Each of the campers had a sibling who had died of cancer within the past 3 years. Camp activities addressed four specific goals: reducing the campers' feelings of isolation; helping campers express themselves; educating campers about the grief process; and facilitating the campers in moving forward in their process (p. 17). On the last day of camp, the children's families were invited to participate in a closing event.

With the exception of a musician and an artist, all staff members and counselors were volunteers (e.g., social workers, nurses, bereavement nurse coordinator, child life specialist) with specific training and education in the grief process of children. Campers, staff, and parents completed written evaluations at the conclusion of the program.

The clinical staff of the camp identified several changes they hoped to incorporate into their program, including extending the admissions criteria beyond 3 years. They recognize that grief is not time-limited, and parents and campers have expressed a desire to return to the camp after the three-year period.

Pilot Study of the Effectiveness of a Grief Camp for Children

Nabors and colleagues (2004) describe a 3-day hospice-sponsored sleepover camp for bereaved children between the ages of 6 and 12 years (N = 18) who had lost a parent or grandparent. The aim of this pilot study was to evaluate children's perceptions of the effectiveness of a grief camp. Staffing for the camp included trained counselors and volunteers from hospice and similar programs. Volunteer training was conducted through a manual developed by a hospice program.

The camp included bereavement and recreational activities. The bereavement activities included writing letters to the deceased loved one and participating in a ceremony to honor the memory of the person. Three key activities were identified in the study: making feeling masks; developing a board game to explore feelings of grief; and a question-answer session with a physician.

Researchers used a 4-point Likert scale and open-ended questions to evaluate the effectiveness of the camp experience. Parents completed a Likert scale survey before the camp and a similar survey after the camp. During the camp, campers used a Likert scale to evaluate the activities. At the end of camp, counselors helped the children answer open-ended questions related to their experience. Some of the children were also surveyed by phone 6 months later.

Before the camp, parents reported children's distress in the form of sadness, anxiety, and low grades since the death of their loved one. Most of the children were still feeling sad or anxious after the camp, and some had emotional reactions to the camp experience that triggered their grief. The surveys showed that despite distress in many areas of their lives, children's friendships were a strong source of support and comfort to them. The children reported that they were helped by the camp experience, particularly the peer support and counseling activities. Most of the children were very satisfied with the feelings mask activity but not with the board game activity.

The session with the physician proved to be very useful to the children. The campers were divided into two groups by age. The younger children asked about changes that occur to the body during death and whether the cause of death of their loved one was contagious. Some younger children asked whether people can come back to life. The older group wondered about the physical changes they saw in the body after the death and what they meant.

The camp had many benefits for the bereaved children and for the parents who came to observe some of the activities over the weekend. Children benefited from meeting peers who shared a similar loss and from having a supportive space to express their feelings. Friendship and play were important aspects of the experience.

The authors strongly suggest maintaining contact with children after such a camp and providing families with referrals for further grief counseling. On the basis of the positive responses they received from both children and parents, they see a potential value in family grief camps as a way of helping children adjust to their loss.

CALVARY HOSPITAL

Calvary Hospital in the Bronx was established in 1899 by the Women of Calvary, a group of 11 Catholic widows who initially cared for indigent and terminally ill women. These women were assisted first by the Dominican Sisters of Blauvet and later by the Dominican Sisters of the Sick Poor. Since 1974, a lay administration has led the program (Cimino & Brescia, 1998).

This one-of-a-kind hospital has 200 beds devoted to palliative care for adults with advanced cancer. The hospital has approximately 4,000 cancer deaths a year, which is about 15% of all the cancer deaths in New York City (Schachter, 2007). A 25-bed satellite program in Brooklyn provides the same services and philosophy of care to families in that location. In addition, Calvary Hospital has a home hospice program, initiated in 1998, with a census of approximately 185 patients a day. Embedded in the hospital's mission is the philosophy of nonabandonment. This is evidenced by the numerous bereavement services the hospital provides without charge to family members and the community. The need to facilitate healthy bereavement, from cancer deaths as well as sudden or violent deaths, is great. [*The authors of this chapter are the director of bereavement services (SRS) and the bereavement counselor (MG) for Calvary Hospital and Calvary Hospice. They coordinate all the bereavement programs for the institution.*]

Bereavement Services for Children and Teens

Calvary Hospital has a long tradition of providing bereavement services for adults in the community. Adult bereavement programs began in the 1960s; the children's and teen programs followed in 1991 and 2001, respectively. Precious Moments is a weekly support group for bereaved children ages 6–11 years; teen groups are available for adolescents 12–18 years. In response to increasing demand, the hospital has created additional groups.

Studies have shown that peer interactions become more important during middle childhood and preadolescence (Mitchell et al., 2007), and take on a special role in adolescence, as the child builds on previous experiences and skills (Englund, Levy, Hyson, & Croufe, 2000). The teen groups allow older children to interact with bereaved peers, which helps them realize that they are not alone (Mitchell et al., 2007; Webb, 1993). The teens participate in art therapy and other expressive opportunities as effective methods of facilitating their grief (Mitchell et al., 2007; McIntyre, 1992). Providing opportunities for the bereaved child or teen to participate in support groups helps the child and can also relieve the grieving parent (Christ & Christ, 2006).

The Bronx (1 of the 5 boroughs of New York City) is an urban area; the children and teens who live there reflect the diversity of the city. Many are economically disadvantaged and live in poor neighborhoods. More than two-thirds are Latino and African American. In many cases, family ties are tenuous. While many of the hospital's bereaved children come from the families of patients, referrals also come from a variety of other sources: parents and guardians, social workers in the community and at other hospitals, school guidance counselors, and case workers from the New York City Administration for Children's Services. In some instances, the hospital receives referrals from the courts, which may mandate that a troubled child attend bereavement groups. Families in this population experience many sources of stress in addition to the death of a loved one (e.g., teen pregnancy, a higher incidence of divorce and separation) (Opie et al., 1992). Clinicians and researchers often recommend participation in support groups as an appropriate intervention for bereavement.

The children Calvary serves are often dealing with multiple traumas and losses within the family that may be unrelated to the death of a loved one. In working with the children, it is necessary to address these traumas and losses, because they complicate their development as well as their grief process. The following story illustrates this situation.

One of our teens had suffered losses on many levels at a very young age. Both of his biological parents were alcoholics. When he was 2 years old, his father took him out of the country to live with him and his girlfriend. The child grew up believing these were his biological parents. He was privy to their constant arguing and was frequently physically and verbally abused by his father. At the age of 12, he witnessed his father stabbing the girlfriend. At the same time, his father told him that this woman was not his mother. He was sent to live with his biological mother, who had gotten sober and married. He felt confused and vulnerable in this new home in a new country, and overwhelmed by the trauma he had experienced. A few years later, his mother relapsed. Over the next three years, she was in and out of rehabilitation centers, and the boy was left with an enormous amount of responsibility for maintaining the household and caring for his younger siblings. When he was 16, his mother was diagnosed with ovarian cancer. During her illness, the boy was her primary caregiver until she died a year later.

Needless to say, this boy's grief was greatly complicated by the dynamics of his family situation. It took him many months in the support group to get in touch with all the different variables of his grief and address all the losses he has experienced. Slowly but steadily, he came to trust the consistency of the weekly group, which has given him a safe place to explore his feelings. His identification with his peers has helped him discuss the anger and shame he felt about his family situation and share more honestly about the dynamics of his family. He has been able to review his relationship with his mother and to grieve both the positive and negative aspects of it. By the end of the first year, his school attendance and grades had improved enough so that he could graduate from high school and start college.

Camp Courageous

In 1997, Calvary initiated Camp Courageous. Although Precious Moments and the teen groups meet throughout the year, the idea was to provide a safe environment where children and teens could come together in a different venue and where intensive activities could be planned to further their growth. Each year since then, the program has expanded, with new activities that are congruent with current research. The weeklong day camp is supported by the hospital and by corporate donations and grants. (All bereavement groups and Camp Courageous are free.) Attendance is restricted to children and teens who have attended the hospital's support groups or are known to the staff.

In the summer of 2007, Camp Courageous celebrated its 10th year, with 37 campers and 21 counselors in attendance. In addition to children and teens in this year's support groups, we invited alumni campers from 2006 to join us for the week. Campers ranged in age from 5 to 18 years. Most counselors were staff members from Calvary Hospital's nursing and hospice departments; they were joined by others from pastoral care, the laboratory, the pharmacy, and even the security department. Because many of the children live in households headed by women, we recognize the need to have male counselors who can act as role models for the campers. An orientation was conducted to educate the counselors on the grief process of children and to provide important information on each child's progress in the support groups during the year. Counselors were matched with campers according to the needs of the children and the interests/specialties of the counselors. The counselor:camper ratio was 1:2—we believe it is important for campers to receive individual attention from counselors and have an opportunity to share their stories with counselors as well as with their peers. Campers and counselors participated in various bereavement and recreational activities throughout the week. On the last day, campers, parents/guardians, and counselors completed evaluations.

A debriefing session was held with the counselors a week later to discuss the experience and gather suggestions for changes and improvements. An important aspect of this meeting was to allow the counselors to reflect on their own emotions and the issues the camp raised for them. Calvary Hospital treats only cancer patients; therefore, staff are accustomed to working with patients who are dying from natural causes. But the bereavement services are open to the community, and many of the campers are coping with the loss of a loved one from suicide, murder, or a violent accident. Providing opportunities for the staff to process and talk about these experiences is essential for their own mental health.

At the 10th anniversary session of Camp Courageous, a different bereavement activity was facilitated every day to address a variety of grief issues and expose campers to different methods of expressing themselves. Campers participated in an age-appropriate variation of the activity. For most activities, the campers were divided into two large groups (6–11 years and 12–18 years) and then into smaller groups with counselors. However, in many instances, the whole group came together for an activity, to promote intimacy and allow the campers to see the similarities in their experiences across age groups.

The group circle was a daily part of the camp experience. After breakfast, campers and counselors gathered in a circle to discuss how they were feeling that morning and to hear about the schedule for the day. At the end of the day, they again gathered in a circle to recap the day's events, including their emotional reactions to the activities. After the first few years, we had decided to divide the group into two circles by age. The smaller groups were less intimidating and the campers were more expressive. We retained the large group for the first day (for introductions) and the last day (for closure). The group circle experience helped the campers see the universality of their feelings and helped them form bonds with one another. It also gave the counselors an opportunity to interact with all the campers and to model appropriate group behavior.

In the evaluations, both campers and counselors ranked building, painting, and filling wooden memory boxes as one of the most helpful bereavement activities. The memory box helps the campers connect with the experiences they shared with their loved one who died. It gives them an opportunity to reflect on the relationship and a place to store important keepsakes. This activity was led by a carpenter who had worked with terminally ill children for many years. The children worked on their boxes throughout the week and shared their work with the whole group on the last day. The counselors also made memory boxes, which helped them relate to the campers and model that it is safe and acceptable to express feelings through different mediums. One camper who had experienced the death of both parents wanted everyone at the camp to sign her memory box; she said the camp will always be a special memory for her and one she would have wanted to share with her mother. Campers are encouraged to keep their box in a special place and look through it when they want to revisit special memories of the loved one.

Campers and counselors also worked together on a wooden jigsaw puzzle in the shape of a heart. This activity focused on the many feelings that arise when a loved one dies, and how your heart can feel as though it is broken in many different pieces. Each camper and counselor was given a piece of the puzzle and asked to think about what helps them mend their broken heart. Campers and counselors were randomly separated into groups of five or six and spent some time sanding the edges of their puzzle pieces, acknowledging that loss leaves us with a lot of rough edges and that different supports can help smooth out some of those rough edges. Everyone decorated their puzzle pieces with pictures of their feelings or the names of their loved ones who died and talked about their pieces within their group. This activity facilitated interactions among children and teens in the group and created greater intimacy for the whole group. At the end of the activity, each camper or counselor took home someone else's puzzle piece—emphasizing their shared loss by taking with them a piece of another's story. The therapeutic value of this activity rested heavily on showing campers how to identify appropriate support networks and teaching them the importance of reaching out for help when they need it.

Tree planting was a way for the campers to memorialize their loved one. Each child was paired up with a buddy from a local Christian community to plant a tree in the forest surrounding the camp area. The physical aspect of digging in the earth and putting energy into tasks related to planting a tree was very healing for the campers, and many spontaneously shared their feelings as they prepared the land for their tree. The idea of leaving a living thing behind in memory of their loved one was very appealing; they labeled their trees and marked them with stones so they would remember which tree was theirs. This activity showed the campers that although their loved ones will not return, they can find ways to remember them.

One of the most poignant therapeutic interventions of the week was a candle ceremony held spontaneously on the last day of camp. The previous day, one of the campers had told a counselor that the 1-year anniversary of his sister's death was the following day. The counselor asked if he would like to acknowledge the day with a ritual and he agreed. He chose several other campers and counselors who were part of his support network to light candles with him as he read passages about memorializing a loved one. The experience was very emotional and moving. As his tears flowed, several of his peers surrounded him and simply held him, acknowledging that this was a difficult moment and affirming their presence while he grieved. He later said that the candle ceremony validated his painful feelings, and he felt that his peers and the counselors gave him permission to express his sadness for his loss. He also said that he had feared that no one would remember his sister's life; this experience showed him that people will not forget and that he can keep her memory alive by talking about her. In addition to the therapeutic value for this particular camper, this intervention greatly strengthened the bond among the group as a whole.

Another bereavement activity that received very positive evaluation comments from both campers and counselors was the balloon release on the final day. Everyone gathered at the lake to pick a balloon and write a special message on it. Campers were encouraged to write things they would like to have said to their loved one or feelings in their heart for their loved one. Campers picked quiet spots to think about the words they wanted to use; their messages were very powerful. For some campers, this was a very private activity; others wanted to share their messages. One camper wrote a message to her father saying that he shouldn't worry when she cries. She wrote that although she feels sad, she will be okay. Another camper wrote about an interaction she regretted with her mother and told the group that she wanted to let her guilt go with the wind that took away her balloon. A 10-year-old camper asked why a stranger had murdered her mother. She said that she knew no answer would be good enough to justify this killing, so she was trying to let her question float up into the sky so she could feel better. This intervention was a release for all the campers, providing them with an opportunity to let go of some of their pain and questions about the meaning of the death.

An important factor of the Calvary program is the continuity of care. In the earlier literature review, we found no indication that the organizations facilitating the camps follow up with the children on a consistent basis, which we believe holds great therapeutic value. At Calvary, children and teens participate in ongoing support groups throughout the year, giving staff and counselors a chance to form bonds with them and to assess their progress through grief. As part of our work, we coordinate care with other systems, such as their families, schools, and mental health organizations. Parents, guardians, and school staff often ask for guidance in helping children through their grief work—we believe it is important to address the child's grief issues with them, so we can collectively work toward the well-being of the child.

The full impact of the camp experience is too vast to explore here. One camper experienced menstruation for the first time during the week; she expressed sadness that her mother was not there but also gratitude for the counselors who helped her through this fragile time. A young camper had lost a tooth and wondered why the tooth fairy did not visit her as she had when her mother was alive. A few thoughtful counselors left a letter and a special present for her to find—she was overjoyed that the tooth fairy had not forgotten her after all. Countless other moments and interactions throughout that week had a positive effect on the lives of the campers.

CONCLUSION

Bereavement camps provide clinicians with a special opportunity to work with children who are experiencing loss. Children may be put off by formal therapeutic settings because of their overwhelming need to be "normal"— the informal setting of camp allows them to express themselves more freely. Combining bereavement activities with recreational activities addresses the nature of bereavement for children. They can only endure a certain amount of grieving at one time—they need to take breaks from their painful feelings and experience a balance of fun and grief work. Giving children time to play and form friendships with peers is also very important for their development. For any therapeutic intervention to have value, it must fit the needs of a particular population. Bereavement camps fit well into the world of children.

Sherry R. Schachter, Ph.D., FT, is the Director of Bereavement Services for Calvary Hospital/Hospice where she develops, coordinates, and facilitates educational and clinical services for staff and families. She facilitates weekly bereavement groups for bereaved spouses/partners, adults whose parents have died and parents who have lost children. Dr. Schachter is a recipient of the Lane Adams Award for Excellence in Cancer Nursing from the American Cancer Society. She has worked with with dying patients and their family caregivers for more than 27 years. In addition, Dr. Schachter has a private practice and writes and lectures on issues related to dying, death and loss. She is the past president of the Association for Death Education and Counseling (ADEC).

Maria Georgopoulos, M.A., obtained her Master's Degree in Applied Psychology at New York University. She currently works as a Bereavement Counselor at Calvary Hospital/Hospice, where she facilitates weekly bereavement groups for children and adolescents who have experienced a death in the family. She also facilitates bereavement groups for adult children whose parents have died. Ms. Georgopoulos coordinates care with the families of the children and adolescents that participate in the groups to assure that they are receiving appropriate services. In addition, in 2007 she facilitated a bereavement group in a local high school as part of a pilot program to address adolescent bereavement needs in schools. She also facilitates educational presentations for Calvary on death and bereavement related issues. She previously worked with adults suffering from mental illness, assisting them with integration back into the community. She is an ADEC member.

REFERENCES

Cerel, J., Fristad, M. A., Verducci, J., Weller, R. A., & Weller, E. B. (June 2006). Childhood bereavement: Psychopathology in the 2 years postparental death. *Journal of the American Academy of Child and Adolescent Psychiatry, 45*(6), 681–690.

Charkow, W. B. (1998, December). Inviting children to grieve. *ASCA Professional School Counselor, 2*(2), 117–122.

Christ, G. H. (2000, March/April). Impact of development on children's mourning. *Cancer Practice, 8*(2), 72–81.

Christ, G. H., & Christ, A. E. (2006, July/August). Current approaches to helping children cope with a parent's terminal illness. *CA: A Cancer Journal for Clinicians, 56*, 197–212.

Cimino, J. E., & Brescia, M. J. (1998). *Calvary Hospital—Model for palliative care in advanced cancer.* Merrick, NY: Palliative Care Institute.

Corr, C. A. (2000). What do we know about grieving children and adolescents? In K. J. Doka (Ed.), *Living with grief: Children, adolescents, and loss* (pp. 21–32). New York: Hospice Foundation of America.

Creed, J., Ruffin, J. E., & Ward, M. (2001, July/August). A weekend camp for bereaved siblings. *Cancer Practice, 9*(4), 176–182.

DeSpelder, L. A., & Strickland, A. L. (2002). *The Last Dance* (6th ed.). Boston: McGraw Hill.

Dowdney, L. (2000). Childhood bereavement following parental death. *Journal of Child Psychology and Psychiatry and Allied Disciplines, 41*, 819–830.

Dowdney, L., Wilson, R., Maughan, B., Allerton, M., Schofield, P., & Skuse, D. (1999, August). Psychological disturbance and service provision in parentally bereaved children: Prospective case-control study. *British Medical Journal, 319*, 354–357.

Englund, M. M., Levy, A. K., Hyson, D. M., & Croufe, L. A. (2000, July/August). Adolescent social competence: Effectiveness in a group setting. *Child Development, 71*(4), 1049–1060.

Geis, H. K., Whittlesey, S. W., McDonald, N. B., Smith, K. L., & Pfefferbaum, B. (1998, January). Bereavement and loss in childhood. *Child and Adolescent Psychiatric Clinics of North America, 7*(1), 73–85.

Kirwin, K. M., & Hamrin, V. (2005, April–June). Decreasing the risk of complicated bereavement and future psychiatric disorders in children. *Journal of Child and Adolescent Psychiatric Nursing, 18*(2), 62–78.

LoCicero, J. P., Burkhart, J., & Gray, S. (1998, January/February). Camp Carousel: A weekend grief retreat. *American Journal of Hospice and Palliative Care, 15*(1), 25–27.

Lohan, J. A. (2006, February). School nurses' support for bereaved students: A pilot study. *Journal of School Nursing, 22*(1), 48–52.

McDonald, S. K. (2006, March). A time for healing. Retrieved August 19, 2007 from www.comfortzonecamp.org/news/200603_richmond_magazine.pdf

McIntyre, B. B. (1992, May). Art therapy with bereaved children. *Caring Magazine, 11*(5), 62–67.

Mitchell, A. M., Wesner, S., Garand, L., Gayle, D., Havill, A., & Brownson, L. (2007, February). A support group intervention for children bereaved by parental suicide. *Journal of Child and Adolescent Psychiatric Nursing, 20*(1), 3–13.

Nabors, L., Ohms, M., Buchanan, N., Kirsh, K. L., Nash, T., Passik, S. D., et al. (2004). A pilot study of the impact of a grief camp for children. *Palliative and Supportive Care, 2*, 403–408.

Opie, N. D., Goodwin, T., Finke, L. M., Beattey, J. M., Lee, B., & Van Epps, J. (1992). The effect of a bereavement group experience on bereaved children's and adolescents' affective and somatic distress. *Journal of Child Adolescent Psychiatric Mental Health Nursing, 5*(1), 20–26.

Rando, T. A. (1984). *Grief, dying, and death: Clinical interventions for caregivers.* Champaign, IL: Research Press Company.

Sanders, C. M. (1998) *Grief: The mourning after* (2nd ed.). New York: John Wiley & Sons.

Sandler, I. N., Ayers, T. S. & Wolchik, S. A. (2003). The family bereavement program: Efficacy evaluation of a theory-based prevention program for parentally bereaved children and adolescents. *Journal of Consulting and Clinical Practice, 71*, 587–600.

Schachter, S. R. (2007). Bereavement summer camp for children and teens: A reflection of nine years. *Palliative and Supportive Care, 5*, 315–323.

Steen, K. F. (1998, March). A comprehensive approach to bereavement. *The Nurse Practitioner, 23*(3), 54–68.

Summers, K. H. (1993, May/June). Camp Sunrise: Supporting bereaved children. *American Journal of Hospice and Palliative Care, 10*(3), 24–27.

Webb, N. (1993). *Helping bereaved children: A handbook for practitioners.* New York: Guilford Press.

Wolchik, S. A., Tein, J. Y., Sandler, I. N., & Ayers, T. S. (2006, April). Stressors, quality of the child-caregiver relationship, and children's mental heath problems after parental death: The mediating role of self-systems beliefs. *Journal of Abnormal Child Psychology, 34*(2), 221–238.

Wolfert, A. D. (1996). *Healing the bereaved child.* Fort Collins, CO: Companion Press.

Woodgate, R. L. (2006, September/October). Siblings' experiences with childhood cancer: A different way of being in the family. *Cancer Nursing, 29*(5), 406–414.

Worden, J. W. (1996). *Children and grief: When a parent dies.* New York: John Wiley & Sons.

Worden, J. W. (1991). *Grief counseling and grief therapy.* New York: Springer Publishing Company.

Zambelli, G. C., & DeRosa, A. P. (1992, October). Bereavement support groups for school-age children: Theory, intervention, and case example. *American Journal of Orthopsychiatry, 62*(4), 484–493.

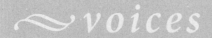

The Right Feeling

Rebecca Wayne

Shock. That was the first feeling I encountered when I was told the news of my daddy's death. It felt as though life had ended and I was the only survivor. As the days passed it definitely did not get any easier, and I went through emotion after emotion. Once the news settled in to a certain extent, I felt helpless and alone, and an overwhelming current of grief washed over me. No one could make me feel any better by the things they said, and the hole in my heart seemed to increase in size. I went through overpowering amounts of sadness doing everyday things, because everything would tie in with my dad. Anger swept over my heart, and I found myself yelling at God when I would cry. I actually ended up not going to church for months because I couldn't understand why He would take my daddy from me. I was only 13 at the time and had so many things to look forward to doing with my dad: father-daughter dances, learning to drive the ATV, volleyball practice, Friday night parties at the dance studio, a new family portrait, high school graduation, being walked down the aisle on my wedding day. Now that he was gone, I couldn't do those things, and I took my anger out on God. I was often drenched with envy when my friends would speak of their dads and when I would go to dinner or the movies and see a little girl with her dad.

A few weeks after my dad died, a woman named Paula visited me at my school. She became my counselor and I saw her every week. She explained to me that my feelings were a normal part of the grieving process, and it was okay to have them. I looked forward to Paula's visits—she was the one person I could really talk to, the one person who understood how I felt and the things I was going through. She knew the words to say when it seemed that comforting words didn't exist anymore. After a year or so, the weekly counseling sessions stopped, but I often got phone calls and letters from her, checking up on me.

A year after our sessions ended, I went to a weekend camp called Camp Triple L: Live, Laugh, Love. It's hard to describe the emotional help I received at the camp. I met other kids who had gone through the same thing I had, and I learned that no matter how alone I felt, I really wasn't. We were all in different places in our grief, and we did activities that could help each of us. Every single one of the counselors at the camp was understanding and comforting. No one ever went unnoticed, because they recognized how you felt and found ways to connect with you.

During my sophomore year of high school, I felt like I needed counseling again, and an angel named Katie was there every 2 weeks to sit with me for a class period and talk with me. New feelings had surfaced and old ones were coming back, but Katie explained (just as Paula had at our first meeting) that my feelings were normal and were part of the grieving process. We did an activity once where we made a key chain. Katie gave me a piece of paper and told me to write down a memory of me and my dad. Then she rolled the paper up around a wire and put a special kind of sealer on it to keep it rolled up and glossy. I strung beads onto the wire. Once my "memory" had dried, we attached it to the key chain. I carried it around with me everywhere—it was always in my purse or my hand or my pocket. Eventually I misplaced it; I was very upset at first, but I've come to realize that I'll always have that memory in my heart.

It's been 2½ years since my daddy suddenly lost his beautiful life, and I still miss him very, very much. But the people of hospice—my angels—have made those 2 years so much easier than they could have been. No one at hospice allows you to face anything alone;

they're only a phone call away, and they'll always be there for you, no matter what.

If there's one thing I'd like to tell other people who have lost a loved one, it's that no matter what happens, that person will always be a part of you. They will always live in your heart and they'll never leave and you'll never forget them. It's okay to be angry with them and frustrated with them and with God. It's okay to be envious when you see a child with a grandparent or a father or a mother or a sibling. It's okay to let out the tears and cry, because you should never have to keep your feelings locked away inside. And it's okay to feel helpless and alone. After all, you just lost someone you'll never be able to get back—a piece of your heart is missing and a piece of your soul is empty. I've learned from my angels at hospice that whatever you're feeling in your heart is the right feeling.

Rebecca Wayne is a high school junior in Clearwater, Florida where she enjoys dancing, writing, and being with her friends.

CHAPTER 14

Grief Groups for Grieving Children and Adolescents

Donna Schuurman

I n 1982, former nurse Beverly Chappell founded the first peer support group program for children and teens impacted by death—The Dougy Center. She was told by the chief physician of a local pediatric unit that her plan sounded like "voodoo medicine," and that he didn't want anyone "messing" with his patients' heads.

Twenty-five years later, more than 165 children's grief support programs in 47 states, and at least 18 in nine other countries, are based on The Dougy Center's model. Additionally, other children's bereavement programs and models have evolved to the degree that an umbrella non-profit organization, the National Alliance for Grieving Children (NAGC), was formed in 2004 to "promote awareness of the needs of children and teens grieving a death and provide education and resources for anyone who wants to support them" (NAGC, 2007). This alliance also sponsors an annual Children's Grief Symposium hosted at a different site each year.

Indeed, multiple service organizations have evolved to serve bereaved children or adults bereaved as children, among them the Lone Twin Network (founded in Birmingham, UK in 1989); American WWII Orphans Network; Voices of September 11 for Kids, founded in December 2006; Families of September 11, founded in October 2001; Tragedy Assistance Program for Survivors, Inc., described on their website as "America's only nonprofit Veterans Service Organization chartered solely to assist the surviving families of military members who have died while serving our nation," including Good Grief Camps for children from 18 months to 21 years old (TAPS, 2007).

Since 1982, The Dougy Center in Portland, Oregon has served more than 20,000 grieving children, teens, young adults, and their parents. When she founded the center, Chappell was inspired by a young boy named Dougy Turno. Dougy was terminally ill from an inoperable brain tumor when he wrote to Elisabeth Kübler-Ross to ask her why the adults around him refused to talk about, or accept, that he was dying. She responded with a personal storybook filled with poetry and drawings. Dougy promptly returned it to her, asking her to make copies for his friends in the hospital. Kübler-Ross later published this as a booklet, *A Letter to a Child With Cancer: The Dougy Letter*. (Although the booklet itself is out of print, it is included in Kübler-Ross, 1999.)

The essence of Chappell's observations of Dougy was that he helped other children who were ill or dying by being honest. "Don't you think it's unfair that we'll never get to graduate from college?" he'd ask his buddies, while the adults around him withdrew from the pain of his truth. "Have you ever kissed a girl?" he'd ask his friends, and "Do you think you'll get to before you die?" While his blunt discussion of his impending death astonished and sometimes threatened the medical personnel, the children opened up freely with their fears and concerns.

Currently The Dougy Center provides 24 age-specific groups for children ages 3 to 5, 6 to 12, 10 to 14, teens, young adults, and concurrent groups for their adult family members. Some of the groups are loss-specific, including for those impacted by parent death, sibling death, murder, suicide, sudden death, and death following a long-term illness.

Over the years, many programs serving grieving children and adolescents have developed through hospices, hospitals, community health centers, and independent non-profits. Whether geared toward providing one-on-one therapy, peer support, or both, they all serve a common goal: to assist young people in their grief following a death.

Although still occasionally referred to as the "forgotten grievers," young people's voices are finally beginning to be heard. They cry out, and often "act out," to inform the adults around them of their pain. Most professionals would agree that not all children or adolescents who experience a death need professional help. But regardless, they all need support.

For some, the support of family, friends, and extended community may provide the healing validation they need. For others, "the web of relationships that once naturalistically provided many sources of resilience—the extended family, the church, the synagogue, the neighborhood, the union hall—is eroding" (Butler, 1997, 29). Many young people who have solid family support still express feelings of estrangement, loneliness, and the sense of not fitting in with their peers.

All of these increased services for bereaved children and adolescents beg the question: *Do they work? And...If so why, how and for whom?*

Grief therapy as a profession has received increasing criticism in the popular press (Brody, 2004; Zaslow, 2005), as well as in professional literature (Curtis and Newman, 2001; Currier, Holland and Neimeyer, 2007).

Curtis and Newman, (2001) reviewed nine studies of programs for bereaved children, concluding that there were only moderate positive program effects. They underscored that methodological weaknesses, including small sample sizes, lack of control groups, high attrition rates, and short-term evaluation, hampered most of the studies. Currier, Holland and Neimeyer (2007) conducted a meta-analytic review of controlled outcome research on the effectiveness of bereavement interventions with children, analyzing the few available studies. "Unfortunately, the fact that the total controlled outcome literature on bereavement interventions with children appears to consist of a mere 13 studies restricted the number of questions that could be legitimately examined in this review and reduced the level of confidence that could be placed in the results" (p. 258).

Clearly more research is needed. Currier et al. conclude that "as for future research, the first priority is to develop well-validated and clinically relevant measures of child grief. Second, researchers need to flesh out the theoretical underpinnings and the operational implementation of their interventions." (p. 258). Although they state that "...it is evident that the experience of bereavement during childhood constitutes a risk factor for concurrent and sometimes chronic distress" (p. 253), "the overall results (of the meta-analysis) do not support the assumption that the bereavement interventions with children have a significant influence on adjustment" (p. 257). Admittedly, the small number of published studies, the relative youth of the childhood bereavement field, and the frequent chasm between researchers and practitioners contribute to this assessment.

This assessment ought not discourage those of us engaged in bereavement services for children, adolescents and families. Rather, it may serve as a springboard to encourage more research, collaboration, evaluation and interest in our work. After all, the study of psychology is a relatively young field, hotly contested since Freud's bold assertions and fueled with controversy in the current atmosphere of managed care and evidence-based practice.

In 1940, British developmental psychologist John Bowlby began to develop his theory of attachment, much to the consternation of his psychoanalytic colleagues. (See Bowlby, 1969, 1973, 1980, 1988.) One of the tenets of this theory is that separation anxiety in children may result from adverse family experiences, including death. His pioneering thinking forms the foundation of much of the current practice with children, including in the field of death, dying and bereavement.

Many psychologists and researchers have built on Bowlby's work. Child psychiatrist Daniel Siegel's insights to the developing mind and brain chemistry suggest that "our most important relationships fire into being the neural circuits of the brain that allow us to understand and empathize with others and feel their feelings" (Wylie, 2004, 30). Siegel expressed in an interview what he believed to be the most important element in the therapeutic relationship. The concept came from a young woman he was seeing in therapy who "was suffering from unresolved grief and guilt at the loss of a parent. Eventually, she got better, and when she was ready to leave, Siegel asked her what had been most helpful about her treatment. She thought for a minute and then said, 'When I'm with you, I feel *felt*'" (p. 33).

Our role—whether as play therapists or counselors, grief support practitioners or psychologists, funeral directors or medical staff—is to help the children and families we serve to *make meaning* through *feeling felt*. It's that simple, and that complex (Schuurman & DeCristofaro, 2007).

As we develop and implement bereavement services for children, adolescents and their families, we also do well to bear in mind who is at risk, what they are at risk for, and how, therefore, our services apply to their needs. Once again, the research is sketchy, though most agree at minimum that there are *some* children and adolescents who are at greater risk for future difficulties without some kind of intervention. Defining this group or the specific risk factors is subject to debate among practitioners and researchers. Currier, Holland and Neimeyer (2007) note that the less than stellar results from their meta-analytic review of program outcomes "could derive in part from a more general tendency to 'pathologize' grief.

Although bereavement makes many children vulnerable to acute and sometimes ongoing difficulties in life, this does not justify the indiscriminate provision of grief therapy to children who show neither clinically elevated distress following a loss or other 'objective' risk factors associated with death itself...Our results suggest the potential value of early screening in cases of childhood bereavement and focusing interventions on the high-risk group, such as those showing the beginning signs of 'childhood traumatic grief'" (p. 258).

Cohen and Mannarino (2004) define childhood traumatic grief (CTG) as a condition in which trauma symptoms interfere with the child's ability to negotiate the grieving process. Although this author takes issue with the specific terminology—which perpetuates a pathologizing of grief and suggests that grief follows a universal progression —the idea that problematic symptoms associated with grieving and loss may, in some situations, need professional intervention, is undeniable. Clearly, more research needs to be done in this area as well.

While it is outside the scope of this chapter to review the literature on the needs and risk factors of grieving children, most clinicians and practitioners would agree that social isolation places this population at increased risk. Siegel emphasizes that "attachment relationships that offer children experiences that provide them with emotional connection and safety, both in the home and in the community, may be able to confer resilience and more flexible modes of adaptation in the face of adversity" (Siegel, 1999, 59).

How Groups May Help Grieving Youth

In this light, providing grief therapy or support in a group setting may help alleviate the sense of aloneness many children and teens report following the death of a parent, sibling or close friend. The following five statements, commonly voiced by grieving youth, illustrate how groups can assist them.

1. "Hey, maybe I'm not crazy"

One of the most commonly expressed fears of children and adolescents at The Dougy Center is the fear that they are "going crazy." Grievers often experience frightening or unwelcome grief symptoms including nightmares, voices, aches and pains in their body, uncontrollable shaking, or waves or heat or cold. As 14-year-old Heather shared, "I was experiencing stuff I couldn't control and didn't understand—weird dreams, stomachaches, seeing my father's ghost in my room at night. I thought I was losing it, and I was afraid to tell anyone."

Many normal manifestations of grief feel, look, or seem "crazy" to the young griever. One of the benefits of sharing in a group setting is the de-pathologizing of normal grief reactions. Kids find out, through listening and sharing with others their age, that much of what they fear is common and normal.

2. "I'm not alone."

"I thought I had this big mark on my forehead," bemoaned 12-year-old Stephen. "It said, 'Look, my mom died and I'm different from you.' I had friends whose parents divorced, but no one who'd had a parent die. It seemed like I was the only one this had ever happened to, and I felt completely alone."

One of the benefits of participating in a group of peers who have experienced a death is the knowledge that others have experienced, and survived, the loss of a family member or close friend. Katie, 10, expressed it this way: "I can talk to other kids who had a parent die and it helps me feel like I'm not the only one who had a parent die, and I feel less weird and different."

3. "Someone else cares what I'm going through."

Children need validation for who they are, what they feel, and what they experience. While attempting to make sense of their new world following a death, they too frequently do not receive support or validation from the adults around them. Young people at The Dougy Center describe encounter after encounter with well-meaning but ill-informed teachers, coaches, ministers, adult family friends, and youth workers who continue to direct them to "put this behind them," "move on," "forget," and "get over it."

A 16-year-old described her teacher's reaction when she did not have a writing assignment completed 4 days after she'd witnessed her brother's death in a drowning accident. "She told me I was using it as an excuse to not do my homework!"

Group support helps children and adolescents know that someone cares and understands. In a society where grieving adults are granted 3 days of bereavement leave and face the avoidance of colleagues who don't know what to say, it is easy for kids to feel they don't have permission to grieve.

4. "My feelings matter and I get to express them."

It's not unusual for grieving children and teens to feel overloaded with emotions, ranging from anger and self-pity to relief and panic. These feelings are experienced in random fashion, leaving the griever confused and feeling out of control. Sometimes adults, disturbed by their kids' actions or consumed by wanting to alleviate their pain, actually complicate the healing process by short-circuiting, making light of, or attempting to take away feelings they don't want children to have to experience. "People kept telling me not to be so mad after my dad got killed," said 8-year-old Jeremy. "But it wasn't their dad that was gone. I was mad, and still am. It isn't fair that I don't get to have a dad."

Group settings for youth that include appropriate boundaries and supervision provide an opportunity for all feelings to be validated, even ones that don't feel good.

5. "I get to express—or not express—what I feel in ways that help me."

Many young people express verbally or by their actions that they don't know what to do with the feelings raging inside them. These feelings frequently wind up being expressed in unhealthy ways through self-destructive behaviors or behaviors pejoratively called "acting out." Accused of "trying to get attention" through crying, withdrawing, substance abuse, reckless sexual behavior, lying, stealing, or aggression, kids who don't get the attention they need are driven to find increasingly reckless ways of seeking it. What they need is adults who will help them express their feelings, even the tough or uncomfortable ones, in healthy ways.

For some, talking in a safe setting—being listened to and validated—provides the support they need. Adults are often more comfortable with the grief of children and adolescents with strong verbal skills because it is clearer what the young person is experiencing than it is with non-talkers. But many children and teens are not comfortable putting their feelings into words or don't have the vocabulary to adequately capture their experience. For them, talk therapy or talk support that only includes verbal processing may prove frustrating.

Play is children's natural activity and a primary way to make sense of their emotional life and experiences. Providing a range of mediums for expression—art, music, dress-up clothes, playhouses, puppets, sandtrays, punching bags, toys and games—allows each child or teen to find his or her own methods to express the feelings inside. It also allows them to regain a sense of control by guiding their own route through grief when so many events have left them feeling powerless and out of control.

How do our group interventions support these and other issues expressed by grieving children and youth? A model of childhood mourning including "12 prescriptive tasks for treatment of childhood traumatic grief" (Crenshaw, 2006-2007), includes many of the goals of group therapy or support, which I would propose are applicable to all grievers, not just those labeled with "traumatic grief." These goals include creating a sense of safety; identifying, embracing and expressing the emotions of grief; commemorating the loss; acknowledging ambivalence; and recovering and preserving positive memories.

Considerations for Running Successful Groups for Grieving Children and Teens

There are numerous models and methods of working effectively with grieving children and teens in the group setting. What follows are some of the practical considerations in determining what model best suits your philosophical framework, available resources, setting, and population.

1. Should we run therapy, education, or support groups—or some combination of these?

The decision about whether to run therapy groups, educational groups, support groups, or some combination of the three depends on a number of factors, including but not limited to the population with which you intend to work. If your population is youth in a mental health setting, a residential treatment program, or those whose emotional problems are severely limiting their ability to function, you may elect to run therapy/educational groups led by professionals. Whatever methodology you use, consider what you intend for the goals of the groups to be: Providing support during a difficult time? Changing behavior? Teaching about healthy grief?

2. Should groups be ongoing or time-limited?

Deciding whether to hold ongoing groups or time-limited groups depends on a combination of factors including resources. Many school-based groups elect to run time-limited groups, most frequently in the six, eight or ten-week range. These groups usually are closed groups, with the same participants attending for the full number of sessions. Most often, they include specific themes or activities for each session. Sometimes time-limited groups are chosen because of resource restraints imposed by an umbrella agency. Sometimes they are the method of choice because they can reach more children than ongoing groups might reach.

Ongoing or open-ended groups tend to allow the participants to guide their own choices and process, as well as decision-making about how long they wish to participate. Though therapeutic, they are not educational in design. Unlike most time-limited groups, they allow for the flux of newcomers.

3. Should we run curriculum-driven groups or non-directive groups?

Curriculum-driven groups select topics for each of the allotted sessions and tend to be education-based. Topics may include identifying and coping with feelings or experiences in funerals or memorialization, and are frequently activity-based. A growing number of curriculum materials for grief groups may be found through resources like the Association for Death Education and Counseling, Compassion Books, and Centering Corporation.

Non-directive groups tend to be on-going and allow for some participant-led choices about how their time will be spent. At The Dougy Center, each group has an opening circle to share names and whatever the participants would like to share about who died. Sometimes an activity is proposed; other times discussions evolve naturally from anniversary or holiday times or topics shared in the circle. An unstructured time follows where children select from a range of activities throughout the Center's grounds, which includes art rooms and "big energy rooms" like The Volcano Room or air hockey and foosball game areas. Part of the philosophy that guides non-directive groups is that by allowing children and teens to decide what they wish to do, we are helping to re-empower them after events that made life seem out of control.

4. Who should facilitate these groups, and what kinds of skills and training should they have?

Some grief groups for children and teens are led entirely by professional counselors or therapists; others by trained volunteers with oversight by professionals. Regardless of the model used, the safety and therapeutic relationship of trust is likely the most important component on which to build. Each of the 165 national programs listed on The Dougy Center's website has some kind of volunteer training program, ranging from 2 to 5 days, as well as ongoing training and supervision. Contact information for these sites is listed as well, and a wealth of information available through these sources.

5. How do we determine which children and teens are appropriate for groups?

Some children function better in group settings and some would benefit more from individual therapy. There are several ways to determine whether they are appropriate for groups, the most commonsense way being to try it out. Some children need therapy in addition to or instead of support groups; some need the individual attention of a single therapist; others may feel overwhelmed by the collective stories of others.

Some children are unable or unwilling to engage productively in group settings because of emotional problems, shyness, fear, or other factors. We have found, however, that many children deemed "inappropriate" for groups have successfully engaged in groups when given clear safety rules and boundaries.

6. What ages should we work with, and should we group by age?

Most thanatologists agree that even infants are capable of grieving. The Dougy Center provides support groups for children beginning at the age of three. They're more labor-intensive than the older kids, but no less capable of expressing what they feel and think. We have found it helpful to group by age as the developmental issues tend to be more similar, but it is not necessary to do so with smaller populations. Younger kids can learn from the older ones, and vice versa.

7. Can we run groups with mixed losses—parent and sibling, impending death, and post-death?

The simple answer to this question is yes. Even without a large enough population to divide by age or type of loss, mixed groups still have much to offer. Some programs group by age but not according to the child's relationship to the person who died. Others group into parent death, sibling death, healing from a suicide death, murder or violent death, etc. Our experience indicates that the children or teens have fewer issues with this than the concurrent parent/adult groups we run. Children who've had a parent die or a sibling die still have much in common based on their age and developmental issues. Adults who have had a spouse die or a child die frequently face very different challenges. For these reasons, and because we have a large population of children and teens, we have mixed groups and loss-specific groups for families to choose from. For example, if a father died of suicide, a child may choose to participate in a parent death group or a suicide death-specific group. Some programs have groups for children anticipating an impending death as well as post-death groups. A challenge in these groups is what to do when the death occurs: does the child stay in the group of children he or she has come to know, or transition into a bereavement loss group?

8. What locations or settings are most conducive to effective groups?

While it is nice to have a comfortable setting in which to run groups, the setting is less important than the atmosphere and attitudes of the leaders. Effective groups can happen in borrowed buildings, homes, or school classrooms. Some families have expressed resistance to attending groups in hospitals or funeral homes because of the painful memories they may have attached to those sites. Some have expressed not wanting to meet in a religious setting, either because of their struggles with spiritual issues and conventional religion, or simply because they're uncomfortable in religious buildings outside of their own faith. At the same time, there are religion-based programs operating successfully in church settings which are open to members and community alike.

9. What size group is best?

Appropriate group size depends on what ages you are working with, how many leaders or facilitators you have, and how much individual attention you intend to provide within the group format. In general, the younger the child, the more adult assistance required, or the smaller a "manageable" group can be. Most of the groups at The Dougy Center have up to 15 children or teens, with adult facilitators ranging from a 1-to-2 ratio for 3-to-5-year-olds, a 1-to-3 ratio for

6-to-12-year-olds, and a 1-to-5 ratio for teens. You may have larger or smaller groups depending on your setting, the activities you include, and the level of human resources you engage. In general though, it's best to have at least two facilitators in every group.

10. Should we include parents or adult caregivers in these groups?

If at all possible, absolutely. Resiliency studies suggest that adult influence is important in children's success, and other studies (Lutzke, Ayers, Sandler, & Barr, 1997; Kalter, Lohnes, Chasin, Cain, Dunning & Rowan, 2002; Silverman, 2000; Worden, 1996) suggest that one of the most influential predictors of how children will cope following a parent's death is how the surviving parent is coping. Concurrent adult groups allow parents and caregivers to have some time off from parenting, enable them to discuss the challenges of raising grieving children with other adults, and provide the opportunity to be heard and to give and receive support and advice as requested.

Donna L. Schuurman, Ed.D., is the Executive Director of The Dougy Center in Portland, Oregon. She is a Past President of the Association for Death Education and Counseling, Vice-Chair of the National Alliance for Grieving Children, and a member of the International Work Group on Death, Dying and Bereavement. Her publications include *Never the Same: Coming to Terms with the Death of a Parent.*

REFERENCES

Bowlby, J. (1969). *Attachment and loss: Vol. 1. Attachment.* New York: Basic Books.

Bowlby, J. (1973). *Attachment and loss: Vol. 2. Separation: Anxiety and anger.* New York: Basic Books.

Bowlby, J. (1980). *Attachment and loss: Vol. 3. Loss: Sadness and depression.* New York: Basic Books.

Bowlby, J. (1988). *A secure base: Parent-child attachment and healthy human development.* New York: Basic Books.

Brody, J. (2004). Often, time beats therapy in treating grief. *The New York Times*, Jan. 27, 2004.

Butler, K. (1997). The anatomy of resilience. *Family Therapy Networker, 27.*

Cohen, J. & Mannarino, A. (2004). Treatment of childhood traumatic grief. *Journal of Clinical Child and Adolescent Psychology, 33*, 819–831.

Crenshaw, D. (2006–2007). An interpersonal neurobiological-informed treatment model for childhood traumatic grief. *Omega: Journal of Death and Dying, 54*, 319–335.

Currier, J.M., Holland, J.M., & Neimeyer, R.A. (2007.) The effectiveness of bereavement interventions with children: A meta-analytic review of controlled outcome research. *Journal of Clinical Child and Adolescent Psychology, 36*, 253–259.

Curtis, K., & Newman, T. (2001). Do community-based support services benefit bereaved children? A review of empirical evidence. *Child: Care, Health, and Development, 27(6)*, 487–495.

Kalter, N., Lohnes, K.L., Chasin, J., Cain, A.C., Dunning, S., & Rowan, J. (2002). The adjustment of parentally bereaved children: Factors associated with short-term adjustment. *Omega: Journal of Death and Dying, 46*, 15–34.

Kubler Ross, E. (1999.) *The Tunnel and the light: Essential insights on living & dying.* New York: Marlowe & Co.

Lutzke, J.R., Ayers, T.S., Sandler, I.N., & Barr, A. (1997). Risks and interventions for the parentally bereaved child. In S.A. Wolchik & I.N. Sandler (Eds.), *Handbook of children's coping with common life stressors: Linking theory, research and interventions* (pp. 215–243). New York: Plenum Press.

National Alliance for Grieving Children. (n.d.). *Our mission.* Retrieved December 15, 2007 from http://www.nationalallianceforgrievingchildren.org

Schuurman, D., & DeCristofaro, J. (2007). After a Parent's Death: Group, Family and Individual Therapy to Help Children. In N.B.Webb (Ed.), *Play therapy with children in crisis*, 3rd ed. (173–196). New York: Guilford Press.

Siegel, D. (1999). *The developing mind: How relationships and the brain interact to shape who we are.* New York: Guilford Press.

Silverman, P. (2000). *Never too young to know.* New York: Oxford University Press.

Tragedy Assistance Program for Survivors. (2007). *Youth program.* Retrieved December 15, 2007 from http://www.taps.org/youth/

Worden, J.W. (1996). *Children and grief: When a parent dies.* New York: Guilford Press.

Wylie, M. (2004). Mindsight. *Psychotherapy Networker*, 29–39.

Zaslow, J. (2005). Moving on: The case for not facing death head on. *The Wall Street Journal*, June 2, 2005.

CHAPTER 15

Play Therapy to Help Bereaved Children

Nancy Boyd Webb

I n many ways, death is the last taboo. Many adults find the subject of death more intimidating to discuss with children than other formidable topics, such as sex. Finding the right words is one obstacle, but finding the inner strength to tell a child that a loved person has died can be even more daunting. Often the adult's own emotional response of denial or outrage contributes to the difficulty; in fact, a frequent response to news of a death is "I just can't believe it." Later, when the reality of the death sinks in, the adult may move from disbelief to a state of temporary paralysis, in which he or she carries on routine activities but still cannot verbalize feelings about the death or permit emotional responses to it. In this state of emotional turmoil, many adults have neither the energy nor the capacity to translate the news of a death into simple and compassionate language that a child will understand.

If adults consider death so overwhelming, it is not surprising that children have even greater difficulty comprehending and coping with the reality and the emotional impact of the end of a life. Bereaved children usually have had little or no previous experience with death, and they simply do not have the vocabulary to describe their complex emotions. Often they are uncertain about what death means, because the brains of young children do not comprehend its finality, even if they have attended a burial. Young children typically expect the dead person to return sometime in the future, and they become confused and angry when this does not happen.

The literature increasingly recognizes that children's bereavement differs from that of adults (Corr & Corr, 1996; Crenshaw, 2002; Goldman, 1996; Webb, 2002). Children's grief responses depend strongly on their age and developmental level, which affect their ability to comprehend irreversibility and other characteristics associated with death. Experts agree that a child's understanding of death develops gradually; studies indicate that most children achieve partial or mature understanding between the ages of 7 and 9 years (Speece & Brent, 1996). For example, a preschooler who was told that her father had died and gone to heaven expected him to return "when he's finished being dead." Her 9-year-old brother became irritated and angry with his little sister's repeated statements that "Daddy's coming back soon." Because he understood that dead people don't come back, his sister's frequent references to their father's return only served to remind him of his painful loss. Both these children benefited from individual play therapy sessions that allowed them to express their grief through the symbolic displacement of play. The boy drew pictures of volcanoes erupting, and the girl played with a dollhouse and female dolls, having them announce, "We can't find the daddy—he's lost." (Webb, 2000).

This chapter addresses the circumstances that may result in a bereaved child's need for therapy and reviews the use of play as a way to communicate with the child through individual, family, or group therapy. The goals of helping will be addressed, as will the role of the bereavement counselor.

Support Versus Therapy: What Is the Difference?

How can teachers, family members, and friends determine how to help a bereaved child deal with mourning? Do all bereaved children need therapy? If not, what considerations might lead to a referral for therapy?

There is no clear formula for answering this question. Each child is different, and each will respond to a death on the basis of a number of factors, such as temperament, age, relationship with the deceased, and the manner of death. Many bereaved children go through the grief process with little or no assistance. Often these children benefit from the compassionate and informal supportive responses of teachers, religious leaders, nurses, and youth group leaders, who may or may not have had training in grief counseling. Sometimes referrals to hospice provide the child with relief and the support of knowing that other children are also grieving losses. The group format helps children overcome feelings of being different from their peers because a death has occurred in their family. Because of the belief that grief is a normal response after a death, hospice refers to its services as "support," not "therapy."

In my opinion, most bereaved children probably do not require referral for mental health counseling, but this in no way implies that they do not grieve. Sometimes children have been referred to as "disenfranchised" (Crenshaw, 2002) because the general public may minimize the extent of their mourning. Children *do* grieve, and many benefit greatly from attending a short-term support group, such as those offered by some schools or by hospice. The fact that many children may not require the help of a therapist does not mean that they do not mourn.

However, supportive services are not sufficient to meet the needs of all children. Therapy with a mental heath professional often proves beneficial for children who have had previous difficulties and for whom the death is the "last straw," exhausting their already depleted coping abilities. Other factors can cause a child's functioning to become impaired after a death. They may relate to the sudden or gruesome nature of the death. Traumatic circumstances associated with murders, terrorism, and school bombings can totally shatter a child's sense of security. These traumatic events may also deeply compromise the ability of adults in the affected community to promise children security and safety. In these circumstances, some children develop understandable fears about going outside and carrying on their usual activities. Because of growing public awareness regarding the impact on children of traumatic and violent deaths, referrals to trauma specialists are becoming more common. But how can a parent, teacher, or other concerned adult decide whether to refer a bereaved child in less obvious circumstances?

Assessing a Child's Need for Therapy

Many factors affect the reaction of a particular child to a specific death situation. Webb (1994, pp. 30–41) devised a chart and accompanying forms to help weigh the influence of various factors. The chart—Tripartite Assessment of the Bereaved Child—outlines three groups of factors that interact to influence a child's response to a death:

1. Factors pertaining to the child's personal background and experience.
2. Factors related to the particulars of the death and the nature of the child's involvement with it.

3. Characteristics of the family/culture and community, and the nature of their response to the child.

I will not list the numerous items contained in each of these three broad categories. Rather, I will identify specific circumstances that often create concerns because of the nature of the death or the child's particular bereavement response.

Referral of the child for an assessment and possible individual therapy should be considered when

- a family member or peer commits suicide;

- the child witnesses a mutilating death or multiple deaths;

- the child develops severe nightmares or sleep disorders;

- the child develops difficulty completing schoolwork;

- the child develops psychosomatic complaints;

- the child's eating patterns become altered;

- the child becomes withdrawn and disinterested in participating in activities; or

- the child's overall behavior regresses.

Some of these behaviors occur in "normal" bereavement, but when several occur together, or when their intensity interferes with the child's usual activities, it is appropriate to seek the opinion of a specialist who is familiar with normal and disabling bereavement in children. Rando (1991) says that when there is a question, it is better to err on the side of obtaining a professional opinion. A referral is not meant to "pathologize" bereavement; rather, it is a preventive intervention to avoid the possible development of even more serious and intransigent problems.

Thus, the answer to the question about whether all bereaved children need therapy is no, but evaluation for therapy definitely should be considered in certain circumstances. I use the term "disabling grief" (Webb, 1994) to refer to grief responses that justify the need for assessment and therapy. Such responses include those already listed, as well as situations in which the child remains "in shock" after most grievers have resumed their usual activities, or when the child has drastically different interpersonal reactions with family and peers than before the death.

No one protocol describes "normal grief." Professional judgment is required to evaluate whether a child's reactions raise a red flag. It is the combination of behaviors and circumstances and the "degree of intrusiveness into the child's life created by the grieving" that must be evaluated (Webb, 2002, p. 21). The following case examples illustrate different responses to bereavement and the role of therapy in helping the child resolve grief.

"Normal" Bereavement

This is an example (Webb, 2002) of a 9-year-old boy, Todd, whose grief reactions could be considered within the normal range following the progressive illness and death of his 79-year-old grandmother from cancer. Todd was already engaged in play therapy related to his learning difficulties (attention deficit disorder) when his grandmother's condition worsened and she became terminal. This case illustrates a frequent occurrence in child therapy—the incidence of a death during the child's treatment for other problems. In this case, the focus of the original referral was on the family's reaction to the grandmother's impending death; some work had been done with the parents on family stresses and their responses to them. At the point of the grandmother's final decline and death, the work with Todd had shifted from family issues to the boy's academic and social problems. The case illustrates bereavement counseling with parents to help them prepare their children for an anticipated death and, later, play therapy with a boy and his father following the grandmother's death.

Anticipatory bereavement counseling

In my role as a child and family therapist, I advised the parents to prepare their children gradually for the grandmother's impending death. In a separate session with the parents, I advised them to begin to comment to Todd and his two sisters, ages 5 and 11, that despite all the doctors' best efforts, Grammy was getting sicker, and soon she might not be able to speak to them. Therefore, they should tell her whatever they wanted to *now*, while she could still hear them.

The parents prepared their children accordingly, and Todd rode his bike over to his grandparents' house and initiated a quiet time with his bedridden grandmother. He told his mother that he whispered in Grammy's ear that he loved her, and that he knew she heard him because she nodded her head and smiled.

Ten days later Grammy died, and Todd was distraught. He screamed and cried, and only the rabbi could comfort him. After the rabbi's intervention, Todd told his parents that he wanted to go to his friend's house for a sleepover, as previously planned for that evening. Furthermore, he wanted to go with his class on a planned trip to see "The Nutcracker" 2 days later, which happened to be the day of the funeral. The parents agreed to Todd's requests, fearing that he would become uncontrollable if they did not. Consequently, he did not attend his grandmother's funeral or burial.

Family sessions following the death

For a family session a week after the death, I suggested that the parents bring family photographs as a basis for talking about their memories of Grammy. This was a productive session. At one point, the sibling rivalry between Todd and his older sister became apparent as they argued about who had spent more time with Grammy. The mother stepped in as the voice of reason; she said that of course the sister had had more time (and more photos) with Grammy, because she was 2 years older than Todd.

Parent-child play therapy session

Several weeks after this session, in a play therapy session with Todd and his father, we played Gardner's (1988) Storytelling Card Game. The game requires the player to put family figures into a picture and make up a story about what is happening. Todd selected the picture of a cemetery rather than any of three other pictures of more neutral neighborhood and home settings. The story he told clearly reflected his understanding of what had occurred at his grandmother's burial, even though he had not been there. This was his story:

> "Somebody has just died, and the family is here to throw dirt on the casket. The rabbi says prayers. The family all say things about the person. They feel very sad, and some of them are crying."

I asked Todd what happened next, and he said, "They go home, because they are still a family."

The story clearly conveyed Todd's understanding about the details of his grandmother's burial and his conviction that his family would survive despite the loss. The stimulus and structure of the game enabled Todd to express his feelings in a way he probably could not have in response to a direct question. The story he told was especially reassuring to his father.

I believe this case illustrates normal grief, in which the child could have managed without professional assistance. At the time of his grandmother's death, I was already working with Todd on issues related to school, friends, and his relationship with his older sister. Because of my ongoing contact with him, I engaged him in some grief-related play therapy sessions; however, I am confident that Todd could have managed his grief without professional counseling.

It is notable that the rabbi's comforting on the evening of the grandmother's death seemed sufficient to relieve Todd and free him to carry out his previous plans. This is an example of a child's *short sadness span*; Todd cried and had a tantrum when he first learned about his grandmother's death, but he quickly moved on. The parents' efforts to prepare the children for the death of their grandmother also probably helped Todd anticipate her death and say good-bye to her.

COMPLICATED GRIEF

The case of the Martini sisters (Webb, 2002) illustrates the increased complexity of grief resolution when two or more loss situations occur at the same time. Different authors have used the term "complicated bereavement" to refer to difficulties in expressing grief due to one or more of the following situations:

- The nature of the death (sudden, traumatic, stigmatized)
- Multiple losses
- Ambivalent relationship with the deceased
- Confusing or ambiguous responses of other mourners
- Distorted, compromised, or absent mourning process (adapted from Goldman, 1996, and Rando, 1993).

The sisters in this case were Amanda, 8, and Linda, 10. Their parents were initiating a divorce at the same time Linda's godfather was hospitalized with pancreatic cancer. Because of the close relationship between the two families and the Martini family's desire to provide maximum support to the family of the dying man, the marital separation was temporarily delayed. Everyone rallied to make hospital visits, to babysit for the godfather's children, and to offer moral support to his wife. The original referral from the mother had requested counseling and therapy for the girls because of the impending separation and divorce; it quickly became apparent that the girls would be losing two important male figures in their life.

My original plan was to have joint biweekly sessions with the girls and to provide counseling to the parents in alternating sessions. The focus was to provide support to the girls at a time of disequilibrium and crisis in their lives, to prepare them for their godfather's death, and to help with the bereavement associated with both losses.

It soon became clear that the girls were embroiled in a hostile, intense relationship that made sibling sessions unfeasible. They were about to be abandoned by the two most important men in their lives—their father would leave home, and their godfather would die. Because they could not direct their anger about the anticipated losses at either of the men, they directed it at each other. We know that anger is an expected component of grief following both divorce and death. Raphael (1983) stated that responses to divorce resemble those of bereavement, although in divorce "the bereaved must mourn someone who has not died" (p. 228). At one point, the girls acknowledged that they fought a lot, both verbally and physically, and Linda said, "I guess we should get a divorce!" I acknowledged that each of them had a right to feel very upset and angry about all the very serious changes in their lives over which they had no control. I commented that they needed to find ways to release their anger without hurting anyone or getting into trouble. I mentioned that playing can sometimes help. These statements made a direct connection to their lives without condoning or encouraging the expression of anger toward people.

WHAT IS PLAY THERAPY AND HOW DOES IT HELP?

Definition of Play Therapy

Play therapy is an interaction between a trained adult and a child that seeks to relieve the child's emotional distress through the symbolic communication of play. It rests on the assumption that the child expresses and works through emotional conflicts—especially those that cannot be openly discussed—within the metaphor of play. Children typically "play out" their feelings rather than talking about them, so play therapy is the method of choice for helping bereaved children express their feelings. Grief counselors and other adults who understand the symbolic nature of children's play communications can respond appropriately to bereaved children using the "language of play."

Orienting the Child to the Play Therapy Process

Ideally, the therapist tells the child in the first session that he or she is someone who helps children and families with their troubles and worries. The therapist in a bereavement situation further acknowledges that someone special has died and that this would cause many people to have some worried reactions. Another important component of orienting the child to the process is to say, "Sometimes we talk, and sometimes we play." This implicitly gives the child control and a choice about how to convey his or her concerns.

Play therapy is different from "just playing" by virtue of the therapist's deliberate attempts to communicate with the child through the process. For example, an 8-year-old girl repeatedly chose to play the board game Operation during the terminal phase of her mother's progressive decline from cancer. The therapist understood that the child was attempting to gain some comprehension and sense of mastery related to her mother's medical condition and repeated surgeries. As she played the game with the girl, the therapist helped validate the child's feelings through comments such as "Oh, this poor man; he's had to have so many operations, and he doesn't seem to be getting any better. The doctors keep trying to help him, but he's just getting weaker and weaker. This is so upsetting and sad; it's not fair! It's so hard on his family." Obviously, the therapist was addressing the child's own experience, but she did not say, "This is like what happened to your mother." Such a statement might make the child very upset and anxious, and she might not want to continue playing. It is important to stay within the metaphor of play communication.

How Play Therapy Helps

Children in play therapy use dolls, drawings, games, and other toys as shields to protect them from the frightening things have happened and may still be happening. In play therapy, "an entire treatment through play may be engineered without stepping far beyond the metaphor of the 'game'" (Terr, 1989, p. 14). Some children will themselves make the connection between the play scenario and their own lives; this initiative should always come from the child, not the therapist. In most instances, though, the child prefers to maintain a comfort zone of distance between the play content and his or her own life circumstances, and the therapist should respect this preference. The play "disguise" allows the child to express anger, jealousy, and fear through the mouths of puppets or dolls instead of admitting that these are the child's own feelings.

Sometimes children can talk about the deceased person and their feelings directly, and in these instances the therapist listens supportively. Children may initially express their feelings but then become uncomfortable and retreat into the world of play. When children are able to talk, the play therapist encourages it, but he or she accepts their need to gain sporadic relief through the less emotionally demanding outlet of play.

In summary, the rationale for the use of play therapy with bereaved children is based on the following three factors:

1. Children have limited verbal ability for describing their feelings.
2. Children have limited emotional capacity to tolerate stress and the pain of loss (they have a short sadness span).
3. Children communicate their feelings, wishes, fears, and their attempted resolutions to their problems through play.

Goals of Play Therapy with Bereaved Children

The goals of play therapy with bereaved children involve

- helping to facilitate the child's mourning process;
- helping to clarify any cognitive confusion the child may have about the death; and
- helping the child return to his or her usual routine.

Role and Function of the Play Therapist

The play therapist tries to establish a helping relationship with the child for the purpose of carrying out the therapy process. Playful methods, including the use of expressive arts such as drawing and sand play, facilitate the engagement and therapy process by encouraging the child's expression of feelings. Depending on the therapist's philosophy and training, the interactions with the child may be somewhat directive or totally nondirective. The play therapist seeks to return the child to an age-appropriate level of functioning.

When the child has experienced traumatic grief, the play therapist may attempt to involve him or her in the creation of a "trauma narrative" to reduce the feelings of helplessness and fright and help the child understand that he or she could not have avoided or transformed the traumatic situation. (This is illustrated below in the case of Susan.)

THE MARTINI CASE (CONTINUED)

Play Therapy Sessions

In individual play therapy sessions, each girl benefited from the opportunity to express some of her anger symbolically, through expressive art activities. Although these girls were old enough to express themselves verbally, their verbal and physical expressions toward one another were aggressive and negative, resulting in disapproval and restrictions from their parents. They needed an outlet where they could vent their anger safely, where they could receive therapeutic understanding about the validity of their feelings, and where they would not suffer penalties for the appropriate expression of anger. At the time of the sessions described below, the godfather had died and the girls' father had moved out (although he maintained regular visitation with them).

Amanda

Eight-year-old Amanda's preferred play therapy modality was modeling clay. I offered it to her knowing that it is a productive method for discharging anger. The clay can be shaped, pounded, poked, and destroyed, providing a very useful outlet for angry feelings. Amanda's clay productions began cautiously as jars/vases or animals. Her anger came out in the way she worked the clay—rolling, poking, and ripping it according to her mood. The final object might be a nice vase, but Amanda's physical involvement with the clay during its creation permitted considerable expression of aggression, including destruction of a previous construction.

Amanda could not verbally stand up to her sister, who was 2 years older. Through the "clay therapy," she expressed feelings of frustration and anger that seemed related to her lack of control about important aspects of her life. Several years later, Amanda accepted my invitation to appear for a follow-up session that would be videotaped for training purposes (Webb, 1994). The video demonstrates different play therapy techniques with a number of children of different ages. Amanda's segment showed her working with clay and talking about her previous conflicted relationship with her sister.

Linda

Ten-year-old Linda was very aggressive, and her anger caused many problems in her family. In play therapy, she used drawings to convey her awareness and fear of her anger and to demonstrate her need for help in controlling her aggression.

In most sessions, I have drawing materials readily available on a table, and I invite children to draw as we talk (although I try to stay quiet while they are drawing). Linda was very interested in drawing. Her drawings depicted mostly threatening themes; for example, two sharks swimming toward one another with their sharp teeth bared, and a teddy bear with claws on all his paws and his tongue stuck out. One picture was of a fearsome werewolf with sharp, threatening teeth. Linda had drawn it during a 20-minute wait for her sister, whose session came after Linda's. When Linda showed me the werewolf drawing (Webb, 2004, p. 83), I commented about how scary and dangerous it looked, and how I hoped it wouldn't hurt anybody. She said it might kill somebody. Linda agreed to my suggestion that I keep the drawing in my locked file cabinet, where it couldn't hurt anybody. Thus, I conveyed to her that it was all right for her to express her anger symbolically in my office but that she should not permit it to get dangerously out of control in her everyday life.

The girls used drawings and modeling material to express their anger related to mourning the dual losses of their godfather and their father. Over several months of individual play therapy sessions, their expressions of anger toward one another greatly diminished, and they were gradually able to refocus their lives on school and recreational activities. They had participated appropriately and meaningfully in their godfather's memorial service, and their lives had settled into a regular routine, with ongoing contact with their father through visits and telephone calls. While they did "lose" the family of their early childhood, they were beginning to realize that their lives were calmer now that their parents were not arguing. Play therapy had been effective in providing an acceptable means for them to learn to both express and control their anger.

PLAY THERAPY WITH TRAUMATICALLY BEREAVED CHILDREN

"Although virtually any death may be perceived by the mourner as personally traumatic because of the internal, subjective feeling involved... circumstances that are objectively traumatic are associated with five factors known to increase complications for mourners" (Rando, 1993, pp. 568–569):

- Suddenness and lack of anticipation

- Violence, mutilation, and destruction

- Preventability and/or randomness

- Multiple deaths

- Personal encounter of the mourner (i.e., personal threat or shocking confrontation)

Of all types of bereavement, traumatic death requires the most specialized management and presents the greatest challenge to the therapist. Because of the interaction between trauma and grief, this type of therapy should be undertaken only by professionals who understand trauma reactions and who have been trained to help people recover following traumatic bereavement.

As a rule, it is imperative to help the child with issues related to the trauma before attempting to assist with the mourning process. Because an integral part of bereavement involves remembering the person who died, this process can be terribly painful when the death was traumatic. Every time the child thinks about the beloved person, he or she also imagines the circumstances of death and the associated details of fear, pain, or violence/mutilation. These mental images frighten the child and lead him or her to want to avoid all memories of the dead person. The symptoms of posttraumatic stress disorder include numbed responses, hyperarousal, avoidance, and altered functioning (American Psychiatric Association, 2000).

The Case of Susan

A 9-year-old girl (Webb, 2004) whose friend had suffered fatal, mutilating head injuries in a car accident refused to visit the boy's home and became panic-stricken whenever her mother drove even close to his neighborhood. She had nightmares and had become withdrawn and irritable, and her schoolwork had deteriorated. The treatment of this child (which predated much of our current knowledge about posttraumatic therapy) included the use of drawings, stories, and board games. Although many of her symptoms abated, she continued to avoid discussing her friend, and although she signed a release permitting me to write about her therapy, she said that she did not want to read what I wrote.

If this child were beginning therapy today, I would use some directive play therapy methods to help her think in a detailed way about the circumstances of the trauma, so she could begin to realize that she could have done nothing to prevent it. Specifically, I would ask her to draw the trauma scene as she imagined it, as well as pictures of her friend before and as she thinks he looked at the time of his death. This would be accomplished slowly and with relaxation exercises to help her deal with any associated anxiety. While she was creating the drawings, I would ask her to make up a story about what she thinks happened. We would either tape record or write down the story and include it with the pictures in a homemade "book." This method is referred to as creating the "trauma narrative" (Cohen, Mannarino, & Deblinger, 2006). The principle is that helping the traumatized person deal with the details of the traumatic event allows him or her to begin the tasks of mourning. For those who worry about "re-traumatizing" the child, we know that children (and adults) whose lives have been touched by traumatic deaths already have created pictures in their heads of what they think happened. Once these pictures come into the open and are shared with a trusted therapist, the child often feels tremendous relief.

In play therapy with traumatized children, the therapist uses cognitive-behavioral techniques before initiating the recall of the event. The therapist teaches the child methods to reduce anxiety and to sooth themselves, explaining that they will help both now and in the future. Some examples of self-soothing behaviors are singing, engaging in physical activity, and thinking of a quiet, special place that is safe and private, and where no harm can ever come to them. Traumatized children sometimes are afraid that violence can happen to them if the perpetrator finds them. Therefore making the safe place private, and even secret, reassures the children that nothing bad will happen.

As the play reconstruction of the event begins under the therapist's direction, the child might choose to depart from distressing memories and "change the channel" to more relaxing, happy thoughts. The therapist moves at the child's pace, encouraging the child to reveal all fears and sensory memories. The ultimate therapeutic aim is for the child to put those frightening memories in the past and to identify him- or herself as a "survivor." Bevin (1999) presents a good example of play therapy reconstruction with a traumatized 9-year-old boy who almost drowned and then witnessed his mother's rape.

Preventing the Vicarious Traumatization of the Therapist

Working with traumatized persons is very stressful for the therapist, who may suffer secondary traumatization from listening to graphic details of violent deaths. Recently, increased attention has been paid to self-help techniques for therapists to prevent "compassion fatigue" and burnout (Gamble, 2002; Pearlman and Saakvitne, 1995; Ryan, 1999). Some suggestions for therapists include having their own support group, arranging a varied caseload that is not excessively weighted with trauma victims, and using the same self-soothing techniques they teach their clients. Therapists also benefit from play/recreation, which helps them maintain an emotional balance that will ultimately help their clients.

Conclusion

The general public and the professional community may not realize the extent to which death affects children and can interfere with their current and future development. Children do suffer pain over the loss of a loved one, although they usually cannot put their feelings into words. Play therapy offers the ideal method for helping bereaved children, since it does not require that they express themselves verbally.

This chapter has been written with the hope that it will sensitize and educate teachers, parents, religious counselors, and others who have contact with children about the tremendous relief that is available through play therapy. The child communicates his or her anxieties through play, and play therapists understand how to respond helpfully, using the child's play language. Although not all bereaved children may require this specialized assistance, in situations of complicated and traumatic bereavement, play therapists can assess and treat children in a manner that provides the best hope for grief processing and resolution. We must be certain that children receive the help they need to cope with their losses and proceed with their development.

Nancy Boyd Webb, Ph.D., holds the titles of Distinguished Professor of Social Work and James R. Dumpson Chair in Child Welfare Studies at Fordham University Graduate School of Social Service in New York where she has been on the faculty since 1979. Dr. Webb is a leading authority on play therapy with children who have experienced trauma and loss and her books are considered essential references. Her works include *Play Therapy with Children in Crisis: Individual, Family and Group Treatment; Helping Bereaved Children: A Handbook for Practitioners; Mass Trauma and Violence, Helping Families and Children Cope; Working with Traumatized Youth in Child Welfare; Social Work Practice with Children* (all with Guilford Press), and *Culturally Diverse Parent-Child and Family Relationships* (Columbia University Press). In addition she has produced a prize-winning video/DVD, *Techniques of Play Therapy. A Clinical Demonstration.* In April 2000, Dr. Webb appeared as one of four panelists in a teleconference sponsored by The Hospice Foundation of America.

REFERENCES

American Psychiatric Association. (2000). *Diagnostic and statistical manual of mental disorders* (4th ed., text rev.). Washington, DC: Author.

Bevin, T. (1999). Multiple traumas of refugees. Near drowning and witnessing of maternal rape: Case of Sergio, age 9 and follow-up at age 16. In N. B. Webb (Ed.), *Play therapy with children in crisis* (2nd ed.) (pp. 131–163). New York: Guilford Press.

Cohen, J. A., Mannarino, A. P., & Deblinger, E. (2006). *Treating trauma and traumatic grief in children and adolescents.* New York: Guilford Press.

Corr, C. A., & Corr, D. M. (Eds.). (1996). *Handbook of childhood death and bereavement.* New York: Springer.

Crenshaw, D. A. (2002). The disenfranchised grief of children. In K. J. Doka (Ed.), *Disenfranchised grief. New directions, challenges, and strategies for practice* (pp. 293–306). Champaign, IL: Research Press.

Doka, K. J. (Ed.). (2002). *Disenfranchised grief. New directions, challenges, and strategies for practice.* Champaign, IL: Research Press.

Gamble, S. J. (2002). Self-care for bereavement counselors. In N. B. Webb (Ed.), *Helping bereaved children. A handbook for practitioners* (pp.346–362). New York: Guilford Press.

Gardner, R. A. (1988). *The Storytelling Card Game.* Creskill, NJ: Creative Therapeutics.

Goldman, L. (1996). *Breaking the silence. A guide to help children with complicated grief.* Philadelphia, PA: Taylor and Francis Publishers.

Pearlman, L. A., & Saakvitne, K. (1995). *Trauma and the therapist.* New York: Norton.

Rando, T. A. (1991). *How to go on living when someone you love dies.* New York: Bantam. (Original work published in 1988.).

Rando, T. A. (1993). *Treatment of complicated mourning.* Champaign, IL: Research Press.

Raphael, B. (1983). *The anatomy of bereavement.* New York: Basic Books.

Ryan, K. (1999). Self-help for the helpers: Preventing vicarious traumatization. In N. B. Webb (Ed.), *Play therapy with children in crisis* (2nd ed.) (pp. 471–491). New York: Guilford Press.

Speece, M. W., & Brent, S. B. (1996). The development of children's understanding of death. In C . A. Corr & D. M. Corr (Eds.), *Handbook of childhood death and bereavement* (pp. 29–50). New York: Springer Publishing.

Terr, L. C. (1989). Treating psychic trauma in children: A preliminary discussion. *Journal of Traumatic Stress, 2*(1), 3–20.

Webb, N. B. (Ed.). (1999). *Play therapy with children in crisis. Individual, family and group treatment* (2nd ed). New York: Guilford Press.

Webb, N. B. (2000). Death of a parent. In A. Gitterman (Ed.), *Handbook of social work practice with vulnerable and resilient populations* (2nd ed.) (pp. 481–499). New York: Columbia University Press.

Webb, N. B. (Ed.). (2002). *Helping bereaved children. A handbook for practitioners* (2nd ed.). New York: Guilford Press.

Webb, N. B. (2003). *Social work practice with children* (2nd ed.). New York: Guilford Press.

Webb, N. B. (1994). *Techniques of play therapy. A clinical demonstration.* Videotape and DVD. New York: Guilford Press. (Republished in 2006.)

CHAPTER 16

The Power of Ritual: A Gift for Children and Adolescents

Kenneth J. Doka

When 7-year-old Toni's grandmother died, Toni did not attend the funeral because her parents thought it would be too upsetting. Instead, she spent the days of the visitation, funeral service, and burial with various friends.

Paul, age 12, did attend his sister's funeral. Although he and his sister had been close, his parents never took him to the cemetery, despite his frequent requests. This no longer matters much to him. With the help of a friend, Paul created a memorial Web page for his sister, unknown to his parents, that he frequently visits. His parents marvel at his resilience, proud that he has "moved on" so well and is now back at his computer games.

After Narita was struck by a car and killed on the way home from her elementary school, the school administration decided not to hold a service or put up a plaque, despite student requests. Her classmates, however, continually visit a makeshift shrine at the intersection where Narita died. They leave stuffed animals, candy, and small presents.

Not only do we protect children from death, we often seek to shield them from the rituals that surround the deaths of others. These efforts are well-intentioned—parents and guardians do not want to upset children and remind them of the loss. In some cases, adults also wish to avoid the troubling prospect of dealing with a child's grief as well as their own.

But sheltering children and adolescents from the rituals of death may deprive them of a critical form of support as they cope with loss. Rituals are powerful. Throughout history, our ancestors knew the power of rituals and memorials as they sought comfort and support in their grief. The rituals and memorials may take on new forms, but they continue to offer support, comfort, and meaning.

"Protecting" young people from the rituals associated with death does more than isolate them from the sustenance ritual offers. Ultimately, it deprives them of a resource that can help them cope with the inevitable losses humans experience throughout life.

This chapter explores the power of ritual. It begins with an examination of the therapeutic role of ritual in coping with loss and grief, which is most evident in the funeral. The chapter documents the value of funerals and offers specific guidelines to help parents and guardians enhance their therapeutic benefits for children and adolescents. It discusses the use of ritual as a strategy for therapeutic interventions. If rituals are a sacred time, memorials are a sacred place—the chapter concludes with a discussion of the role of memorials, both real and virtual, in adapting to loss and grief.

THE NATURE OF RITUAL

The term *ritual* can be used in many ways. It can refer to regularized activities, such as reading the morning paper or pledging allegiance to the flag. Shorter (1996) calls such activities *ceremonies* or *habits*; he reserves the word "ritual" for special acts that are invested with meaning. For example, a person goes into a restaurant and orders a glass of wine. The wine is served along with a basket of bread. There is nothing unusual or special here. Yet these same elements—bread and wine—served in a church and blessed by a member of the clergy, become a most sacred act: the sacrament of communion. Similarly, there is nothing inherently special in lighting candles, but when a Jewish mother lights a candle and invokes a blessing on the night of the Sabbath, she is completing a sacred act.

Rituals are powerful. Gennep (1960) describes rituals as "liminal," meaning they are transitional events that exist at the threshold between consciousness and unconsciousness. As a person goes through the steps of a particular ritual, strong feelings and reactions may emerge from the unconscious. For example, one may experience goose bumps or become tearful without being fully aware of what is creating these reactions.

The effect of rituals may be intrapsychic as well as psychosocial or social. Depending on the nature of the ritual, it may confer and reaffirm a changed state or status for the participants. For example, a boy leaves his bar mitzvah as a man, and two single people leave their wedding as a couple. Public rituals such as these have an additional social component: The transition is witnessed by others, who are expected to affirm their support (Romanoff & Terenzio, 1998).

THE FUNERAL RITUAL

The power of ritual is evident in funerals. Rando (1984) delineates the many benefits of funerals. For one, they allow people to behave in structured ways at a highly emotional time. Following the steps of a ritual at an otherwise chaotic time can be very therapeutic (Doka, 1984; Martin & Doka, 2000). Funerals provide a safe venue for the physical and emotional expression of grief, because the ritual contains that grief. They offer a chance for family, friends, and the larger community to come together in support. Funeral rituals provoke remembrances that help bereaved persons find meaning in the life of the person they are mourning. Finally, funerals allow grieving people to apply spiritual and philosophical frameworks that help them interpret the loss or find comfort within it. A large body of research has reaffirmed the therapeutic role of ritual (e.g., Bolton & Camp, 1987, 1989; Doka, 1984; Gross & Klass, 1997; Reeves & Boersma, 1990).

Children also benefit from the ritual of a funeral. The Harvard Child Bereavement Study found that children saw great value (especially retrospectively) in having attended a parent's funeral, where they found comfort and support (Silverman & Worden, 1992). Fristad and her associates (2001) reported that children whose families did not have funerals or who were not permitted to attend them fared less well over time than children who experienced the funeral.

There are ways to help children and adolescents participate in funerals. A child who is old enough to understand a funeral and sit through a ceremony should have a choice about how he or she wishes to participate in the rituals. For that choice to be meaningful, the child needs information, options, and support.

Depending on their age, developmental level, and previous experiences, children may have all sorts of fantasies about what happens at a funeral. The adult can help the child understand what will occur, including the purpose of the funeral, the physical setting, and the kinds of behaviors that the child may observe. It is critical to talk about the different ways others may act, from tears and sadness, to simple reconnections of relatives and friends, and even to reminiscences that elicit laughter. Explore any cultural or spiritual aspects of the funeral that might be confusing to the child. Funeral directors can be helpful here—most are willing to show the child the facility before the funeral and answer any questions the child might have.

Children also need options, as well as assurance that their decisions will be understood and respected. If the child decides not to attend some or any parts of the funeral, a viable alternative should be available. For example, it is not a true choice to either attend a funeral event or stay alone in an empty or unfamiliar house. The option might be to stay with a trusted adult.

Older children can process information about familial and cultural expectations that frame participation in the funeral events, but their choices also should be supported. In many cultural groups, funerals are multifaceted events. They may include a visitation period, a formal funeral service, an interment, and perhaps a postfuneral meal or reception. Children should be allowed to decide which events they want to attend.

A parent who is deeply involved in the funeral may not be able to provide support to children in their decisions. Here it may be useful to assign an adult who is not intimately involved in the funeral to oversee the child—even to remove the child if the event becomes too upsetting. Older children and adolescents can benefit from peer support.

Research indicates that planning and participating in rituals facilitates the grieving process (Doka, 1984). Children and adolescents can contribute to this planning. It may be useful to solicit their ideas about the rituals, and they may even be assigned responsibility for certain choices. In one case, for example, a bereaved 12-year-old child was comforted when his mother allowed him to make the final choice for his deceased father's casket.

Children and adolescents can participate as well. One of the most meaningful funerals I have attended was for a young girl who was killed in a bicycling accident. Her middle school peers were deeply involved in the service—as singers and instrumentalists, readers, and ushers. Their participation facilitated their grief and reaffirmed to the parents the impact their daughter had had, even in her short life.

Even very young children can participate. A widow described how meaningful it was to watch her 4-year-old great-grandson somberly handing out flowers at a graveside service. Participation does not have to be public. Children can be encouraged to write letters, draw pictures, or place objects in the casket. They can help select photos for display at the funeral or tape tributes and reminiscences. Such opportunities allow children and adolescents to be more than passive observers; they extend the benefit of a therapeutic funeral to even the youngest participants.

RITUAL AS A THERAPEUTIC TOOL

Because rituals are so beneficial, there is value in harnessing their power as a therapeutic tool. Rituals can be developed for use by individuals, families, or groups—such as school classes—to facilitate the grieving process. Different rituals convey different meanings. Building on the work of Gennep (1960), Rando (1993), and Martin and Doka (2000), we can delineate four kinds of rituals.

Rituals of continuity emphasize the continuing bond with the deceased. These can be quite simple. For example, a family might light a candle on the anniversary of the death or some other significant time to evoke the memory and continued bond with the deceased. Groups can use this kind of ritual, too: In the spring after Tyrone's death, his third-grade classmates planted a tree in his honor on the school grounds. Even years later, family and classmates return to the tree on Tyrone's birthday and the anniversary of his death.

Rituals of transition mark some movement or change in the grieving process. For example, before Jason's father essentially abandoned his family, Jason had made a plaque in his middle school ceramics class that said "Daddy's Garage." The divorce and subsequent paternal disinterest troubled Jason deeply. After a few months, he took the plaque down from the garage wall and carefully pulverized it. He proudly announced to his mom that it was no longer "Daddy's Garage" and took over the space himself. Rituals of transition mark times of change.

Rituals of reconciliation tend to finish business; that is, they allow the grieving child or adolescent to express or receive forgiveness, or to offer a last message or a simple farewell. Two cases illustrate these rituals. Joe's grandfather died suddenly when Joe was 5 years old. Three years later, Joe was troubled by the fact that he never told his grandfather how much he loved him. His counselor helped him understand the many ways he had conveyed that love—like running to meet him when he visited—and the many special moments they shared. But Joe was not satisfied. He and his therapist created a ritual in which Joe saved money to dedicate flowers at church in loving memory of his grandfather. After church, he laid them on his grandfather's grave and said, "I love you."

Eight-year-old Maria had a different issue. Her mother was an intravenous drug user, in and out of jail or rehabilitation. Maria lived much of her life with her godmother—a very loving and stable presence in her life. When her mother died, Maria believed that she had become a ghost. Ghosts, Maria explained, were neither good enough to go to heaven nor bad enough to go to hell. Ghosts had opportunities to do either good or harm, which would determine their eventual fate. One day, Maria announced that her mother was now ready to go to heaven. She and her therapist created a ritual in which Maria pasted angel wings on her mother's photo and then burned the photo, which freed her mother to enter heaven.

Rituals of affirmation allow the bereaved child or adolescent to thank the lost person for his or her presence and legacies. Ten-year-old Kieran and his father had often fished together—a sport they both loved. For a long time after his father's death, Kieran did not fish. When he decided to fish again, he reverently buried the first fish he caught near his father's grave, thanking his dad for teaching him the sport and promising that whenever he fished, he would remember his father and the special moments they shared.

A few principles should guide the creation of these therapeutic rituals. First, they should not be imposed but should be developed from the child's own narrative of loss and grief. That narrative will suggest the appropriate kind of ritual and offer clues as to who should participate or witness it and what objects should be included. Rituals can be private or witnessed by small or even large audiences. The second principle is that rituals should include objects; they serve as visual reminders with highly symbolic significance. Third, rituals should be fully planned and carefully processed. Finally, rituals are likely to be more powerful if they include primal elements; for example, fire, water, music or chimes as wind, and flowers as earth. Because they are liminal, rituals can harness power in a therapeutic environment.

MEMORIALS—REAL AND VIRTUAL

If rituals are sacred times, memorials are sacred places. Not only are they places where the remains of the deceased rest, they may have significant familial, spiritual, and cultural connections. For example, cemeteries may host many generations of the family. They also may be organized by ethnicity or religion, offering a tie to a specific faith or culture. They are a perfect setting for rituals.

But there may be value simply in visiting the memorial. The same basic principles that govern funerals apply to children's visits to cemeteries or mausoleums. Children should have a choice about whether they participate, and that choice requires information, options, and support. In some cases, children may have irrational fears about cemeteries; once addressed, these fears are often easily controlled. In other cases, the child may simply not feel any connection to the deceased person in the cemetery. There may be other "sacred" places where the child feels more of a connection; he or she should be encouraged to visit those places, share memories, and honor the deceased.

Children and adolescents often fashion spontaneous memorials, such as a shrine at the site of an accident or another significant place. For example, when Marco was killed in a car collision, his adolescent friends placed a cross on the side of the highway.

Virtual memorials on sites like *MySpace* are increasingly common. While most adults are "digital immigrants" (meaning that they learned how to use computers later in life), children are "digital natives," having grown up with computers and the Internet. It is not surprising that they turn to the Internet for meaning and support. Virtual memorials allow adolescents to remember and mourn together, even if they are geographically separated, and to feel that they honor a friend. However, because of the unregulated nature of the Internet and its invisibility to many adults, the therapeutic role of such memorials can be compromised if other adolescents post negative stories or rumors about the deceased peer. Like many innovations, virtual memorials can have a dark side.

Conclusion

Rituals and memorials are legacies from prehistory that still hold great power. Using rituals and memorials with children and adolescents imparts an ancient wisdom that is helpful today, empowering us when we come together at special times and places to mourn our losses. This power and purpose should not be denied to the youngest and most vulnerable mourners.

Kenneth J. Doka, Ph.D., is a Professor of Gerontology at the Graduate School of The College of New Rochelle and Senior Consultant to the Hospice Foundation of America. A prolific editor and author, Dr. Doka's books include *Living with Grief: Before and After Death; Death, Dying and Bereavement: Major Themes in Health and Social Welfare; Pain Management at the End-of-Life: Bridging the Gap between Knowledge and Practice; Living with Grief: Ethical Dilemmas at the End of Life; Living with Grief: Alzheimer's Disease; Living with Grief: Coping with Public Tragedy; Men Don't Cry, Women Do: Transcending Gender Stereotypes of Grief; Living with Grief: Loss in Later Life; Disenfranchised Grief: Recognizing Hidden Sorrow; Living with Life Threatening Illness; Children Mourning, Mourning Children; Death and Spirituality; Living with Grief: After Sudden Loss; Living with Grief: When Illness is Prolonged; Living with Grief: Who We Are, How We Grieve; Living with Grief: At Work, School and Worship; Living with Grief: Children, Adolescents and Loss; Caregiving and Loss: Family Needs, Professional Responses; AIDS, Fear and Society; Aging and Developmental Disabilities;* and *Disenfranchised Grief: New Directions, Challenges, and Strategies for Practice.* In addition, Dr. Doka has published more than 60 articles and book chapters. Dr. Doka is editor of *Omega* and *Journeys: A newsletter to help in bereavement.*

Dr. Doka was elected President of the Association for Death Education and Counseling in 1993 and elected to the Board of Directors of the International Work Group on Dying, Death and Bereavement in 1995 and served as its chair from 1997-1999. He has received numerous awards for his work in thanatology and hospice. In 2006, Dr. Doka was grandfathered in as a mental health counselor under New York's first licensure of counselors. Dr. Doka is an ordained Lutheran minister.

REFERENCES

Bolton, C., & Camp, D. (1987). Funeral rituals and the facilitation of grief work. *Omega: The Journal of Death and Dying, 17,* 343–351.

Bolton, C., & Camp, D. (1989). The post-funeral ritual in bereavement counseling and grief work. *Journal of Gerontological Social Work, 13,* 49–59.

Doka, K. (1984). Expectation of death, participation in funeral rituals, and grief adjustment. *Omega: The Journal of Death and Dying, 15,* 119–130.

Fristad, M., Cerel, J., Goldman, M., Weller, E., & Weller, R. (2001). The role of ritual in children's bereavement. *Omega: The Journal of Death and Dying, 42,* 321–340.

Gennep, A. (1960). *The rites of passage.* Chicago: University of Chicago Press.

Gross, R., & Klass, D. (1997). Tibetan Buddhism and the resolution of grief: The Bardo-Thodell for the living and the grieving. *Death Studies, 21,* 377–398.

Martin, T., & Doka, K. (2000). *Men don't cry, women do: Transcending gender stereotypes of grief.* Philadelphia, PA: Brunner/Mazel.

Rando, T. A. (1984). *Grief, dying and death: Clinical interventions for caregivers.* Champaign, IL: Research Press.

Rando, T. A. (1993). *The treatment of complicated mourning.* Champaign, IL: Research Press.

Reeves, N., & Boersma, F. (1990). The therapeutic use of ritual in maladaptive grieving. *Omega: The Journal of Death and Dying, 20,* 281–291.

Romanoff, B., & Terenzio, M. (1998). Rituals and the grieving process. *Death Studies, 22,* 697–712.

Shorter, B. (1996). *Susceptible to the sacred: The psychological experience of ritual.* New York: Routledge.

Silverman, P., & Worden, J. W. (1992). Children's understanding of the funeral ritual. *Omega: The Journal of Death and Dying, 25,* 319–332.

Sincerely

Michael Santoro

To My Teachers:

As you are aware, it is December. Many joyous things are associated with the month of December. Snow days, Christmas, Chanukah, and the start of the new year.

Unfortunately, the first thing that comes to my mind when December rolls around is not so joyous and cheerful. My twin sister, Paula, died on December 10, 2000, from the complications of Cushing's syndrome.

My sister's death affected many people, and it continues to hurt today.

Next Wednesday, when I come to school, I may feel upset, or my temper might spark, or I might not participate in class as much as I should. Last year, nobody mentioned my sister to me all day at school. I don't know if it was purposefully or if they just were not informed, but it made me feel worse.

When I talk about my sister, or when someone mentions her, it doesn't hurt. It makes me feel better. It hurts when no one mentions her to me.

Please mention her name anytime you want, but especially next Wednesday.

This letter was written on December 4, 2003, by then-seventh-grader Michael Santoro of Morristown, New Jersey, to his teachers. He read it to them at a teachers meeting to express how he would feel at school and how they could help them on his grief journey. Michael and his family attended a Compassionate Friends support group following Paula's death.

Today, Michael is 17 and a junior in high school. He is a skilled trombone and sitar player and an avid outdoorsman. What follows is his view of his sister's death years after he wrote the letter to his teachers.

Hello, I'm Mike. I turned 17 earlier this month, and I am a junior in high school.

For almost 7 years now, I've had to deal with one of the most difficult things a kid can be asked to deal with. That's the loss of my twin sister, Paula. She died on December 10, 2000 from the complications of a rare disease, called Cushing's syndrome. She was sick, and had a serious operation, but she was recovering and back home when her pancreas failed and she died suddenly. Mom and Dad were at the hospital when Paula died. I was taken there by a neighbor but didn't arrive until after she had passed away.

Grief is always hard, but maybe the hardest part comes after some time passes. After a few months or so, my friends thought that they shouldn't even mention my sister's name, because they were afraid that even hearing her name would upset me. So I began to think that they didn't care about Paula, but in reality, they did. They just didn't know how to help. It got even harder when I graduated from the grade school that Paula and I went to, and went on to middle school. None of the teachers there really knew Paula, and on the anniversary of her death, no one mentioned her to me. It seemed like everyone had already forgotten about her. The next year, I wrote a letter to my teachers, and read it at a teacher's meeting. I explained that Paula's anniversary was coming up, and that I might have trouble concentrating in school. I said it was alright for people to mention Paula and to share memories about her. In fact, it made me feel better when people remembered her. The teachers were really helpful when they knew what was on my mind.

People want to help—sometimes, they just don't know how. So we have to "say" and "do"—*say* what's on our mind and how people can help us, and *do* things to honor our brother or sister.

In the "say" category, I am part of a support group called The Compassionate Friends. I go to the conventions. There I meet with kids my age who are experiencing the same feelings I am experiencing. I also go to a counselor every so often to talk about how things are going. My current counselor also lost a sibling so he knows what I am going through.

In the "do" category, I asked my parents if we could have a fundraiser to help people with the disease that killed Paula. I came up with a "Bike and Hike with Mike." It takes a lot of work but we've raised about $65,000 for research. It is always a good day, with lots of friends and family who remember Paula and who want to help.

So in dealing with grief, my advice is to "say" and "do." Always find a way to say what's on your mind. Try to find things to do to keep memories alive. And never forget that most people want to help you—but they sometimes need you to show the way.

CHAPTER 17

Grieving Adolescents: The Paradox of Using Technology for Support

Libba James, Kevin Ann Oltjenbruns, and Peggy Whiting

INTRODUCTION

Anyone who reads this volume will know that at any given moment, significant numbers of adolescents are grieving the loss of a loved one. What adult helpers might not know is the extent to which this age group uses the Internet to seek information about grief, memorialize those who have died, express their emotions, and seek or offer support. And many helpers might not realize how text messaging provides opportunities for almost constant communication as young persons interact following a loss.

The intent of this chapter is fourfold: First, we will share a perspective on how many adolescents access technology on a regular basis, although any snapshot of usage is a rapidly moving target. Second, we will give a brief summary of developmental characteristics to provide insight on why adolescents regard technology as such a powerful tool for dealing with life's challenges. Third, we will discuss numerous examples of how adolescents are using technology. Finally, we will discuss some fundamental issues (positive and negative) with regard to using these tools to offer and gain support in grief.

HOW MANY ADOLESCENTS USE TECHNOLOGY?

In 2005, the Pew report on adolescent usage of the Internet (Pew Foundation, 2005) found that approximately 93% of U.S. teens (ages 12–17) used the Internet. Seventy-four percent of online teens use instant messaging, and 55% have an online profile and use social networking Web sites. These numbers had increased significantly since the 2000 Pew report. MySpace and

Facebook, popular networking sites, have contributed dramatically to the growing cyberworld populated by teens. In addition, approximately 79% of American teens ages 15 to17 have cell phones (Elder, 2007). These constantly changing forms of technology provide adolescent users with 24/7 links with friends and immediate access to unlimited amounts of information.

DEVELOPMENTAL CHARACTERISTICS: WHY DO ADOLESCENTS USE TECHNOLOGY?

Adolescence has been characterized as a developmental stage filled with unique biological, psychological, and social influences (Corr, Nabe, & Corr, 2006). Changes occur in attitudes, values, behavior, self-concept, self-esteem, social connectedness, and developmental sophistication. A bereavement crisis in adolescence may overtax the developmental resources and threaten the mastery of developmental tasks associated with this period (Collins & Collins, 2005). Adolescents can gain maturity or suffer increased vulnerability when dealing with bereavement, a paradox of the opportunity and risk inherent in incorporating and adapting to events that produce disequilibrium (Balk, 2007). Elsewhere in this chapter, we will highlight another paradox: While technology can help some adolescents deal with their grief, the same technology can be fraught with danger.

Collins and Collins (2005) discuss the developmental-ecological perspective as a framework for understanding crisis response. These authors suggest that development offers a context for a person's cognitive, affective, and behavioral response to crisis. When the developmental-ecological model is applied to grieving adolescents, it suggests that the crucial developmental tasks of becoming autonomous, sustaining intimate peer relationships, and defining identity and future direction for oneself form the backdrop of an adolescent's world when bereavement is a part of the experience (Balk, 2000). Balk lists some of the developmental tasks that may lead adolescents to use technology at such a high level; primarily, strengthening autonomy (i.e., the need to do things for themselves, without the scrutiny and supervision of adults) and strengthening peer relations.

Some teens seek "virtual" relationships as often as they seek face-to-face relationships, and the ability to form cyber-relationships provides a tool for the task of defining their identity. An adolescent who explores various possible identities in the real world of relationships runs the risk of being regarded as strange or weak. While risk is also involved on the Internet, the adolescent can put forth different personas under cover of anonymity. In a chat room, one can make up a name, a history, and a set of experiences that either parallel reality or have little to do with it. Teens may get various reactions from peers who intersect with them in cyberspace. They can decide whether a particular experimental identity was met with the reaction they hoped for in terms of respect, support, closeness, and so on. On the other hand, they can see which shared emotions or requests for help were ignored or condemned.

During adolescence, teens create relationships that are qualitatively different from those at earlier life stages. Peers help define one's identity, offer support, and perform many other important functions. However, adolescents may confuse meaningful relationships with the number of connections or interactions. Which is more beneficial: time spent communicating with a few trusted friends who know you well and challenge you to grow in a safe environment, or time spent interacting online with hundreds of people you do not really know? A collection of "Internet friends" may camouflage a lack of real closeness or intimacy. The intensity of grief expressed in less authentic relationships is a phenomenon of today's technological structures; it requires processing or mediation by a caring adult.

With the ability to think in the abstract, adolescents who care deeply about belonging may be prone to exaggerate the attention of the imaginary audience and embrace the idea that peers are watching and evaluating them at all times (Oltjenbruns, 2007). This belief contributes to an increased fear of being perceived as different, being denied coveted social status or acceptance by others. In the real world, teens may censor their true feelings if they think those feelings will be unacceptable to their peers. Technology offers teens a way to experiment with expressing feelings and thoughts without the self-consciousness inherent in face-to-face interaction.

The adolescent belief in a personal fable is another relevant developmental characteristic, because it affects the way adolescents deal with life situations. The belief that something "cannot happen to me" can make a teen especially vulnerable to negative outcomes in cyberspace. Adults are likely to be appropriately cautious in giving personal information over the

Internet, but adolescents often see no harm in providing personal details. Confidence in the personal fable can result in a young person's minimizing the potential dangers of Internet advice from strangers. It is crucial that caring adults discuss with teens what is and is not appropriate to share and what precautions they should take. For example, rather than identifying the school she attends, a teen could simply say she lives in Colorado.

Cognitively, the adolescent is shifting toward greater sophistication in comprehending the finality, causality, and universality of death through the onset of abstract reasoning. With cognitive maturation comes a thirst for information. Technology allows access to information at any hour of the day. In the past, a teen could have been stymied in the search for information, because parents don't want their children wandering the streets at night and because libraries have limited hours of operation. Today, however, teens can find information on the Internet at all hours, and they can do so anonymously. For example, a young person who does not want to ask directly what a "normal grief response" is for fear of not being "normal" can easily access that information online.

How Are Adolescents Using Technology for Grief Support?

The scope and complexity of the Internet make it a breeding ground for an unlimited number of cyber-connections. It allows the existence of millions of information-packed Web sites and in recent years has fostered an explosion of sites created for social interaction. These sites were created to play a networking function, but they have also become an extremely powerful tool in adolescents' search for support in times of loss. Web memorials and access to information, grief support groups, and online counseling are instantly available on the Internet. For example, on April 16, 2007—the day of the Virginia Tech shootings—hundreds of students used Facebook to inform their families and friends that they were safe. Since the shootings, thousands of Web sites about the tragedy have emerged. The Internet provided an instant support system for those who were affected, directly or indirectly, by this tragedy.

Search Engines

One of the most powerful advantages of the Internet is easy access to information in a manner that was impossible in the past (although the mere existence of this information does not ensure that it is accurate or helpful). Search engines, such as Google and Yahoo, are a starting point for gaining information on any topic, including grief. A grieving adolescent can use these tools to seek information and support. For example, a teenager who just lost a mother can use a search engine to find online resources that may assist in the grieving process. If he or she uses the keyword "grief" as a starting point, the search engine will filter more than 26 million Web sites on grief-related topics (including sites that simply include the word "grief" in some form). Web sites are listed in order according to how many people have visited them (how many "hits" they have received). Figure 1 shows some of the Web sites that emerge from a simple search on the keyword "grief."

FIGURE 1. GOOGLE SEARCH WITH KEYWORD *GRIEF*

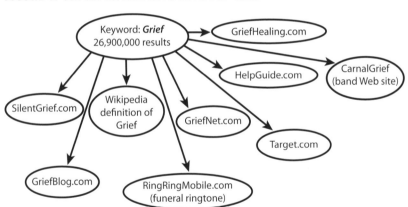

Certainly, some of the Web sites that surface through keyword searches can be helpful to grieving adolescents. They may find useful information on the grieving process or contacts for support services offered in their area. However, some links may be more damaging than helpful, providing inaccurate information or misleading offers of support. For example, it is easy to find sites that offer online counseling for a fee. Some of these services are provided by credentialed helping professionals, but others are facilitated by persons who are not trained in ethical and effective counseling techniques and may even be online predators. As professionals, we need to educate ourselves about the many Web sites that are useful in dealing with grief. It is our responsibility to refer our young clients to good online resources that may offer support outside the traditional counseling arena and to explain why we recommend some Web sites over others. An online comparison, with the teen involved in the search and evaluation, can be a helpful teaching tool.

Search engines can lead to various "blogs" (Web logs)—essentially, personal diaries that can be publicly viewed. Blogs often include not only the writer's thoughts but also responses from readers. For an adolescent, a blog may trigger an uncontrolled dialogue that may do emotional harm. For example, the authors easily accessed a number of blogs, written about the deaths of loved ones, to which readers had responded in unhelpful, negative, and derogatory ways. These damaging responses could result in a teen's not seeking any other type of support for fear of being condemned or verbally abused.

Situations such as these demonstrate the importance of keeping open lines of communication with adolescents about their use of technology for grief support and how they feel about what is transpiring online. These conversations are possible only if the teen already has a trusting relationship with the adult.

Social Networking Sites

The Internet is a virtual world where strangers can meet, lost friends can reconnect, and relationships can strengthen. Social networking sites, such as MySpace, are an example of online communities that foster personal connections. MySpace is a widely popular Web site that provides a free networking forum for members. It has been estimated to contain more than 106 million profiles, mostly of young adults (Faultline, 2006). Profiles may contain personal information, photos, music, and videos, making a very attractive display of one's personality. In the MySpace world, a member can communicate directly with networks of existing friends (real person-to-person contacts in the member's physical world) and can enter into new friendships that may or may not extend outside the virtual community. Most of us consider a friend to be a person with whom we have an intimate and significant relationship; in the virtual MySpace world, the meaning of the word changes.

As a member, you may search profiles in the community and may solicit another member to be your "friend." This simply means that you now have an online connection with this person, and he or she can be listed on your "friend list," which can be viewed on your profile. Unfortunately, some adolescents may define their worth by the number of people on their friend list. To increase that number, they may seek out strangers or respond to strangers' requests, making them susceptible to online predators. The authors also question whether the amount of time spent online in virtual relationships dilutes the amount of time and energy available for face-to-face interactions.

MySpace offers public and private interest groups that any member may join. Group topics are wide-ranging, from popular music to grief support. Let us explore one example. Suicide affects many teens around the world, and MySpace offers resources—good and bad—for a teenager who may be contemplating suicide. Suppose an adolescent has suicidal thoughts and explores MySpace interest groups with the hope of tapping into resources and gaining support for options other than ending his or her life. Figure 2 illustrates the sequence of Web pages that an adolescent might discover in his or her search for suicide support groups.

FIGURE 2. MYSPACE INTEREST GROUP SEARCH WITH KEYWORD *SUICIDE*

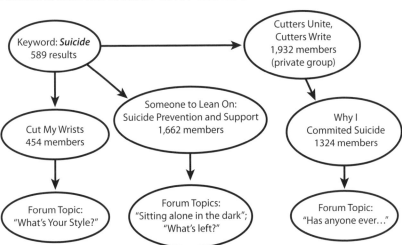

With just three clicks of a mouse, a vulnerable teenager might find helpful sites; on the other hand, the same adolescent might inadvertently enter into an online group discussing different styles of self-mutilation or other dangerous topics. With minimal investigation, it is evident that many so-called support groups can be more harmful than helpful. A group member might post a question, or "forum topic," to which other members can respond. Often, these forum topics are of a desperate nature and very alarming. Sometimes a question is met with derogatory, hateful, or damaging responses. Other times, a request for help does not receive any supportive messages at all. How do teens feel when no one bothers to respond in their time of need? Because there is no credentialed mediator, it is impossible to know if grieving adolescents are being contacted by well-meaning (even if untrained), supportive people or by persons with more selfish or darker motives. The continuum of possible contacts might range from a person who hopes to recruit new clients into his or her own "counseling" practice to someone who sets up a face-to-face meeting that could result in some sort of violence.

Figure 3 illustrates how an adolescent can easily find groups that may offer support in response to death-related losses. Many of the online support groups are composed of members who are similar in age and experiences, which can make for a seemingly safe forum to talk about personal losses and listen to others' stories of loss. These groups can offer a way to normalize the grief process for adolescents who are confused and uncomfortable in their own grief. However, many support groups that appear to be helpful may actually be based in deceit. In exploring several grief support groups on MySpace, the authors observed that many of the same "helpers" were members of many different groups. Often these people attempted to recruit grieving individuals to join a group in which they served as a facilitator. These facilitators claimed to be "experts" in grief counseling, but they did not have any kind of formal training or endorsement in this area. Because grief work is such a delicate and personal experience, it is alarming that these kinds of people are gaining the attention of adolescents.

FIGURE 3. MYSPACE INTEREST GROUP SEARCH WITH KEYWORD *GRIEF*

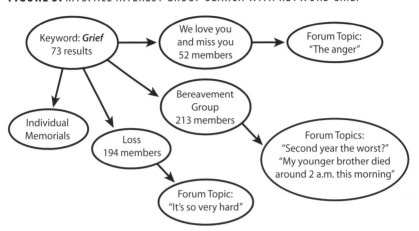

Because of this threat, we must also examine the growing number of adults using networking Web sites such as MySpace. While it may be completely appropriate for an adult to use MySpace to connect with friends and co-workers, danger may exist when the adult cyberworld overlaps with that of the adolescent.

There is much debate about how helping professionals can use the Internet to work with grieving teenagers. Many adults approach sites like MySpace as a wonderful tool to connect with teens. However, some adults may use the site as a way to "spy" on adolescents or, even more alarming, to take advantage of vulnerable teens.

Some helping professionals have succeeded in building strong relationships with their young clients through online connections. But because there are no established ethical guidelines or standards for this practice, it is a risky tool.

Online Memorials

One of the most interesting phenomena on Web sites such as MySpace is the creation of memorials. In many cases, young adults use the profiles of friends who have died as a forum for people to come together to honor the one they have lost (e.g., victims of the Virginia Tech shootings or fallen soldiers). Online memorials provide a meeting place where teens can gain support from their peers and receive confirmation that grief is a normal and universal process.

A 17-year-old high school student told us how MySpace has served as a memorial for a classmate who was murdered. She said that the murdered boy's peers used his MySpace profile as a place to verbalize their sorrow and fear. "I think it definitely benefited his grieving friends to have a place to center their attention and...to express themselves and connect with other people who could relate," the student told us. She added, "It surprised me how much people are doing over the Internet to help cope with the grief, but it made me realize how big a role the Internet plays in my generation" (S. Harlan, personal communication, July 5, 2006). This phenomenon is one more example of how important technology is in the lives of adolescents.

Online memorials have recently been the subject of media discussion. One question relates to the idea of "ownership" of memorial sites, as a concern has surfaced among family members of deceased persons who do not want their loved one's profile to become a memorial site. Currently, no policies or procedures are in place for deleting online profiles of users who have died. As people continue to send messages, some grieving families may become distressed at the ongoing contact. Others, however, are comforted to see how many people cared about their loved one. Discussion has focused on whether or not family members have the authority to close an online profile created by their now-deceased loved one.

In some cases, entirely new profiles are created specifically to memorialize the deceased. While online memorials can be wonderful ways to remember lost loved ones, they can also be a dangerous sounding board for anyone who may have negative feelings about the person who has died. We have seen several online memorials in which comments moved from honoring the dead to attacking or belittling the person or his or her family and friends. As with all forms of Internet grief support, we must be aware of the pros and cons of online memorials.

Text Messaging

Text messaging is real-time interaction via cell phone; it is a popular form of technology that is widely used by adolescents. An estimated 2.5 billion text messages are sent each month, mostly by adolescents and young adults (CBS, 2005). Teenagers have made texting an artful skill, executed with amazing speed and often without ever looking at the keypad. Cell phones and text messaging have created numerous problems in schools, as they often detract from the learning environment. However, as we have observed with other forms of technology, not all use is damaging. The following scenario is an example of how an adolescent used text messaging to gain support in a time of loss.

> Ms. L, a high school counselor, was talking with C, a 17-year-old student who was grieving the death of her grandmother. C had just received a call from her mother informing her of the death. Ms. L listened as C talked about her grandmother's recent illness and the fear she had experienced about her inevitable death. As the two talked, the conversation was continually interrupted by the alert signal on C's cell phone. As a steady stream of text messages came through, Ms. L became frustrated by the distraction, but C appeared more and more at ease. Later, Ms. L discovered that C was receiving text messages from her classmates offering their sympathy. C felt supported and cared for as these messages poured in from her friends. Ms. L reevaluated her experience during this session and realized that C was receiving the support she needed in this nontraditional way.

Many helping professionals have had a similar experience when working with adolescents. Technology is a central element in adolescents' lives—they use it to gain instant information, instant communication, and instant support. Some counselors can appreciate the importance of technology in the life of teens, while others find the constant interruptions to be inconsiderate or even rude. We should view this type of interaction as both an opportunity to educate ourselves and a chance to teach adolescents about the impact—positive and negative—of their use of technology on interpersonal relationships.

Summary

Many social changes affect adolescents today as they work through the normative developmental tasks of their life stage. Society has moved from limited sources of delayed information to an overload of immediate information; from delayed and monitored social interactions to spontaneous, independent encounters with unfamiliar persons; and from greater to lesser accountability to adults. These collective changes are producing risks for the current generation of adolescents, particularly as they confront the crisis of bereavement. We must try to determine what provides value and what promotes vulnerability for adolescents, with their unique developmental tasks and perspective, as they reach out through technology for assistance with their grief.

The environment holds possibilities for recovery and adaptation after a significant loss; it can also create a pathway toward vulnerability during a grief crisis. For adolescents, cyberspace is one of the major contextual environments in which they deal with grief. It has become a place for self-expression and social networking, limited though it is in terms of promoting truly authentic and supportive relationships. Like generations past, the current generation of teens will seek ways to connect and communicate with their peers when facing a crisis. Grieving adolescents can seek comfort, express vulnerable feelings, and receive feedback anonymously and without adult supervision. And they can do this spontaneously—they do not have to arrange to meet with others; through technology, help is immediately accessible.

Earlier, we noted that adolescents will seek avenues within their technological environment to experiment with who they are, which may create an increase in risky behaviors and open the door to predatory relationships. Adults have reason for concern about the impulsivity and lack of discernment many adolescents display when they are seeking immediate relief and solace around the complex issue of bereavement.

Adolescents have a social and interpersonal style focused on group acceptance and independence from adult figures. Experimentation with intimacy through peer relationships is a central issue (Balk, 2007), and adolescents desire some anonymity and privacy in this endeavor, so adult monitoring may be difficult or perceived as intrusive (Oltjenbruns & James, 2006). This reality is in conflict with the accepted notion that the best predictor of a positive outcome for an adolescent's grief is the availability of a responsible and responsive adult (Worden, 1996). In fact, adults may find themselves with little or no knowledge of an adolescent's friendship network and without face time to help the teen deal with the grief.

The stark reality of bereavement can affect the way an adolescent copes with the core issues of predictability, personal control, justice and fairness, self-confidence, and connections symbolic of belonging (Fleming & Adolph, 1986). Grief counselors and other caring adults must consider the possibility that the adolescent who reaches out for Internet support and comfort may be met with responses that contribute to increased fears, social dismissal, and self-doubt rather than a sense of acceptance and support. Much depends on who and what are encountered during an online search—some interactions clearly make a positive, long-lasting difference, and some do not.

Adolescents are well served when they are guided to what Stroebe and Schut (1999) describe as a "restoration orientation"—a perspective that holds hope and promise for the future. Desetta and Wolin (2000) define resiliencies such as insight (asking tough questions and confronting the truth of a situation), independence (making action decisions), relationships (seeking sources of support), and initiative (taking action to meet challenges) as critical elements for adolescents in their struggle to be strong in the face of adversity. These processes are not likely to be facilitated on the Web to the extent they would be with one-on-one interaction between the teen and a parent, counselor, teacher, minister, or other caring adult. Direct interaction offers more hope of authenticity and the advantage of picking up on nonverbal cues that are missing in virtual communication.

Because they turn to the Internet for information and solace, adolescents in grief often become less available for direct interactions with adults, who have a wider perspective on living and dying and on reconciling personal losses. Technology may increase the availability of certain types of support, but the Internet lacks the necessary protection and continuity as the grief process unfolds. There is no easy solution to this dilemma. As part of a face-to-face interaction, an adult might ask a teenager what he is accessing on the Web and view the sites he is entering. The ensuing conversation might then focus on such things as—

- whether the information on a site is accurate or misleading, including guidance for determining the quality of a particular resource;

- whether interpersonal communications on a blog or other interactive site are appropriate, sensitive, hurtful, honest, etc.; and

- whether responses from peers in cyberspace are comforting (and why) or hurtful (and why).

How willing should we be as helping professionals to extend ourselves to teenagers through the use of technology? The authors advocate as much direct interaction between teens and caring adults as possible, although we understand the limitations. An adult who already has a relationship with the bereaved teen might see the value of meeting him or her in cyberspace. If one believes that the best, most time-efficient, or only way to enter a conversation is through e-mail or texting, then it should be pursued. At least that adult can still share valuable information, make referrals, challenge beliefs, and probe more deeply. When trust is built in this fashion, opportunities for more direct interaction may ultimately unfold.

Adolescents will continue to increase their use of technological tools and will discover new ways to connect with the world around them. To offer strong support in times of loss, adults must meet young people where they are with technology. But how do we regulate the endless avenues that are available through technology? There are no ethical guidelines for using technology to work with adolescent clients—conversations are needed in our professional communities to address this issue. The task is enormous, but ignoring the complex debate is not an option if we want to ensure the safety and welfare of our children and adolescents.

Schaefer and Moos (2001) proposed appraisal-focused, problem-focused, and emotion-focused coping skills as resources for mastering adaptive tasks associated with bereavement. They argue that an adolescent's skillfulness in cognitive redefinition, identification of action options, finding sources of support, and exercising emotional control and release will enable him or her to successfully complete the tasks of establishing the meaning of the death, confronting the realities of the event, sustaining relational connection, maintaining affective balance, and preserving self-efficacy. In this context, how does technology help and hinder the successful transmission of an orientation toward restoration, resilience, and coping skill for the adolescent who is confronting grief? We do not pretend to know the answer but suggest that significant research remains to be done in the area of adolescents using technology for grief support.

Libba James is a school counselor at Windsor High School in Windsor, Colorado. She also works part time at Hospice of Larimer County's "Pathways" grief and loss programs facilitating support groups for grieving adolescents. Ms. James is currently working toward earning her Ph.D. in Education and Human Resource Studies concentrating in Human Development and Family Studies at Colorado State University in Fort Collins.

Kevin Ann Oltjenbruns, Ph.D., was a longtime faculty member (31 years) in the Department of Human Development and Family Studies at Colorado State University where she served as Vice Provost for Undergraduate Studies for three years prior to her retirement in June 2005. She served in many other administrative roles at the University, including serving the Associate Dean in the College of Applied Human Sciences.

Dr. Oltjenbruns' major professional focus was in the area of grief and loss. She co-authored a textbook entitled *Dying and Grieving: Lifespan and Family Perspectives* and has written numerous articles and chapters, focusing primarily on various issues related to developmental stages and grief. In addition to many other community volunteer activities over the years, Dr. Oltjenbruns has been involved with Hospice of Larimer County and is a frequent guest speaker on topics related to grief. Currently, she is serving as a Co-Director of the Osher Lifelong Learning Institute through the Division of Continuing Education at Colorado State University.

Peggy P. Whiting, Ed.D., is a professor in the Department of Counselor Education at North Carolina Central University. She is a nationally certified thanatologist, a K–12 licensed school counselor, a licensed professional counselor and earned a doctorate in human development counseling. Dr. Whiting's scholarship activities have primarily followed a thematic focus around the impact of loss situations upon development. She has strong interests in the role of systems such as schools and faith communities in providing environments for the teaching of life skills contributing to resilience and loss adaptation in children and youth. Dr. Whiting has maintained a grief counseling private practice for 20 years while serving as faculty in counselor education programs at both Vanderbilt and Winthrop Universities. She is the author or co-author of more than 100 articles, presentations, videotapes and manuals focused upon loss. Dr. Whiting has designed and implemented graduate grief counseling and human development courses at three universities. She is the 1998 recipient of the Distinguished Service Award given by the South Carolina Counseling Association for prolonged accomplishment to counseling and for her contribution to crisis response with school-age children.

REFERENCES

Balk, D. E. (2000). Adolescents, grief, and loss. In K. J. Doka (Ed.), *Living with grief: Children, adolescents, and loss* (pp. 35–49). Washington, DC: Hospice Foundation of America.

Balk, D. E. (2007). Working with children and adolescents. In K. J. Doka (Ed.), *Living with grief: Before and after the death* (pp. 209–227). Washington, DC: Hospice Foundation of America.

CBS. (2005, January 18). Teen texters' tabs take off. Retrieved September 2, 2007, from www.cbsnews.com/stories/2005/01/18/earlyshow/living/ ConsumerWatch/main667428.shtml.

Collins, B. G., & Collins, T. M. (2005). *Crisis and trauma, developmental-ecological intervention.* Boston, MA: Lahaska Press.

Corr, C. A., Nabe, C. M., & Corr, D. M. (2006). *Death and dying, life and living* (5th edition). Belmont, CA: Wadsworth.

Desetta, A., & Wolin, S. (Eds.). (2000). *The struggle to be strong.* Minneapolis, MN: Free Spirit Publishing, Inc.

Elder, J. (2007). New web site lets parents monitor teen cell-phone use. Retrieved September 3, 2007, from www.freep.com/apps/pbcs.dll/ article?AID=/20070903/NEWS09/70903030

Faultline. (2006). MySpace music deal poses multiple threats. Retrieved September 2, 2007, from www.theregister.co.uk/2006/09/08/myspace_ threatens_record_labels

Fleming, S., & Adolph, R. (1986). Helping bereaved adolescents: Needs and responses. In C. Corr & J. McNeil (Eds.), *Children and death* (pp. 97–118). New York: Springer Publishing Co.

Oltjenbruns, K. A., & James, L. (2006). Adolescents' use of the Internet as a modality of grief support. *The Forum, 32*(4), 5–6.

Oltjenbruns, K. A. (2007). The importance of a developmental context: Childhood and adolescence as an example. In D. Balk (Ed.), *Handbook of thanatology* (pp. 143–149). Northbrook, IL: Association for Death Education and Counseling, Thanatology Association.

Pew Foundation. (2005). Teens and technology. Retreived September 1, 2007, from www.pewInternet.org/PPF/r/162/report_display.asp

Schaefer, J. A., & Moos, R. H. (2001). Bereavement experiences and personal growth. In M. S. Stroebe, R. O. Hansson, W. Stroebe, & H. Schut (Eds.), *Handbook of bereavement research: Consequences, coping, and caring* (pp. 145–167). Washington, DC: American Psychological Association.

Stroebe, M., & Schut, H. (1999). The dual process of coping with bereavement: Rationale and description. *Death Studies, 23,* 197–224.

Worden, J. W. (1996). *Children and grief: When a parent dies.* New York: Guilford Press.

CHAPTER 18

Helping Students Cope with Grief

Robert G. Stevenson

T he topic of grief as it relates to children and adolescents raises questions among parents, teachers, counselors, mental health professionals, and other caring adults. What do children know about death? How do they learn it? What should they be told?

Some people believe that children should be "spared" dealing with such questions and that there is no need to answer them, or even look at possible answers, until a death occurs. This position is typically taken by parents and educators who are unsure that anything they say or do will help when youngsters face grief. They also fear that what they do say or do, if incorrect, will cause more harm than good. These questions have been discussed for decades, and it seems that there *are* helpful things that can be said and done to teach children about death and to help grieving children. While adults cannot take away the pain of a loss, they can help a young person cope with the grief process and relieve anxiety based on the unfamiliar nature of the experience.

STUDENTS AND DEATH

In the 25 years I have spent as a death educator and counselor, the most frequently asked question has been "Why?" When it follows a death, the question is especially poignant. "Why did he (she) die?" "Why do things like this happen?" When death educators attempt to answer these questions, others arise. "Why are you teaching this in school?" "Why do you think you are qualified to teach this topic?" "If the goal is to prepare students to cope with loss, why teach this to children before they need to know it?"

If it were possible to spare children the pain associated with loss, it would be tempting to do so. However, loss is something that young people confront almost daily. It may be the loss of a feeling (such as safety or self-confidence). It may be the loss of future plans (failure to achieve admission to a certain college or to earn a spot on an athletic team) or the loss of a condition or state (such as good health). Or it may be the loss of a person (through death or divorce). All these losses have certain things in common. The coping skills that can help students face smaller losses (smaller, at least, to others) can also be used to cope with the losses caused by death or divorce and can assist them in the recovery process known as grief.

Many children and adolescents experience major losses and the accompanying grief. And yet, some schools act as though grieving students, when they return to the classroom, should return to business as usual. Students may even be disciplined by parents or teachers for a drop in grades after a death occurs. The grief of these students can be complicated by guilt about not maintaining previous levels of academic achievement when, in fact, they may be performing quite a feat simply by returning to school.

Death education (or "loss education" as it is called in some schools) is not just for children. It must also include professional staff. Many classroom teachers and counselors do not understand how grief affects children. They are not aware that grades often fall after the loss of a loved one, or that such a drop can take place even years after the loss. Students may exhibit behavior changes or may self-medicate with alcohol or drugs (Stevenson, 2000). Educators may not realize when they are dealing with the unresolved pain of a student's earlier loss. It is not just that students don't tell their teachers what is happening to them—the students may not be aware of the nature of the grief process or how it is affecting their lives.

The most difficult time to try to learn to cope with grief—or to help others cope—is right after the loss occurs. There is a phenomenon known as "psychic annulment," in which a person who is experiencing extreme stress or anxiety might be told everything that is happening and what needs to be done, but be unable to process or retain the information. If schools are to play a positive role in helping students cope with the losses they will inevitably encounter—and with deaths that might occur—it is best to take action before and not after the fact.

When a death affects students, it takes time for the school staff to identify what has happened and decide on an appropriate response. It is difficult to make such decisions in the midst of a crisis. State regulations require public schools to hold regularly scheduled fire drills, even though most schools have never had a serious fire and never will. On the other hand, many schools have experienced the death of a student, parent, teacher, or prominent figure known to the students, and still they have no clear plan for responding to an event that prompts community grief.

By acknowledging the reality of loss and grief, educators, parents, and students can develop guidelines for dealing with them in the school setting. In the school where I taught a death education course, my students discussed many issues related to death and grief. They asked other students and teachers to recall the questions they had when a death took place. In our class, we developed guidelines around these questions. These questions formed the basis for a protocol that was designed to help educators when they must inform students of a death (Stevenson & Powers, 1987).

Who should tell students that a death has occurred?

The students believed that it should be someone in authority, but it should *not* be done over the public address system or at a school assembly. The best person to convey such information is a classroom teacher or counselor—someone with whom students have developed a relationship. This can help control rumors and avoid some of the anxiety and feelings of uncertainty.

Where should the students be told?

An individual student should be told about a death in a private place—such as the school nurse's office or a counselor's office—where the student can remain after hearing the news. A loss that affects the entire school community should be announced in individual classes by the teachers. If possible, all classes should be informed simultaneously, which would necessitate having a plan in place for such announcements.

What should the students be told?

The student answer to this was a simple one: the truth. Tell them what happened in an honest, direct, age-appropriate manner.

How should the students be told?

The information should be kept simple. The meaning of words should be clear. The teacher or counselor should make sure that students understand what has been said. Misunderstanding can cause distress or lead to rumors. Students should be allowed to ask questions, and the questions should be answered honestly.

WHAT IS DEATH EDUCATION?

The label "death education" has been applied to a wide range of student experiences. It does not refer to any course in which the word "death" is mentioned or discussed. An English class that is reading Shakespeare's *Romeo and Juliet* or a history class that is studying the Holocaust may not be exploring these topics in the context of death education. Death education is defined as a *formal curriculum that deals with dying, death, grief, and loss, and their impact on the individual and on humankind.*

A death education curriculum must be shaped to the developmental level of the students for whom it is intended. The first high school death education course was offered in New Jersey in 1972. Programs for children were established in elementary schools in the 1980s, typically in response to a particular death. The differences between programs offered to adolescents in secondary schools and those intended for use with younger children have not always been clear. The lessons taught to the two age groups are not interchangeable. Materials developed for younger children can be adapted for use with adolescents, but the reverse is not true. Young children may not be able to understand or benefit from materials and classes developed for older students. In fact, these materials may be so upsetting that the negative impact is greater than any possible benefit. Just as one cannot bring college material into a high school classroom without evaluation and modification, high school content and methodology cannot be moved into elementary school.

The death education course I developed was a separate social studies offering. It began as a 9-week elective and was expanded to 18 weeks (one semester) and paired with a psychology elective to give students a full-year program. For schools that cannot devote an entire course to issues of loss and grief, modules are available for use in health, social studies, English, and science courses. Family living courses often deal with this topic. Some time ago, the state of New Jersey mandated that family living courses teach the "full life cycle" from birth to death, although it never offered any suggestions or provided any materials to help educators implement this directive. Death education units fit the bill quite nicely, either as a complete course, or as units or modules that cover various aspects of loss and grief, and can be placed in existing courses.

At the elementary school level, complete units or modules on loss or grief have not become popular with educators. However, books that deal with themes of death or loss in an age-appropriate way are used regularly. In every death education class below the college level, it is important to encourage students to discuss what they are learning in class with family members. At the elementary level, it is essential that parents be informed when material related to loss and grief is being used in school. This allows them to be supportive and to monitor the impact of this material on their child and avoids possible negative reactions when these topics are discussed without the knowledge of parents.

Because of the strong emotional component of death education, teachers must be properly prepared to deal with this sensitive subject. When potential exists to offer great help to students, there is usually also a possibility that inappropriate action might cause damage. Schools that establish death education courses should maintain an ongoing program of evaluation and revision to monitor these courses and the faculty members who teach them. The school should seek input from educators, counselors, students, parents, and community members to evaluate death education and its place in the school.

Students can speak about their beliefs, but that is not the same as a presentation by a caring adult who can answer the questions that may follow such a presentation. If educational institutions allow their content to be censored—even indirectly—it is even more important that parents have current, accurate information to share with their children. For this reason, it is recommended that schools that offer death education also offer programs for parents.

Courses on death and grief are not the only contribution that schools can make to grieving students. (See pages 322–23 for sample course outline.)

PERSPECTIVES ON DEATH AND LOSS

The following is a syllabus of a death education course for high school students.

COURSE DESCRIPTION: This course will give students a fuller understanding of death and loss. It provides knowledge of the ways people cope with loss in their lives. Grief is the process of coming to understand a loss and incorporating it in one's life. Grief may also be an underlying cause of behavior and emotions. The content of this course can be of special use to counselors, educators, and parents. A textbook used in this course is *The Last Dance: Encountering Death and Dying* by L. A. DeSpelder and A. L. Strickland (Mayfield Publishing).

COURSE OBJECTIVES: At the conclusion of this course, students will be able to:

- Describe significant historic, scientific, artistic, and religious views of death.
- Identify the possible social, psychological, biological and economic impacts of a death.
- Define the grief process.
- Describe the possible impact of grief on behavior, memory and the learning process.
- Compare and contrast types of grief, including normal, destructive, unrecognized and complicated grief.
- Identify major coping styles of individuals.
- Identify personal coping behavior.

COURSE OUTLINE: The topics of death and grief cannot be addressed without recognizing the fact that for many students a strong affective component (emotions, attitudes, values) accompanies the cognitive component (intellect, knowledge and abilities) in an examination of the topics of death, dying, loss and grief. This is addressed through use of a confluent curriculum based on:

1. Participation—shared responsibility for research and presentations
2. Integration—of thoughts, feelings and actions
3. Relevance—of course content to the intellectual and emotional needs of the participants
4. Self—the "self" is seen as a legitimate object of study since personal issues can impact the interpretation and utilization of course material
5. Goal—the ultimate goal of this course is to assist the student in becoming a functioning member of his/her professional (counseling, education) community and his/her personal community.

THE COURSE IS DIVIDED INTO TWELVE SEPARATE UNITS:

1. Introduction: Draw a Picture of Death

2. Death and Grief: Definitions and Meanings:
   - Definitions of key terms and their connotations.
   - Examination of the way language has been used in some cultures as a masking behavior in discussing death and grief.

3. Death and the Child:
   - Age and the child's perception of death
   - Misunderstandings of children
   - Children and death-related rituals

4. Explanations of "Why" Do We Die?
   - Religion
   - Philosophy
   - Art

5. Ethical / Moral Issues:
   - The "hour" of death— when does death occur?
   - Abortion
   - Euthanasia
   - Capital punishment
   - The "right to die"

6. Death and Beyond
   - Life after death
   - Reincarnation
   - The "near-death" and the "out-of-body" experiences

7. The Grief Process
   - Models of the grief process
   - Types of grief (normal, destructive, unrecognized, complicated)
   - Impact of the cause of death on the grief process

8. Possible Intervention Techniques
   - Symbols and art therapy
   - Bibliotherapy
   - Play therapy
   - Journal keeping
   - Dream therapy

9. Rituals
   - Wakes / Shiva
   - Funerals
   - Cultural differences

10. Suicide and Suicide Prevention
    - Dynamics and statistics of suicide
    - The role of a "gatekeeper"

11. Death and Grief in Film and Television

12. Family and Support

The above course outline is provided by author Robert G. Stevenson, past recipient of the Death Educator Award by the Association of Death Education and Counseling.

Many schools have established bereavement support groups for students, and special continuing education programs are offered to counselors and teachers concerning ways to help students deal with grief, both inside and outside school. This task should not be left to schools alone. The ability to work with parents to help their children cope with grief and to act as a resource for students and parents can make a school a focal point for support in times of grief and crisis.

BENEFITS OF DEATH EDUCATION FOR STUDENTS

Any death education program should be judged on the basis of its impact on students. What are the specific benefits to students of studying these topics? These benefits have been shown to include the following:

- Improved communication
- Increased knowledge and academic skills
- Lessening of death-related fear and anxiety
- Preparation for coping with future losses
- Greater feelings of personal control of life

Improved Communication

For many years in this country, death was considered a taboo topic. As students study it and discuss it, the taboo falls away. The discussions take place in the classroom and in the home. The majority of students and parents cited improved communication as the first and greatest benefit of death education. The channels of communication, once opened, were used to discuss other topics that may formerly have been "taboo" as well.

Increased Knowledge and Academic Skills

The academic tools used to measure increased knowledge (in the areas of psychology, sociology, and history) include testing student knowledge in each area and measuring improvement in academic skills (such as reading, essay writing, and forming effective generalizations) and problem-solving strategies. Students showed greater increases in knowledge and skills in death education classes than they did in the English, history, and social science courses they were taking at the same time.

Lessening of Death-Related Fear and Anxiety

For death education students who reported a high degree of death-related fear, there was a lessening of such fears. As one student said, "I used to think about death all the time, but I could never talk about it. Now I talk about it all the time, so I don't have to be afraid of it any more." Students who had not previously thought much about the topic at first reported an increase in death-related fear, then a reduction in such fear as time passed and they had an opportunity to process the experience.

Greater Feelings of Personal Control of Life

Grieving students may feel that their lives are beyond their control. The emotions associated with grief can magnify feelings of helplessness, and these feelings can spill over and affect academic work. Adult silence in the face of grief also magnifies such feelings. The student may wonder whether adults are not acknowledging the loss because they, too, are helpless. Or maybe there's nothing they can say, and the situation is truly hopeless. Or—worst of all—maybe the student did something to make the teachers and counselors think he or she is worthless. Feelings of helplessness, hopelessness, and loneliness are part of normal grief. When they are combined with feelings of worthlessness, they constitute the emotions present in many suicide attempts. Adding feelings of worthlessness to the other strong emotions a child or adolescent may feel in response to a death can create a situation in which there is only pain and from which there seems to be no escape. Adult silence can reinforce and strengthen these feelings—it is clear that silence is not an effective way to deal with student grief.

Students who have learned the physical and emotional effects of grief report that they still hurt after a loss, but they feel less isolated and afraid. Because they understand what they are experiencing, they feel that their lives are less out of control when a death or other major loss occurs.

Greater Appreciation for Life

Although not at the top of the list, this point is made by some students in every death education class. Students say that each day becomes more precious to them and they are less likely to take it for granted. In postcourse evaluations, students speak of telling family members that they love them, visiting relatives they may have avoided in the past, and becoming involved in community service projects or charity fund raising. Student stories of stronger bonds with their families counter criticism from political groups (such as the Eagle Forum) that death education courses undermine family authority. If anything, students who have looked at death say they appreciate life and see the importance of family in that life.

Greater Appreciation of Cultural Diversity

As they study the different ways people mourn their dead and express their grief, students can see the similarities and differences among cultures. Very different ceremonies can have the same goals—removal of the deceased's body, recognition (and, possibly, celebration) of the life that has been lived, acceptance that that life is now ended, and the beginning of the grieving process for the survivors. Death and grief are universal experiences; studying different expressions of grief gives students a basis for appreciating cultures other than their own.

The Possibility of Therapeutic Effects

When we look at the possible benefits of death education, it is important to recognize the limits of such courses. Death education courses are academic courses with established curricula and trained teachers. Even if some students experience therapeutic effects, these courses are not therapy for troubled persons. Some students in a death education course may have problems that are best addressed through referral to the school counselors and, at some schools, to a psychologist or consulting psychiatrist. Mental health and counseling centers in the community work with schools and regularly accept referrals made in consultation with parents or guardians.

GUIDELINES FOR SCHOOLS

The school is a natural support system. Students and teachers work together, play together, and share the knowledge they gain about life. In such close proximity, it is easy to come to know others very well. Students may say they are there because they have to be, but this does not explain the hours they spend there with classmates and teachers outside regular class time. It does not explain why some students who have lost a loved one want to return to school as soon as possible—even on the day they learn of the death—to be with their friends and teachers. They see the school as a place where they will receive support in dealing with important issues in their lives (Stevenson, 2008).

The following guidelines are for educators who seek to create a supportive atmosphere for young people coping with grief. These are not just things to do after a death. Educators and parents should start now to develop a plan that can be implemented when it is needed.

Be sure that students, educators, and parents know what support exists in the school and the community.

All students, teachers, counselors, and parents should know the people in the school who can help grieving students. The protocols that are followed after a death should also be known (or available) to everyone. In addition to the support within the school, there are support organizations in the local community. Their contact information should be part of the school's response plan.

National organizations, such as the Hospice Foundation of America, have programs for the bereaved and for those who are helping the bereaved. The Association for Death Education and Counseling (ADEC) can provide help in creating an atmosphere of support in a school following a loss. ADEC is an important resource for educators. Many programs are available that can be used in schools, such as the Rainbows Program, used across the United States and Canada to join family and educators in support of young people who have suffered a loss or death.

The Center for Education about Death and Bereavement at the University of Wisconsin–LaCrosse sponsors annual conferences on aspects of loss and grief. The main topic is different each year, but the discussion regularly includes young people and grief.

Teach all staff and parents in advance how to speak to a young person when a death or other loss occurs, and inform them of the need to do so as soon as possible after the event.

News of a death is painful no matter what is said or done; however, planning for such an event can help minimize the pain by avoiding mistakes (often well-intentioned) that could make the situation worse. Hearing what happened in a timely manner is important for children of all ages.

Provide positive role models.

Parents and other concerned adults model ways to deal with loss and sadness. They can show children that grief hurts, tears are normal, and emotions need not be avoided. Such an experience can reduce the fears of both children and parents.

Avoid silence.

Silence can magnify the feelings of helplessness, hopelessness, loneliness, anger, and guilt that are, in varying degrees, part of all grief reactions (Stevenson, 1987). Silence about a death after the young person has been informed may strengthen these painful emotions, causing children to think they are alone in confronting loss, dying, death, and the feelings they generate.

Be aware of the importance of nonverbal communication.

We communicate in many ways. Our attempts to speak with young people can be influenced by location (where we speak), time (when we speak), and space (distance between us as we speak). Adults should be aware of all of the factors that can have an effect on our communications with children.

Establish a place and a protocol for telling students about a death when it must be done in school.

The location for such communication should be a place where students feel most comfortable or least threatened, such as the office of a counselor or the school nurse. The best time to speak about a death is as soon as those involved know the facts. It is not good to postpone such communication.

Create rituals to acknowledge the changes that take place when a death occurs.

Rituals and memorials need not be traditional or formal, but it is important to show young people that a death does not simply happen without other changes taking place as well. By taking time for a ritual or rite of passage, we confirm that the change has happened and the child's reactions to it are justified. If we try to deny that a change has taken place, we should not be surprised when children adopt coping mechanisms that attempt to do the same. In some cases, young people may act out to block "business as usual" until some recognition of the death takes place. Parents should be informed of any rituals that take place in the school so they can remain the primary support for their children. Classroom rituals have involved lighting candles, drawing pictures, sharing memories, and creating a memory book as a gift for the parents and family of a deceased student. Other rituals may involve donation of books or other equipment in the name of the deceased (with an accompanying ceremony), a gift to charity in the name of the deceased, or a ceremony or memorial of the students' design.

Give concrete form to the abstract concepts of "death" and "grief."

Death and grief can be difficult concepts for students, especially preadolescents, to grasp. Often a small item can provide comfort and courage to grieving children and adolescents. A cross or other religious symbol, a polished stone, a doll, or some other object can be an amulet (warding off evil) or a talisman (helping the possessor to accomplish some difficult task). The power in such an object or ritual comes not from the thing itself but from the caring person who introduces it and from the way it is used. If nothing else, it serves as a reminder to students that people care about them and are there to help them.

Encourage students to help others as a way to overcome feelings of helplessness or worthlessness.

Helping others is a powerful tool for overcoming feelings of helplessness. Parents can allow their children to help with tasks during the period immediately after a death. The young people should be given the option of participating in any death ritual as long as they are able to understand and process what they may see or experience. A tearful adult can be a positive role model in the expression of sorrow.

The school plays a role at this time. Some schools close, or grieving children are kept at home, when a major loss or death occurs, but this is not recommended (Stevenson, 2007). Closing a school is a form of denial—it says that the school has nothing to offer at such a time. The reality is that students who have suffered a loss look to their friends as an important part of their support system in times of crisis. Some students attend school, at least briefly, on the same day as a wake or funeral. They want to do so because at school they feel safe from what has happened to them in the outside world. They should not be cut off from this support.

Provide security and structure.

With one part of life out of control because of a death, children and adolescents need to feel that they still have some control in other areas of life. It is not unusual for a young person to try to go through the day in as normal a manner as possible. However, to force children to behave in a routine manner after a death or other major loss, when they do not wish to do so, removes the very feelings of control we are trying to reinforce.

Take the student's developmental level into account.

Materials are available to help children and adolescents understand and cope with grief. Books about death and grief are geared to many ages and developmental levels, and to specific cultural/ethnic groups. A book that is very good for one age group may miss the mark entirely if it is offered to much older or younger children. Adults must know in advance what is contained in any story they share with a child.

Help students externalize their thoughts and feelings.

Provide young people with ways to express the thoughts and feelings they may otherwise keep bottled up inside. Drawing pictures, writing, reading stories related to loss or grief (bibliotherapy), or storytelling can all be helpful techniques to offer grieving students an opportunity for catharsis—an emotional cleaning out.

Acknowledge that the impact of a death may also affect the adults in the school community.

As time passes, most members of a school community will grieve, recover, and move on from a death and its aftermath. The impact on a grieving child's parents and adult relatives goes without saying, but teachers and school counselors are also affected. Teachers in the role of caregiver may have difficulty taking time to tend to their own needs. When a child, or a child's loved one, dies, teachers often spend long hours helping children and their parents, and they may also seek training to be more effective in that role. Schools need to acknowledge the fact that the death of a student or a student's loved one has an impact on staff as well as other students.

Become partners.

Educators and parents should become partners. Parents should try to be open to the efforts of others to help them and their children after a death. If help is not forthcoming, they should be willing to reach out and let others know what they need. The partnership of parents with teachers and other members of the community is vital to ensure a caring atmosphere for grieving children and adolescents.

SIGNS THAT A GRIEVING CHILD NEEDS EXTRA HELP

Even if the school has programs in place to help grieving students and parents, some children will need extra support. The American Academy of Child and Adolescent Psychiatry (1998) cautions parents and teachers that, although most children grieve less over time, counseling should be considered if a child exhibits *several* of these behaviors *over an extended period*:

- Depression so severe that the child shows little interest in daily activities

- Inability to sleep, eat normally, or be alone

- Regression in behavior to that of a less mature child

- Imitation of the deceased person

- Repeatedly wishing to join the deceased

- Loss of interest in friends or play

- Refusal to attend school or a persistent and marked drop in school achievement

- In such cases, the child might be referred to a professional grief counselor.

Researchers have studied a condition known as complicated grief (CG) in children and adolescents, which is marked by a constellation of symptoms that includes longing and searching for the deceased, preoccupation with thoughts of the deceased, purposelessness and futility about the future, numbness and detachment from others, difficulty accepting the death, lost sense of security and control, and anger and bitterness over the death (Prigerson, Shaw, Jacobs, 1999). CG is more likely to occur if the young person believes that others are to blame for the death or that others blame him or her for the death (Melhem, Moritz, Walker, Shear, & Brent, 2007). If CG is suspected, parents should explore the young person's beliefs about the cause of the death and deal with any misperceptions. In some cases of CG, parental or family support is not sufficient.

Parents should not hesitate to seek professional help if they think their child may be suffering from complicated grief. In today's world, with all we have learned, there is no need for a child to go it alone.

Final Thoughts

Grieving students have special needs. Parents, family members, and educators have found it helpful to have a plan in place to use when the need arises. Such plans are best made in advance, when the pressures of time and emotional distress are at a minimum. They should include ways to speak with children and adolescents about death and grief, and about the feelings they may experience. Conversations between children and parents/guardians, teachers, and counselors can free children from isolation and offer support at a difficult time. Open communication can lessen the pain that isolation magnifies. It reflects love and caring in a way young people can understand and appreciate.

Robert Stevenson is a professor in the M.S. Counseling program at Mercy College, NY. An educator with 40 years experience, he holds a B.A. (College of the Holy Cross), M.A. (Montclair State University), and an M.A.T. and Ed.D. (Fairleigh Dickinson University). He is a member of the International Work Group on Death, Dying and Bereavement and the Association for Death Education and Counseling. He is the author of over 60 books and articles related to loss and grief. He has received numerous awards including the ADEC Death Educator Award and the New York State Defense of Liberty medal for his work following the events of 9/11/2001.

REFERENCES

American Academy of Child and Adolescent Psychiatry. (1998). Quoted in *Children and grief.* Retrieved August 6, 2007, from PsycARTICLES database (www.athealth.com/consumer/disorders/childgrief.htm).

Melhem, N. M., Moritz, G., Walker, M., Shear, K., & Brent, D. (2007, April). Phenomenology and correlates of complicated grief in children and adolescents. *Journal of the American Academy of Child and Adolescent Psychiatry, 46*(4), 493–499.

Morgan, J., & Laugani, P. (Eds.). (2002). *Death and bereavement around the world* (Vols. 1–3). Amityville, NY: Baywood Press.

Prigerson, H. G., Shear, M. K., & Jacobs, S. C. (1999). Consensus criteria for traumatic grief: A preliminary empirical test. *British Journal of Psychiatry, 174,* 67–73. Cited in N. M. Melhem, G. Moritz, M. Walker, K. Shear, & D. Brent (2007, April). Phenomenology and correlates of complicated grief in children and adolescents. *Journal of the American Academy of Child and Adolescent Psychiatry, 46*(4), 493–499.

Stevenson, R. G. (2008). *Perspectives on violence and violent death.* Amityville, NY: Baywood Press.

Stevenson, R. G. (2007). Children and death around the world. In J. D. Morgan, & P. Laungani (Eds.), *Death and bereavement around the world* (Vol. 5, pp. 84-112). Amityville, NY: Baywood Press.

Stevenson, R. G. (1987). The fear of death in childhood. In J. E. Schowalter, P. Buschman, P. R. Patterson, A.H. Kutscher, M.T. Tallmer, & R. G. Stevenson (Eds.), *Children and death: Perspectives from birth through adolescence.* New York: Praeger.

Stevenson, R. G., & Powers, H. (1987, May). How to handle death in the school: Ways to help grieving students. *Education Digest, LII*(9), pp. 42–44.

CHAPTER 19

When Tragedy Strikes: Response and Prevention

Marcia Lattanzi Licht

CULTURAL CONTEXT

This is the age of information and technology. Children as young as 7 or 8 years old are computer literate. Adolescents rely on text messaging, cell phone contact, and a constant stream of electronic music, information, and communication. The irony of our ever-present means of communication is the lack of meaningful personal contact. Never have young people had such access to instant communication, and yet many feel significant isolation.

As our communities and schools become more diverse, there is a tendency for people to focus on a small reference group. Most neighbors see each other very little. Children play indoors much more than in the past. Most people rely on television for a never-ending stream of detailed, often speculative information. Twenty-four-hour news coverage and the Internet bring the world into our homes. The constant flow of news is both seductive in bringing problems to our awareness and overwhelming in the magnitude and impact of all this information.

There is a tension between our wish for contact and our awareness of our absolute isolation (Yalom, 1980). At times of tragedy, we long to be part of a larger whole. A sense of connectedness and belonging binds a school community together and encourages students, staff, and the community to be invested in their school (National Association of School Psychologists, 2006). In an effort to understand the tragedies that affect schools and universities, we must focus on the important themes of relationships, community, and responsiveness in painful times.

Responding to Tragedy

Although the majority of violence involving children and adolescents occurs in the home and in the community at large (Cornell, 2007; Eron, Gentry & Schlege, 1993), school tragedies capture significant media attention. Each school and university community should have an integrated plan to respond to a tragedy that affects it directly, as well as a plan for responding to students when tragedies occur elsewhere.

A bedrock principle in the response to traumatic events is organized planning and preparation. The first step is to review school/university policies to ensure that they cover a wide range of potential situations. Plans and policies must address safety, information exchange, and telecommunications. Plans also need to address the physical and mental health needs of students, faculty, and parents who are involved in the crisis; in some cases, assistance is needed for a considerable period afterward.

Typically, educators do not receive training in responding to trauma (American Academy of Experts in Traumatic Stress, 1999). Few school districts have staff members who are adequately trained to deal with the consequences of a crisis such as a school shooting. School districts often rely on a crisis response team made up of counseling professionals and psychologists, medical or nursing staff, administrators, and community health professionals. Every school district and university should designate and train a person or group to act as lead official(s) for the response to a crisis situation (U.S. Department of Education, 2002). For a school that is directly involved in a shooting or other active threat, the response must include the ability to assess the situation promptly and effectively, and to notify and mobilize key personnel to ensure safety. For example, the lead person or group must be able to make a decision quickly to evacuate a building or close an entire campus.

Support Networks

School district and university officials need to develop relationships with law enforcement officials and other emergency service agencies to establish clear lines of authority in the event of a crisis. It is equally important for school districts and universities to develop connections with community mental health organizations that can address the needs of those affected by a crisis.

Following the April 2006 shootings at Virginia Tech, a Mental Health Advisory Group was formed that included counselor-educators and representatives from the university's counseling center, the psychology department, the New River Valley Community Services Board, and the American Red Cross. The group met the day after the shooting to develop a plan to provide mental health support for the entire Virginia Tech community (Kennedy, 2007). The group decided that most of the counseling would be done by community and American Red Cross volunteers and would be essentially supportive. Those in need of additional counseling were referred to the university counseling center. Mental health professionals wearing badges and purple armbands passed out fliers outlining what people might experience in the days following the traumatic event. They established a prevention perspective and communicated that counseling services would be available to everyone who wanted them (Kennedy, 2007).

The administration at Virginia Tech cancelled classes for the remainder of the week, and many students went home. The Mental Health Advisory Group began to make preparations for the students' return. A refresher course on brief trauma counseling was organized for volunteers. When classes resumed a week after the shootings, 200 mental health volunteers were on campus. Working in teams of two, they were in each class that had lost a student, and they walked the grounds and halls offering support. The message to students was "We will try to help you with anything you want or need to support your recovery" (Kennedy, 2007). The assumption was that not everyone would need critical care and that the response would be an ongoing process. Volunteers also were available to support the mental health staff at graduation ceremonies in May.

It is important for schools and universities to initiate conversations with local health and mental health providers and develop agreements that outline roles and responsibilities in times of crisis (USDOE, 2002). National organizations representing mental health providers can help identify local resources. While a school or university that is experiencing a crisis needs outside help from community law enforcement and mental health professionals, a flood of volunteers who want to help can add to the chaos. School districts and universities should develop a coordinated plan, in conjunction with law enforcement and mental health partners, to screen for qualified and suitable volunteers. The best plan is to have a group of experts and other service providers identified and prescreened, so they can be available immediately during a crisis (USDOE, 2002).

In challenging situations, children and university students turn to their natural support systems. For most young people, these systems include family members, peers, and faith community leaders. For example, in the aftermath of the Columbine shootings in Colorado, many students turned to their faith communities for support.

Communication

The way an experience is handled largely determines its consequences. This definitely applies to school tragedies. The presence of trusted, responsive leadership is crucial. Timely, accurate information must be provided to students, family members, and faculty during a crisis. In the absence of information, fears and rumors are likely to spread, causing additional problems for school officials and law enforcement. Detailed procedures for providing information in a crisis are essential (USDOE, 2002).

Major communication disruptions can occur in large-scale disasters or tragedies, such as hurricanes, floods, or the September 11 attacks. Schools and universities should work with telecommunications experts to determine what communication systems and links are likely to be affected in various circumstances; they should investigate backup plans, including low-tech or nontraditional communication approaches (USDOE, 2002).

Many communities in Colorado and elsewhere established networks and plans in the aftermath of the Columbine shootings, but it proved difficult to sustain interest and participation over time. The challenge is to continue to develop and implement these programs through ongoing communication and practice, including annual reviews and updates. For schools and universities, plans are best reviewed at the start of each academic year. Any significant changes to the plan or to the support network should be communicated to staff, faculty, and other key stakeholders when they are made.

Responding to the Media

Local tragedies quickly become public tragedies because of media involvement. The reality of 24-hour news coverage means that intensive focus and attention to events is the norm. Schools and universities should have a designated person to speak to the media during the crisis. The ideal spokesperson is a leader, a person of strength and warmth with whom students and the public can identify during the initial stages of a crisis. School and university officials can also encourage the media to contribute to the collective understanding rather than creating greater stress during a tragedy (Dolan, 2003). For example, students can be further traumatized if the media constantly rebroadcast violent events (USDOE, 2002). Hospice professionals who work with grief can help schools and communities deal with the media by sharing information on short- and long-term grief, coping strategies, supportive efforts, and so on.

Supporting Students

Loss and grief are realities in schools. After a tragedy, schools have several key areas of responsibility:

1. Use a previously identified school response team to handle safety and mental health concerns and communication.

2. Educate teachers and school personnel about at-risk students, posttraumatic stress reactions and posttraumatic stress disorder, and recommend school and classroom involvement strategies (Bouton, 2003).

3. Create opportunities for students to cope with the tragedy through information and classroom activities.

4. Use a community support network that plans for and provides backup and support during the crisis and in the short- and long-term aftermath.

A tragedy can affect children and adolescents on many levels. They may have difficulty sleeping, experience physical symptoms and illness, become easily distracted, or develop fears about the future. Support responses must be geared to the developmental needs of students. For example, when adolescents lose their sense of predictability and safety, they can be helped to construct new assumptions (Matthews, 1999). School districts and universities can work with mental health and hospice professionals to establish guidelines and approaches for supportive responses that fit the developmental needs of students.

Finally, it is important to consider the concept of resilience in the context of responses to tragic events. Masten and Coatsworth (1998) define resilience as "manifested competence in the context of significant challenges to adaptation or development." According to Rutter (1987), resilience may reside in the social context as well as in the individual. Schools and parents can foster resilience in students by planning supportive responses that encourage competence in the face of vulnerability. There is a growing need for multifaceted, culturally competent programs that focus on young people, families, schools, and communities (Davies, 1999). School and university responses must focus in informed, thoughtful, and compassionate ways on safety and on promoting understanding and the capacity to cope.

Rituals and Public Memorials

School and university tragedies, as well as other public tragedies, often trigger spontaneous memorialization by students and the community at large. The memorials at Columbine High School in Littleton, Colorado, filled nearby Clement Park. It was estimated that 200,000 people visited them before they were removed. In September 2007, 3,000 people attended the dedication ceremony for the permanent flagstone and granite memorial to the Columbine victims. The memorial includes six fountains and individual testimonials to the 13 who died (Vaughan, 2007).

Condolences at Virginia Tech included more than 60,000 objects and message boards for each person who died in the shooting. These ritual acts of remembrance—like those after Princess Diana's death and the attacks on September 11—in some way parallel traditional attempts to help, like taking food to a grieving neighbor. They are ways for people to come together, to mourn, and to feel a sense of connection. Memorialization provides a way for many people to symbolically acknowledge the tragedy and to offer help.

Rituals like the Virginia Tech convocation and the Columbine dedication can provide comfort to those affected by tragedy and to the public at large. Doka (2003) notes two important functions of rituals—they permit meaningful action in a time of disorganization and they affirm community. Memorials and public rituals often contain a message or themes intended to find meaning in the experience. Prayers and religious beliefs are often offered as a source of consolation and meaning for those who believe. It is important to ensure that memorial events and anniversary events are inclusive and ecumenical.

School and university officials at Virginia Tech held a memorial convocation two days after the tragedy. National and state officials attended, along with a majority of students and faculty. There were many condolences and prayers, and celebrated poet and Virginia Tech English professor Nikki Giovanni addressed the gathering and closed with these encouraging words: "We are the Hokies. We will prevail. We will prevail. We are Virginia Tech." At the close of the convocation, students gave a resounding Hokie cheer. One student who knew five of the victims believed that the students who died would have wanted the cheer—that the cheer was for them (Kennedy, 2007).

The theme "We Are Columbine" reverberated after the 1999 shootings. The "We Are Virginia Tech" and "We Are Columbine" messages carried meaning-related themes of strength in the face of adversity, identifying with the larger group, and the tradition of the university/school. The "we" message offers a sense of belonging and solidarity with those who died and those who grieve. Standing together in tragedy and loss is one of the most important ways humans can show support.

Case Example

In the aftermath of the Virginia Tech shootings, school officials closed the school and students were given the opportunity to return home. Amber was a freshman at Virginia Tech, an honor student from Kansas. She was an only child whose mother had died of breast cancer less than 2 years earlier. It was important for Amber and her dad to spend a long weekend together after the shootings. Both of them experienced a heightened sense of vulnerability, and the time at home together was reassuring for them. Amber was shaken by the experience, particularly because a classmate in one of her courses had been killed. She spent considerable time talking with her family and friends and riding her horse. Amber told her father that she was a bit afraid to go back to campus, but she was also glad to be going back to finish the year and spend time with friends.

When she returned home for the summer, she talked about the fact that the shootings had stirred up memories of her mother and her fears about loss. She and her dad spent time together at the cemetery, where they talked about the emotional connections between the loss of Amber's mom and the shootings.

Prevention

The most powerful focal point in the aftermath of a tragedy is the desire to prevent similar tragedies in the future. Almost universally, families grieving tragic deaths wish to spare others similar suffering; they often devote themselves to prevention efforts.

Schools are communities, and prevention efforts must be aimed at building a responsive, safe environment for all students. The most effective approach to averting school violence and protecting students is a balanced one that combines physical safety, educational practices, and programs that support students' social, emotional, and behavioral needs (NASP, 2006).

Identifying Problems

The actual incidence of violent acts against students and school staff is low; however, the occurrence of pre-violent behavior such as bullying, threats, and classroom disruptions is more common (Walker et al., 1996). Faculty and staff need to learn the early warning signs and patterns of a student who is troubled, so they can intervene and keep these behaviors from escalating. Programs may include training for staff, students, and families in understanding the factors that can trigger or exacerbate aggressive flare-ups (Walker et al., 1996). Children can learn problem-solving and anger management skills (Zangoza, Vaughn, & McIntosh, 1991). Families can be referred to community-based services for skill training, therapeutic assistance, and other support (Epstein, Kutash, & Duchnowski, 1998). Finally, it is essential for families to ensure that children and adolescents do not possess or have access to firearms (Heide, 1997).

Key Elements in Prevention

In the aftermath of school tragedies like Columbine and Virginia Tech, significant resources have been invested in prevention. A large percentage of these resources goes to law enforcement and security efforts—additional police presence, key lock doors on campuses, video surveillance, and closed campuses. But there is a limit to what physical security measures can achieve, and research has not shown these methods to be the most effective long-term strategy (Center for Collaborative and Effective Practice, 2002).

Government officials have identified the following key elements for preventing violence and assessing threats (Leavitt, Spellings & Gonzales, 2007):

1. **Sharing critical information**

   Key people (including education officials, law enforcement personnel, and mental health professionals) are often not fully informed or are confused about when and how to share information on persons who are likely to be dangerous.

2. **Accurate and complete information prohibiting gun ownership**

   Current state laws and sale practices do not ensure that guns are kept out of the wrong hands.

3. **Improved communication and awareness**

   Teachers, parents, and students can learn to recognize warning signs and encourage those who need help to get it.

4. **Access to mental health services**

   Communities are responsible for integrating people with mental illness. The challenge is to coordinate services and to ensure that providers are sensitive to the important aspects of providing care, privacy, and safety.

On the whole, prevention efforts have been effective in decreasing the frequency and intensity of behavior problems in school communities (Hunter & Elias, 1998), but prevention programs will not help the 5–10% of students who need more intensive interventions (Sugai & Horner, 1999).

The most powerful prevention effort for schools is to establish trust and communication with students and to encourage them to notify officials about threats or violent behavior (Cornell, 2007). Often, disturbed students communicate their distress and violent intentions in advance of a tragedy. Shooters in recent school tragedies have been marginalized, isolated, avoided, and sometimes ridiculed by other students. Violent students often feel rejected and socially victimized. Research shows that a responsive, safe community helps all students and that it is possible for schools to provide effective additional support to students who need it. (Cotton, 1995; Quinn, Osher, Hoffman, & Hanley, 1998). Intensive individual interventions are necessary for students with severe behavioral problems.

It is not always possible to predict when a child will be violent. However, experts suggest the following steps that schools and parents can take (CCEP, 2001):

1. **Identify problems and assess progress toward improvement.** Situations that are potentially dangerous, or in which students and staff feel threatened or intimidated, must be objectively addressed and progress assessed on an ongoing basis (Eron et al., 1993; Trump, 1998).

2. **Understand the context of violence and aggression.** Violence and pre-violent aggressive behavior can be triggered by elements in the environment or the situation (Mayer, 1995). At-risk students may be prone to violence under high-stress situations, if they lack adequate coping skills, or if aggression is a learned response for them.

3. **Avoid stereotypes.** Labeling students can limit or damage the school's capacity to identify and help them. Schools need to be vigilant and avoid false cues triggered by race, socioeconomic status, academic ability, or physical appearance (Axelson, 1999). School or community action in response to a stereotype can harm students.

4. **View warning signals from a developmental perspective.** Emotional and social capacities and the ability to express needs differ for children and adolescents according to their developmental level. Understanding developmentally appropriate behavior helps prevent misunderstanding and misreading of conduct.

5. **Understand that troubled children typically exhibit multiple warning signs.** Children who are troubled commonly exhibit multiple warning signs and repeat them, with greater intensity, over time (Loeber & Farrington, 1998). Avoid overreacting to a single sign or action.

Schools and universities need to develop approaches that address various aspects of prevention. Diversity training and programs that address bullying and teasing can have an effect on the marginalization and isolation of students. The experience of African-American students in Jena, Louisiana, speaks to the potential for bias among faculty and students, and shows how violence can be triggered and can escalate.

Threat Assessment

Threat assessment is a process of learning about threats, investigating, and following up with corrective action. School teams can conduct standard threat assessments. Thorough assessments and personal knowledge of students can prevent overreactions to pranks or rash statements. School-based teams can quickly manage transient threats and take preventive action on substantive threats (Cornell, 2007).

School districts, colleges, and universities need to look for early warning signs related to violence and other disturbing behaviors. Universities must balance the importance of privacy, individual freedom, and assisting students with mental health needs against security and safety concerns. The actions of Cho Seung-Hui at Virginia Tech were not predictable, but a significant number of people at the school had recognized that he was deeply disturbed. Persons with serious mental health conditions—including severe depression and paranoia—can come to believe that suicide or homicide is justified in response to their suffering. Schools and universities need to provide effective interventions for troubled students. These interventions must be multiple, sustained, and coordinated efforts.

In the absence of threats or unusual behaviors, it is extremely difficult to predict whether a person will commit a serious act of violence. Early warning signs are signals that a student needs help, but profiles or lists of characteristics are not useful to identify potentially violent students. In fact, a likely consequence of this approach is the identification of innocent students as dangerous (NASP, 2006).

Communication is a critical element in responding to and preventing tragedy. Authorities, including researchers and law enforcement groups, have determined that close communication and trust among students, parents, and the community are the most effective elements in preventing school violence.

Guns

Guns are used in almost every major episode of school violence. In the United States, where gun ownership is considered a right, a discussion of this topic can be politically charged. Gun-related deaths are a major, continuing tragedy in our society. Each year, more than 30,000 people die from suicide or homicide involving guns—more than 82 deaths each day (Virginia Youth Violence Project, 2007). A small fraction of these deaths occur in schools. Our society has not adequately addressed the issue of access to guns by young people, and the problem of access to weapons by antisocial or emotionally disturbed persons is a serious public health matter (Cornell, 2007).

There is a long-standing conflict between gun-rights advocates and gun-control advocates. The two groups see the issue from very different perspectives: Gun-rights advocates focus on motive (people kill people), and gun-control advocates focus on method (killings usually involve guns). Our communities and our country need to find ways to limit the widespread availability of guns, particularly large military weapons. Guns should not be available to people who are unable or unwilling to use them responsibly (Cornell, 2007).

Conclusion

High-functioning schools foster learning, safety, socially appropriate behaviors, and meaningful relationships. When tragedy strikes, schools need to have comprehensive, collaborative plans for crisis response and intervention. The response—in both the crisis and the aftermath—should focus on getting appropriate help for students. Schools and universities also must be skilled in prevention and in addressing early warning signs of violence. The best prevention approach focuses on communication and on creating inclusive, responsive school communities.

Marcia Lattanzi Licht, M.A., RN, LPC, is a psychotherapist and consultant, and co-founder of HospiceCare of Boulder, Colorado (1976). Ms. Licht's publications include *The Hospice Choice*, and *Coping with Public Tragedy* (co-editor). An internationally known educator, she was awarded an honorary doctorate from the University of Colorado in 2005, the 1984 Winston Churchill Traveling Fellowship, the 2002 ADEC Educator Award, and the National Hospice and Palliative Care Organizaton's 1995 Heart of Hospice.

References

American Academy of Experts in Traumatic Stress (AAETS). (1999). *Practical guide for crisis response in our schools* (4th ed.). Commack, NY: American Academy of Experts in Traumatic Stress.

Axelson, J. A. (1999). *Counseling and development in a multicultural society* (3rd ed.). Pacific Grove, CA: Brooks/Cole.

Bouton, B. L. (2003). Schools, children and public tragedy. In M. Lattanzi-Licht & K. J. Doka (Eds.). *Coping with public tragedy*, pp. 151–164. Washington, DC: Hospice Foundation of America.

Center for Collaborative and Effective Practice (CCEP). (2001). *Early warning signs, timely response: A guide to safe schools*. Washington, DC: American Institutes for Research. Accessed July 2007 at http://cecp.air.org/guide.

Cornell, D. G. (2007, June). Virginia Tech: What can we do? *APA Monitor on Psychology, 38*(6). Accessed July 2007 at www.apa.org/monitor/jun07/ceo.html

Cotton, K. (1995). *Effective schooling practices: A research synthesis* (1995 update). Portland: Northwest Regional Educational Laboratory. Education Commission of the States.

Davies, N. J. (1999). *Resilience: Status of the research and research-based programs*. Rockville, MD: Center for Mental Health Services, Substance Abuse and Mental Health Services Administration. Accessed July 2007 at http://mentalhealth.samhsa.gov/schoolviolence/5-28Resilience.asp

Doka, K. J. (2003). Memorialization, ritual, and public tragedy. In M. Lattanzi-Licht & K. J. Doka (Eds.), *Coping with public tragedy*, pp. 179–190. Washington, DC: Hospice Foundation of America.

Dolan, P. (2003). Public grief and the new media. In M. Lattanzi-Licht & K. J. Doka (Eds.), *Coping with public tragedy*, pp. 85–90, Washington, DC: Hospice Foundation of America.

Epstein, M. H., Kutash, K., & Duchnowski, A. (1998). Outcomes for children and youth with behavioral and emotional disorders and their families. *Programs and evaluation best practices*. Austin, TX: ProEd.

Eron, L. D., Gentry, J.H., Schlege, P. (1993). *Reason to hope. A psychosocial perspective on violence and youth*. Washington, DC: American Psychological Association.

Heide, K. M. (1997). Juvenile homicide in America: How can we stop the killing? *Behavioral Sciences and the Law, 15*, 203–220.

Hunter, L., & Elias, M., (1998). School violence: Prevalence, policies, and prevention. In A. R. Roberts (Ed.), *Juvenile justice: Policies, programs, and services* (pp. 71–92). Chicago: Nelson-Hall.

Kennedy, A. (2007, June). We Are Virginia Tech. *Counseling Today*. Vol. 49, No. 12, 46–47.

Leavitt, M. O., Spellings, M., & Gonzales, A. (2007, June 13). *Report to the President on issues raised by the Virginia Tech tragedy*, Washington, DC: United States Department of Health and Human Services. Accessed July 2007 at www.hhs.gov/vtreport.html

Loeber, R., & Farrington, D. (1998). *Serious and violent juvenile offenders: Risk factors and successful interventions*. Beverly Hills, CA: Sage.

Masten, A. S., & Coatsworth, J. D. (1998, February). The development of competence in favorable and unfavorable environments: Lessons from research on successful children, *American Psychologist, 53*(2): 205–220.

Matthews, J. D. (1999). The grieving child in the school environment. In J. D. Davidson and K. J. Doka (Eds.), *Living with grief: At work, at school, at worship*, pp. 95–114. Washington, DC: Hospice Foundation of America.

Mayer, G. R. (1995). Preventing antisocial behavior in the schools. *Journal of Applied Behavior Analysis, 28*, 467–478.

National Association of School Psychologists (NASP). (2006, October 27). *Fall 2006 school shootings position statement*. Bethesda, MD: National Consortium of School Violence Prevention Researchers and Practitioners. Accessed July 2007 at www.nasponline.org/press/jointshootingspos_state.pdf

Rutter, M. (1987). Psychosocial resilience and protective mechanisms. *American Journal of Orthopsychiatry, 57*(3): 316–330.

Quinn, M. M., Osher, D., Hoffman, C. C., & Hanley, T. V. (1998). *Safe, drug-free, and effective schools for ALL students: What works!* Washington, DC: Center for Effective Collaboration and Practice, American Institutes for Research.

Sugai, G., & Horner, R. (1999). Antisocial behavior, discipline, and behavioral support: A look from the schoolhouse door. *Archives of Pediatric and Adolescent Medicine, 17*(4): 10–22.

Trump, K. S. (1998). *Practical school security: Basic guidelines for safe and secure schools.* Thousand Oaks, CA: Corwin Press.

U.S. Department of Education (USDOE). (2002). *The three R's to dealing with trauma in schools: Readiness, response, recovery.* Washington, DC: USDOE, Harvard School of Public Health, Prevention Institute, Inc., & Education Development Center, Inc. Accessed July 2007 at www.walcoff. com/prevention/docs/participant_packet.doc

Vaughan, K. (2007). This is a good day. *Rocky Mountain News,* September 22, p. 2.

Virginia Youth Violence Project (2007). The Virginia Tech shooting: Why did it happen? What should we do? Charlottesville, VA: School of Education, University of Virginia. Accessed August 2007 at http://youthviolence.edschool.virginia.edu/vtech.htm

Walker, H. M., Horner, R. H., Sugai, G., Bullis, M., Sprague, J. R., Bricker, D., & Kaufman, J. J. (1996) Integrated approaches to preventing antisocial behavior patterns among school-age children and youth. *Journal of Emotional and Behavioral Disorders, 4,* 194–209.

Yalom, I. D. (1980). *Existential psychotherapy.* New York: Basic Books.

Zangoza, N., Vaughn, S., & McIntosh, R. (1991). Social skills interventions and children with behavior problems: A review. *Behavioral Disorders, 16,* 260–275.

CHAPTER 20

The Problem of Child and Adolescent Suicide

Lillian M. Range

Suicide is tragic no matter what age the victim; among young people, it is the third leading cause of death (Centers for Disease Control and Prevention, 2007). The rate of suicidal deaths increases steadily from the ages of 11 to 21 (Conner & Goldston, 2007). In 2004 in the United States, for children aged 10–14 years, the suicide rate was 1.6 per 100,000. For teens aged 15–19, the suicide rate increased to 8.9 per 100,000. For young adults aged 20–24, it was 13.6 per 100,000. In comparison, for all U.S. citizens, the rate was 10.93 per 100,000 in 2004 (National Center for Injury Prevention and Control, 2004).

The number of youth who consider or attempt suicide is also alarming. The National Youth Risk Behavior Survey includes a representative sample of high school students who answered anonymously about the previous 12 months. Among respondents in grades 9 through 12, in 2005, 16.9% seriously considered suicide, 13.0% planned suicide, and 8.4% attempted suicide (CDC, 2006). Further, in a review of several research studies, some 20% to 30% of adolescents reported suicidal thoughts, including 19% in the year before the survey (Evans, Hawton, & Rodham, 2005). Suicidal thoughts and behaviors are relatively common in adolescence.

In examining the problem of youth suicide, it is important to consider risk factors that may contribute to suicide rates, suicide prevention, interventions with suicidal youth, and responding after the tragedy of a youth suicide. Information about adults is relevant, but the focus of this chapter is on children and adolescents.

Risk/Protective Factors

Factors associated with increased risk can be grouped in various ways. The American Psychiatric Association's (2003) grouping is comprehensive and will be used to guide the following discussion.

Suicidal thoughts and behaviors are a bad sign. Thoughts shape, and ultimately determine, whether young people swallow pills, pull a trigger, or act in some other way to cause their own death (Shea, 1999). More is worse: More thoughts, plans, or attempts mean greater risk of death by suicide. Lethality and intent to die in previous attempts also increase risk.

Psychiatric diagnoses associated with increased suicide risk include major depression, bipolar disorder, schizophrenia, anorexia, alcohol use disorder, other substance use disorders, and personality disorders (particularly borderline). Among a representative sample of children and adolescents aged 9–16 from the southeastern United States, interviewed on multiple occasions from 1993 through 2000, suicide risk was greatest in association with current depression plus anxiety, specifically generalized anxiety disorder, or depression plus a disruptive disorder, primarily oppositional-defiant disorder (Foley, Goldston, Costello, & Angold, 2006). Among a sample of homeless persons in England who had contacted mental health services within the past year, suicide risk was greatest among young people who displayed schizophrenia, personality disorder, unemployment, and substance misuse (Bickley et al., 2006). Psychiatric diagnoses increase suicide risk, and comorbidity is especially risky.

Physical illnesses associated with suicide include nervous system illnesses, cancer, and HIV/AIDS (American Psychiatric Association, 2003). The association of physical illness and suicide is characteristic of older persons but has not been noted in youth.

Psychosocial features associated with suicide include recent lack of social support, drop in socioeconomic status, poor relationship with family, domestic partner violence, and recent stressful events. For adolescents, social support usually means peers. Among teens hospitalized because of concerns about suicide, greater levels of perceived peer rejection and lower levels of close friendship support were directly associated with more severe suicidal ideation (Prinstein, Boergers, Spirito, Little, & Grapentine, 2000).

Other psychosocial features associated with youth suicide include poor relationship with family (Slap, Vorters, Chaudhuri, & Centor, 1989). Among adults, suicide risk increases with loss of a close personal relationship, often a domestic partner (Conner, Duberstein, & Conwell, 2000), and poverty (Foley et al., 2006). With youth, the risk is more likely to be associated with the breakup of a romantic relationship. Typically, suicidal thoughts and attempts are preceded by common, stressful life events (Spirito, Overholser, & Stark, 1989). The ways youth perceive and think about stressors may be an important consideration in identifying those who are potentially suicidal (Nock & Kazdin, 2002).

Abuse is associated with suicide. A research review of 10 studies on physical and sexual abuse and suicide indicated that adolescents who had been physically or sexually abused were significantly more likely to experience suicidal thoughts and behaviors than other adolescents (Evans, Hawton, Rodham, & Deeks, 2005). Early childhood abuse and neglect appear to contribute to the familial transmission of suicidal behavior by compounding genetic vulnerability (Brent & Mann, 2006).

Genetic and familial factors contribute to suicide. Many teenagers who attempt suicide show evidence of an inability to regulate their mood or tolerate distress. The tendency toward such behavior is often familial, so it likely has a genetic component (Brent & Mann, 2006).

Psychological features associated with suicide include hopelessness and anhedonia, psychic pain, anxiety, panic, shame, turmoil, decreased self-esteem, psychic vulnerability, impulsiveness, aggression, and agitation. These features are associated with suicide with or without the presence of psychiatric diagnoses.

Cognitive features associated with suicide include negative automatic thoughts (Nock & Kazdin, 2002), loss of executive function, thought constriction (tunnel vision), polarized thinking, and rigidity. Reasons for living, in contrast, are cognitive protective factors against suicide. In a 2-year follow-up study, depressed inpatients were assessed for reasons for living; they were assessed again at 3 months, 1 year, and 2 years postdischarge. High reasons for living scores predicted fewer suicide attempts within 2 years in women but not in men (Lizardi et al., 2007).

Demographic features make a difference in suicide risk. Risk increases if the child or adolescent is male, white, and/or gay or bisexual. As with adults, suicide risk increases for males and whites. Sexual minority youths are more likely than their peers to think about and attempt suicide (Russell & Joyner, 2001).

Alcohol use increases suicide risk. Alcohol abuse impairs judgment, reduces impulse control, and lowers mood. Multiple studies show substantial suicide risk associated with alcohol consumption (King, 1997), and more than one third of adolescent suicide attempters had consumed alcohol within 6 hours prior to their attempt (Hawton, Fagg & McKeown, 1989).

The *presence of firearms* increases suicide risk, particularly when the firearm is stored unsafely (Hardy, 2006). One review concluded that up to 40% of children, and even more adolescents, have access to firearms in their homes (Hardy, 2006). Further, children's (especially boys') fascination with guns has been well documented and appears resistant to intervention. In addition, young children lack the cognitive maturity to generalize lessons about safety, and older children and adolescents believe themselves to be invulnerable to injury.

Why the increase in rate of suicide, particularly among boys and young men? Depression increases in adolescence, and drug use generally increases between the ages of 11 and 21. These developmental patterns suggest that drug use and dependence may account for the increase of suicide in young men (Conner & Goldston, 2007). Depression in combination with drug use may be particularly potent in this group. Minor acts of aggression and physical fighting decline over the course of adolescence (Conner & Goldston, 2007), but severe acts of aggression increase (U.S. Department of Health and Human Services, 2005). Because the rate of severe aggression parallels the rate of suicide, it is likely that aggression is a contributing factor to the increased suicide rate among boys and young men (Conner & Goldston, 2007). Firearms are the most commonly used method of homicide and suicide (National Center for Injury Prevention and Control, 2004). Increased depression and aggression, in combination with access to guns, probably account for increased suicide rates, particularly among adolescent boys.

Many of these risk factors, such as hopelessness and psychiatric diagnoses, occur together. But the presence of numerous risk factors does not necessarily mean that the person is an immediate risk. The three most useful indicators are presenting for treatment immediately after seriously attempting suicide, psychotic processes, and planning or intent (Shea, 1999).

Prevention

For youth and adolescents, prevention efforts typically occur either in schools or in the community. Efforts in both arenas can reduce suicide rates.

Schools can make a difference. One major depression prevention study involved suburban middle school students who were randomly assigned to one of three groups (Gillham et al., 2007). A cognitive-behavioral and social problem-solving skills group taught students to think flexibly and accurately about their challenges and problems. Students learned about pessimistic explanatory styles; cognitive restructuring skills (including how to challenge negative thinking by evaluating the accuracy of beliefs and generating alternative interpretations); and the links among beliefs, feelings, and behaviors. They practiced techniques for coping and problem solving, including assertiveness, negotiation, decision making, and relaxation. A life enhancement group used structured activities, role-playing, and guided discussion to cover important life topics, including peer pressure, ethical dilemmas, trust and betrayal, improving communication, friendships, family conflict, setting and achieving goals, self-esteem, and body image. A control group had no special training but completed the same assessments. In both treatment groups (groups size from 6 to 14 participants), students met for 90 minutes after school for 12 weeks; the groups were led by teachers, school counselors, and trained graduate students. Parents received $5 per session that their child attended and a $15 bonus if their child attended at least eight sessions. Children in all three groups completed questionnaires at baseline, at 2 weeks postintervention, and every 6 months thereafter for 3 years. Results were mixed. In two schools, cognitive-behavioral and social problem-solving skills significantly reduced depressive symptoms at 30-month follow-up (Gillham et al., 2007). However, cognitive-behavioral and social problem-solving skills did not help in the third school. The benefits of these skills are strongest when group leaders are the intervention developers, members of the developers' research team, or extensively trained and supervised graduate students. Effects are often smaller or nonsignificant when group leaders are teachers, clinicians, or other researchers (Gillham, Hamilton, Freres, Patton, & Gallop, 2006).

Given the overlap of depression and suicidal thoughts and behaviors, it is reasonable to expect that a cognitive-behavioral intervention would reduce suicidal thinking and acts. If teachers and counselors are to lead cognitive-behavioral and social problem-solving skills groups, they need training and supervision. Schools are a viable setting in which to teach depression prevention skills.

Communities also can make a difference in suicidal behaviors. Crisis lines are important community mental health resources. In one study, those who called a crisis line were typically young women aged 16 to 18, and they rated the crisis line as helpful (Meehan & Broom, 2007). In another study, independent raters measured young people's suicidality and mental state at the beginning and end of 100 taped phone counseling sessions. Callers were significantly less suicidal and likely to have an improved mental state by the end of the phone call (King, Nurcombe, Bickman, Hides, & Reid, 2003). Another study reports similar results, as well as reduced hopelessness and psychological pain among callers, but the age of these callers was not ascertained (Gould, Kalafat, Munfakh, & Kleinman, 2007). Seriously suicidal youth reach out to telephone crisis services, and these services can help them.

Other prevention strategies include screening at-risk youths, educating primary care physicians, and educating the media (Gould, Greenberg, Velting, & Shaffer, 2003). When youth contact mental health services, the suicide prevention measures likely to benefit them include targeting schizophrenia, dual diagnosis, and loss of service contact (Bickley et al., 2006). Because community-based education, media campaigns, access prevention laws, and physician-based counseling have little significant impact on parents' gun ownership and safe storage practices, preventing firearm injuries and deaths among children and adolescents should be depoliticized and reframed as a public health issue (Hardy, 2006).

Efforts to reduce youth suicide can start in the school or in the community. At school, recommendations include training in optimism, cognitive strategies, and problem solving. In the community, recommendations include implementing crisis lines, screening, educating contact persons such as physicians and the media, and passing laws to restrict access to guns.

Intervention

Intervention includes assessment and treatment of suicidal youth. Assessment might involve clinical interviews, structured interviews, or questionnaires.

Assessment often starts with interviews containing open-ended questions about suicide. Much information is conveyed nonverbally, so interviews are very important. In an interview, experts recommend asking directly about suicide, in simple language (Shea, 1999). Unstructured interviews allow the interviewer to follow up as needed, to provide in-depth information about the potentially suicidal youth.

Structured interviews can be quite informative as well. One structured interview designed specifically for adolescents contains 169 items in five modules that assess the presence, frequency, and characteristics of suicidal ideas, plans, gestures, and attempts (Nock, Holmberg, Photos, & Michel, 2007). Among adolescent volunteers, this interview has excellent interrater and strong test-retest reliability, and strong parent-adolescent agreement.

Health professionals can supplement interviews with questionnaires. Many suicide questionnaires, such as the Scale for Suicide Ideation (Beck, Kovacs & Weissman, 1979), are designed for adults, but a few target children and adolescents. Copyrighted questionnaires designed specifically for youth or adolescents include the Inventory of Suicide Ideation–30 (ISI–30) (King & Kowalchuk, 1994), which can be used as a screening tool or with outpatient adolescents; the Suicide Probability Scale (Cull & Gill, 1982), also for adolescents and more widely used than the ISI-30; the Suicide Ideation Questionnaire (Reynolds, 1987), which has junior high and senior high versions; and the Child-Adolescent Suicidal Potential Index (Pfeffer, Jiang, & Kakuma, 2000), which is designed for adolescents but can be read to children as young as 6 years.

Available in noncopyrighted form are the Multi-Attitude Suicidal Tendency Scale (Orbach et al., 1991), which asks multiple-choice questions about four suicide-related attitudes (attraction to life and death, and repulsion by life and death); the Fairy Tales Test (Orbach, Feshbach, Carlson, Glaubman, & Gross, 1983), which uses stories (i.e., Pinocchio) to illustrate these four suicide-related attitudes; the Juvenile Suicide Assessment (Galloucis & Francek, 2002), a structured interview designed for a juvenile justice setting; and Reasons for Living for Young Adults (Gutierrez et al., 2002), a list of 32 reasons not to commit suicide should the thought occur. A comprehensive, well-organized book on assessment is *Measuring Suicidal Behavior and Risk in Children and Adolescents* (Goldston, 2003). All these instruments are reasonable tools. The Reasons for Living list has a uniquely positive focus.

Using questionnaires to assess for suicidality carries advantages and disadvantages. Advantages include speed, ease, norms, and access to information that might be difficult to obtain in a face-to-face interview and is useful for discussion. Disadvantages include the temptation to view responses uncritically or believe that the person's suicidal state is static, and the danger of relying on questionnaires instead of developing a strong therapeutic relationship (Range, 2005a). There is no substitute for sound clinical judgment in assessing a potentially suicidal child or adolescent.

Assessment is the antecedent to treatment. Treatment typically involves some combination of therapy and medical intervention.

Psychotherapy to reduce suicide risk may take the form of cognitive therapy, dialectical behavior therapy, or interpersonal psychotherapy. Therapy might also include outreach interventions, such as sending caring letters.

Cognitive-behavioral therapy (CBT) targets the automatic thoughts and core beliefs that were activated right before the person's suicide attempt. In the beginning phases, the therapist teaches specific cognitive and behavioral techniques with the goal of decreasing suicidal thoughts and preventing future suicide attempts. In the middle phases, the therapist focuses on cognitions and behavioral change, using techniques such as Socratic questioning, dysfunctional thought records, behavioral experiments, and role-playing. In the later phases, the therapist works on relapse prevention (Berk, Henriques, Warman, Brown, & Beck, 2004). CBT is multidimensional; it acknowledges behavioral, affective, social, and environmental factors associated with vulnerability for suicide. A meta-analysis of treatment yielded four studies on cognitive-behavioral therapies that showed a significant preventive effect on repeated suicide attempts (van der Sande, Buskens, Allart, van der Graaf, & van Engeland, 1997). However, initial findings have not been uniformly positive, the number of randomized trials is small, sample sizes are limited, treatment gains are not necessarily maintained (Reinecke & Didie, 2005), and intervention efforts have generally focused on adults rather than youth or adolescents.

Dialectical behavior therapy (DBT) was originally designed for older adolescents and young adults but has been modified for suicidal adolescents. The adolescent modification of DBT is a regimen including individual therapy that aims for a balance between acceptance and change; group-formatted skills training emphasizing mindfulness, emotional regulation, interpersonal effectiveness, distress tolerance, and balance; telephone consultation; family therapy; and a consultation team (Miller, Rathus, & Linehan, 2007). Individual therapy includes diary cards that ask about problems with self-harm, suicidal thoughts and actions, alcohol and drug urges and use, medicine, cutting class, risky sex, and emotions. The length is 16 weeks, with an optional 16 weeks of graduate group work (Miller et al., 2007). The core of DBT for adolescents as well as adults is acknowledging that their actions make sense in the context of their current lives, and challenging them to change their lives. DBT presents a hierarchy of treatment targets, starting with decreasing life-threatening behaviors and ending with finding freedom and joy. Miller and colleagues believe that this multimodal approach offers enormous hope for effective interventions with suicidal adolescents.

Interpersonal therapy stresses autonomy. The therapist expresses empathy and honors the client's self- and worldviews. The therapist provides choices and explains them, avoiding reassurance even though the client seeks it. Interpersonal therapy for adolescents addresses issues specific to the age group, such as disputes with parents and friends, difficulties with life transitions, initial experiences with grief, and stresses related to single-parent families (Mufson, Dorta, Olfson, Weissman, & Hoagwood, 2004).

An aspect of therapy with suicidal youth is life-maintenance agreements, also known as safety agreements, no-suicide contracts, stay-alive understandings, and suicide prevention agreements. The potentially suicidal youth agrees to refrain from any type of self-harm for a specified period and to seek help when he or she is in a suicidal state and unable to honor this agreement. The first published report of life-maintenance agreements described training 31 clinicians to make them (Drye, Goulding, & Goulding, 1973). In current practice, life-maintenance agreements are common therapeutic tools for psychologists (Motto, 1999), psychiatrists (Kroll, 2000), nurses (Farrow, 2002), crisis line workers (Mishara & Daigle, 1997), and other mental health professionals.

Arguments for using life-maintenance agreements are that they can strengthen the therapeutic alliance, instill hope, slow the pace of the suicidal crisis, and lower anxiety. Arguments against using life-maintenance agreements are that they can inhibit the therapeutic alliance, introduce coercion, and imply that the suicidal state is static or that the therapist is more interested in administrative details than in the client. In using them, it is important to develop a relationship with the suicidal person first, collaborate on the agreement, attend to the context, keep the wording simple, avoid the term *contract*, consult and document, and remember that alternatives are available (Range, 2005b). Most mental health practitioners have a positive opinion about no-suicide contracts and agree that they should be used with adolescents and adults but not with children (Davidson, Wagner, & Range, 1995). Overall, suicidal persons and those treating them are generally positive toward life-maintenance agreements, although some suicidal youth may be unwilling or unable to uphold the agreement. Surveys of adolescent users are needed to see if they have the same attitudes as adults.

Outreach interventions such as letters of concern may reduce suicide risk. Adults who had refused ongoing care after being hospitalized for suicidality or depression were randomly divided into two groups: The experimental group received personal letters at least four times a year for 5 years; the control group received no further contact. Patients in the contact group had a significantly lower suicide rate in the first 2 years (Motto & Bostrom, 2001). The procedure was designed for adults but could be modified for use with adolescents.

A different kind of outreach intervention focused on social support for suicidal adolescents. Project staff helped adolescents nominate up to four potential support persons, one of whom could be a peer. Support persons had an education session and were asked to contact the adolescents weekly to discuss concerns and encourage activities in support of treatment goals. Intervention specialists contacted support persons regularly. Compared with treatment as usual, girls (but not boys) reported fewer suicidal ideas and reduced mood-related functional impairment (King et al., 2006). Bolstering social support helped reduce suicidal thoughts in suicidal teenage girls.

Medicines that are potentially helpful include antidepressants, which may reduce suicide ideation in depressed youth. Prescribing medicine for depression is on the upswing. From 1988 to 1994, there was a three- to fivefold increase in the United States in antidepressant treatment of youths under 20 years of age (Zito et al., 2002). Antidepressants, however, are not necessarily given for suicide ideas or attempts. Meta-analyses indicate no significantly higher number of suicides among children and adolescents who take antidepressants, but a higher number of nonfatal attempts and thoughts was found (Sakinofsky, 2007). A huge problem in research on antidepressants is that most studies are retrospective and not designed with suicide as the outcome of interest (Sakinofsky, 2007). Antidepressants may prevent suicide through their beneficial effect on depression, but controversy exists about whether antidepressants increase suicide risk.

Other medicines may have an impact on suicide rates as well. Lithium, an antimania drug, appears to reduce rates of suicide attempts and completions in people with bipolar disorder and recurrent depression (Sakinofsky, 2007). Antipsychotics reduce suicide in persons diagnosed with schizophrenia, particularly if they are highly agitated (APA, 2003). Antianxiety agents have the potential to reduce suicide because they reduce anxiety, but they can also lower inhibitions and enhance impulsivity (APA, 2003). Also, they can be lethal in combination with alcohol.

Other medically focused interventions are sometimes used to treat suicidality. Inpatient treatment is the current standard of care, but it has never been found efficacious in clinical trials (Comtois & Linehan, 2006). Electroconvulsive therapy may reduce suicide ideas in the short term (APA, 2003).

Guidelines for medicine and medical procedures for suicidal youth include using adequate doses and maintaining them after initial symptoms have resolved or moderated, introducing medical procedures in the context of an empathic therapeutic relationship, and monitoring closely (Salzman, 1999). Medicine is not a cure for suicide, but it can be part of a comprehensive treatment program.

Controlled studies indicate that, as a whole, psychosocial treatments reduce the risk of suicide attempts and completions (Comtois & Linehan, 2006). In one study with adolescents, the combination of Prozac and CBT was more effective than Prozac alone in treating depression (Emslie et al., 2006).

Interventions can reduce suicide risk, but there is no routine treatment. Rather, intervention should be tailored to specific youth, taking into consideration their preferences, tolerances, and abilities.

POSTVENTION

"Postvention" is a term coined by Shneidman (1972) to describe appropriate and helpful acts that come after a dire event. After the suicidal death of a child or adolescent, postvention can focus on friends and family who knew the youth directly or on the community at large, which knew the youth indirectly. Suicidal contagion is a particular concern.

Research with adults indicates that reactions to the suicide of a significant other may involve a wider repertoire of grief responses than those elicited after other modes of death (Ellenbogen & Gratton, 2001). Themes in grief following a suicidal death include questions of meaning, feelings of responsibility, and feelings of rejection or abandonment (Jordan, 2001). It is reasonable to conceptualize bereavement by suicide as a posttraumatic reaction (Callahan, 2000). In view of these possibilities, mental health professionals may need to be more proactive in offering help than is usual in most health care systems (de Groot, Keijser, & Neeleman, 2006). However, they should avoid naive optimism or banal platitudes (Leenaars & Wenckstern, 1998) and should use language that all can understand. It is helpful to encourage bereaved persons to develop ways of coping with distressing flashbacks, visual images, or other horrific sensations, and of confronting painful, avoided memories (Callahan, 2000).

Group approaches may be beneficial for those bereaved by suicide. In one study with adults, two forms of group intervention helped over time, regardless of the focus of the group (Constantino, Sekula, & Rubinstein, 2001). These results suggest that the very process of interacting with a group of other survivors of suicide death helps, but research is needed that focuses on youth.

Journaling may be helpful for those bereaved by the suicidal death of a loved young person. One Internet-based journaling intervention focused on people suffering from complicated grief (Wagner, Knaevelsrud, & Maercker, 2006). Bereaved persons—some of whom had lost a loved one to suicide—wrote for 45 minutes twice a week for 5 weeks, focusing on exposure, intrusion, and recovery. *Exposure* included writing all their fears and thoughts about the event, including sensory perceptions, in as much detail as possible. They wrote using the present tense and the first person, without regard to grammar, style, or logical chronology. *Intrusion* involved concentrating on one intensely distressing moment that kept coming to mind. In this exercise, the instructions encouraged cognitive reappraisal and writing a supportive, encouraging letter to a hypothetical friend that reflected guilt feelings, challenged dysfunctional automatic thinking and behavior, and corrected unrealistic assumptions. *Recovery* included developing rituals to remember the deceased, focusing on positive memories of the deceased, and using resources such as social contacts. The goal was to cope now and in the future. Those who participated in this intervention had significantly less intrusion and avoidance, and significantly more adaptation than those in the wait-listed control group. Journaling may help youth as well as adults.

Narrative strategies that promote meaning-making regarding loss can mitigate bereavement complications (Neimeyer, 2002) and may be especially relevant when the circumstances of the death are violent. For example, one research project involved participants telling and retelling the story of the loss in the context of reviewing and revisiting life goals (Shear, Frank, Houck, & Reynolds, 2005). They imagined a conversation with the deceased, recalled (mostly) positive memories about the deceased, defined life goals, considered what they would like for themselves if their grief were not so intense, identified ways to know that they were working toward their goals, made concrete plans to put goals into action, and reengaged in meaningful relationships. Bereaved persons suffering from complicated grief responded more strongly and more quickly to this narrative strategy than to standard psychotherapy (Shear et al., 2005).

Identifying risk factors, making prevention efforts, and actively intervening with suicidal youth can make a difference in the long term. Suicidal youth can recover and go on to lead productive, happy lives. Postvention efforts after a suicide can help bereaved persons deal with their responses and draw some meaning from the tragedy.

Lillian M. Range, Ph.D., is Professor of Psychology at Our Lady of Holy Cross College, New Orleans, Louisiana, and Professor Emeritus, The University of Southern Mississippi. Her research interests are suicide, bereavement, and health promotion. She is Associate Editor of *Death Studies*, and editorial board member of *Journal of Personality Assessment, Suicide and Life-Threatening Behavior, Journal of Psychopathology and Behavioral Assessment,* and *Journal of Loss and Trauma.* She is a licensed psychologist in Louisiana and Mississippi, a fellow of the American Psychological Association, and 2007 president of Southeastern Psychological Association. Recent book chapter topics include suicide prevention, women and suicide, and no-suicide contracts. Recent article topics include perceptions of college student suicide, psychological impact of writing about abuse or positive experiences, suicidal thoughts and interrogative suggestibility, responding to suicidal crisis line phone calls, an overview of suicide assessment instruments, collecting health data at faith-based institutions, and community coalitions for preventing tobacco use.

REFERENCES

American Psychiatric Association (APA). (2003). *Practice guideline for the assessment and treatment of patients with suicidal behaviors.* Washington, DC: Author. Retrieved September 11, 2007, from www.psych.org/psych_pract/treatg/quick_ref_guide/Suibehavs_QRG.pdf

Beck, A. T., Kovacs, M., & Weissman, A. (1979). Assessment of suicidal intention: The Scale for Suicidal Ideation. *Journal of Consulting and Clinical Psychology, 47,* 343–352.

Berk, M. S., Henriques, G. R., Warman, D. M., Brown, G. K., & Beck, A. T. (2004). A cognitive therapy intervention for suicide attempters: An overview of the treatment and case examples. *Cognitive and Behavioral Practice, 11,* 265–277.

Bickley, H., Kapur, N., Hunt, I. M., Robinson, J., Meehan, J., Parsons, R., et al. (2006). Suicide in the homeless within 12 months of contact with mental health services. *Social Psychiatry and Psychiatric Epidemiology, 41,* 686–691.

Brent, D. A., & Mann, J. J. (2006). Familial pathways to suicidal behavior: Understanding and preventing suicide among adolescents. *New England Journal of Medicine, 355,* 2719–2721.

Callahan, J. (2000). Predictors and correlated of bereavement in suicide support group participants. *Suicide and Life-Threatening Behavior, 30,* 104–124.

Centers for Disease Control and Prevention. (2006). National youth risk behavior survey: 1991–2005. Retrieved October 1, 2007, from www.cdc.gov/HealthyYouth/YRBS/trends.htm

Centers for Disease Control and Prevention. (2007). Suicide trends among youths and young adults aged 10–24 years, United States, 1990–2004. *Morbidity and Mortality Weekly Reports, 56*(35), 905–908.

Comtois, K. A., & Linehan, M. M. (2006). Psychosocial treatments of suicidal behaviors: A practice-friendly review. *Journal of Clinical Psychology, 62,* 161–170.

Conner, K. R., Duberstein, P. R., & Conwell, Y. (2000). Domestic violence, separation and suicide in young men with early onset alcoholism: Reanalyses of Murphy's data. *Suicide and Life-Threatening Behavior, 30,* 354–359.

Conner, K. R., & Goldston, D. B. (2007). Rates of suicide among males increase steadily from age 11 to 21: Developmental framework and outline for prevention. *Aggression and Violent Behavior, 12,* 193–207.

Constantino, R. E., Sekula, K., & Rubinstein, E. N. (2001). Group intervention for widowed survivors of suicide. *Suicide and Life-Threatening Behavior, 31,* 428–441.

Cull, J., & Gill, W. (1982). *Suicide Probability Scale manual.* Los Angeles: Western Psychological Services.

Davidson, M., Wagner, W., & Range, L. M. (1995). Clinicians' attitudes toward no-suicide agreements. *Suicide and Life-Threatening Behavior, 25,* 410–414.

De Groot, M. H., Keijser, J., & Neeleman, J. (2006). Grief shortly after suicide and natural death: A comparative study among spouses and first-degree relatives. *Suicide and Life-Threatening Behavior, 36,* 418–431.

Drye, R. C., Goulding, R. L., & Goulding, M. E. (1973). No-suicide decisions: Patient monitoring of suicidal risk. *American Journal of Psychiatry, 130,* 171–174.

Ellenbogen, S., & Gratton, F. (2001). Do they suffer more? Reflections on research comparing suicide survivors to other survivors. *Suicide and Life-Threatening Behavior, 31,* 83–90.

Emslie, G., Kratochvil, C., Vitiello, B., Silva, S., Mayes, T., McNulty, S., et al. (2006). Treatment for adolescents with depression study (TADS): Safety results. *Journal of the American Academy of Child & Adolescent Psychiatry, 45*, 1440–1455.

Evans, E., Hawton, K., & Rodham, K. (2005). Suicidal phenomena and abuse in adolescents: A review of epidemiological studies. *Child Abuse and Neglect, 29*, 45–58.

Evans, E., Hawton, K., Rodham, K., & Deeks, J. (2005). The prevalence of suicidal phenomena in adolescents: A systematic review of population-based studies. *Suicide and Life-Threatening Behavior, 35*, 239–250.

Farrow, T. L. (2002). Owning their expertise: Why nurses use "no suicide contracts" rather than their own assessments. *International Journal of Mental Health Nursing, 11*, 214–219.

Foley, D. L., Goldston, D. B., Costello, E. J., & Angold, A. (2006). Proximal psychiatric risk factors for suicidality in youth: The Great Smoky Mountains Study. *Archives of General Psychiatry, 63*, 1017–1024.

Galloucis, M., & Francek, H. (2002). The juvenile suicide assessment: An instrument for the assessment and management of suicide risk with incarcerated juveniles. *International Journal of Emergency Mental Health, 4*, 181–200.

Gillham, J. E., Hamilton, J., Freres, D. R., Patton, K., & Gallop, R. (2006). Preventing depression among early adolescents in the primary care setting: A randomized controlled study of the Penn Resiliency Program. *Journal of Abnormal Child Psychology, 34*, 195–211.

Gillham, J. E., Reivich, K. J., Freres, D. R., Chaplin, T., Shatte, A. J., Samuels, B., et al. (2007). School-based prevention of depressive symptoms: A randomized controlled study of the effectiveness and specificity of the Penn Resiliency Program. *Journal of Consulting and Clinical Psychology, 75*, 9–19.

Goldston, D. B. (2003). *Measuring suicidal behavior and risk in children and adolescents.* Washington, DC: American Psychological Association.

Gould, M. S., Greenberg, T., Velting, D. M., & Shaffer, D. (2003). Youth suicide risk and preventive interventions: A review of the past 10 years. *Journal of the American Academy of Child & Adolescent Psychiatry, 42,* 386–405.

Gould, M. S., Kalafat, J., Munfakh, J., & Kleinman, M. (2007). An evaluation of crisis hotline outcomes: Part 2: Suicidal callers. *Suicide and Life-Threatening Behavior, 37,* 338–352.

Gutierrez, P., Osman, A., Barrios, F., Kopper, B., Baker, M., & Haraburda, C. (2002). Development of the Reasons for Living Inventory for Young Adults. *Journal of Clinical Psychology, 58,* 339–357

Hardy, M. S. (2006). Keeping children safe around guns: Pitfalls and promises. *Aggression and Violent Behavior, 11,* 352–366.

Hawton, K., Fagg, J., & McKeown, S. P. (1989). Alcoholism, alcohol and attempted suicide. *Alcohol and Alcoholism, 24,* 3–9.

Jordan, J. R. (2001). Is suicide bereavement different? A reassessment of the literature. *Suicide and Life-Threatening Behavior, 31,* 91–102.

King, C. A. (1997). Suicidal behavior in adolescence. In R. W. Maris, M. M. Silverman, & S. S. Canetto (Eds.), *Review of suicidology* (pp. 61–95). New York: Guilford Press.

King, C., Kramer, A., Preuss, L., Kerr, Weisse, L., & Venkataraman, S. (2006). Youth-nominated support team for suicidal adolescents (Version 1): A randomized controlled trial. *Journal of Consulting and Clinical Psychology, 74,* 199–206.

King, J., & Kowalchuk, B. (1994). *Manual for Inventory of Suicide Ideation–30.* Minneapolis, MN: National Computer Systems.

King, R., Nurcombe, B., Bickman, L., Hides, L., & Reid, W. (2003). Telephone counselling for adolescent suicide prevention: Changes in suicidality and mental state from beginning to end of a counselling session. *Suicide and Life-Threatening Behavior, 33,* 400–411.

Kroll J. (2000). Use of no-suicide contracts by psychiatrists in Minnesota. *American Journal of Psychiatry, 157,* 1684–1686.

Leenaars, A. A., & Wenchstern, S. (1998). Principles of postvention: Applications to suicide and trauma in schools. *Death Studies, 22*, 357–391.

Lizardi, D., Currier, D., Galfalvy, H., Sher, L., Burke, A., Mann, J., et al. (2007). Perceived reasons for living at index hospitalization and future suicide attempt. *Journal of Nervous and Mental Disease, 195*, 451–455.

Meehan, S., & Broom, Y. (2007). Analysis of a national toll free suicide crisis line in South Africa. *Suicide and Life-Threatening Behavior, 37*, 66–78.

Miller, A. L., Rathus, J. H., & Linehan, M. M. (2007). *Dialectical behavior therapy with suicidal adolescents.* New York: Guilford.

Mishara, B. L., & Daigle, M. S. (1997). Effects of different telephone intervention styles with suicidal callers at two suicide prevention centers: An empirical investigation. *American Journal of Community Psychology, 25*, 861–885.

Motto, J. A. (1999). Critical points in the assessment and management of suicide risk. In D. G. Jacobs (Ed.), *The Harvard Medical School guide to suicide assessment and intervention* (pp. 224–248). San Francisco: Jossey-Bass.

Motto, J. A., & Bostrom, A. G. (2001). A randomized controlled trial of postcrisis suicide prevention. *Psychiatric Services, 52*, 828–833.

Mufson, L. H., Dorta, K. P., Olfson, M., Weissman, M., & Hoagwood, K. (2004). Effectiveness research: Transporting interpersonal psychotherapy for depressed adolescents (IPT-A) from the lab to school-based health clinics. *Clinical Child and Family Psychology Review, 7*, 251–261.

National Center for Injury Prevention and Control. (2004). United States suicide injury deaths and rates per 100,000. Retrieved September 21, 2007, from: http://webappa.cdc.gov/cgi-bin/broker.exe

Neimeyer, R. A. (2002). Traumatic loss and the reconstruction of meaning. *Journal of Palliative Medicine, 5*, 935–942.

Nock, M. K., Holmberg, E. B., Photos, V. I., & Michel, B. D. (2007). Self-Injurious Thoughts and Behaviors Interview: Development, reliability, and validity in an adolescent sample. *Psychological Assessment, 19*, 309–317.

Nock, M. K., & Kazdin, A. E. (2002). Examination of affective, cognitive, and behavioral factors and suicide-related outcomes in children and young adolescents. *Journal of Clinical Child and Adolescent Psychology, 31*, 48–58.

Orbach, I., Feshbach, S., Carlson, G., Glaubman, H., & Gross, Y. (1983). Attraction and repulsion by life and death in suicidal and in normal children. *Journal of Consulting and Clinical Psychology, 51*, 661–670.

Orbach, I., Milstein, I., Har-Even, D., Apter, A., Tiano, S., & Elizur, A. (1991). A multi-attitude suicide tendency scale for adolescents. *Journal of Consulting and Clinical Psychology, 3*, 389–404.

Pfeffer, C., Jiang, H., & Kakuma, T. (2000). Child-Adolescent Suicidal Potential Index (CASPI): A screen for risk for early onset suicidal behavior. *Psychological Assessment, 12*, 304–318.

Prinstein, M. J., Boergers, J., Spirito, A., Little, T. D., & Grapentine, W. L. (2000). Peer functioning, family dysfunction, and psychological symptoms in a risk factor model for adolescent inpatients' suicidal ideation severity. *Journal of Clinical Child Psychology, 29*(3), 392–405.

Range, L. M. (2005a). The family of instruments that assess suicide risk. *Journal of Psychopathology and Behavioral Assessment, 27*, 133–140.

Range, L. M. (2005b). No-suicide contracts. In R. I. Yufit & D. Lester (Eds.), *Assessment, treatment, and prevention of suicidal behavior* (pp. 181–203). Hoboken, NJ: Wiley.

Reinecke, M. A., & Didie, E. R. (2005). Cognitive-behavioral therapy with suicidal patients. In R. I. Yufit & D. Lester (Eds.), *Assessment, treatment and prevention of suicidal behavior* (pp. 205–234). Hoboken, NJ: Wiley.

Reynolds, W. M. (1987). The Suicide Ideation Questionnaire. Odessa, FL: Psychological Assessment Resources, Inc.

Russell, S. T., & Joyner, K. (2001). Adolescent sexual orientation and suicide risk: Evidence from a national study. *American Journal of Public Health, 91*, 1276–1281.

Sakinofsky, I. (2007). Treating suicidality in depressive illness: Part 2: Does treatment cure or cause suicidality? *Canadian Journal of Psychiatry, 52*(Supplement 1), 85S–101S.

Salzman, C. (1999). Treatment of the suicidal patient with psychotropic drugs and ECT. In D. G. Jacobs (Ed.), *The Harvard Medical School guide to suicide assessment and intervention* (pp. 372–382). San Francisco: Jossey-Bass.

Shea, S. C. (1999). *The practical art of suicide assessment.* New York: Wiley.

Shear, K., Frank, E., Houck, P. R., & Reynolds, C. F. (2005). Treatment of complicated grief: A randomized controlled trial. *Journal of the American Medical Association, 293*, 2601–2608.

Shneidman, E. S. (1972). Foreword. In A. C. Cain (Ed.), *Survivors of suicide* (pp. ix–xi). Springfield, IL: Charles C. Thomas.

Slap, G. B., Vorters, D. F., Chaudhuri, S., & Centor, R. M. (1989). Risk factors for attempted suicide during adolescence. *Pediatrics, 84*, 762–772.

Spirito, A., Overholser, J. C., & Stark, L. J. (1989). Common problems and coping strategies: II. Findings with adolescent suicide attempters. *Journal of Abnormal Child Psychology, 17*, 213–221.

U. S. Department of Health and Human Services. (2005). *Youth violence: A report of the Surgeon General.* Washington, DC: Author.

van der Sande, R., Buskens, E., Allart, E., van der Graaf, Y., & van Engeland, H. (1997). Psychosocial intervention following suicide attempt: A systematic review of treatment interventions. *Acta Psychiatrica Scandinavica, 96*, 43–50.

Wagner, B., Knaevelsrud, C., & Maercker, A. (2006). Internet-based cognitive-behavioral therapy for complicated grief: A randomized controlled trial. *Death Studies, 30*, 429–453.

Zito, J. M., Safer, D. J., dosReis, S., Gardner, J. F., Soeken, K., Boles, M., et al. (2002). Prevalence of antidepressants among U. S. youths. *Pediatrics, 109*, 721–726.

Bibliographical Resources— Children, Adolescents, and Grief

Charles A. Corr

PICTURE AND ACTIVITY BOOKS FOR PRESCHOOLERS AND BEGINNING READERS

Brown, M. W. (1958). *The Dead Bird*. Reading, MA: Addison-Wesley. Some children find a wild bird that is dead, touch its body, bury it in a simple ceremony, and return to the site each day to mourn ("until they forgot"). Sadness need not last forever; life can go on again. An early classic.

Carney, K. L. (1997–2001). *Barklay and Eve Activity and Coloring Book Series*. Dragonfly Publishing Company, Wethersfield, CT. This series currently has eight titles. Each book tells a story and offers drawings to color or blank spaces to draw pictures about a loss-related topic that adults may find difficult to discuss with children. In each book, two curious Portuguese water dogs learn lessons like: loss and sadness do happen; those events are not their fault; it is OK to have strong feelings as long as they are expressed in constructive ways; and "we can get through anything with the love and support of family and friends" (Book 1, p. 5).

De Paola, T. (1973; 1998). *Nana Upstairs and Nana Downstairs*. New York: Putnam. Tommy likes visiting "Nana Upstairs" (his great-grandmother). When told that she has died, he does not believe it until he sees her empty bed. A few nights later when Tommy sees a falling star, his mother suggests that perhaps it represents a kiss from Nana who is now "upstairs" in a new way. Later, an older Tommy repeats the experience and interpretation after the death of "Nana Downstairs" (his grandmother).

Ewart, C. (2003). *The Giant*. New York: Walker & Co. Before she died, a young girl's mother said that a giant would look after her. As the seasons pass on the family farm, the girl misses her mother and searches for the giant. Her hardworking Pa says there is no such thing as a giant, but the girl keeps searching everywhere until she finally realizes that her tall, strong Pa is the giant looking after her.

Fox, M. (1994). *Tough Boris*. New York: Harcourt Brace. Boris von der Borch is a scruffy, scary pirate. But when his parrot dies, Boris cries and cries just like everyone else. A simple story and pictures give children permission to experience and express their grief.

Gryte, M. (1988). *No New Baby: For Siblings Who Have a Brother or Sister Die before Birth*. Omaha, NE: Centering Corporation (Spanish edition, *No Tenremos Un Nuevo Bebé*). A young child tells about her reactions when the anticipated birth of a new sibling does not happen. Grandma picks up a young bud off the ground and uses it to explain that while most buds keep growing and become flowers, some, like this one, don't. The girl realizes that something like this happened to their baby. Grandma says no one is to blame and we do not always have answers.

Harris, R. H. (2001). *Goodbye Mousie*. New York: Margaret K. McElderry Books (Simon & Schuster). A boy finds it hard to believe that his pet Mousie has died. Over time, he comes to understand that Mousie is dead and will not be coming back. The boy shares his grief with his father and mother. Together they prepare a shoebox in which they bury Mousie.

Heegaard, M. E. (1988). *When Someone Very Special Dies*. Minneapolis, MN: Woodland Press. This activity book discusses loss and death to encourage children to share thoughts and feelings through coloring and drawing.

Hemery, K. M. (1998). *The Brightest Star*. Omaha, NE: Centering Corporation. Before Mommy died, Molly and her parents used to go to the beach and look at the stars. After Mommy died, Molly is troubled when Ms. Baylor asks the children to draw a picture of their families at school. Daddy helps by taking Molly to the beach and pointing out the brightest star, which reminds her of her mother's love.

Hodge, J. (1999). *Finding Grandpa Everywhere: A Young Child Discovers Memories of a Grandparent*. Omaha, NE: Centering Corporation. A little boy realizes that Grandpa is dead, not "lost" as the adults keep saying. But he consoles himself and his Grandma with this thought: Grandpa always said "to do something for someone you have to put a little of yourself into it." So memories of Grandpa and his love live on everywhere the boy looks.

Krasny Brown, L., & Brown, M. (1998). *When Dinosaurs Die: A Guide to Understanding Death*. Boston: Little, Brown. A cartoon format introduces young children to issues of death and loss.

Muñoz-Kiehne, M. (2000). *Since My Brother Died/Desde Que Murió Mi Hermano*. Omaha, NE: Centering Corporation. With text in both English and Spanish, a child wonders if a brother's death is only a dream or if anything could have been done to keep him from dying. The child reports sadness in the family as well the child's own physical reactions. Afraid of forgetting this brother, the child begins to paint, with simple watercolor illustrations gradually turning into rainbows and the confidence that life can go forward.

O'Toole, D. (1988). *Aarvy Aardvark Finds Hope*. Burnsville, NC: Compassion Books. Designed to be read aloud, this is a story about how Aarvy Aardvark comes to terms with the loss of his mother and brother. Many animals offer unhelpful advice to Aarvy; only one friend, Ralphy Rabbit, who really listens to Aarvy as the two of them share their losses, is truly helpful.

Simon, J. (2001). *This Book Is for All Kids, but Especially My Sister Libby. Libby Died*. Austin, TX: Idea University Press. Five-year-old Jack struggled to understand the death of his young sister. This book frames his questions and comments with dramatic, colorful illustrations.

Woodson, J. (2000). *Sweet, Sweet Memory*. New York: Hyperion Books for Children. When Grandpa dies, a young African-American girl named Sarah and her grandmother are consoled by stories and funny memories of him. They recall that he always said, "The earth changes … . Like us it lives, it grows. Like us … a part of it never dies. Everything and everyone goes on and on."

Zolotow, C. (1974). *My Grandson Lew*. New York: Harper & Row. When 6-year-old Lewis wonders why his grandfather has not visited lately, his mother says she did not tell Lewis that his grandfather had died because he had never asked. The boy says that he hadn't needed to ask; his grandfather just appeared. Son and mother share warm memories of someone they both miss: Lewis says, "He gave me eye hugs"; his mother concludes, "Now we will remember him together and neither of us will be so lonely as we would be if we had to remember him alone."

STORYBOOKS AND OTHER TEXTS
FOR PRIMARY SCHOOL READERS

Alexander, A. K. (2002). *A Mural for Mamita/Un Mural Para Mamita*. Omaha, NE: Centering Corporation. A young girl, her family, and the whole neighborhood plan a fiesta to celebrate the life of her grandmother who has recently died after a long illness. Mamita was well known and greatly loved in the neighborhood as the proprietor of the local bodega or store. The girl's special contribution to the celebration is a brilliant mural painted on the side of Mamita's store. The text of this book appears in both English and Spanish.

Alexander-Greene, A. (1999). *Sunflowers and Rainbows for Tia: Saying Goodbye to Daddy*. Omaha, NE: Centering Corporation. A 10-year-old African-American girl named Tia describes how she and other family members feel when her Daddy dies suddenly. Tia tells about her sadness and grief, along with her fears that Mama might also die and leave the children alone. She also explains how people came over to the house to share their love for Daddy, support her family, and bring food. Being involved in many of the preparations for the funeral and taking part in the funeral itself helps Tia, especially when she is allowed to bring Daddy's favorite sunflowers to the ceremony and a big rainbow comes shining.

Barron, T. A. (2000). *Where Is Grandpa?* New York: Philomel Books. After Grandpa dies, family members share memories. When a young boy wants to know where Grandpa is now, they decide that Grandpa is in heaven and that "heaven is any place where people who love each other have shared some time together." He is comforted by the thought of Grandpa way off in the Never Summer range of the Rockies, where they used to look "as far as we can possibly see" from the tree house they built together.

Bunting, E. (1999). *Rudi's Pond.* New York: Clarion. While Rudi is sick, his classmates send cards and make a big "GET WELL RUDI" banner for his hospital room. After Rudi dies, the children write poems and make a memorial pond in the schoolyard that attracts a beautiful hummingbird.

Bunting, E. (2000). *The Memory String.* New York: Clarion. Laura's grief three years after her mother's death is still vivid and it is difficult for her to accept her new stepmother, Jane. Laura consoles herself with a string of buttons going back three generations in her family, especially with the buttons from Mom's prom and wedding dresses and from the nightgown she was wearing when she died. When the string breaks, the 43 buttons are scattered all over the yard. Laura, Dad, and Jane find all but one button. Dad proposes to Jane that they substitute a twin for the missing button, but Laura overhears Jane wisely saying, "It's like a mother. No substitute allowed" (p. 25). When Jane finds the missing button, Laura asks her to help restring her buttons.

Coerr, E. (1977). *Sadako and the Thousand Paper Cranes.* New York: Putnam's. This book is based on a true story about a Japanese girl who died of leukemia in 1955 as one of the long-term results of the atomic bombing of Hiroshima (which occurred when Sadako was 2 years old). In the hospital, a friend reminds Sadako of the legend that the crane is supposed to live for a thousand years and that good health will be granted to a person who folds 1,000 origami paper cranes. With family members and friends, they begin folding. Sadako died before the project was finished, but her classmates completed the work and children all over Japan have since contributed money to erect a statue in her memory.

Copeland, K. M. (2005). *Mama's Going to Heaven Soon.* Minneapolis, MN: Augsburg Fortress. Vivid colors and minimal text in this storybook for young readers describe reactions of two children when their Mama becomes ill and their Daddy says she will soon go to heaven to live with God and the angels. Mama will be gone forever but she will always love her children. Remembering her love and talking about feelings with Daddy can help.

Ferguson, D. (1992). *A Bunch of Balloons*. Omaha, NE: Centering Corporation. This book begins as a story about a child who loves to play with balloons. One day when the string slips out of his hand, the child loses his balloon. Then the book shifts to the reader who may also have lost someone or something. Many different types of grief reactions that the reader may be experiencing are described and two pages offer blank balloons in which the reader can write or draw what has been lost and what is still left.

Goble, P. (1993). *Beyond the Ridge*. New York: Aladdin/Simon & Schuster. At her death, while her family members prepare her body according to their custom, an elderly Plains Indian woman experiences the afterlife believed in by her people. She makes the long climb up a difficult slope to see the Spirit World beyond the ridge.

Grollman, E., & Johnson, J. (2006). *A Complete Book about Death for Kids*. Omaha, NE: Centering Corporation. The three main parts of this book address death and feelings, funerals and cemeteries, and cremation, respectively. Almost every page has two photos and a few simple sentences directed to child readers and adults who might interact with those children. The authors are two well-known experts in this field who are sensitive to the needs of children and insightful in how to address those needs.

Hanson, R. (2005). *A Season for Mangoes*. New York: Clarion. In Jamaica, Sareen is concerned about participating in her first sit-up, a ritual in which villagers share food and tell stories to celebrate the life of her recently deceased grandmother. Sareen discovers that sharing her stories of Nana's passion for mangoes helps ease her sadness.

Johnson, J. (2001). *The Very Beautiful Dragon*. Omaha, NE: Centering Corporation. Two young boys are scared when they first encounter a dragon and become more frightened when they see it again on other occasions. It isn't enough to show them there actually is no dragon present. What really helps is a neighbor who teaches the boys that they have to face their fears and get to know what scares them. That's the way to face down one's dragons and recognize one's own strengths and power. The *Beautiful Dragons and Other Fears Workbook* accompanies this title.

McLaughlin, K. (2001). *The Memory Box*. Omaha, NE: Centering Corporation. A young boy is mad at Grandpa for dying when he had promised to take the boy fishing. Mommy agrees the boy will miss doing some things with Grandpa, but she tells him to hold onto his good memories of all they had shared. One way to do that is to make a memory box and to put into it lots of objects that help the boy remember this special relationship.

Newman, L. (1995). *Too Far Away to Touch*. New York: Clarion. Uncle Leonard is Zoe's favorite relative. He takes her to special places, tells her jokes, and makes her laugh, but now he is sick and has less energy (gradually, we learn that he has AIDS). Nevertheless, one day he takes Zoe to a planetarium. Afterwards, he explains that if he dies he will be like the stars, "too far away to touch, but close enough to see." Another evening at the seashore confirms the lesson as they again watch the night sky and witness a shooting star.

Old, W. (1995). *Stacy Had a Baby Sister*. Morton Grove, IL: Albert Whitman. Stacy liked her baby sister sometimes, but not always. The baby took up a lot of her parents' time and Stacy was jealous until one night she woke up to find the baby had died from SIDS. Stacy wonders if she caused the baby to die and if she will get SIDS. She also has trouble sleeping until she talks with her parents about it.

Plourde, L. (2003). *Thank You, Grandpa*. New York: Dutton Children's Books. Over the years, a girl and her grandfather enjoy walking in the woods together. They share discoveries of a bird, a bee sipping nectar, a sneaky snake, a squirrel waving his tail at them, a butterfly, and a mouse. One day when they find a dead grasshopper, the girl asks, "What can we do?" Grandpa says: "We can say thank you and good-bye." In time, Grandpa becomes too old to walk and one day the girl finds herself walking alone. When she finds a dandelion, she says to herself: "Thank you, Grandpa, for our walks. You kept me steady when I wasn't so steady. You let me run ahead when I was ready to run ahead. Thank you for sharing spiderweb tears and firefly flashes. But most of all, thank you for teaching me the words I need to say.... . Grandpa, I love you and I'll miss you. But I will never forget you. Thank you and good-bye."

Rosen, M. (2004). *Michael Rosen's Sad Book*. Cambridge, MA: Candlewick Press. Michael Rosen pretends to be happy when he is sad "because I think people won't like me if I look sad." Michael is sad because his son, Eddie, died. Sometimes he wants to talk about this and sometimes not. Sometimes he does crazy things because life just isn't the same as it used to be. Michael knows that being sad isn't the same as being bad, so he tries to figure out ways of being sad that don't hurt so much. He also tries to do one thing each day that involves a good time—it can be anything so long as it doesn't make anyone else unhappy. Memories of Eddie and good times seem to help. Bright illustrations illuminate a spare, achingly honest text.

Smith, H. I., & Johnson, J. (2006). *What Does that Mean? A Dictionary of Death, Dying and Grief Terms for Grieving Children and Those Who Love Them*. Omaha, NE: Centering Corporation. It is important to find the right words to use in talking with children, especially so when the subjects involve loss and death. This book identifies more than 70 important words, explains how to pronounce them and what they mean, and offers guidance about how to use these words and discuss these subjects with children.

Tamberrino, S. S. (2001). *Grunt*. Omaha, NE: Centering Corporation. Grunt is an old dog, now blind, in pain, and sick with both cancer and arthritis. A boy and Dad agree that it will be best for Grunt to be euthanized. Still, it isn't easy to carry out that decision, to take Grunt in the car to the veterinarian's office and hold him on the table while the shot takes effect. They bury Grunt in a box in the back yard under a big oak tree, and then just sit together for a long time while they talk about happy times with Grunt and good memories of a good dog.

Vogel, R. H. (2002). *The Snowman* (rev. ed.). Omaha, NE: Centering Corporation. Two brothers are building their first snowman since their Dad died. Talking about their father's illness and how he died helps answer some of 8-year-old Buddy's questions. It also lets 12-year-old Tommy release some of his internal anger and guilt. Using Dad's old pipe, hat, and favorite scarf, the two boys finish the snowman and share good memories of Dad.

Wood, R. (2004). *Now Caitlin Can: A Donated Organ Helps a Child Get Well*. El Dorado, AR: Abc Press. Freddie's little sister was born with kidney problems. When Caitlin was old enough and had gained enough weight, she was able to receive a transplanted kidney. That changed Caitlin's life and made it possible for her to do many things that she had previously been unable to do.

Literature for Middle School Readers

Blume, J. (1981). *Tiger Eyes*. Scarsdale, NY: Bradbury. After Davey's father is killed during a holdup of his convenience store in Atlantic City, Davey (age 15), her mother, and her younger brother all react differently and are unable to help each other in their grief. They attempt a change of location to live temporarily with Davey's aunt in Los Alamos, but they eventually decide to move back to New Jersey to rebuild their lives.

Brisson, P. (1999). *Sky Memories*. New York: Delacorte. While her mother struggles with cancer and before she dies, Emily (age 10) and Mom develop a ritual to celebrate and commemorate their relationship. Together they gather "sky memories," mental pictures of the ever-changing sky in all its variety and wonder. The sky seems to reflect the phases of Mom's illness and the vitality of her soul.

Dragonwagon, C. (1990). *Winter Holding Spring*. New York: Atheneum/Simon & Schuster. At first, nothing is the same for 11-year-old Sarah and her father after her mother dies. Each is in great pain, but gradually they begin to share their experiences and their memories of Sarah's mother. Eventually, they realize together that "nothing just ends without beginning the next thing at the same time" (p. 11). Each season somehow contains its successor; life and love and grief can continue together, for winter always holds spring. And Sarah knows that "love is alive in me and always will be" (p. 31).

Gignoux, J. H. (1998). *Some Folk Say: Stories of Life, Death, and Beyond*. New York: FoulkeTale Publishing. Here are 38 legends, retold in prose and poetry, that different cultures have used to come to terms with the reality of death and hopes for life beyond the grave. Brief comments from the author introduce each section and follow each story. The book is also enlivened by 8 dramatic illustrations. A treasury of global culture to stimulate the imagination and to use in working with children.

Hemery, I. M. (2005). *Sunflower Promise*. Omaha, NE: Centering Corporation. Willow and Davy are best friends. One day as they are teasing, Davy accidentally tears the big, floppy, cloth sunflower off her lovely new hat. Willow is furious and won't play with Davy any more even though he promises that someday he will make it up to her. Willow even punches Davy on the arm, but she is regretful when his bruises don't go away and he becomes so tired that he misses school. Willow worries when Davy goes to the hospital for testing. Will he never get better? Did she cause it? Ultimately, Davy does die, but not before arranging a surprise for Willow to fulfill his promise: a gorgeous field of sunflowers in the field where they used to play.

Henkes, K. (1997). *Sun and Spoon*. New York: Greenwillow Books (Puffin, 1998). Shortly after the death of his grandmother, 10-year-old "Spoon" Gilmore searches for something special of hers to keep. While visiting his grandfather's house, Spoon finds the deck of cards that Gram, Pa, and he used to play with. Without asking, Spoon takes the deck. A few days later, Spoon learns that the same cards also are a source of solace to Pa, who thinks he has misplaced them. Eventually, Spoon puts the cards back and confesses that he had taken them. Pa understands, and gives Spoon the cards to keep.

Jukes, M. (1985). *Blackberries in the Dark*. New York: Dell Yearling. Everything seems so different when Austin comes to visit his Grandma on the farm after Grandpa died. In previous summers, Austin and his Grandpa would do things together, like go fishing or pick blackberries in the dark and eat them for dinner. This summer, Austin had looked forward to Grandpa teaching him to fly-fish. Still, when Grandma joins Austin at the stream, they help each other learn to fly-fish, pick blackberries together, and begin some new traditions of their own.

Little, J. (1984). *Mama's Going to Buy You a Mockingbird*. New York: Viking Kestrel. Jeremy and Sarah only learn their father is dying from cancer by overhearing people talk about it. They share many losses, large and small, that accompany his dying and death, often compounded by lack of information and control over their situation. Their need for support from others is clear.

Park, B. (1995). *Mick Harte Was Here*. New York: Knopf (Random House Bullseye Books, 1996). Phoebe Harte tells about the death of her brother, Mick, who was hit by a truck while riding his bicycle. Phoebe relates many memories from her relationship with Mick and describes her profound grief after his death. Phoebe and her parents are each alone in their grief. She wants very much to know where Mick is now; in time she decides that if Mick is with God (as people keep saying) and God is everywhere, then Mick is everywhere, too. Mick's body is cremated, there is a memorial service with lots of funny stories about Mick, Phoebe speaks about bike safety at a school assembly, and she prints the following in the fresh concrete at the new soccer field bleachers: "M-I-C-K H-A-R-T-E W-A-S H-E-R-E."

Paterson, K. (1977). *Bridge to Terabithia*. New York: Crowell. Jess and Leslie have a special, secret meeting place in the woods, called Terabithia. But when Leslie is killed one day in an accidental fall, the magic of their play and friendship is disrupted. Jess mourns the loss of this special relationship, is supported by his family, and ultimately is able to initiate new relationships that will share friendship in a similar way with others.

Smith, D. B. (1973). *A Taste of Blackberries*. New York: HarperCollins. After Jamie dies from an allergic reaction to a bee sting, his best friend (the book's unnamed narrator) reflects on this unexpected event: Did it really happen or is it just another of Jamie's pranks? Could it have been prevented? Is it disloyal to go on eating and living when Jamie is dead? He decides that no one could have prevented this death, "some questions just don't have answers," and life can go on.

Stickney, D. (1985). *Water Bugs and Dragonflies*. New York: Pilgrim Press. This little book focuses on transformations in life as a metaphor for transformations between life and death. One key point is that the water bug that is transformed into a dragonfly is no longer able to return to the underwater colony to explain what has happened. Each individual must wait for his or her own transformation in order to appreciate what it entails.

Traisman, E. S. (1992). *Fire in My Heart, Ice in My Veins: A Journal for Teenagers Experiencing a Loss*. Omaha, NE: Centering Corporation. This book offers a journal framework for teenagers who have had a loss. A line or two of text on each page and many small drawings offer age-appropriate prompts for this purpose.

White, E. B. (1952). *Charlotte's Web*. New York: Harper. A classic story of friendship on two levels: that of a young girl named Fern who lives on a farm and saves Wilbur, the runt of the pig litter; and that of Charlotte, the spider, who spins fabulous webs to save an older and fatter Wilbur from the butcher's knife. In the end, Charlotte dies of natural causes, but her accomplishments and her offspring live on.

Wiener, L. S., Best, A., & Pizzo, P. A. (Comps.). (1994). *Be a Friend: Children Who Live with HIV Speak*. Morton Grove, IL: Albert Whitman. The vivid colors, drawings, and layout in this book seek to permit children living with HIV infection to speak in their own voices. The result is sometimes poignant, often charming, and always compelling. For example, one 11-year-old writes: "I often wonder how other children without AIDS learn to appreciate life. That's the best part about having AIDS" (p. 13).

LITERATURE FOR HIGH SCHOOL READERS

Craven, M. (1973). *I Heard the Owl Call My Name*. New York: Dell. This novel describes a young Episcopal priest with a terminal illness. He is sent by his bishop to live with Native Americans in British Columbia, who believe that death will come when the owl calls someone's name. From them, the bishop hopes that the young priest will learn to face his own death.

Deaver, J. R. (1988). *Say Goodnight, Gracie*. New York: Harper & Row. When her close friend, Jimmy, is killed by a drunken driver in an automobile accident, Morgan is so disoriented by the extent of her loss that she is unable to face her feelings, attend Jimmy's funeral, or speak to his parents. Her own parents offer support and tolerate Morgan's withdrawal from the world, but it is not until a wise aunt intervenes that Morgan is able to confront her feelings in a way that leads her to more constructive coping and to decide to go on with living.

Draper, S. M. (1994). *Tears of a Tiger*. New York: Atheneum. Without any narrative, this book uses excerpts from official statements, newspaper articles, letters, diaries, homework, phone calls and conversations to describe the aftermath of the death of Robert Washington, captain of the high school basketball team, in a fiery automobile accident. The car's driver, Andrew Jackson, cannot get over Rob's death and his feelings of guilt. Two other friends in the car do well, but Andy sinks gradually into a deeper and more desperate depression. Smiling on the surface, he offers lots of clues about his inner trauma, but his parents, friends, teachers, and even a psychologist do not realize what is happening until he eventually takes his own life.

Grollman, E., & Malikow, M. (1999). *Living when a Young Friend Commits Suicide*. Boston: Beacon Press. This book is intended to help adolescents by guiding them through typical reactions and questions after a friend completes a suicide. It offers suggestions for how to cope and how to help suicidal people. Also addressed are religious questions, popular misconceptions about suicide, and getting on with one's life. A final chapter lists helpful resources.

Guest, J. (1976). *Ordinary People*. New York: Viking. This impressive novel gradually reveals that Conrad Jarrett has many problems after his older brother drowns in a boating accident. Conrad's grief is compounded by the guilt that he feels for not saving the life of his sibling. An overprotective father and a cold mother are little help, but a therapist eventually helps Conrad realize that he is not to blame for his brother's death because he lived through the accident.

Lewis, C. S. (1976). *A Grief Observed*. New York: Bantam. The author, a celebrated British writer and lay theologian, recorded his experiences of grief following the death of his wife on notebooks lying around the house. The published result is an unusual and extraordinary document, a direct and honest expression of one individual's grief that has helped innumerable readers by normalizing their own experiences in bereavement.

Martin, C. (2004). *The Dead Don't Dance: A Novel of Awakening*. Nashville: WestBow Press. The expectations of Dylan Styles and his wife for the birth of their first child turn into tragedy when the baby dies at birth and Maggie is left comatose for many months. Eventually she recovers and there is a happy ending, but the real strength of this novel is how it conveys the pall that hangs over lives affected by grief, guilt, anger, and frustration. Dylan would end his life if it weren't for the seemingly unlikely possibility that Maggie might recover. His friends, teaching a writing course at a local college, students, and a pregnant nursing aide named Amanda all help. Only after a terrible automobile accident involving Dylan's best friend and Amanda, during which her baby is born, is Dylan's faith restored and he sees a way forward.

O'Toole, D. (1995). *Facing Change: Falling Apart and Coming Together Again in the Teen Years*. Burnsville, NC: Compassion Books (477 Hannah Branch Road, Burnsville, NC 28714). This little book is intended to help adolescents understand loss, grief, and change, and to think about how they might respond to those experiences.

Scrivani, M. (1991). *When Death Walks In*. Omaha, NE: Centering Corporation. This little booklet was written to help teen readers explore the many facets of grief and how one might cope with them in productive ways.

Tolstoy, L. (1960). *The Death of Ivan Ilych and Other Stories*. New York: New American Library. The title story is an exceptional piece of world literature in which a Russian magistrate in the prime of his life is afflicted with a grave illness that becomes steadily more serious. As his health deteriorates, Ivan suddenly realizes that glib talk in college about mortality does not apply only to other people or humanity in general. He also discovers that many around him gradually withdraw and become more guarded in what they say to him; only one servant and his young son treat him with real compassion and candor.

Voigt, C. (1983). *Dicey's song*. New York: Atheneum. Dicey Tillerman's father disappeared when she was 7 and her mother is now institutionalized. At 13, she feels responsible for her 3 younger siblings and for Gram with whom they have come to live. Often, Dicey has to "hold on" to let others solve problems when she really wants to jump in herself. Gram and the children need love, trust, and courage to face their new beginnings and many challenges. Overshadowing everything are the losses they have all suffered. That becomes clearest when Gram and Dicey fly up to Boston to be a Momma's bedside when she dies, after which they bring her ashes back to Maryland for burial in the yard.

Establishing Protocols to Respond to Death and Grief in Schools

Kenneth J. Doka

School teachers, administrators and other personnel can play a critical role in helping students with loss and grief after a death has occurred. Because school is central to a child's life, both in terms of time spent and social networks established, school employees will inevitably encounter situations in which a student is touched by death. In all cases, a designated crisis response team of critical school personnel can be helpful, and at times essential, in determining and organizing a proper action plan for the school and its students. The crisis response team should be able to address situations of death and grief, and it should be trained to respond in an age-appropriate manner. Possible circumstances and suggested responses follow:

DEATH NOTIFICATION

When a student must be notified of a death during school hours, it is preferable for the child to be informed of the death by family members, police, or other persons trained in death notification. It is best to have a school policy in effect that enables teachers and administrators to sensitively and appropriately respond to such an event. It is critical that the student's location be established once the information is received by the school, but the student should not be pulled from his or her environment until the person notifying the student is available. There is value in forewarning the child, particularly an older child or adolescent, when he or she is escorted to the location where notification will be given. A simple, calmly delivered and situation-appropriate statement, such as, "Your father is waiting for you, there has been a family emergency," warns the child to prepare for bad news. It is essential that the child be told in a private room. If family members are not present, another trusted adult should be available to offer support. The school's crisis team should be informed so that plans can be made to provide follow-up support when the student returns to school.

ASSISTING THE GRIEVING STUDENT

Acknowledge loss—When a student returns to school following a death, have a private conversation with the child and acknowledge his or her loss. Offer support in a straightforward way. A simple, "I'm sorry to hear about your Dad," for example, conveys caring and concern. Monitor the student's demeanor in the days, weeks and months following. For example, if the child seems to be having a difficult time, talk privately to the child again, assess his or her state of mind, and take additional action (such as referral to the school counselor or other key personnel) as necessary.

Understand grief—A student's grief may be manifested in many ways. Some children may have emotional outbursts; some may withdraw. Others may act out their grief, getting into fights or arguments. Younger children may exhibit regressive behavior, clinging to adults or thumb sucking. Because grief may have cognitive effects, the child may be overly distracted or unable to concentrate. Nightmares and other sleep disturbances may make the child tired or listless in class. Grades may decline. Observe the ways that grief may be affecting the child. Keep parents or guardians informed, and when necessary, confer with support staff, including guidance counselors, school social workers, the school nurse, school psychologists or appropriate administrators. Remember that anger or punishment is an inappropriate response in such situations.

Offer support—The most tangible way you can show support is by helping the child keep up with schoolwork and other school activities. In addition, there may be services you can offer to the child and the family. Does the school offer any support groups for grieving students? Does the school library have any appropriate books that might be offered to the child? There may be services within your community, such as grief groups or camps for grieving children and adolescents. Your local hospice may either offer such services or be a source for information and referrals.

Empower natural networks—The child's best support will come from his or her natural networks. While schools and teachers are certainly one important network, so are family and peers. When possible, gently empower the peer network—teaching children ways to reach out and support a grieving peer. Discuss with families the ways the child is progressing since the loss, assess the parent or guardian ability to cope, and offer parent or guardian support. Keep the lines of communication open with surviving family members or guardians.

Recognize developmental needs—Always keep in mind the child's developmental level in offering support and assessing needs and services. For example, some adolescents may be reluctant to speak of their grief and do not wish to be treated in any way that is different. Children with developmental delays or special needs may have difficulty comprehending and coping with the loss. Confer with the support team to develop strategies to support these children.

Problem solve—Since grief does have cognitive implications, children, especially older children and adolescents, may have difficulty in keeping up with their schoolwork. Work with these children and adolescents—assisting them in prioritizing tasks and finding extra help when needed.

Show sensitivity with projects/events—Some events and projects, such as making Mother's Day and Father's Day gifts, or events such as father/son games or father/ daughter dances, can isolate the child who has experienced the death of a parent. One of the techniques I have developed for such events and projects is to broaden the scope. For example, for a Mother's Day project begin by brainstorming "What mothers do." Once the responses have been written on a blackboard or other surface, affirm that this is "mothering." Ask the class list all the people who "mother" them—listing perhaps aunts, grandparents, sisters, neighbors and friends, step-mothers, even fathers. You can then affirm that this is a day we honor the people who mother us. The project then recognizes and honors such people.

Be sensitive to classmates—Watch the behavior of classmates. Quietly intervene when a classmate makes an insensitive remark. Classmates may also need assistance on how to respond. Seize opportunities to teach caring and compassion. Know, too, that the death of a significant person, such as a parent, may make other children feel vulnerable and anxious.

Refer when necessary—Know your limits. When a child exhibits signs of severe problems—repeated failure with school work, aggressiveness, delinquency, truancy, substance abuse, depression, apathy, or self-destructive behaviors—make appropriate referrals.

If a Suicide Occurs: A Protocol for Schools

Suicide is a leading cause of death for adolescents. Schools should have a protocol or plan to provide postvention (supportive intervention following a suicide). This is particularly essential with adolescents, as sometimes there is a "cluster effect" with adolescent suicides—a number of suicides that follow in a given area and time. As you plan a protocol for suicide:

Develop a communication plan and chain—Someone should be assigned to verify information and assess what the family wishes to be shared. If there are discrepancies between what the family would like to be shared and the public story, sensitively discuss these differences. Information should be shared as soon as possible with the school's crisis team, and staff should be informed as early as possible so that they are ready to assist.

Develop a media plan—Depending on the situation, local media may visit the school after a suicide. One person should be designated to speak to media and other staff should be fully trained as to how to respond. School staff should know who will accompany media if they are in the facility and know who is delegated to handle media inquiries. Recognize, too, the limits to your control. There is little you can do, for example, if reporters interview students outside of school grounds.

Inform students—Students should be informed of the suicide in their classrooms once information is verified. It is important that staff share factual information that the school crisis team has prepared. All staff should speak with one consistent, agreed upon message. Consistent information deters rumors.

Review the student's life and death—The crisis team should lead a discussion of the student's life, death, and the decision to take his or her life. Such a discussion has a number of purposes. First, a discussion validates grief and reminds students of the terrible consequences of suicide. Second, such a review can emphasize that there was no reason to take one's own life—alternatives and assistance are always available. Third, it can avoid isolating individuals who might be "blamed" for the death, such as a teacher who gave the student a failing grade or a partner who terminated a romantic relationship. The team can emphasize that such experiences are normal, albeit painful, events in adolescents and find ways to cope with such situations.

Identify "at-risk" students—As the crisis team sets up counseling, check in with students particularly deemed "at risk." This may include students who were close friends of the student who died. Attachments do not only have to be positive—others such as enemies, persons who bullied, or were bullied by the victim may also be struggling with the death. Be aware, too, of other students who have attempted to commit suicide in the past.

Set up counseling—Counseling services should be available to the school's students and staff. There may be value in having group sessions for friends, classmates, club-mates, or teammates. Students should self-select counseling because some students who have no apparent connection to the deceased student may feel vulnerable.

Remember staff—Teachers and other staff, including secretaries and other school-based personnel, may also need help. They may struggle with beliefs that their comments and actions may have contributed to the death or that they failed to assess the need or otherwise failed the student. Crisis plans should reach out to staff.

Memorialize carefully—It is important to provide opportunities to memorialize the person who died. However, such memorials should take into account the circumstances of the death in a way that does not glorify the victim or manner of death. For example, in one school, a memorial collection of self-help books was dedicated to a young woman who had committed suicide in order to "prevent such needless deaths."

Inform parents—Parents need to know what has occurred. A letter should inform parents of what happened, what the school did, what parents should do, and where to obtain additional information and assistance.

Monitor Internet communication—This is an Internet generation. As you monitor memorials and comments on such popular sites as MySpace or Facebook, you may gain additional insight into the ways your students understand and cope with their loss.

School Response to Traumatic Loss

Traumatic loss can mean many things—a national public tragedy such as 9/11, the Space Shuttle Challenger disaster, or a more localized event, such as a school bus accident or a tornado. Schools need to develop response protocols suitable to the developmental levels of their students. Similar to responses to suicide, these protocols should include the following elements.

Develop a communication plan and chain—Someone should be assigned to verify information and monitor the media. As with suicide, information should be shared as soon as possible with the crisis team, and staff should be informed as early as possible. Should a crisis unfold during the school day, school personnel should respond to code established for such events.

Develop a media plan—There may be situations where local media come to the school. One person should be designated to speak to media and other staff should be fully trained as to how to respond. All staff should know who will accompany media in the facility and who is delegated to handle media inquiries.

Inform students—Students should be informed of the event in their classrooms once information is verified. It is important that staff is trained to share factual information that the crisis team has supplied. Consistent information deters rumors.

Validate and explore responses—Acknowledge that this will not be a "normal" school day. Depending on the nature of the traumatic event, there may be some value in maintaining a degree of normalcy and viable routines. Nonetheless, some time will need to be set aside for students to explore their reactions and have their responses validated.

Shape a group response—In tragic and traumatic events, there is a need to "do something," or to offer support and show concern. Students may need to memorialize the event or find tangible ways to show support. Depending on the age and circumstances, this may involve a number of different actions—collecting funds, writing letters, or even, with older students, donating blood.

Identify students "at-risk"—As the crises team sets up counseling, check in with students particularly deemed "at risk." This may include students who were close friends of the adolescent who were personally affected by the tragedy or had experienced prior traumatic losses.

Make counseling available—It is important that counseling services be available. There may be value in having open group sessions or sessions for those personally affected. Personal counseling should also be available. In such counseling, there should be opportunities for students to self-select into counseling as some students may feel especially vulnerable.

Remember staff—Teachers and other staff may also need help. Crisis plans should reach out to staff. Traumatic events affect everyone in the community. Staff cannot be expected to constantly support their students unless they, too, are supported.

Inform parents—Parents as well need to know how the school has responded to the tragedy. A letter should be sent out informing parents what happened, what the school did, what parents should do, and where to obtain additional information and assistance.

Include stakeholders in plans to develop on-school memorials—Should the tragedy or traumatic event be centered in a school, such as a school bus accident, there may be a desire, even a deeply felt need, to commemorate such events. Different stakeholders in the schools may have distinct desires in such commemorations. Parents, for example, of children who died may want extensive memorializations while other parents may wish to move beyond the event. It is critical to create committees that will allow such dialogues to occur and consensus to be reached so that any subsequent rancor or conflict may be minimized. This is best done by having committees that include all stakeholders—surviving and other parents, school administrators, staff and teachers, as well as other community representatives.

WHEN A STUDENT OR STAFF MEMBER DIES

An Action Plan for Schools

Schools should have a protocol in place to follow if a member of the school community dies. This plan should be periodically reviewed and modified. Central to any plan is a crisis team consisting of trained administrators, teachers and support staff. This team is the key to effective response. All response should be age appropriate. Here are suggestions for the components of devising a protocol.

As soon as school officials are aware of a death, the crisis team should meet—The initial work of the team is to ascertain the correct information regarding the death as well as the communication wishes of the family of the deceased. Once this information is clarified, the team can plan to respond. In this response, the team should identify students, faculty, and staff most at risk. In assessing risk, the team should remember that strong attachments do not have to be positive. Friends and foes alike may be affected.

Inform classes in a uniform, calm manner—It is important that the same information is shared and that its delivery is controlled. Rumors are much less likely to occur when the information shared is accurate, uniform and complete.

Encourage discussion—Recognize that the day when notification is given will not be a normal day. Students and staff will need to discuss and review the life and death of the person as well as process their own reactions.

Have help available—It is helpful to have counselors available for students and staff most affected by the loss. These counselors should reach out to students and staff with strong attachments. However, the team should allow students and staff to self-select counseling. The death of someone can raise a sense of vulnerability in people with no visible connection to the deceased.

Encourage students and staff to reach out to the family—Students may need help in knowing what to say and what to do. The crisis team and counselors can help students find the right words. School personnel should have a presence at the funeral.

Shape a group response—It may be helpful to students and staff to respond as a group. Depending on the needs, circumstances, and culture, these can include contributing for flowers, or memorializing in some other appropriate way.

Inform parents—Parents should receive a letter of informing them of what has happened, how the school responded, how the can help their children, and where they can receive help if help is needed.

Remove the deceased's personal effects, such as papers, in a normal cycle—Papers, artwork and desk or locker contents should be offered to family. In some cases, family may not know what they want in the early phases of grief. It is better to hold these for a year, even if family does not express initial interest. Never send the effects without consulting with the family. In addition, remove the family from any automatic communications. For example, in one case, parents continued to receive absence notes after their daughter died.

Do not ignore the needs of staff—Their needs and grief must be recognized even as they reach out to others.

Organizational Resources

Lisa McGahey Veglahn

H ospice Foundation of America offers the following list of selected resources, helpful for bereavement professionals or concerned family members helping a child cope with grief. Professional associations may also offer resources and training about children and bereavement. Remember that your local hospice can serve as an excellent community resource.

American Hospice Foundation
www.americanhospice.org
2120 L Street, NW, Suite 200
Washington, DC 20037
800-347-1413
ahf@americanhospice.org

The American Hospice Foundation supports programs that serve the needs of terminally ill and grieving individuals of all ages. The Foundation advances hospice concepts by training school professionals who work with grieving students; educating employers and managers about the needs of grieving employees; creating tools to help hospices reach out to their communities; promoting improved hospice benefits in managed care organizations; and initiating research on consumer needs and preferences in end-of-life care.

Association for Death Education and Counseling

www.adec.org
60 Revere Drive, Suite 500
Northbrook, IL 60062
847-509-0403
adec@adec.org

The Association for Death Education and Counseling is a professional organization dedicated to promoting excellence and recognizing diversity in death education, care of the dying, grief counseling and research in thanatology. Based on quality research and theory, the association provides information, support and resources to its international, multicultural, multidisciplinary membership and through it, to the public.

Children's Hospice International

www.chionline.org
1101 King Street, Suite 360
Alexandria, VA 22314
800-24-CHILD
info@chionline.org

Children's Hospice International (CHI) was founded to promote hospice support through pediatric care facilities, encourage the inclusion of children in existing and developing hospice, palliative, and home care programs, and to include the hospice perspectives in all areas of pediatric care, education, and the public arena. CHI provides education, training and technical assistance to those who care for children with life-threatening conditions and their families.

The Compassionate Friends, Inc.

www.compassionatefriends.org
PO Box 3696
Oak Brook, IL 60522-3696
877-969-0010
nationaloffice@compassionatefriends.org

The Compassionate Friends is a national self-help support organization that offers friendship, understanding, and hope to bereaved parents, grandparents and siblings. There is no religious affiliation and there are no membership dues or fees.

The Dougy Center
www.dougy.org
PO Box 86852
Portland, OR 97286
866-775-5683
help@dougy.org

The mission of The Dougy Center for Grieving Children is to provide support in a safe place where children, teens and their families grieving a death can share their experiences as they move through their grief process. The Dougy Center provides support groups for grieving children that are age specific (3-5, 6-12, teens) and loss specific (parent death, sibling death, survivors of homicide/violent death, survivors of suicide.) Additional services include national trainings, consultations to schools and organizations, crisis-line information, and referrals.

Growth House
www.growthhouse.org
415-863-3045
info@growthhouse.org

Growth House, Inc. serves as a portal to resources for life-threatening illness and end-of-life care. Its primary mission is to improve the quality of compassionate care for people who are dying through public education and global professional collaboration. Growth House has a search engine that offers access to the Internet's most comprehensive collection of reviewed resources for end-of-life care and bereavement, including resources on children and grief.

Hospice Foundation of America

www.hospicefoundation.org
1621 Connecticut Ave., NW, Suite 300
Washington, DC 20009
800-854-3402
info@hospicefoundation.org

Hospice Foundation of America provides leadership in the development and application of hospice and its philosophy of care with the goal of enhancing the American health care system and the role of hospice within it. Hospice Foundation of America meets its mission by conducting programs of professional development, public education and information, research, publications and health policy issues. HFA's programs for heath care professionals assist those who cope either personally or professionally with terminal illness, death, and the process of grief, and are offered on a national or regional basis. HFA's programs for the public assist individual consumers of health care who are coping with issues of caregiving, terminal illness, and grief.

The Initiative for Pediatric Palliative Care

www.ippcweb.org
The Initiative for Pediatric Palliative Care at
The Center for Applied Ethics and Professional Practice (CAEPP)
Education Development Center, Inc.
55 Chapel Street
Newton MA, 02458-1060
617-618-2454
jdoherty@edc.org

The Initiative for Pediatric Palliative Care (IPPC) is both an education and a quality improvement effort, aimed at enhancing family-centered care for children living with life-threatening conditions. IPPC's comprehensive, interdisciplinary curriculum addresses knowledge, attitudes and skills that health care professionals need in order to better serve children and families. The IPPC's curriculum includes training on grief and bereavement.

KidsAid

www.kidsaid.com

cendra@griefnet.org

KidsAid is a safe place for kids to help each other deal with grief and loss. KidsAid is a companion site of GriefNet.org, an Internet community of persons dealing with grief, death, and major loss. KidsAid offers email support groups, online opportunities to share stories and artwork, and resources for parents and educators.

The MISS Foundation

www.missfoundation.org

PO Box 5333

Peoria, AZ 85385-5333

888-455-MISS (6477)

info@missfoundation.org

The MISS Foundation is a volunteer-based organization committed to providing crisis support and long-term aid to families after the death of a child from any cause. MISS also participates in legislative and advocacy issues, community engagement and volunteerism, and culturally competent, multidisciplinary, education opportunities.

National Alliance for Grieving Children

www.nationalallianceforgrievingchildren.org

info@nationalallianceforgrievingchildren.org

The mission of The National Alliance of Grieving Children is to provide resources and education to anyone who supports children and teens grieving a death. The NAGC is a non-profit organization that heightens awareness of the needs of grieving children, and connects resources with individuals and organizations serving the needs of grieving children, teens and families. NAGC has a searchable state-by-state database of children's grief centers and programs.

National Child Traumatic Stress Network

www.nctsn.org
Program Office of the National Child Traumatic Stress Initiative
Center for Mental Health Services
Substance Abuse and Mental Health Services Administration
US Department of Health and Human Services
5600 Fishers Lane
Parklawn Building, Room 17C-26
Rockville, MD 20857
301-443-2940

Established by Congress in 2000, the National Child Traumatic Stress Network (NCTSN) is a unique collaboration of academic and community-based service centers whose mission is to raise the standard of care and increase access to services for traumatized children and their families across the United States. Combining knowledge of child development, expertise in the full range of child traumatic experiences, and attention to cultural perspectives, NCTSN serves as a national resource for developing and disseminating evidence-based interventions, trauma-informed services, and public and professional education.

National Hospice and Palliative Care Organization

www.nhpco.org
1700 Diagonal Rd., Suite 625
Alexandria, VA 22314
703-837-1500
Consumer HelpLine: 800-658-8898
nhpco_info@nhpco.org

National Hospice and Palliative Care Organization (NHPCO) is the largest nonprofit membership organization representing hospice and palliative care programs and professionals in the United States. The organization is committed to improving end of life care and expanding access to hospice. NHPCO offers educational programs and materials for professionals and the public. One program of NHPCO is the ChiPPS program (Children's Project on Palliative/Hospice Services), which is working to increase the availability of state of the art services to families.

Partnership For Parents
www.partnershipforparents.org
65 Nielson St #108
Watsonville, CA 95076
831-763-3070

This site offers online support for parents of children with serious illnesses. The site has sections for physical care, emotional issues, dealing with the medical system, and helping siblings and other family members. There is a partner site in Spanish, www.padrescompadres.org/

SuperSibs!
www.supersibs.org
4300 Lincoln Ave, Suite I
Rolling Meadows, IL 60008
866-444-SIBS

The goal of SuperSibs! is to reach out to the brothers and sisters of over 12,600 children in the U.S. and Canada who are diagnosed with cancer each year. SuperSibs! helps children redefine the "cancer sibling" experience—by providing needed support services and by helping to draw out the greater and important lessons that may benefit these children later in their own lives.

Tragedy Assistance Program for Survivors, Inc. (TAPS)
www.taps.org
910 17th Street, NW Suite 800
Washington, DC 20006
800-959-TAPS
info@taps.org

TAPS is a national non-profit organization made up of, and providing services at no cost to, all those who have suffered the loss of a loved one in the Armed Forces. The heart of TAPS is its national military survivor peer support network called SurvivorLINK, which links together the families, friends, and coworkers of those who are grieving. TAPS also offers bereavement counseling referral, hosts the nation's only annual National Military Survivor Seminar and Kids Camp, publishes a quarterly journal, and offers a toll-free crisis and information line available 24 hours a day.

Index

A

ABCDE. *See* Assess, Believe, Choose, Deliver, Empower

Achenbach Child Behavior Checklist
  Harvard Child Bereavement Study assessment tool, 125, 126

ADEC. *See* Association for Death Education and Counseling

Adolescents
  causes of death, 18, 29, 86, 179, 388
  children's hospice care and, 64
  clique membership, 181
  cognitive maturation, 302
  competence issues, 87
  computer literacy, 335
  dating interactions, 182
  fear of being perceived as different, 301
  friendship characteristics, 181–182, 181–183
  grief counseling after the loss of a parent, 134, 135, 141–157
  Harvard Child Bereavement Study, 125–137
  involvement in pain assessment and care plans, 87
  journaling and, 88
  literature for high school readers, 382–384
  literature for middle school readers, 379–382
  oversedation issues, 88–89
  pain diaries, 87
  pain management issues, 86–89
  paradoxical response to medications, 89
  peer relationships, 181–182, 301
  regression, depression, and opposition, 88
  siblings' deaths and, 34, 159–174
  surrogate decision making issues, 109
  use of technology for support, 299–315

Adolescents' encounters with death. *See also* Helping students cope with grief; Schools
  adolescent development phases, 25–27, 34, 175, 300–302
  appraisal-focused, problem-focused, and emotion-focused coping skills associated with bereavement, 312
  bereavement among adolescent girls who have lost a parent, 126–127, 142–143

bereavement during adolescence, 33–34, 299–315
communication importance, 31–32, 34–35, 87
complicating factors for bereaved adolescents, 34–35
creating an individual identity and, 44
decline in adolescents' life expectancy, 25
developmental-ecological model for adolescents' response to crisis, 300
developmental tasks of adolescence and, 26, 27, 183, 300
egocentric thought processes of adolescents, 27, 28, 301–302
face-to-face interactions with adults and, 311
friends' deaths, 175, 182–185
HIV/AIDS and, 29
holistic template for, 36
implications for those who work with adolescents, 34–36
interpersonal issues, 30, 35
isolation issues, 30, 44
issues hindering adolescents' understanding of death, 27–28
life-threatening illness, 29–33
paradox associated with, 300
parenting issues, 34
personal fables and, 27, 28, 301–302
personalization of death, 52–53
present-orientation of adolescents and, 44–45
prolonged grief disorder, 35–36
resiliencies in coping with death, 311
responsive adults and, 310–311
"restoration orientation" and, 311
spiritual issues, 2–3, 31, 184–185
support from friends rather than family, 184
surviving friend's identification with the one who died, 183–184
violence as a cause of death, 28–29

Adolph, R.
  conflicts in phases of adolescent development, 26

The dying child
    children's hospice care, 57, 59–74
    ethical issues in pediatric palliative care, 58, 99–119
    management of end-of-life pain and suffering, 57–58, 75–98

E

Edmarc Hospice for Children program
    description, 61

Education and Training Curriculum for Pediatric Palliative Care, 69

Elkind, David
    egocentric thought processes of adolescents, 27

End-of-Life Nursing Education Consortium
    education and training curriculum, 69

England
    children's hospice care programs, 61, 65

Epidural infusions
    infants and, 78

Erikson, E.
    life review process, 52
    midlife "generativity vs. stagnation," 46
    young adults' perspectives on death, 45

F

F-Copes. *See* Family coping assessment

Face, Legs, Activity, Cry, and Consolability
    pain assessment in toddler-age children, 80

Facebook
    increase in the number of adolescents using, 299–300
    Virginia Tech shootings and, 302

FACES III
    Harvard Child Bereavement Study assessment tool, 125

FACES pain rating scale. *See* Wong-Baker FACES pain rating scale

Fairy Tales Test
    suicide assessment, 357

Families of September 11
    grieving children and, 255

Family Bereavement Program
    strategies for grief counseling after the loss of a parent, 141–157

Family coping assessment
    Harvard Child Bereavement Study assessment tool, 125–126

Family Inventory of Life Events
    Harvard Child Bereavement Study assessment tool, 126

Fentanyl
    infants and, 78

Field, M.J.
    When Children Die: Improving Palliative and End-of-Life Care for Children and their Families, 69

FILE. *See* Family Inventory of Life Events

Finality concept
    adolescents' understanding of death and, 27, 28
    causability, 12, 44, 142
    description, 8–9
    irreversibility element, 11–12, 28, 43, 142
    nonfunctionality element, 12, 27, 28, 142

FLACC. *See* Face, Legs, Activity, Cry, and Consolability

Fleming, S.S.
    conflicts in phases of adolescent development, 26

Frankel, L.
    Institute of Medicine report on end-of-life care, 75

Freud, Sigmund
    adults' awareness of mortality, 46

Friends' deaths
    adolescent friendship characteristics, 181–182
    adolescents and, 182–185
    childhood friendship characteristics, 176–178
    communication importance, 181
    compared with sibling grief and the loss of a pet, 179–180
    counseling strategies, 185–187
    funeral attendance and, 181
    importance of acknowledging the grief children and adolescents feel, 121
    importance of friendships, 121, 175
    infants and children and, 178–181
    lack of support for grief, 180, 185–186
    maintaining a connection to the one who died, 186
    parental support for and acknowledgment of grief, 180–181
    racial and ethnic background and response to, 186
    resilience factors, 187
    self-definition and self-worth and, 178